ELAINE HOBBY is a Welshwoman, born in Reading, Berkshire in 1956, where she grew up. Having earned her B.A. from the University of Birmingham and her M.A. from Essex, she spent several years doing research into seventeenth-century women's writing in the USA under the sponsorship of Harkness and Huntington Library Fellowships. In 1984 she was awarded her PhD. from Birmingham. She has written and lectured widely on her subject and is now working on a study of seventeenth-century female sexuality. Elaine Hobby is a lecturer in Women's Studies at Loughborough University of Technology in Leicestershire and lives in Nottingham.

In this scholarly and entertaining book, Elaine Hobby examines the writing of more than two hundred women whose work appeared between the years 1649–88. *Virtue of Necessity* makes a major contribution to our understanding of women's literary activity and lives in the seventeenth century.

Virtue
of
Necessity

English Women's Writing
1646–1688

ELAINE HOBBY

Published by VIRAGO PRESS Limited 1988
20–23 Mandela Street, Camden Town, London NW1 0HQ

British Library Cataloguing in Publication Data

Hobby, Elaine, *1956–*
Virtue of necessity : English women's
writing, 1649–1688.
1. English literature. Women writers,
1649–1688. Critical studies
I. Title
820.9'9287

ISBN 0–86068–831–3

Typeset by Florencetype Ltd, Kewstoke, Avon
Printed in Great Britain by Billings & Sons Ltd

CONTENTS

Acknowledgements vii

Note on Quotations from Seventeenth-Century Texts ix

INTRODUCTION: Making A Virtue Of Necessity 1

CHAPTER ONE: Prophets and Prophecies 26

CHAPTER TWO: Religious Poetry, Meditations and
Conversion Narratives 54

CHAPTER THREE: Autobiographies and Biographies of
Husbands 76

CHAPTER FOUR: Romantic Love – Prose Fiction 85

CHAPTER FIVE: Romantic Love – Plays 102

CHAPTER SIX: Romantic Love – Poetry 128

CHAPTER SEVEN: Skills Books – Housewifery,
Medicine, Midwifery 165

CHAPTER EIGHT: Education 190

POSTSCRIPT: Beginning Again 204

Notes 208

Bibliography: Primary Sources 228

Selected Background and Further Reading 252

Index 261

For Edna and Vernon Hobby

ACKNOWLEDGEMENTS

MANY thanks to the friends and colleagues who have given me access to their unpublished research, and discussed mine with me: Wendy Ayotte, Nazife Bashar, Maureen Bell, Beat Carre, David Cressy, Moira Ferguson, Sandy Findley, Elizabeth Hampsten, Paul Hardacre, Hilary Hinds, Suzanne Hull, Suzanne Lebsock, John Loftis, Paddy Lyons, Phyllis Mack, Gerald MacLean, Mitzi Myers, Tom O'Malley, Kate Pahl, Dolores Paloma, Lyndal Roper, Simon Shepherd, Robbie Smith, Jane Spencer, Lawrence Stone, Ann Tobin, Charles Webster, Rachel Weil; and thanks to Anne Buckley, who helped with the typing, again.

Gratitude, too, for the stimulation received from the Birmingham Rape Crisis Centre Collective, 1980–81; the English Studies Group at the Centre for Contemporary Cultural Studies, 1979–81; the members of Lawrence Stone's graduate seminar, Autumn 1981; and all those who have come to hear my talks these last eight years.

I have received specific help from John Morrison and Carolyn Nelson of the Wing *Short-Title Catalogue* Revision Office, who have dealt patiently and promptly with my many communications; librarians in some twenty different places, especially those of the British Library, Friends' Library, London, and the Huntington Library, California; and from Tony Davies, who supervised the original research with his customary energy, intellectual integrity and political clarity.

For their work on the index, thanks to Katelyn Adler and Maggie Hammond. And thank you to Ruthie Petrie of Virago Press for her professional expertise and personal support.

Most centrally, Jim Killbery, Kathryn Harriss and Bill Flatman, who supported me financially, politically and emotionally through the years of research; Jan Sellers, who lent her typewriter, proofread and sent flowers; Christine White, who saw me through the last stages; to you all, my love and gratitude, as ever.

Crucially, the Women's Liberation Movement. Without my sisters, this project would have been, quite literally, unthinkable.

The errors, of course, are mine.

NOTE ON QUOTATIONS FROM
SEVENTEENTH-CENTURY TEXTS

NOT to alter quotations from seventeenth-century texts gives a false and distancing sense of quaintness. To alter them at all nonetheless distorts them. My solution to this dilemma is an unhappy compromise. Generally, I have not meddled with punctuation, but have modernised spellings (except in the titles of works, where modernisation could give problems to anyone trying to find a text). In some cases I have also silently exchanged full-stops for seventeenth-century colons or commas. We need good modern editions of these women's works, to make such piecemeal solutions unnecessary.

INTRODUCTION

MAKING A VIRTUE OF NECESSITY

BETWEEN 1649 and 1688 writings by more than 200 women were published on every conceivable topic, from Katherine Philips' joyful celebration of women's friendship, to Hester Biddle's furious desire to burn the two university towns to the ground. Women wrote religio-political propaganda and poetry, autobiography and midwifery manuals, novels, poetry and plays: a constant source of surprises. Who today would have imagined that they could have been so funny or so angry or so clear?

Writing was not without its problems or its cost. Women were not supposed to enter the public world in any form, and that prohibition extended to a ban on 'making public' their words. They had to find ways of making their writing acceptable, both to themselves and to others. As a result, not only do their works discuss politics and love, household management and education, they also examine, repeatedly, the problem of being a woman writer in their society. This book is therefore presented as a beginning: a guide to women's writing in that period of social upheaval and change, and an analysis of the strategies they were bound to use to have their voices heard.

MAKING A VIRTUE OF NECESSITY:
A VERY WOMANLY THING TO DO

How can we find out what life might have been like for the seventeenth-century woman writer, and so work out what her writing might have meant to her and her contemporaries? One way in (used by some historians and literary critics) is through assertions and descriptions by their male contemporaries, but we need to be wary. In *A Collection of English Proverbs*, 1670, John Ray explains why he has omitted from his book most of the proverbial expressions he has come across concerning women.

England is the paradise of women. And well may it be called so, as might easily be demonstrated in many particulars, were not all the world already therein satisfied. Hence it hath been said that if a bridge were made over the narrow seas,

· 1 ·

all the women in Europe would come over hither. Yet it is worth noting, that though in no country of the world, the men are so fond of, so much governed by, so wedded to their wives, yet hath no language, so many proverbial invectives against women. (p. 54)

This passage tells us several things, some through what it says, and some through what it omits. It makes it clear that what gets onto the page is selected. Even a text that purports to be a simple 'collection of proverbs' is put together according to more or less conscious principles. We need to read between the lines, as well as reading the lines themselves, if we are to deduce from these words the gaps between what Ray wants to believe and wants his reader to believe about the status of women and men's treatment of them; and what his written evidence might suggest. A writer (including this one, and including the women studied in this book) has preconceptions that determine what is written. The reader – especially if s/he comes from a different culture or from a different position within the same society – can see things that the writer cannot; or can see things that are supposed to be invisible. This passage from John Ray indicates at least that there is some kind of dispute going on in seventeenth-century England about women's role, and that some people believed or wished to believe, in jingoistic fashion, that 'in no country of the world, the men are so fond of, so much governed by, so wedded to their wives'. The existence of this assertion suggests a need to assert it. It does not tell us much about whether readers then would have agreed with it.

Bearing in mind that caution, it is nonetheless possible to examine written sources from the period to try to establish at least the limits of what women were supposed to be like. There are three main issues, and I shall take them in turn: a woman's position in the family; her access to education; and her role in the churches.

The Family

Surveys of conduct books (early etiquette books) have shown that there were two central commandments for women in the period.[1] First and foremost, a woman must preserve her family's honour: that is, she must protect her reputation for sexual chastity or 'honesty'. She must be a virgin on marriage, and then be sexually faithful to her husband. These injunctions, familiar to women in other ages too, had a particular resonance then because women were also perceived as the more lustful sex. It was commonly asserted that women's carnal appetite was voracious, and widows were stereotypically portrayed as sexually predatory. Adolescent depression and lethargy, known as 'green-sickness', were also attributed to sexual frustration, and masturbation or early marriage frequently urged as cures. A chaste reputation was therefore hard to gain and easy to lose, and its centrality in men's view of women is succinctly expressed in a statement from Luis Vives's *The Instruction of a Christen Woman.*

No man will look for any other thing of a woman, but her honesty [i.e. chastity]: the which thing only, if it be lacked, is like as in a man, if he lack all that he should have. For in a woman the honesty is instead of all. (p. xvii)

If chastity was the first commandment, it was not, in fact, 'instead of all'. In addition, women were constantly exhorted to restrict their attention to their proper concerns. The precise definition of these varied, but Richard Brathwait's frequently reprinted *The English Gentlewoman* is fairly typical in its declaration that female discussion of household matters is permissible, while debating divinity or state affairs is not (p. 81). Sometimes, this prohibition extended to the assertion that *any* talking is unfitting for a woman: 'they should be seen and not heard . . . Their best setting out is silence,' Brathwait says (p. 41). While this would be a problem for any woman, clearly it presented a specific dilemma for aspiring writers.

Such admonitions appear throughout the early-modern period, but their precise effects on women's lives probably varied since, as historians studying the family have shown, in the seventeenth century a divide grew up between 'public' and 'private' spheres.[2] For the middle and upper classes at least, the family became a private place, a shift that had quite different implications for women and men. For men, the family became a haven they could retreat to for solace. For women, it was supposed to map out the limits of their world. Although this picture is an over-simplification – women did, after all, maintain their own social networks, and economic (that is, 'public') considerations continued to play an important role in deciding who married whom – it does draw attention to the possible effects of such transitions. As Alice Clark points out in *The Working Life of Women*, during the seventeenth century women's work in the home also changed, becoming increasingly restricted to final-stage production and consumption, making it very difficult for single women to be economically independent.[3] The 'privatisation' of the home therefore had very different effects on women from those it had on men.

Another preoccupation of family historians is with the establishment of what Lawrence Stone (*The Family, Sex and Marriage*) calls the 'companionate marriage'.[4] Stone believes that people's increasing rights to choose their marriage partners in this period led to greater equality and affection between husband and wife. The argument clearly does not connect: deciding whom you are going to marry does not reduce that person's power over you once you are married, and an initial attraction ('falling in love') is not necessarily very long-lived. The evidence from women's writing in the period suggests in fact that women did not have *fewer* problems as the century progressed: they just had different ones.

Central to the question of how relationships between wives and husbands might have changed in the seventeenth century, though, is the fact that there was little alteration in the legal definition of marriage.[5] Husband and wife were one person, and that person was the husband. In 1632, T.E., the (male) author of *The Lawes Resolution of Women's Rights*, explained that the 'locking together' of wedlock should not be considered an equal bonding.

It is true, that man and wife are one person, but understand in what manner. When a small brook or little river incorporateth with Rhodanus [Rhone], Humber or Thames, the poor rivulet loseth her name: it is carried and recarried with the new associate; it beareth no sway . . . I may more truly, far away, say to a married woman, her new self is her superior, her companion, her master. (p. 125)

Women were under no illusion that, however much they might care for their husbands, once they were married their relationship would change from the courtship pattern of 'mistress' and 'servant' to man and wife (see Chapters Five and Six). A particularly clear example of this is one of the few well-known pieces of writing by a seventeenth-century woman: Dorothy Osborne's letters to her fiancé, William Temple. In her letters, Osborne uses to the utmost the opportunity to negotiate the terms of their ('freely chosen') match while she is still legally free from him. She repeatedly urges Temple to treat her with the directness of a friend, and not play the games of 'mistress' and 'servant'. It is no idle enquiry, either, when she asks him how he would treat someone over whom he had absolute power: that was to be his future relationship to her.

There is also material for a study of the realities of women's legal rights in the personal petitions published by women in the mid seventeenth century concerning non-payment of legacies from the estates of their deceased relatives. (These pamphlets were legally worded, and probably drafted by lawyers.) One of these petitioners, Katherine Pettus, was so frustrated in her attempt to obtain money due to her from the executor of her husband's will that she had the executor's widow, Margaret Bancroft, jailed for debt. This did not solve the problem, since after one year's imprisonment Bancroft had still not produced her inheritance. As part of her continuing campaign, Pettus published a petition addressed to the parliamentary committee drafting new laws concerning debtors, asking them to be sympathetic to the creditors' point of view, and that 'there may be some special provision made for suchlike cases'.[6] Anne Smyth also appealed in print to parliament, asking them to intervene in her dispute with the executor of her late father's will and force him to release her legacy, an estate worth £1000.[7] Published petitions in a dispute between Mary Alexander the Countess of Stirling and her relative Anne Levingston concerning the countess's inheritance from her aunt, Lady Powell, also exist. The pamphlets include accusations against Levingston of using both witchcraft and force against Lady Powell at the instigation of the latter's estranged husband, causing her to exclude the countess from her bequests. The details of this case – finally won by the countess's descendants after her death – might well provide material for a study of conflicts around married women's legal and financial rights and stratagems.[8]

Education

If the family was one major institution through which women's subordination was achieved and maintained, another key factor was their access to education. Little is yet known about the reading ability of people in the past: how do you measure whether someone could read? Inability to write is obviously easier to prove. Nonetheless, the large sales of almanacs and bibles throughout the period does suggest that reading might have been much more widespread than was once thought, and the popularity of cookery books, in particular, implies that many women could read.[9] When it comes to writing, on the other hand, there are many examples of women's spelling, grammar and even their handwriting being idiosyncratic (more so than men's), and so difficult to understand. To take one instance: the one sample the British Library owns of the handwriting of the prolific Margaret Cavendish is a postscript she added to her letter to the painter Constantin Huygens. It reads

Sr i would have writt my letters to you in my own hand but be reson my hand written in not legabell i though you might rather have gest at what i would say then had read what i had writt this is the reson they wer writt by an other hand.[10]

The figures concerning people's ability to write are the subject of some controversy, but all sides agree that men were far more likely to be able to write than women.

Reading and writing are only the first step, of course. Chapter Eight describes in greater detail the ways in which women's education differed from men's, preventing them engaging in most contemporary public debate.

Religion

To have any inkling of the importance of Christianity in people's lives in the seventeenth century, we need to remember that attendance at church was compulsory through most of the period (though many people broke that law), and that the major political and social issues of the day were argued out in terms not of 'what people want' but 'what God wants'. (I shall return to this below.) According to the doctrinal texts referred to by widely differing religious groups, women's position was clear enough. 'Let your women keep silence in the churches: for it is not permitted unto them to speak; but they are commanded to be under obedience, as also saith the Law' (1 Cor. 14. 34–35). These words are quoted and discussed so frequently in mid seventeenth-century tracts that it seems likely that they were regularly thrust at women during Sunday sermons. The injunction to silence is accompanied by an explicit assertion of male authority: 'And if they will learn anything, let them ask their husbands at home: for it is a shame for women to speak in the church'; and this is expanded in St Paul's first letter to Timothy: 'Let the woman learn in silence with all subjection. But I suffer not a woman to teach nor to usurp authority over the man, but to be in silence' (1 Tim. 2. 11–12). A basis for male authority and female obedience and silence was firmly established in the scriptures.

In the light of all these restrictions, how did seventeenth-century women manage to write and publish? How could they bring themselves to believe that these were acceptable activities, and how could they persuade their readers that such acts were not entirely reprehensible? There are many answers to these questions, and this book is, in part, a whole series of different answers, showing how different women faced with different circumstances managed to write. This Introduction mentions various women who, confronted with the upsets of civil war, published their petitions to parliament. In Chapters One and Two I describe the activities of other civil-war women: members of radical religio-political groups who wrote their own life stories, or published pamphlets expressing opinions on affairs of state. In the years that followed the Restoration of the Monarchy, female poetry- and novel-writing began really to flourish, and Aphra Behn and her fellow dramatists started to have their plays staged. Their writings form the subject-matter of the middle chapters of this book, followed by an examination of texts written by women to defend female control of cookery and midwifery against male incursions. I end with a discussion of defences of women's education. This great variety in subject-mattter and literary form, and the fact that this book is based on the writings of some two hundred women, might lead one to think that the constraints placed on women were less crippling than I have suggested. We need to bear in mind, however, that very few women, compared with men, wrote for publication: their works form less than one per cent of the total number of texts published in the period.[11] To understand how women could believe they were entitled to write, and to make sense of the justifications they address to their readers, we need to see their works as a series of strategies that 'make a virtue of necessity'. In their different ways, they transformed proscriptions into a kind of permission.

There are various ways of describing women's oppression. One popular method is what might be called a repression-liberation model: it is suggested that women's true nature is fenced in and denied in patriarchal societies, and that 'all' that is needed is for women to help one another shrug off their conditioning so that they can become their 'real selves'. (Some tendencies in the politics of Greenham women, or of Women Against Violence Against Women, belong to this framework, as do a lot of writings by US radical feminists.) Coming to consciousness as a feminist can feel like this, especially at first. In consciousness-raising groups or in conversations with female friends, women begin to recognise ways in which we have not been allowed, or not allowed ourselves, to be strong, independent, self-directed. It does feel at first as if something 'repressed' has been 'liberated'. 'Femininity' seems like something imposed from the outside, something we have escaped from. This is not the end of the story, though. The next stage for a new feminist is often an ebbing of energy, as a sense of direction is lost. There no longer seems to be an 'inner self' driving her on, but a sense of confusion. Some women regain a feeling of purpose through their involvement with the women's liberation movement; others return to a life closely akin to the one they had rejected; others take other directions. I think this happens because 'femininity' is not simply an imposition from the outside onto a 'true self': that there is no 'true self' to recapture. Who we are is created by the world we live in, and although there are choices available to us, those choices are set up by the world we inhabit, and what anyone feels able to choose depends on how that world has made us into who we are. 'Femininity', therefore – or 'being a woman' – is something that is constantly being redefined, in both the world at large and the life of each of us, as circumstances change and we struggle to change circumstances.[12]

Femininity, then, is not like a restraining garment forced onto the body of an unwilling or acquiescent victim, which entirely controls her movements until it is shrugged off when the 'real woman' inside it is set free. It is both more accurate and more productive to see patriarchal domination as a dynamic (that is, constantly changing and constantly challenged) process. 'Femininity' is produced only partly through women being placed in subordinate positions in key social institutions – the family, education and (in the seventeenth century) the church – which support the power and authority of men, and justify their dominance in legal status and the economy. Recapturing the outlines of these structures is not the end of the story, since this male control only sets the limits of what is possible for women. It does not prescribe the specific content of ideas or precisely determine the details of 'femininity', since these limits are constantly being fought against. Women find ways of coping with their oppression and ways of resisting it, but this capitulation or resistance is not free or self-determined: it can normally only occur within the limits and on the terms of the framework set by the dominant group, men. Different amounts and different kinds of challenge are possible at different times, but there is no 'female essence' that is being confined or denied, and no imposition of a rigid 'femininity' that can simply be identified and rejected. The framework is being constantly challenged, and to some extent renegotiated, by women 'making a virtue of necessity'.

Law guidebooks, conduct books, sermons and other explicitly ideological texts can only tell us about the *limits* of femininity – about what women were meant to be like, according to these dominant ideas. It is common today for people to assume that women in the past were as passive and modest – or as lusty and immoral – as such sources suggest. Although books written by seventeenth-century women do not and cannot give us the 'truth' either, they do give us information that suggests that women then (like other oppressed groups in other societies) resisted the demands of those who would control them by 'making a virtue of necessity'. Women's legal and economic position, and the ideological statements made justifying their subjection are the 'necessity' they lived under. In different ways, their own writings show us, they were able to 'make a virtue' of this: to turn constraints into permissions, into little pockets of liberty or autonomy. Depending on how radical this resistance was, they either forced their oppressors to redefine the terms of the argument so as to continue to control them; or appeared to fit neatly and invisibly into the status quo, apparently changing nothing but making their oppression less stifling.

It is because the struggles against the dominant order are continual, although also continuously changing, that I am not looking for heroines or amazons or 'great writers' in the past (though it is good occasionally to find such figures). Instead, I am interested in the full range of women's writing, and the very diverse strategies it reveals women using to make writing for publication permissible. In their texts we see 'femininity' being constantly defined and redefined, its limits shifting and being reimposed, as the struggles of domination and subordination are played out: different women, in different ways, 'making a virtue of necessity'.

A few examples of the ways in which women justify their writing, and one slightly longer examination of writings by Hester Shaw, will show how this dynamic worked in practice.

The primary 'necessity' for women was that they be 'modest': that is, first and foremost, sexually chaste, but also 'modest' in its more general sense too. Women belonged in the increasingly private sphere of the home: they were not supposed to be so bold – or so immodest – as to venture into the public world of print. The charge of 'immodesty' was a serious one. Whatever the initial grounds of the attack on a woman's reputation, an association with sexual misbehaviour, with a lack of concern for her family's 'honour', was always in danger of following. The terms 'honour', 'reputation', 'modesty', 'chastity' formed such a tight group when applied to women that the use of one of these words – or its opposite – would inevitably bring the others to mind, and into question. As a result, women had to find a repertoire of devices to make their writing a 'modest' act: they 'made a virtue of necessity' by claiming that the dictates of modesty were prompting them to write and publish. Many women, as we will see in Chapters One and Two, assert that they are commanded by God to write: that they are proving their obedience (and hence their modesty) by doing as they are told. Other women have other justifications. Margaret Cavendish runs through a wide variety of 'proofs' that writing is virtuous, including asserting that it is better for her to write than to gossip; and saying that she would spin or sew instead of writing if she could, but since she lacks the skill she writes to prevent unwomanly idleness.[13] Two pamphlets by Hester Shaw, published in 1653, provide a clear demonstration of how the injunction to women to defend their 'modesty' and 'honesty' could be used as perfect justification for the immodest act of writing.

It is possible that Hester Shaw had played a part in the 1630s in resisting attempts by the College of Physicians and the Chamberlen brothers to take control of midwifery (see Chapter Seven). If so, it might have been through this experience that she learned the effectiveness of stirring up public sympathy. Certainly as a midwife she had a public profile, something that made her particularly vulnerable to charges of dishonesty, since her job required her word to be inviolate. (Women's inheritance rights were inextricably bound up with their ability to produce at least one living child, so it was always possible that a still-born baby would be secretly exchanged for another child. The midwife's oath included an undertaking to prevent such deceit, and her employment was dependent upon the reliability of her word. Her involvement with childbirth also made her the easy butt of sexual jokes and scandal.) Hester Shaw's excursion into print occurred when her word on another matter had been brought into doubt by no less a person than the local church minister, Mr Clendon.

The circumstances of their dispute were simple enough. On 4 January 1650, the gunpowder Mistress Shaw's neighbour kept stored in his home exploded, destroying five houses including Hester Shaw's, and killing her son-in-law, her maid and three of her grandchildren. The newssheet report of the incident describes Hester Shaw as 'a midwife of good esteem and quality', and while it does not estimate the specific cost to her of the subsequent fire, it calculates that the overall loss of the five houses must have totalled £60,000.[14] The money and possessions scattered by the blast were collected up and taken for safekeeping to various nearby addresses, including the house of the minister, Mr Clendon. The point at issue between Shaw and Clendon is whether some bags of her money to the value of at least £950 were among the items deposited with him. There is no firm evidence as to what occurred in the next three years, but subsequent events make it highly probable that Mrs Shaw left the local community in no doubt that she believed Mr Clendon had stolen her money. What is certain is that he used the privileged access to print that his status as a church minister gave him to challenge her as a 'malicious slanderer' in the dedicatory epistle to one of his published sermons. In doing so, he removed the adjudication of the matter from the realm of gossip, a quintessentially female domain, and took it into the male, public world. (A dominant meaning of 'gossip' at this time was 'a woman's female friends invited to be present at a birth' (*OED*).) Her honesty challenged, Hester Shaw had no option, she claimed, but to follow him into print, and in so doing jeopardised her reputation for modesty. To offset this, she made it quite apparent that she knew that a woman should be silent, appealing to the reader's sympathy for her as a 'weak woman'.

Finding myself crowded into print with calumny and reproach, I was the rather prevailed upon by some of my best friends not to be silent lest my innocency suffer. I have therefore according to my capacity, in the plain style of a weak woman, (with all sincerity and meekness, however provoked) . . . (Hester Shaw, *A Plaine Relation*, p. 1)

Weak or not, Hester Shaw was an efficient businesswoman. This first text, giving her side of the story, was swiftly followed by a second, which included a whole series of affidavits from witnesses. Abraham Perrott testifies that he had repaid her a loan of £953 6s 8d on 8 December. Mary Saunders reports being told by two men that they had taken bags of silver to Mr Clendon's house. Others tell how they went with Shaw in her unsuccessful attempt to reclaim her money. She is so confident that 'all rational persons' will judge in her favour that she even reprints Mr Clendon's declaration that she is characterised by 'volubility of tongue, and natural boldness, and confidence . . . and much impudency' (*Mrs Shaw's Innocency restored*, p. 3). With such a charge against her, she had no choice but to challenge him on his own ground, in the public world. (Unless the case went to settlement at court it appears to have rested there, since no further pamphlets, on either side, were published.) Because she was not the naturally inferior creature the ideologues of the day would wish to make her, she was able to marshall considerable forces in her defence. This was done, however, not by rejecting the dictates concerning proper feminine behaviour, but by using them to justify to herself, her neighbours and her readers her incursion into print.

VIRTUE OF NECESSITY: WOMEN DRIVEN, OF NECESSITY, BACK TO VIRTUE

It is not of course possible to give a description of all the events of a forty-year period: any account is selective. I will merely sketch the major public issues of the period 1649–88, and indicate women's involvement in them. At the same time, I want to argue that the period is made up of two phases. In the first, challenges being made to the status quo involved new freedoms and activities for women. In the second phase, after the Restoration of the Monarchy, women were driven back into their newly private homes, where they retreated to an espousal of virtue. Of necessity, they made themselves virtuous.

'What really happened' in the seventeenth century is the subject of intense, sometimes angry, debate among twentieth-century historians. Certain events, of course, are beyond dispute. A king (Charles I) was beheaded in 1649. During the 1650s, Oliver Cromwell rose to power and was appointed Lord Protector, while various experiments were made in the selection and composition of parliament. After his death he was succeeded briefly by his son, and in 1660 Charles II came back to England and the monarchy was restored. He in turn was succeeded in 1685 by his brother James II, who after only three years was removed from the throne in a bloodless coup, his distant cousin William of Orange and Mary, James's daughter, being invited to come and reign in his place. None of that is open to debate, although some historians would argue with the exact terms I have used to describe these episodes. The arguments centre on questions like: who wanted the king beheaded, and why did the execution happen?; where were Cromwell's allegiances in the bitterly fought disagreements of the 1650s?; were the various parliaments of the 1650s more or less democratic than one another, and why did they fall?; who wanted Charles II to return, and in whose interests was the restoration?; did the returned monarch live largely in harmony, or in conflict, with his parliaments?; how widespread was the support for the 'Glorious Revolution' of 1688?[15]

On 31 January 1649, Charles I was executed, and within a few days the monarchy, House of Lords and established church were abolished. Later that year England was declared 'a Commonwealth and Free State', and Oliver Cromwell led troops to Catholic Ireland where thousands of Irish people were massacred. The following year, all Acts compelling attendance at church were repealed, all court proceedings changed from Latin to English, and Acts condemning swearing, adultery and 'profanation of the gospel' became law. In September 1651 Charles Stuart (the future Charles II) was beaten by Cromwell's army at the Battle of Worcester, and fled to the Continent.

Two aspects of this series of events are important. Firstly, it is clear that the changes achieved at this time were accompanied by violence and bloodshed: England had had two periods of civil war during the 1640s, while supporters of Charles I and supporters of parliament fought for control of the country. Secondly, it is notable that the key issues on both sides were expressed and perceived in terms of 'God's will'. Charles I had asserted his right to absolute power over his subjects by using the argument that he was appointed by God, and he used compulsory church attendance as one way of reinforcing his claims. Changes in religious services and in the internal layout of churches implemented under Archbishop Laud in the 1630s were seen by many as 'Popish' (that is, Catholic) innovations, and opposition to them gathered support for the parliamentary cause. The parliamentary army perceived itself as a godly force, committed to preventing the incursions of Popery that were associated in the popular mind with strict social hierarchies and monarchs with absolute power over their people.

Such inter-relation between affairs of state and religious commitments becomes clearest in the period 1653–4. In April 1653, Cromwell took it upon himself to dissolve the Rump Parliament, claiming that it was not doing God's will. (Its name came from the fact that its members were the 'rump' left after many had been removed by the parliamentary army in 1648 during Pride's Purge.) It was replaced by a nominated assembly, known as the Barebones Parliament or Parliament of Saints. Who exactly chose its members is disputed. After six months this parliament was also dissolved (while its more radical members were absent early one morning), and power voted to Cromwell, who became Lord Protector for life. The first Protectorate Parliament met in 1654. Each of these assemblies was presented as an attempt to ensure that a Godly Commonwealth was established. The description of the Barebones Parliament as 'Saints' does not mean that they were especially good people, but rather that they perceived themselves as chosen by God to set about creating his kingdom on earth. The idea that Christ's long-promised Second Coming was imminent, and that it was the task of all Christians to make the earth a suitable place to receive him, was widespread in the period. Millenarian enthusiasm, the eager expectation of the arrival of the 'millennium' or 'golden age' characterised many political and religious movements of the time, including some that still survive today but are no longer seen as social revolutionaries. The early Society of Friends, or Quakers as their enemies called them, rejected any reliance on authority of state, church or biblical text, asserting that each person had an Inner Light that could tell them directly God's will. 'God's will' could therefore include very specific demands for changes in the law, the education system, the economy and so on. Similar beliefs were held by some Baptists, and by Seekers, Muggletonians and other radicals. Umbrella-group alliances included the Levellers, who campaigned for wide-ranging social reforms; and the Fifth Monarchists, who interpreted biblical predictions in the Books of Daniel and Revelation as referring to England, and who took up arms to establish by force the Fifth Monarchy, the reign of King Jesus. All these groups were known collectively as Independents (and sometimes as Congregationalists or Separatists) because of their belief that each congregation should be free to establish its own beliefs about God's will. A basic demand of them all was that tithes, a tax on all households to support the national church, be abolished. (This was never achieved, and some Independents regarded this as one clear sign that Cromwell and his followers had betrayed God's people once the actual fighting was over.)

If such groups are seen as the far left of the spectrum of opinion that supported parliament against Charles I, at the right of the parliamentary group are other kinds of Puritans, known as Presbyterians because they wanted to change the structure of the church away from its control by bishops (who were members of the House of Lords and identified as being allied to kingly power), towards a less undemocratic control by the presbytery (church elders). Presbyterians tended to favour continuation of a more national structure to the church than Independents did. Disputes within the parliaments of 1653 and 1654 can be described (with reservations) as battles between Presbyterians and Independents to decide exactly how God's England should be run, and by whom.

Before going on to indicate the incidents and issues of the Restoration and Glorious Revolution, it would be as well to give a few examples of women's contact with affairs of state in the Commonwealth and Protectorate period, since upheavals of war and constitutional change provided the opportunity, or created the necessity, for many women to write and sometimes publish petitions. (The *Commons' Journal* and *Calendar of State Papers Domestic* reveal that many more female petitions were presented than were ever printed.) These fall into two broad groups: those concerning individual grievances or needs; and those addressing more general social issues. The women signatories of such petitions present themselves as creatures driven irresistibly into print by force of circumstances, and whether or not they were successful, very few of them published more than once.

Private petitions to government were presented by women on both sides of the royalist/parliamentarian split. In 1654, Margaret Somerset the Countess of Worcester, Anne Henshaw and Katherine Stone, all dependants of royalists whose estates had been confiscated by parliament, petitioned to claim their rights to one fifth of the property.[16] (Earlier, in 1650, when the House was drawing up legislation to dispose of the estates of such 'delinquents', a joint petition that their dependants be provided for was presented to parliament and published by 'several wives and children of such delinquents'.[17]) As printed texts, these are a very marginal form of women's public writing, and might well have been drafted by lawyers since most are written in legal jargon and cite extensive case law. The accompanying assertion of the women's helplessness, distress and need for protection, however, marks them out as typically female. Texts that might appear to be of interest solely to legal historians in fact have something to show about how carefully negotiated *any* female entry into print had to be, and how the petitioners were 'making a virtue of necessity' when they cited their feminine weakness. Anne Henshaw's case is particularly striking. Describing herself as a 'distressed widow . . . having the sole care of eight children', she persuaded the Commons to release £12,000 – a very considerable sum in those days – from the sequestered estate of the Earl of Carlisle. Since she had in fact been widowed fourteen years before, and her husband had been a wealthy man, it seems unlikely that her circumstances were quite as hopeless as she chose to suggest.

Petitioners who had supported the parliamentary cause included Susannah Bastwick and Mary Blaithwait. When Susannah Bastwick published her broadside *To the High Court of Parliament* (1654), she had already petitioned the Commons on at least eight previous occasions, and so knew that they responded slowly, if at all. In the early 1640s she had petitioned repeatedly for actions taken against her husband by royalists to be overturned, and to have his release negotiated when he was taken prisoner by them. His freedom secured, she had turned her attention to having his promised reparation paid. In the published petition, Bastwick, by this time widowed, reminds parliament of her husband John's great sufferings for the parliamentary cause, and appeals for a pension to be paid to her. This was finally agreed, after a further presentation of her petition, in 1657, although an entry in the *Commons' Journal* for March 1659 shows that payment had already fallen into arrears.[18]

In contrast with such legally worded texts, the petition published by Mary Blaithwait bears the hallmarks of female composition. In May 1654, a few months after Cromwell had been appointed Lord Protector, Mary Blaithwait turned publicly to him with the case that she had tried to put to the Parliament of Saints. In 1644 she was arrested in her native Cumberland for distributing parliamentary propaganda, having already been subjected to constant harassment from the local royalist gentry. The persecution had driven her husband mad, she says, and he 'died in a consuming condition' (*The Complaint*, p. 5). She now seeks protection from the royalists, and demands that compensation be paid her from estates confiscated from Cumberland royalists. It is interesting that even a woman in Blaithwait's position, who as a pamphlet-seller had obvious links with the publishing trade and who had suffered extensively for her political activities, is unable to publish without addressing explicitly the problem that women are not supposed to go into print. The decision to publish is presented as one forced on her by circumstances, and as something almost to be ashamed of. The convention of appealing to her feminine weakness and need for protection is exploited to the full.

[I] am forced after much labour in vain, and many a weary step, to no purpose, to make myself a fool in print, hoping hereby I by [sic] some hand, mouth, or pen, this my complaint may come to the ear of that great man, who hath taken upon him the Protection of Commonwealth etc. to stir him up to come forth and hear the widow's complaint, and give relief unto me and my fatherless children. (*The Complaint*, p. 2)

Oh that I could come to speak with His Highness, that I might say unto him, my Lord Protector, do justice for me a distressed widow and my fatherless children, lest when your wife is a widow, and children fatherless, they cry and be not heard. (pp. 5–6)

The pamphlet ends with 'A Word to the Reader':

If any man shall blame me a poor distressed widow for soliciting His Highness, and petitioning the parliament, let them know that my oppressions are so great and so insufferable, that I cannot do less than crave for justice, from which I have been so long detained. (p. 8)

Other individual petitions in this period include one by Margaret Beck (*The Reward of Oppression*) claiming the Duchy of Lancaster as her son's rightful inheritance; a collection of pamphlets *Love's Name Lives*, edited by Mary Love, calling for the release or reprieve from execution of her husband Christopher (all she won was a stay of execution until after the birth of her baby); and one by Mary Walker complaining about parliament's violation of her dower rights after her royalist husband had died in prison when awaiting trial. All of these texts would repay more detailed study, and each reveals the complex and different ways that women could appeal for support or reparation by making much of their feminine vulnerability. Perhaps the most remarkable of all was *The Petition of the Jewes* (1649), Joanna Cartwright's appeal for Jews to be readmitted to England (they had been excluded by Act of Parliament for many years).

The other major type of women's petition presented in this period is collective texts complaining about particular acts or omissions of the Commons. (Repeatedly during the 1640s, there were specific orders made to the guards of the House to control clamouring women, as ever larger groups gathered to urge specific policies on the law-makers.[19]) In 1650, *The Womens Petition* contended that the aims of the revolution had not yet been accomplished. The petitioners used the metaphor popular among radical groups of the day: although the head of tyranny had been cut off with the king's execution in 1649, its body was still intact in the continuation of an oppressive legal system, the Norman Yoke. (Radicals frequently argued that the Norman Conquest in 1066 had resulted in sweeping changes in English law, and that the native peoples had lost their freedoms as a 'Norman Yoke' of slavery was imposed.) They called for changes in the laws concerning debtors. The petition, presented to Cromwell on 27 October 1651 (six weeks after his victory at Worcester) by K. Frese, D. Trinhale, E. Bassfield and E. Cole, expressed at length a sense of loss and betrayal.

What shall we say? Our hope is even departed, and our expectation of freedom (the fruits of our blood shed, and expense of our estates) is removed far away; yea, the hope of our liberty is cut off like a weaver's thumb. We have for many years (but in especial since 1647) chattered like cranes, and mourned like doves; yea with many sighs and tears have we presented our several complaints against God's and our enemies; but we are hitherto so far from gaining redress, as that our eyes behold them still exalted to bear rule over us: and thus for felicity, we reap bitter grief; for freedom, slavery; for true judgement, justice and mercy, injustice, tyranny and oppression; because the head of tyranny was cut off in 1648 (was expected to die, and be dead) still liveth in and by his ordained members of injustice and oppression; and the Norman laws of the oppressors still bear dominion over us.

In 1649 and again in 1653, when one of the Leveller leaders, John Lilburne, was in prison, groups of radicals petitioned parliament for his release. On both occasions, this included organised petitioning by Leveller women. The stated purpose of these pamphlets is to press for Lilburne's release, since 'what is done or intended against him (being against common right, and in the face thereof) may be done unto every particular person in the nation', but their frame of reference is much wider, raising fundamental questions about the way in which England should be governed.[20] The women warn parliament that not only are all petitioners, women as well as men, equal, but that MPs themselves are no better than anyone else. God deserted the Rump because it caused so much suffering, they maintain, and advise the Parliament of Saints

not to walk in any way of their evil ways, as in pride, in keeping at distance with other people, or in apparel, diet, housing, and fantastic fashions, comliments, couches and congees, clothing in scarlet, and faring deliciously every day, or in covetousness, advancing their estates, families and relations upon the ruins of the people.[21]

Despite the unfeminine range of questions they address, however, these women petitioners continue to emphasise their stereotypically feminine qualities. Reforms must be necessary since 'the thing is so gross, that even women perceive the evil of it'. Lilburne's suffering has had 'our hearts melting in tenderness', and so 'we could not forbear to make this our humble application unto you'. The excuse for petitioning, and its necessity, are one and the same. In their earlier 1649 petition they had explained, using a logic much favoured by the radical sectaries throughout the Commonwealth period, that women's very weakness makes them the most appropriate bearers of truth, 'it being a usual thing with God, by weak means to work mighty effects'.[22] Aspects of the same ideology could be used to make a case to cross its boundaries. This carefully negotiated space marks the petitions out as the work of women, despite Woodhouse's throwaway remark that 'it is improbable that this petition was actually composed by the women'.[23]

Women were combining in an attempt to alter government policy, justifying their actions with the assertion that since they were affected by affairs of state, they should be allowed to express their opinions. This is a wholly different view of women's place in society from that expressed in *The Lawes Resolution of Women's Rights* in 1632. T.E. explains there that women have no voice in parliament because 'they make no laws, they consent to none, they abrogate none' (p. 6). It may be true, as Christopher Hill states, that no one sat down in those years and explicitly and unambiguously formulated the suggestion that not only men, but women, too, should have the vote.[24] Nonetheless, the actual practices of women at the time show that some of them, at least, had no doubt that a voice in parliament was theirs by right.

Women were encroaching a long way into men's territory, and this provoked a male backlash. One sign of this is the fact that parliament's heated debate over the Act of Subscribing the Engagement (a loyalty oath) in 1650 resulted in only one change in the Bill: the word 'persons' was changed to 'men', exempting women from the duty to swear their allegiance to the Commonwealth. In law, they were thus resubsumed into their husbands' identities.[25] The more virulent attack on female petitioning, however, came from the royalists. They produced a whole series of pamphlets in the late 1640s and 1650s, parodying those presented by women. These texts reduce women's complaints to a desire for more sex, and their bargaining power to the threatened withholding of sexual activity from their husbands. The Grand Remonstrance of 1641 (a statement of parliament's grievances) had been a crucial element in the outbreak of the Civil War, containing, as it did, a sweeping indictment of Charles's government. The royalist pamphleteers take the term 'remonstrance' and apply it to women's affairs, producing in 1647 *A Remonstrance of the Shee-Citizens of London. And of many other the free-borne Women of England. Humbly shewing their desires for the attaining of a free trade.* They present the very idea of women objecting to the government as absurd. The 'free trade' that women are missing is not the useful employment of working women, but the sexual prowess of royalist soldiers. This was followed in 1659 by *The Ladies Remonstrance*, which is equally derisory on the subject of women having complaints to make. The 'religious toleration' they sought is explained as a demand to be allowed to 'lie with man of any colour hair or body shape'. This later text is still startling in the vitriolic fury with which it turns on women.[26]

If such a backlash started during the 1650s, however, its main force did not develop until after the restoration of the monarchy in 1660. The court of the returned monarch swiftly established for itself a reputation for profligacy and debauchery. Although an active promotion of sexual pleasure need not necessarily include elements that are woman-hating, the predatory male culture developed at court certainly was. It is therefore not surprising to find that the 1660s also saw the beginnings of home-grown pornography.[27] The re-established monarchy undertook as one of its tasks to beat women back from their uppity behaviour in the 1640s and 1650s. Redefining them simply as 'sex', as the eager objects of male sexual desire, was an integral part of this assault, as I shall argue in more detail in Chapter Four. Faced with such an onslaught – with a shift in the dominant definitions of desirable feminine behaviour – women not only retreated from state politics, but also began, of necessity, to assert their virtue, their lack of interest in male pornographic fantasies. Many of the texts published by women after the restoration advocate celibacy, rejecting any female involvement in sexuality, as I shall explore at greater length in Chapters Four, Five and Six. Here, then, is the second reason for the title of this book: after a period of public female activity, women were forced back into virtue.

It is frequently asserted that Charles II's return to England in 1660 was met with universal rejoicing. It is certainly the case that many pamphlets were published heralding the event, including Rachel Jevon's

Exultationis Carmen, published in both English and Latin. (It was very rare for women to be taught Latin in the period, and almost unknown for them to publish in the language.) Jevon's greeting to the king presents her as his helpless subject, unable to stem an effortless outpouring of joy.

> Dread sovereign Charles! O king of most renown!
> Your country's father; and your kingdom's crown;
> More splendid made by dark affliction's night;
> Live ever monarch in celestial light:
> Before your sacred feet these lines I lay,
> Humbly imploring, that, with glorious ray,
> You'll deign these first unworthy fruits to view,
> Of my dead muse, which from her urn you drew.
> Though for my sex's sake I should deny,
> Yet exultation makes the verse, not I;
> And shouting cries, 'Live ever Charles, and be
> Most dear unto thy people, they to thee.'[28]

The poem was not the naive outpouring that it might at first appear. Two years later, on or around the anniversary of the restoration, she made a personal (unpublished) petition to the king for 'the place of one of the meanest servants about the queen'.[29] It would be interesting to know whether she was successful in what seems a planned strategy of publicising her learning, royalism and humility, and won herself a job.

Another woman who used a printed text as part of a wider plan to gain recognition from the king was Anne Wyndham. In 1667 she published *Claustrum Regale Reseratum*, an account (in English) of her family's role in securing Charles II's escape after the Battle of Worcester in 1651. The text was probably written by her late husband, Colonel Wyndham, who had presented a manuscript version of the story to the king in 1660. After his death in 1666, Anne Wyndham applied for a pension of £400 a year, which was finally granted the same year as *Claustrum Regale Reseratum* appeared in print.[30]

At the time of the restoration itself, in 1660, there was also a brief flurry of shorter individual petitions. Mary Love republished *Loves Name Lives*, and Mary Hewitt, whose husband had also been executed during the Commonwealth period, appealed to the Commons to exempt the man who had tried him from the Act of Oblivion which had given an almost universal pardon to parliamentarians.[31] Mary Wandesford petitioned for lands in Hampshire granted to the family by Charles I to be returned to her.[32] Hewitt's and Wandesford's cases were clearly drafted by lawyers.

Even if it is true that most people did initially feel enthusiastic about the restoration of the monarchy – Charles had after all signed the Declaration of Breda promising to allow people to live according to their own beliefs – it is not the case that that optimism was universal. In 1661 the Fifth Monarchists attempted an armed uprising (swiftly crushed). In the years that followed, a series of intensely restrictive laws were passed (the 'Clarendon Code'), and there were probably few radicals who did not know someone who was fined or imprisoned, and who perhaps died in jail. Although things were far from free under Oliver or Richard Cromwell (in 1657, for instance, after a prominent Quaker, James Nayler, accompanied by a group of women, had ridden into Bristol on a donkey in imitation of Jesus, perhaps heralding the Second Coming, laws were passed reducing the right to freedom of worship, and Nayler was savagely punished), the increase in state repression after 1661 was marked. The picture is complicated, however, by the king's need to establish some toleration for Catholicism – something that could best be achieved by linking it to more general religious liberalism, since the English hostility to 'Popery' was so intense. Acts reducing freedom of worship therefore alternated with declarations granting toleration through much of Charles II's reign.

From 1662, when Charles married the Catholic princess Catherine of Braganza, the court became a centre of Catholicism. In 1670, under a secret treaty with Louis XIV of France (whose authoritarian regime was commonly seen as proof that a 'Popish' king would be tyrannical), Charles undertook to turn England Catholic. In 1673, his brother James, his most probable successor, publicly announced his conversion to Catholicism and married another Catholic princess, Mary of Modena. As Charles's policies seemed to be becoming more pro-Catholic, Lord Shaftesbury was dismissed from his post as Lord Chancellor for opposing them, and the subsequent division of parliament between Whigs (supporters of Shaftesbury) and Tories (followers of the Crown) is usually cited as the beginning of 'party politics'. (In 1681, as agitation against Charles increased, Shaftesbury was imprisoned for treason, but found not guilty and released to much public excitement.) From 1673 until Charles's death in 1685, whenever parliament met it attempted to restrict the constitutional powers of any future Catholic monarch, or to ban Catholics from the throne altogether. Since the right to call, adjourn or dissolve parliament lay with the king, he repeatedly used this power to prevent parliamentary debate, and for the last four years of his reign did not summon one at all. It is not surprising, therefore, that when James came to the throne in 1685 his reign was brief and stormy. He was ejected in the so-called Glorious Revolution of 1688, and his Protestant distant cousin William of Orange and William's wife Mary (James's daughter) invited to come and rule in his place: but to do so within clearly defined limits of monarchical power.

In the midst of the storms of the 1670s erupted the Popish Plot. Great furore was whipped up over Titus Oates's entirely untrue assertion that there was a Catholic plot to murder Charles II and replace him with his brother James. In the panic that followed, many people were jailed and several leading Catholics executed. This sketch of the events of the restoration might best be concluded by a more extended consideration of writings by one woman, Elizabeth Cellier (like Hester Shaw, curiously enough, a midwife; Cellier's writings on midwifery will be discussed in Chapter Seven), who involved herself with the machinations of the Popish Plot, perhaps partly in an attempt to bring some relief to Catholic prisoners.

It might have been the necessary mobility of midwives that helped to divert attention from Elizabeth Cellier in 1678, when she made repeated visits to Catholics imprisoned in the Popish Plot furore. In any case, when she met Thomas Dangerfield (alias Willoughby) in Newgate in 1679, she felt free to employ him to provide her with information on the ill-treatment of his Catholic fellow-prisoners. After she had paid for his release, he also frequented coffeehouses and other Presbyterian meeting places, piecing together, he said, evidence of a Presbyterian Plot to replace Charles II with his illegitimate son, Monmouth. His written reports to Cellier were hidden in a flour tub at her house, their discovery there leading to the affair being christened the Meal-Tub Plot. Dangerfield was arrested and charged with fabricating the story of the Presbyterian Plot and attempting to cast suspicion on Shaftesbury by hiding papers in the room of Mansell, a leading Whig. Dangerfield quickly confessed that there was no truth in the intrigue, claiming that Cellier had employed him to invent it in order to hide the existence of a genuine Popish Plot. Like so many Catholics before her, Cellier was arrested on a charge of treason, but found not guilty when she raised in court Dangerfield's long criminal history, debarring him from giving evidence against her. After her release she published *Malice Defeated*, her account of these events.[33]

The text is quite a patchwork, including sections by Cellier recording her conversion to Catholicism, her prison visiting, and her relationship with Dangerfield. It also contains a copy of the petition she repeatedly tried to have read in parliament, and her account of her trial. In addition, she prints some of the papers found in her mealtub, describing the living conditions and torture of Catholic prisoners, and affidavits from various people asserting the dishonesty of William Stroud, one of the key witnesses against them. The government must have been alarmed by the expected content of *Malice Defeated*, since part of it was seized in the press.[34] When this failed to deter Cellier from publishing her work and selling it from her own home, she was again arrested, this time on a charge of malicious slander, found guilty of lying about the Catholics' prison conditions and sentenced to a hefty fine and the pillory. Two years later she petitioned the king to set aside the fine, since, sick and weak after being stoned almost to death in the pillory, and unable to pay her fine, she was in danger of dying in prison.

Elizabeth Cellier underwent two years' imprisonment and risked death by stoning for a text that she disowned. Official state papers concerning the pamphlet describe its authorship as uncertain, suggesting in one place that Mr Anderson, a priest, might have written *Malice Defeated*, in another naming a Mr Synge as Cellier's amanuensis. During the libel trial,[35] Cellier was questioned at length in an attempt to make her claim authorship of the text, but she steadfastly refused. If she was to be saved from a severe sentence, she had to convince the court that the text was not her work, despite the appearance of her name on the title page. When questioned about John Perry's evidence that she had described the book as hers when he bought a copy from her, she tried at first to escape by putting her remarks down to feminine vanity. When this tactic failed, she continued

My Lord, I hope you will please to remember, he swears, I said only it was mine, not that I was the author . . . I said it was my book, and so it was, because it was in my possession, but not that I writ it. This is my fan, but it does not follow that I made it. (*Malice Defeated*, p. 17)

The court was not convinced.

An examination of *Malice Defeated* suggests that Elizabeth Cellier indeed played a part, at least, in its composition. The problem pre-occupying the author is the typically feminine need to clear Cellier from charges of dishonesty and immodesty in both a general and a specifically sexual sense. A large number of scurrilous ballads and mock petitions were published attacking her, and these make great play of her 'indecent' profession, midwifery. In her case, the commmon slide from condemning a woman for 'immodesty' to questioning her chastity is made easier by her trade. She is portrayed as an immoral Popish bawd, receiving her just deserts in the pillory. *The Tryal of Elizabeth Cellier*, one of several contemporary accounts of the libel trial, shuts her back into her 'proper place'.

As to the prisoner's defence, it was very inconsiderable, her romantic spirit was much abated and she talked abundantly more like a midwife, than such a politician and stateswoman as she would be accounted. (p. 3)

Malice Defeated attempts to counteract this kind of deprecation, con-cluding the account of events leading up to her first trial with a specific appeal to her own sex to forgive and defend her. The appearance of this passage, and the clear dissociation it urges between social bravery and sexual boldness, can be read as evidence that Cellier herself was involved, at least, in the writing of *Malice Defeated*.

Thus I have laid open the truth of my case, to be believed or not believed, as reason, sense and probability shall guide men.

And as to my own sex, I hope they will pardon the errors of my story, as well as those bold attempts of mine that occasioned it . . . though it may be thought too masculine . . .

And in all my defence, none can truly say but that I preserved the modesty, though not the timorousness common to my sex. And I believe there is none, but had they been in my station, would, to their power, have acted like me; for it is more our business than men's to fear; and consequently to prevent the tumults and troubles factions tend to, since we by nature are hindered from sharing any part but the frights and disturbances of them. (p. 31)

It would be a mistake to draw too close a comparison between these words by Cellier and the earlier activities of Leveller women. She was a Catholic, employed in the royal household. The Levellers were radicals, many of them from very poor homes. No one would expect their stance on public issues to be the same. It is noticeable nonetheless that, while women so diverse from one another all assert their virtue when writing, those radicals at the beginning of the period use this as a way of advocating increased female involvement in affairs of state. Cellier, by contrast, exhorts women to quiescence and withdrawal from such matters, 'since it is more our business than men's to fear'. By the end of the period, women were retreating, of necessity, to virtue.

THE PAST AND THE PRESENT

Studying the past feels a little like being a visitor in a foreign culture. When we go abroad, we are limited in what we understand about the country we visit not only by differences in language and our lack of previous experience of its inhabitants, but also by the fact that we look at it through our own cultural preconceptions. Consciously or not, we are only aware of ways in which it is either 'like home' or 'not like home'. This binary (either/or) opposition blinds us to all the ways in which the foreign land is organised according to patterns which are neither exactly 'like' nor 'not like' our own. We constantly misrecognise or distort what we are looking at. People working on the past make similar errors: in many ways, we find what we are looking for. Pushing the argument to its extreme, we could say that history does not study the past at all: that all we can really address ourselves to, whatever we might believe ourselves to be up to, is the here and now. There is a lot of truth in this, but it is not quite accurate. All accounts of the past are not equally true, just as all foreigners' responses to a culture are not equally valid (although differences between such descriptions do tell us about the preconceptions of those making them). The past does produce surprises, setting us puzzles that seem not to make sense. Our attempts to understand things that seem not to add up make us aware of some of the cultural blinkers we wear. The past, like any foreign culture, can educate us about the 'here and now' by making us aware of how it differs from the 'there and then'.

Through studying the past we return with fresh eyes to the present. We can be forced to realise that the way we live here and now is not due to 'human nature' but is socially created, and can only be socially changed. We might also be prompted newly to see ways in which our own culture is organised in the interests of certain groups (whites, men, the middle class, heterosexuals), and against the interests of others (Black people, women, the working class, lesbians and gay men).

Nonetheless, it is true that our own cultural framework predetermines what we look for in the past, and what we find. This is why until recently 'history' has mainly been concerned with the activities of powerful white men (and 'literature' with white male writing). This is changing not because we have suddenly discovered evidence about the lives and ideas of other groups, magically allowing knowledge to progress. Rather, oppressed groups today, such as women, have returned to the past and its writings with new questions, and begun to establish that the evidence has been there all along: but it has been invisible to those whose eyes have encountered it before. (This is not to say that we will find evidence for everything we might wish to know about the past. Many things were never written down; and, as I discuss above, the connections between written texts and people's 'real lives' are anyway not straightforward.)

Finding 'our past' is important to us in far-reaching ways. In the light of arguments going on among feminists today about pornography and male violence, we might see the retreat of our foremothers into an avowal of 'virtue' as a warning that we should not repeat their mistake. Explicit presentation of sexual desire need not be oppressive of women. Heterosexual intercourse is not the same thing as rape. Women are not *naturally* more virtuous or less lascivious than men. Opposing male power need not mean rejecting desire or, necessarily, violence.

Studying the past is part of a process of challenging the values of the society we live in today. Which is more important, knowing about wars or about childbirth?; the fates of kings, or the work of midwives? In the light of such questions, some readers might wonder why I have allowed the chronological limits of this study to be set by two such instantly recognisable dates (in traditional history) as 1649 and 1688. In fact, when I began this work I deliberately avoided these end-dates, intending to look within the arbitrary limits of 1650 to 1680. The texts themselves

– the crucial importance to seventeenth-century writers of both genders of the beheading of the king – led me back to 1649; 1688, since it saw the death of Aphra Behn, later became the end-date. Perhaps future work on the period will reveal how this frame has distorted my work in ways invisible now to me.

A related problem for feminist historians is how we can know whether what we find in the past was new *then*, or whether it is simply 'new to us' because of our present lack of knowledge about the past. Perhaps some of the shifts in women's writing that I chart in this book are not changes at all, or are changes of a different kind from the one I perceive.

One final question about these past writers that has been posed to me repeatedly: were they any good? This question sounds innocent, as if it is asking for an 'objective' response. In fact, the query comes from and is limited by the dominant literary and educational cultures of today. A lot of work has been done in the last ten years or so showing that our ideas about what makes for 'good writing' are connected to and help support many of the values of the 'establishment': of white, heterosexual, middle-class men. We need to ask a different sort of question about writings from the past. I am much more interested in what women's writings show us about female struggles within and against the demands made of them, than I am in their use of rhyme or complexity of characterisation (to take some extreme examples of the narrowness of conventional literary-critical concerns). In asserting this, I might be accused of 'making a virtue of necessity'. I don't believe it.

CHAPTER ONE

PROPHETS AND PROPHECIES

WELL over half the texts published by women between 1649 and 1688 were prophecies. These were written by women who present themselves as divinely inspired counterparts of the Old Testament prophets, whose role was to report and interpret God's messages to His people. They addressed the major issues of national politics of the day, such as the call for the abolition of tithes and establishment of true religious freedom, and engaged in disputes over specific elements of doctrine. This was especially common in the 1650s, when the various radical sects that had mushroomed into existence before and during the English revolution struggled to establish the new form of state that they had fought for in the war.[1] These groups (their members were known as 'sectaries') emphasised the importance of direct divine inspiration as a source of authority that was not dependent on the hierarchies of the national church they had overthrown. Phyllis Mack has shown that women could be perceived as particularly suitable vessels for God's messages. Their lowly status, it was reasoned, would make them less predisposed to the sin of taking pride in their heavenly inspiration, and demonstrated that, with God's help, the last could indeed be made first. In addition, it was felt that women's irrational and emotional essence and lack of strong personal will could make them especially receptive to the external Voice of God. Women prophets were possessed by the Lord, burdened with the duty to speak.

After the Restoration, as persecution of radicals increased under the workings of the Clarendon Code, sectaries were gradually reduced to silence and inertia. During the 1670s, one of the most radical groups, the Quakers, instituted a major internal reorganisation which served to 'temper the Spirit' of its members.[2] These changes included reassigning women to more feminine caring roles, and most of the prophecies published by female Friends in the latter part of the period are quieter, more 'rational' affairs than the enthusiastic *Warnings* and *Messages* of the era of revolutionary potential, more concerned with questions of internal discipline than matters of state.

In assessing the meaning and significance of these pamphlets, I will be questioning the assertions of two schools of thought about women sectaries. The first of these, represented in the work of Keith Thomas and Christopher Hill, presents female prophets as mere auxiliaries to their male counterparts, and fails to understand how the women's activities present a case for their right to be involved in matters of national government.[3] A second interpretation appears in Hilda Smith's *Reason's Disciples*. She asserts that the prophets were not really woman-centred, or concerned with issues of family structure or male power, and so were not challenging patriarchal domination as their later, royalist sisters did. I believe that, on the contrary, they actively and deliberately transcended the bonds of true feminine self-effacement, using the ideas and structures of contemporary thought to negotiate some space and autonomy. The very terms of this rebellion, however – the women described themselves and perhaps perceived themselves as passive instruments of God's Will, mere channels for his Word – also made possible their eventual re-confinement to less noisy, more feminine concerns.

EARLY PROPHETS

During the 1640s and 1650s, more and more women refused to stay silent on the great religio-political questions of the day, and took to prophesying in churches, marketplaces and in the street. Some of them wrote down and published their messages. The most prolific of these early prophets was Lady Eleanor Davies (or Douglas), whose very high social status and knowledge of Latin actually make her atypical. She had risen to prominence in court circles during the 1620s and 1630s as a noted prophet, running into trouble in 1633 when she began to predict the death of Charles I. Her earlier forecasts of the death of her first husband as punishment for destroying her writings, and of the Duke of Buckingham, had proved disturbingly accurate, and she was sentenced to the first of several periods of imprisonment.[4] She continued to publish her messages throughout the 1640s and after the king's execution became particularly prolific, her writings becoming ever more ecstatic and allusive. It would be a mistake, however, to dismiss her prophecies as the spontaneous outpourings of a rambling madwoman. In *From the Lady Eleanor, Her Blessing to her Beloved Daughter*, 1644, Lady Eleanor explains that time is short. This is the period predicted by Daniel, when prophecy would come into its own and be understood

although penned somewhat hastily or unperfectly, etc., being like the honey: and like the honey gathered out of so many parts, I shall the less need to excuse it unto such as have full knowledge of the scriptures, that should it be written at

large a chronicle or a book as ample as those tables of the maps of the world
could I suppose not contain it.

  Not suitable to the little book, being but an epitome as it were, and so much for
being not voluminous, especially when the time so short too. (p. 36)

An examination of several copies of *Elijah the Tishbite's Supplication*,
1650, reveals that identical meticulous corrections of the printed text
have been made in Lady Eleanor's own hand: her prophecy, for all its
obscurity, was an exact one.[5] In *The Appearance or Presence of the Son
of Man*, 1650, she interprets verse eleven of Revelation as referring to a
female deity and creator, who will bring peace and an end of oppressive
religion, a woman superior to 'man' who is associated with death and
hell.

She whose throne heaven, earth her footstool from the uncreated, saying, I am A
and O first and last, both beginning and ending, by whom all things were done:
not without her anything done or made; Trinity in Unity, of manhood the head;
who of death have the keys, and hell: than the Queen of the South a greater, born
a greater not of woman: Malea, by interpretation, Queen of Peace, or She-
Counsellor. And so much for this without contradiction, she his executioner,
made like unto the Son of God, the Ancient of Days' likeness: owner of the title of
tithes, to whom the patriarch offered a tenth.[6]

This 'A' and 'O' (alpha and omega, the first and last letters of the Greek
alphabet) become 'Da.' and 'Do.' in the course of the pamphlet, which
are taken as abbreviations of Lady Eleanor's two married surnames,
Davies and Douglas. She herself, with the voice of God in her, is the deity
described: 'I am A and O' (p. 8).

  Other female radicals might not have claimed to be deities themselves,
but their activities were still seen as dangerously subversive, and many
attacks on them were published. *A List of Some of the Great Blasphemers*, for example, records that many women asserted they were
pregnant with the new Christ of the Second Coming. David Brown's *The
Naked Woman*, 1652, was written in outrage after a woman had
stripped naked in Whitehall to mock a sermon delivered by Peter Sterry
on the theme of Resurrection. Brown was furious that the minister had
failed to reprimand the woman or have her arrested, believing that this
kind of rebellious behaviour was symptomatic of a more general rejection of the new government's authority. She should have been closely
questioned, he asserts, in a manner which would make her proper,
submissive role clear to her.

She ought to have been demanded . . . 4. With what company she walketh? 5.
How long? 6. Whether or not she was sent by them? 7. If not, then by whom? 8.
If by none at all, then did she not run unsent? 9. What her name was? 10. If she
hath a husband? 11. If yea, what his name was? 12. Where he dwelleth? 13. And
if he and she live together? (p. 8)

Although Lady Eleanor's pouring forth of God's word was a highly unusual occurrence when she began to prophesy in the 1620s, by the time of her death in 1652 many women were finding their voice. The popularity of the idea that women could serve as particularly direct funnels for the conveying of divine commands was evident in 1654 when the royalist Arise Evans edited and published *A Message from God (By a Dumb Woman)*. The 'dumb woman' was Elinor Channel, who had been found wandering around the streets of London. She had walked to the city from her Surrey home, leaving behind her husband and many children, driven by the necessity to find someone to write down her prophecy for her. Her message appears to be concerned with one of the great issues of the day: the treatment of debtors. It is distorted by Evans in his marginal notes into a call for Cromwell to align himself with Charles II, and restore the monarchy. Evans seems to have hoped that his version of Channel's prophecy could be used to offset the influence of another divinely inspired woman, the radical sectary Anna Trapnel. Some of Trapnel's hold over her audience had come from the fact that her prophecies, calling for the overthrow of residual monarchical structures in the nation, were spoken in a trance. This could be interpreted as a sure sign that the hand of God was upon her. Channel also exhibited bodily signs of direct divine intervention. When her husband had refused to allow her to travel all the way to London to deliver her message, Evans tells us, she had been struck dumb, and had remained speechless until her husband consented to the journey. Lest the reader should fail to notice the parallel with Trapnel, Evans points it out explicitly.

And though it be but short, yet you shall find more truth and substance in it, than in all Hana Trampenel's songs or sayings, whom some account the Diana of the English, Acts 19.34, as may appear by this that was written for her. (p. 7)

Another woman whose pronouncements produced public controversy was Elizabeth Poole. In 1649 she was granted an audience with the General Council, where she prophesied against their intention to execute Charles I. Agreeing that the king had broken his agreement with the people and been justly overthrown, she nonetheless argued, using an extension of the popular metaphor which likened the nation to a large family, that the country stood in the same relation to the monarch as a wife does to her husband. It was God's will, she proclaimed, that the people not harm the king's body, just as a woman must submit to her husband's body.

You never heard that a wife might put away her husband, as he is the head of her body, but for the Lord's sake suffereth his terror to her flesh, though she be free in the spirit of the Lord. (*A Vision*, 1648/9, p. 5)

In her prophecy she drew on women's experience and elements of feminine duty to define the correct political response of the country in general. Her church (the Baptists led by William Kiffin) responded to this boldness by expelling her, and by publicising charges of immorality against her which would undermine her right to use women's conduct as a basis for ethical decisions. When Poole left London, a warning about her was circulated to various people including John Pendarves, the minister of Abingdon.[7] This was intercepted by his wife Thomasina who, fearing that the accusations were endangering Poole's income –

you cannot be ignorant that she hath no livelihood amongst men, but what she earns by her hands: and your defaming her in this manner cannot in an ordinary way but deprive her of that, and so at last bring her blood upon you[8]

– demanded that Kiffin make a public retraction. 'I have not yet acquainted my husband with your letter' (Elizabeth Poole, *An Alarum*, p. 11), she adds, but explains that this action does not mean that she is a rebellious wife: she is merely God's passive instrument.

A woman prophet could claim a duty to publish, since her writings were not her own works, but God's. Mary Cary's image of her passivity in this arrangement is especially interesting.

I am a very weak, and unworthy instrument, and have not done this work by any strength of my own, but have been often made sensible, that I could do no more herein (wherein any light, or truth could appear) of myself, than a pencil, or pen can do, when no hand guides it.[9]

By using this particular analogy for her impotence, Cary also brings to mind a picture of her own hand guiding the pencil. Her role as writer of the text is actually accented, while she makes the requisite denial of her agency in the matter. Her identity as author is further enhanced when she explains to the reader that she had signed herself as 'Cary' because this is the name she was using when she last published, in 1648. She has since changed her name to Rande, but is publishing under her previous surname so that both texts will be identified as hers. Although there is no way of knowing whether Cary was being deliberately self-effacing to make her writing more acceptable to her audience, the image she chose certainly serves the double function of both confirming her feminine passivity and providing her with access to the status of author. Affirming her femininity might have been especially necessary. *The Little Horns Doom and Downfall* is followed by *A New and More Exact Mappe, or Description of New Jerusalems Glory*. This second part of the text includes a call to war, asserting that the Saints can justly use the 'material sword' to establish the New Jerusalem. Her prophecy thus directly opposes Elizabeth Poole's understanding of the people's duty.

Her vision of the Godly Commonwealth is an especially female one.

She is particularly concerned to portray the new roles open to women in her utopia, where all will be prophets, unlike the contemporary situation where

they are generally very unable to communicate to others, though they would do it many times in their families, among their children and servants: and when they would be communicating to others into whose company they come, though sometimes some sprinklings come from them, yet at other times they find themselves dry and barren. (p. 238)

To use the word 'barren' to refer to a woman's inability to speak confidently in the public world is a direct challenge to an orthodoxy which would see her only significant products as those of her body, her only 'barrenness' a failure to provide an heir for her husband. She also makes a more direct reference to the property relations between husbands and wives. She makes their legal identities as one person into a proof of a woman's right to property, 'for there is nothing that he possesses that she hath not a right unto' (p. 54). In Cary's new world, 'no infant of days shall die' (p. 289), and the laziness of the rich will cease: 'such idle and profane creatures shall then have no allowance or sufferance to live such lives as now they do' (p. 308). Cary's commitment to a radical equality between people extends to her relationship with her readers. She says that her message will only be confirmed as the will of God if others recognise Christ's voice in it (p. 46).[10] God's will, as transmitted by Cary, is that a profoundly egalitarian society be established. In *Twelve Humble Proposals* she warns the government to see to the needs of the poor before worrying about other matters, and calls for an absolute ceiling of £200 a year to be placed on earnings. Lands confiscated from delinquent royalists, she adds, must not be resold into private hands, but kept in the common treasury for the good of all (pp. 8, 12, 13).

ANNA TRAPNEL AND THE FIFTH MONARCHY

Parliament paid no heed to Cary's prophecy, and more women began to speak out against the new government's decisions. If we look in a little more detail at the writings of one of them, we will understand more about how female prophecy was defined and understood. Anna Trapnel's name first appeared in print early in 1654, with the publication of *Strange and Wonderful Newes from White-hall*. This short pamphlet describes her falling into a trance on 11 January that year, and prophesying for eleven days and twelve nights to the crowds who came to hear her. A detailed rendering of some of the verses followed in *The Cry of a Stone*, the text of which was apparently taken down as she was speaking, with a view to publication. She laments the state of the Commonwealth, referring to the present powers as the 'fourth horn' of Daniel's prophecy, which must be overthrown at the imminent arrival of the Fifth Monarchy, the time of Christ's personal reign.[11] Her outpouring was provoked by recent events in the government. The Barebones Parliament (Parliament of Saints), a nominated assembly which had included twelve Fifth Monarchist leaders among its 144 members had been dissolved on 12 December 1653. The arrests of certain Fifth Monarchists (Christopher Feake, John Simpson and Vavasor Powell) had swiftly followed, as they began to prophesy and preach against Cromwell.[12] It was at Powell's trial in Whitehall that Trapnel first fell into her trance.

Shortly after her recovery, Trapnel was called on by God to visit Cornwall. In *Anna Trapnel's Report and Plea* she describes the conversation she had with the divinity on that occasion, and her attempts to talk him out of the idea. The Lord was adamant, however, and so she set off, despite her own misgivings and those of her friends (pp. 1–2). In Cornwall, she visited two Fifth Monarchist members of the Barebones Parliament, Francis Langden and John Bawden, travelling and preaching in the vicinity until she was arrested and imprisoned, first in Plymouth, then in Bridewell, London.[13] While she was in prison, the congregation of her church, All-Hallows the Great, published her account of her conversion, *A Legacy for Saints*. This was followed by her narrative of her visit to Cornwall, and subsequent arrest, in her *Report and Plea*. These publications appear to have helped to bring her plight to public notice, and she was soon released from prison. In August 1657 she again fell into a trance, and her prophecies were recorded in *Voice for the King of Saints*.[14] After August 1658, her prophetic voice fell silent. She does not appear to have written anything at the time of the failed Fifth Monarchist rising in 1661.

Although Trapnel did not actually *write* several of the texts published under her name – they were written down by someone else while she was in her trances – they bear her name on the title page, and we can assume that she approved their contents. *Voice for the King of Saints* even has a final sheet listing printer's errors, indicating that close attention has been paid to the details of the text.

If Anna Trapnel's travels and trances can be understood as a response to the imprisoning of male members of her movement, it is her relationships with women that dominate the writings themselves. The women might have had their own meetings and organisational structures. The Fifth Monarchist congregation led by Thomas Venner certainly did: the 'sisters that meet together' had the task of spreading the rebels' manifesto in preparation for the 1657 uprising.[15] There is so little evidence about these women's meetings that it is difficult to know what to make of them.

Certain references in Trapnel's works, however, suggest the existence of special bonds among female Saints. After her dispute with God over the necessity for her to travel to Cornwall, for instance, she discusses the plan with her 'sisters', and before she sets off ten of them sit up with her all night to pray for a successful outcome (*Report and Plea*, pp. 2, 7). After her arrest, she is visited in Bridewell by women, and one of them, Ursula Adman, moves into the prison with her, staying for seven of the eight weeks of her imprisonment.[16]

The possibility that these women were able to help one another establish some autonomy from their 'brothers' is increased by Trapnel's passing references to marriage. One of her utterances in *Voice of the King of Saints* is addressed to her unnamed 'companions'.

> Hallelujah, Hallelujah Lord,
> For companions I will sing,
> And praises shall be given here,
> Because they have not been
> Carried about, not yet enticed,
> From thee by any means,
> And they shall here meet with reproof,
> If on creatures they lean.
> Hallelujah, Hallelujah for
> Companions that do come,
> And are not wedded to anything,
> But to King Solomon. (p. 23)

In this instance, of course, her use of the term 'not wedded' can be interpreted metaphorically. During her questioning at her arrest in Cornwall, however, she explicitly equates marriage with a loss of freedom – something that she has been saved from.

Lobb: I understand you are not married.

A.T.: Then having no hindrance, why may not I go where I please, if the Lord so will?[17]

Trapnel was careful to make it explicit that God's message was addressed to women as well as men. Rejoicing in salvation, she reflects 'Oh to be in Christ! Who can tell out his or her estate, night and day? How pleasant it is?' (*Legacy*, p. 12). She explicitly proposes that women are included in God's promises, and that their responsibility is directly to him, not to men.

> John thou wilt not offended be
> That handmaids here should sing,
> That they should meddle to declare
> The matters of the King.
> John will not be displeased that

> They sit about the throne,
> And go unto original
> And nothing else will own . . .
> And the handmaids were promised
> Much of that spirit choice,
> And it is, and it shall go forth
> In a rare singing voice.
> (*Voice*, pp. 37, 54)

Her use of other biblical references is also selective. When describing Christ's resurrection. For example, she stresses that it was to women that He first appeared, and that men played a lesser role (*Voice*, pp. 35, 51).

Trapnel's prophecies pour forth in verse. To the modern eye, this might make it hard to believe that such an avalanche could have happened spontaneously. To Trapnel, it was a sure sign that the hand of God was upon her. 'Inflamed with love' for her Creator, she could not help but sing. She sang hymns of praise in every conceivable circumstance, including when on the road to Cornwall, and while in prison in Bridewell. Once she is singing, she enters a state of oblivion, in which she is secure from the physical conditions which might oppress her (*Report and Plea*, p. 42).

Her contemporaries might be uncertain whether to perceive her as God's handmaid, or as mad. John Evelyn mentions a sightseeing visit he made to Bedlam, London's insane asylum, where he saw 'nothing extraordinary, besides some miserable poor creatures in chains; one was mad with making verses'.[18] Trapnel also met her share of doubters. Her preface to her *Report and Plea* explains that she had decided to print her account of her imprisonment because she had been adjudged as mad. In *The Cry of a Stone* she adds that this 'distraction' has been called a kind of 'immodesty', and appeals to God to prove that she acts at his bidding (p. 67).

To be assessed as mad could have caused her to be confined to Bedlam, as Lady Eleanor was. Equally dangerous was the charge that she was a witch, the tool of the devil. *Anna Trapnel's Report and Plea* is centrally concerned with the problem of witchcraft, since this was in fact one of the accusations made against her. While she was in prison, people in Dartmouth reported that she had bewitched the winds, preventing their ships from setting sail (p. 35). She was also threatened with a visit from a 'witch-tryer-woman', and thanked God that he preserved her from this, and 'her great pin which she used to thrust into witches, to try them'.[19] Her description of her trial in Plymouth indeed reveals a great deal of the terror a woman accused of witchcraft was subjected to. When she came to give evidence in court, her ready control of language, which in other circumstances might have condemned her as unfeminine, became imperative. Should she have been too nervous to speak eloquently when publicly questioned, she would have been burnt as a witch.

> The report was, that I would discover myself to be a witch when I came before the justices, by having never a word to answer for myself; for it used to be so among the witches, they could not speak before the magistrates, and so they said, it would be with me; but the Lord quickly defeated them herein, and caused many to be of another mind. (p. 25)

The suspicion of evil magic was dropped once she had proved herself able to speak up for herself: 'And the rude multitude said, "Sure this woman is no witch, for she speaks many good words, which the witches could not" ' (p. 28). Even once this was apparently settled, her skill with words was put to further use. She describes how on another occasion her questioner tried to give his own interpretations to her replies, and she had to struggle to prevent this: 'The Lord kept me out of his ensnarements' (p. 33). It is not surprising that she ascribes her survival to an act of God. Her life was in serious jeopardy, and she had already experienced her inspiration to versify as proof of His control over her. In general, women's command of language was a far more tenuous affair, as the quotations above from Mary Cary's prophecies indicate.

Although Trapnel describes in detail her persecutions, she unfailingly returns to interpret them as having a general, historical significance. It is because she is a Fifth Monarchist, propagating belief in Christ's imminent Second Coming, that she is suffering, not because she is Anna Trapnel. The prophecies she makes during her trances are unequivocal in the alliances she seeks to forge. In *The Cry of a Stone* she calls on Cromwell to abandon his title as Lord Protector, and acknowledge Christ as the only real Protector. She accuses him of having betrayed the revolution, remarking 'If he were not [speaking of the Lord Cromwell] backslidden, he would be ashamed of his great pomp and revenue, whilst the poor are ready to starve' (p. 50). She exhorts the army sergeants to remember that their allegiance should be to the common people, and appeals to soldiers not to attack Saints, but hold fast to their original aims (pp. 20, 56, 65–6). She condemns tithing, and appeals to merchants not to betray the radical aims of the war (pp. 40, 30). In her *Report and Plea* she also describes how she worked long hours to make money to help finance the parliamentary army (p. 50).

Although the major modern study of the Fifth Monarchists, Bernard Capp's *Fifth Monarchy Men* (sic), portrays the movement as elitist, Trapnel's writings clearly show that the apocalypse she longs for will transform the lives of all, not just benefit a blessed few.

> Methinks I see not only foolish virgins slumbering and sleeping, but the wise virgins are also in a slumber, but when the bridegroom's appearance shall be

manifested, shall they still lie in a slumber? I believe otherwise, that there shall be such an awaking of all things, the very foundation of all things shall be shaken by that foundation that shall stand for ever. (*Legacy*, pp. 45–6)

Anna Trapnel, like many of her sisters in the 1650s, was awake, and hurrying to awaken others to the 'true meaning' of God's promises.

RADICALISM AND RETREAT

The vast majority of extant women's prophecies were written by Quakers, which might reflect the particularly active role played by women in the Society of Friends. The large number of female Quaker writings is also no doubt due in part to the decision by the Society in 1672 to acquire and preserve two copies of every text published by Friends since the beginning of their movement.[20] No such efficient collection was made of other prophetical writings, and it seems likely that many were lost. What is clear is that the activism of women sectaries was not originated by Quakerism. Women had played important parts in the development of the Familists and Anabaptists earlier in the century. It has often been observed that George Fox (the Quaker leader) made his first 'steeplehouse' interjection in defence of a woman who had asked a question of the church minister.[21] Women, it is suggested, were drawn to the sexual egalitarianism that Quakerism offered. But presenting the origins of the sect in this manner is a distortion. In the early days, in the 1640s and 1650s, the Society of Friends was not a ready-formed body, with established policies and principles, to which women were attracted. Richard Vann has shown that the first Friends were not 'converts' as such. They recognised one another as like-minded individuals. When Sarah Blackborow recalls how she came to join the Quakers, for example, she describes how she found that their message was consistent with her own beliefs. Perhaps the first person to join Fox in those early days was a woman, Elizabeth Hooton. She was already an established preacher when she met Fox, and subsequently became the first Quaker to be imprisoned for preaching. Such a sequence of events can scarcely be interpreted as evidence of women being secondary in the establishment of Quakerism's ideas.[22] We derive a more accurate impression of their role if we reflect that, while it is true that Fox supported a woman's right to speak in church, the initiative in the much-cited case was taken by the woman who asked the question.

In many respects, the ideas and activities of early Quakerism reveal women's part in its establishment. Quaker emphasis on Inner Light as a source of understanding and guide for action grew out of, and made possible women prophets' challenge to their restriction to the private sphere. Women's freedom to minister and to publish the opinions God had revealed to them swiftly extended into a duty or right to 'witness against' specific men. They could criticise men's views because the equality of Spirit in women and men gave equal validity to their interpretations of God's will. In 1655, for example, Margret Braidley assured the minister John Shopp, 'Thou art no minister of Christ, but a minister of Antichrist.'[23] This practice served as useful training for women like Mary Pennyman, Ann Mudd and Elizabeth Atkinson, who later left the Society of Friends and published attacks on their former allies' beliefs. These women felt confident to discuss in detail specific questions of religious doctrine and cite biblical texts in defence of their conclusions. Elizabeth Atkinson's first criticism of the Quakers, *A Breif and plain discovery of the Labourers in mistery*, was swiftly followed by a second and longer text, after Rebeckah Travers had dismissed her argument as 'so contradictive in itself' as not to be worthy of serious refutation, and Anne Travers and Elizabeth Coleman had suggested that she was not the true author of her work.[24]

These early Quakers also instituted other practices which gave women access to activities that might have been proscribed as unwomanly. In her autobiography, Alice Curwen recollects how, on hearing of the suffering of Quakers in New England, she knew that God wanted her and her husband to travel to Boston and preach against persecution. Her husband was opposed to the idea, and finally she set off without him. Her description of this disagreement is noteworthy. It is not presented (nor, perhaps, perceived) as a clash of their individual, human wills. Her intention to travel is a result of God's bidding, and she is puzzled that God has not yet made this desire known to her husband.

Then I having this testimony sealed in my heart, I laboured with my husband
night and day to know his mind, because it was much with me, that we were to
travel together; but he did not yet see it to be required of him at that time . . . but
the Lord make me willing to leave all (that was near and dear to me) and I . . .
made preparation to go to sea, and having got my bed and clothes on board ship,
it pleased the Lord (in whom was and is my trust) to send my husband to go along
with me.[25]

Alice Curwen's call to travel with her husband was relatively unusual. More commonly, these women journeyed and preached with female Friends. When Joan Brooksop and Elizabeth Hooton went to Boston to warn the rulers to cease persecuting Quakers, Hooton, who was aged about sixty, was already a widow. Brooksop, however, had 'forsaken all my relations, husband, and children' to make the journey. Theophila Townsend's *Testimony* for Jane Whitehead recalls Whitehead's first companion, Frances Raunce, 'who is entered into rest with her, and was a fellow labourer with her in the same work and service'. After her marriage, Whitehead continued to minister, and on one occasion was imprisoned in Ilchester away 'from her husband, and four small children, and one tender child she carried in her arms'. Joan Vokins, who travelled ceaselessly in Ireland, the West Indies and New England despite constant ill-health, also left behind her husband and children, noting in one of her letters home

It is troublesome for me to write, the vessel doth so wave. I desire that Susan Dew, and Mary Elson may see this, or have a copy of it: and also my dear husband and children.[26]

Perhaps the most remarkable travelling fellowship was that between Katherine Evans and Sarah Chevers, who in 1658 set off together for Alexandria, leaving behind their husbands and children. They only got as far as Malta, where they had already been kept in prison by the Inquisition for three years when another Quaker, Daniel Baker, visited them, and published their account of their sufferings.[27] Their courage and determination, and confidence in one another's fortitude, even when kept in solitary confinement for months on end, are compelling. Their identity as prophets gave them a route out of the narrow confines of their families and dependence on their husbands. Their role as God's messengers might also have been the deciding factor in achieving their release. As the period of their incarceration lengthened, they took more and more to fasting and stripping naked to prophesy God's vengeance on their behalf. When a gunpowder store was struck by lightning, causing much damage in the city, Sarah Chevers was accused of witchcraft but was not executed (*A True Account*, pp. 228–30, 236–46, 250–1). Perhaps the Inquisitors were not quite confident of their diagnosis. As negotiations for the release continued, the Inquisition kept reducing its demands, until finally the women were granted their freedom in return for an undertaking that they would go away and not return. As Katherine Evans expressed it, 'We were very dreadful to them' (pp. 229–30). The likelihood that the women convinced the Inquisition of their divine inspiration is increased in the light of subsequent events. After they left Malta they stopped at Tangiers to prophesy. They were arrested, but this time not imprisoned: 'The Governor said, he did lovingly receive our good instructions and admonitions, and promised to follow our counsel' (p. 258). In general, the achievements of all these women were made possible by the power they obtained through being identified as the weak recipients of God's word. Within the confines of femininity, they were able to negotiate a space that allowed for decidedly unfeminine activities.

Quaker writings pass through a series of changes in the period. Among the very first publications are texts written during imprisonment. The women appeal against prison conditions, or reaffirm their belief in the principles for which they were arrested.[28] *The Lambs Defence against*

Lies, 1656, contains Dorothy Waugh's description of what happened when she spoke out in Carlisle marketplace in 1655 'against all deceit and ungodly practices'. She was promptly hauled off to jail. When she was unrepentant, the mayor ordered the scold's bridle to be put on her head to make an example of her. This cruel contraption, which was also used against witches and 'nagging' wives, was a heavy iron mask with three bars across the face and a large piece which, crammed into the woman's mouth, caused her great pain and made her incapable of speech. Dorothy Waugh's jailer tried to make some money from the situation, charging people two pence a time to view her.

And the people to see me so violently abused were broken into tears, but he [the mayor] cried out on them and said 'For foolish pity, one may spoil a whole city'. (p. 30)

Later, she was turned out into the street still wearing the bridle, and ordered to be whipped from city to city until she was home.

From about 1655 onwards, more prophecies were published calling on specific groups of people, such as priests and lawyers, or the inhabitants of particular towns, such as Plymouth, Oxford, Dartmouth or Dover, to repent. The writers dwell less on the specific circumstances of their own sufferings, emphasising the general judgement and overturning that is imminently expected. Some of these simply address 'all the world', explaining that their message is from God, and must be heeded before it is too late.[29] The year 1659 also saw a mass Quaker women's petition, carrying seven thousand signatures, calling for the abolition of tithes and recommending other radical changes.[30] These warnings reach a peak between 1659 and 1662, a period which, as Barry Reay and Alan Cole have shown, was a turning point for Quakerism.[31] The millenarian optimism of early 1659, when Lambert restored the Rump, was swiftly replaced by the spectre of Charles's return and the Restoration. Before 1659, the Society of Friends was not a pacifist movement. Although Quakers firmly believed that the struggle to establish God's kingdom could not be won by the sword alone, they did not scorn its use. Many applied in 1659 to rejoin the armed forces from which they had been expelled. Grace Barwick's petition, carefully addressed *To all present Rulers, whether of Parliament, or whomsoever of England*, reminds General Lambert that her husband had once served as his cornet (cavalry officer). She exhorts the rulers to use force to carry through the long-promised reforms and abolish tithing, assuring them that

being once brought down, and the people eased from it: it can never be supposed, that reasonable men will be so foolish as ever to fight to set it up again, and the people loves liberty, and however that shall come to them, it will be thankfully received, whether by a law or contrary to a law. (p. 3)

As 1659 advanced, hostility towards Quakers grew as it was carefully orchestrated through the pulpit. After the restoration, official persecution intensified, despite the toleration promised in the Declaration of Breda. In 1662, Sarah Blackborow's *Oppressed Prisoners Complaint* reflected

> Is liberty of conscience now a sin,
> Though promised by the word of a king . . .?
> Nine score prisoners in Newgate now doth lie
> For justice, justice, these aloud do cry.

The unsuccessful uprising of the Fifth Monarchists in 1661, and the concentrated persecution of all sectaries under the Clarendon Code, made it necessary for them carefully to bury their involvement in armed radicalism in order to survive. After that date, the character of women's writing slowly changes. Although some continue to rail against persecution, or undertake careful rebuttals of their opponents, by the 1670s many of their publications are concerned either with ending strife within the Society and calling on Friends to stand firm in the faith, or with describing the deathbed testimonies of dying Friends.[32]

The prophecies of the 1650s are very radical texts. Through their relationship with the Spirit, Quaker, Baptist and other radical women can claim a freedom to publish, and they explode into print with rage and joy. This in itself would justify the description 'radical'. In addition, some of the pamphlets exhibit other unconventional or innovative features. The first texts are almost all collective enterprises, written by or on behalf of imprisoned prophets. Most characteristically, they are also jointly written. The most interesting in this respect is *The Saints Testimony Finishing Through Suffering*.[33] The text is a compilation of accounts of the charges against a number of Quakers imprisoned in Banbury. It is prefaced by a description of their subsequent trial, which is written by a body of Friends from Bristol, Gloucester and Berkshire, who travelled to attend it. The pamphlet as a whole shows much evidence that its internal structure and arrangement were carefully discussed by its (mostly anonymous) authors, and the reader is frequently referred from one section to another for further elucidation of specific points. It is surely no coincidence that this work also includes one of the earliest extended Quaker justifications of women's preaching.

This tradition of shared enterprise is also the informing experience that produced Elizabeth Hincks's image of the Body of Christ in *The Poor Widows Mite*, 1671. To describe the church as a body was of course to use a highly conventional image. Hincks's particular vision of the interdependency of its parts, though, and their reliance on one another, is a portrait of collective working.

And so the head it cannot say to the foot, I need not thee;
Nor eke the eye unto the ear, O be thou gone from me:
For that the body is but one, yet members hath it many:
Appear there would deformity, if lack there were of any: . . .
So what is wanting in each one, a supply others have;
To minister unto each wants, by it their souls to save. (p. 7)

The radicalism of the texts extends beyond the circumstances of their actual writing. The world of interdependence and shared labour that the early prophets were heralding would be one without difference of 'degree' (social status). This was succinctly expressed by the Baptist Margaret Abbott, who delivered God's promise to his children that

they shall build houses, and dwell in them; they shall not build, and another possess; they shall plant vineyards, and eat of the fruit of them; they shall not plant, and another eat. (*A Testimony*, p. 8)

Three years later in 1662, Hester Biddle rebuked the new order for its neglect of God's commands.

Oh you high and lofty ones! who spendeth God's creation upon your lusts, and doth not feed the hungry, nor clothe the naked, but they are ready to perish in the streets; both old and young, lame and blind lyeth in your streets, and at your masshouse doors, crying for bread, which even melteth my heart, and maketh the soul of the righteous to mourn: did not the Lord make all men and women upon the earth of one mould, why then should there be so much honour and respect unto some men and women, and not unto others, but they are almost naked for want of clothing, and almost starved for want of bread? (*The Trumpet*, p. 12)

The desire to dispense with class differences also led Anne Clayton, in *A Letter to the King*, to address the returning sovereign as her 'dear Friend' and 'dear Heart'.

The overturning of traditional religious hierarchies and assertion of the Sainthood of all believers could also result in an authorial stance very different from the passive, self-deprecating attitude of Mary Cary quoted above. Hester Biddle's address to the city of Oxford, which was reprinted verbatim as an attack on its twin town of Cambridge, is written in a first-person voice which stands for both Biddle and God. The text opens:

Woe to thee city of Oxford, thy wickedness surmounteth the wickedness of Sodom; therefore repent whilst thou has time, lest I consume thee with fire, as I have done it; therefore harden not your hearts, lest I consume you in my fierce anger, and so be brought to naught.[34]

God's voice and the voice of Hester Biddle are one and the same. The prophecy concludes, 'Remember you are warned in your lifetime, and all left without excuse. Hester Biddle.' Margaret Killin's warning to the 'parish teachers' of Plymouth does not contain such an extended merging of the voice of God and that of his prophet, but it does use similar biblical allusions to dramatic effect.

If ye had stood in my counsel, ye would have turned away from the evil of his doings, but because ye have departed out of my counsel, I will spread dung on your faces, yea I have cast dung on your faces already. (p. 2)

The language of these female prophets also explores in a more diffuse way their relationship with their Lord. God is frequently referred to as a 'nursing mother'. In itself, this phrase is a commonplace in the religious writings of the time. Its meaning when used by men or women differs, however. For the male prophet, it describes a relationship in which he receives care and nourishment, as he did in his relationship with his own mother. For a woman, it also describes an activity which she herself has performed, or might one day perform, when giving suck to her own babies. The dominant, male reading of the image is contested and altered by the female experience. God has qualities that are specifically feminine, and women therefore have a privileged access to understanding those aspects of the divinity. Elizabeth Hincks explains the origin of the term 'nursing mother' by leading the (female) reader into the role of nursing a baby. She also adds a dimension to the arrangement: once the child has fed, the breast feels more comfortable. The relationship is one that provides mutual comfort and benefit.

> And us seeking thus unto God, is as a sucking child,
> That seeketh for its mother's breasts, that is tender and mild.
> And when the child has sucked its fill, the breast likewise is eased,
> The child then it is satisfied, and mother also pleased.
> This figure God made use of when to Israel he did say,
> Her child, can a mother forget, that sucks on her each day? (p. 24)

This can be contrasted with the use made of the image by male preachers in Massachusetts when describing themselves as the 'breasts of God'. Cotton Mather's bizarre expansion of this image – that the *lips* of the ministers are 'the breasts through which the sincere milk of the Word has passed unto you, for your nourishment' – is a purely symbolic use of the metaphor.[35]

The research of present-day feminist linguists has shown that the use of 'man' and 'he' to refer to people of both genders has the effect of eclipsing women, invisibly excluding them from discourse.[36] It is interesting to find, therefore, how frequently the phrases 'he and she' or 'women and men' occur in the visions of the prophets, even though there is no consistent use of such formulations. When they appear however – and they do so remarkably often, as some of the passages quoted above have already shown – they can disrupt the smooth progress of a sentence, drawing the reader's attention to the idea that God's promises were made to women as well as men. Sarah Blackborow, for instance, manages this interruption with the use of parentheses: 'Many there be (sons and daughters) who witness his death and resurrection, who hold forth a true testimony of Jesus to the world' (*Herein is held forth*, p. 4).

The most frequent appearance of images of women in these texts, however, are derogatory descriptions of Popery or the established church as witches or the Whore of Babylon. These comparisons were contemporary commonplaces, and it would be difficult to imagine women condemning the theology of their opponents without using such expressions. Such metaphors were not innocent in their appearance in men's writings, of course. They grew out of, and helped to perpetuate, a perception of women as sexually threatening, and as inherently more sinful than men. The female prophets engage in this implicit debate on the nature of women in their condemnation of the 'harlot'. While agreeing that Popery is abhorrent, they strive to produce a desirable model of femininity which will allow women to escape identification with the Whore. Hester Biddle addresses the women of London, calling their attention to the plight of the poor. Women who ignore these social issues, she suggests, are no better than the Whore of Babylon. Another kind of behaviour is both commendable and attainable.

Yet thou canst pass by them in thy gaudy apparel, and outstretched neck, with thy face decked with black spots, which are the marks of the Whore, the Beast, and the False Prophet, which is not the attire of Sarah, Abraham's wife. (*A Warning*, pp. 10–11)

The Bible was a useful source of examples of the existence of earlier women prophets. (A comprehensive listing of them, with descriptions of their activities, was made by Elizabeth Bathurst in 1683, and published as *The Sayings of Women*.) It was also the authority for the injunction that women should not minister. The most frequently cited text is Paul's first Letter to the Corinthians, verses 34 and 35.

Let your women keep silence in the churches: for it is not permitted unto them to speak; but they are commanded to be under obedience, as also saith the law. And if they will learn anything, let them ask their husbands at home: for it is a shame for women to speak in the church.

It has been suggested that the first published Quaker rebuttal of this text was made in George Fox's pamphlet *The Woman Learning in Silence* in 1656, and that this was later expanded by Margaret Fell in 1666 and 1667 in the two editions of *Women's Speaking Justified*.[37] In fact, the argument predates Fox's contribution. Earlier extended discussions of the matter appear in Richard Farnworth's *A Woman Forbidden to Speak*, 1654, and in Priscilla Cotton's and Mary Cole's pamphlet *To the Priests and People of England* and the collectively written *The Saints Testimony*, both of which appeared in 1655. *The Saints Testimony* cites examples of biblical women prophets, which include some in Paul's own church (p. 16). Cotton and Cole set out more boldly to turn the Bible against itself, quoting other texts which, they say, make it necessary to reinterpret Paul's message.

> Thou tellest the people, women must not speak in a church, whereas it is not spoke only of a female, for we are all one both male and female in Christ Jesus (Gal. 3.27, 28), but it's weakness that is the woman by the scriptures forbidden, for else thou puttest the scriptures at a difference from themselves, as still it's thy practice out of thy ignorance; for the scriptures do say, that all the church may prophesy one by one, and that women were in the church, as well as men. (pp. 6–7)

They insist that the text be interpreted as having metaphorical significance only. 'Woman' is to be read as meaning 'weakness' – one of the qualities most commonly associated with womanliness in contemporary discourse. Since 'man in his best estate is altogether vanity, weakness, a lie', both men and women are forbidden to prophesy if what they speak is merely human, and not divinely inspired. With the help of the Light Within, however, anyone can speak, because their words are no longer 'weak'.

> Here mayst thou see from the scriptures, that the woman or weakness whether male or female, is forbidden to speak in the church . . . Indeed, you yourselves [the church ministers] are the women, that are forbidden to speak in the church, that are become women.[38]

For a woman to minister she had to confront direct biblical prohibition, as Priscilla Cotton and Mary Cole had. Susannah Parr could not countenance such a change, and repeatedly refused to obey the orders of her church minister to speak her opinions in church. As time passed and she grew increasingly unhappy with the doctrinal path her church was pursuing, however, she began to argue with Mr Stucley during the services. Presumably he had not been prepared for the alteration in church practices to have such an effect. Susannah Parr was told that she must not speak for herself, but talk to one of the men, who would then preach for her.[39] After this, she ceased to attend services there, transferring her allegiances to another church. Finally, when Mr Stucley and his congregation separated from the national church she severed all contact with them. When they excommunicated her three years later and published charges against her, she found herself forced into print in her own defence. The book she wrote is formed from the same contradiction as her earlier behaviour. Steadfastly opposed to women speaking in church or publishing their views, she does both while still asserting their immorality. In the dedicatory epistle to *Susanna's Apologie* she tells her reader

> Weakness is entailed upon my sex in general, and for myself in particular, I am a despised worm, a woman full of natural and sinful infirmities, the chiefest of sinners, and least of Saints.

She then proceeds to make a lengthy examination of the doctrines espoused by Mr Stucley, entering into close textual argument with him, in a book that extends to more than one hundred pages. Men like Mr Stucley were taken by surprise by the outcome of their insistence that correct female behaviour should include giving vent to God's word.

Susannah Parr's story demonstrates that a woman could be allowed or even encouraged to prophesy by men who had not considered the possibility that such behaviour would lead them to rebel against male authority. After the Restoration, as I shall demonstrate in more detail below, men's dominance was reasserted. In order to survive, the Society of Friends had to deny many aspects of its early radicalism. One of the most striking of these was the need gradually to abandon the more public roles open to women in the 1650s.

The earliest vindications of women's preaching were written from prison in the mid-1650s. These texts are visionary and extravagant in their use of scripture, turning St Paul's works against themselves to argue that the 'women' who are forbidden to speak are the male church ministers. Firm in their conviction of direct contact with God's meaning and purpose, they give a symbolic reading to biblical commands. Although Quakers continued to advocate women's right to prophesy, as time passed their official stance on the subject became ever more guarded. Margaret Fell's 1666 pamphlet, *Women's Speaking Justified*, which David Latt, its modern editor, wrongly describes as the first radical statement of a woman's right to speak in church, is in fact a far more careful and conservative presentation of the case than that practised and argued for a decade or more before. Her judicious, rational presentation of Bible verses which counter Paul's injunction to silence has none of the ecstatic fervour of Cotton and Cole. Indeed, Fell's pamphlets generally are more measured and 'rational' than those of her Quaker sisters. She addresses readers with a tone of clear authority which has none of the fervour of, for instance, Hester Biddle's early exhortations.

Fell was, however, far more supportive of women's right to prophesy, even though in a muted form, than was the influential Quaker George Keith in 1674. Addressing the question of female prophecy, he admits that such a thing exists, but seeks rigorously to control the circumstances in which it is permissible. Where Cotton and Cole had accused the priests of being 'women' who have no right to speak, George Keith would allow *any* man to ask questions in church or to minister, but only in extreme circumstances permit a sister to break her silence.

If they [women] speak, they are not to do it by permission, but by commandment, whereas it is permitted unto men, at all times, to speak in the church . . . An unlearned man may be permitted to ask a question in the church, which is not permitted unto a woman, nor is it needful, for she may ask her husband at home.[40]

When the special category of 'public ministers' was established by Friends in the 1670s, very few women were given official approval to travel and preach. Earlier, no such corporate licence had been necessary.[41] Women who presumed to claim divine inspiration and defied the ban were dealt with sternly. Margery Clipsham's *The Spirit that works Abomination*, 1685, attacks the activities of Elizabeth Aldridge, who had dared to travel around the country to both men's and women's meetings testifying against Quaker doctrines. Rather than welcoming her as God's enlightened prophet, Clipsham presents her as mentally deranged (hysterical), due to problems experienced in giving birth.[42]

In the time of her lying in, being weak, and disordered in her head (a distemper which divers of her relations have been subject to, and her own mother died in, soon after the time of the birth, as we have been credibly informed), her mind was filled with strong imaginations; and after she was up, she came forth again with a pretence of visions and revelations, wherewith Friends were greatly dissatisfied, and burthened. (p. 4)

The reduction of women's right to deliver the Word is also reflected in the epistles prefacing many of the texts they print in the late 1670s. Isabel Yeamans and Elizabeth Bathurst, for instance, both apologise for the length of their texts, and justify their publishing in more detail than their earlier Sisters had.[43] In 1672, in fact, Quakers had established a censorship system, whereby only those texts approved by the Second Day Morning Meetings were allowed to be published.[44] By this date, some of the more outrageous women – Martha Simmonds, Mary Howgill, Anne Gargill – had left the Society. Margaret Killin had died. When Hester Biddle was arrested in a Quaker meeting in 1662, the court claimed to be shocked to hear of a woman preaching, and the judge reproved her:

'She should ask of her husband at home.' She said, 'If her husband should be a drunkard, or a sot, what should she learn of him, to be as wicked as he was?' R. Brown [the judge] asked if her husband were so? She said no, but if he were so, what could she learn? 'But Christ is my husband, and I learn of Him,' said she. Alderman Brown said she had left her husband two years, and went with a young man into other lands. She told him that was not his business to judge at this time, nor was it fit for him to accuse her, but she went with three women as she was moved of the Lord.[45]

Biddle responded to this attack on her virtue by reminding the judge of his own erstwhile involvement with the sectaries of 'Oliver's days'.

Richard, dost thou not remember that thou prayedst in the camp by Abingdon, and was that an unlawful meeting? Was that not a good day with thee? I am afraid thou wilt never see such another. (p. 37)

After being imprisoned in Newgate in 1665 for speaking in the street, Hester Biddle seems to have fallen silent. Certainly she published no more after 1662, although she did not die until 1696.[46]

The role of women within Quakerism changed radically, in fact, as the century passed. The female prophets retreated to Women's Meetings, the concerns of which were limited to more conventionally feminine tasks. These meetings were introduced as part of Quakerism's administrative structure during the 1670s, although some groups of Quakers, notably those in London, had organised separate women's meetings (which might not have been so restricted in their brief) since about 1657.[47] The duties of the formally established meetings were described by Anne Whitehead in 1680. She uses biblical precedent not to justify women's preaching, but to show that women's task is to be helpmates to men,

> as the good women of old were helpers in the work of the gospel, in such things as are proper to us, as visiting and relieving the sick, the poor more especially and destitute amongst us . . . Again, we being met together, the elder women to instruct the younger to all wholesome things (having their own husbands and children, to be discreet, chaste, sober, keeping at home), that the work of God we profess be not blasphemed, etc., with many other matters pertinent to us.[48]

These 'other matters' included finding work for servant girls and apprenticing the sons of poor Friends, and the investigation and suppression of scandal.[49] It seems unlikely that the women's meetings of the 1650s had such a limited brief. In 1672, the men's and women's meetings in London published jointly *An Exhortation and Admonition*, rebuking unmarried servant girls who had taken to leaving their jobs and living alone in lodgings, 'whence many inconveniences and evils have ensued'. Where early Quakers had suffered beatings and imprisonment for refusing to heed social rituals marking dominance and submission, in 1685 the Women's Meeting at the Bull and Mouth issued *A Tender and Christian Testimony to young People*, counselling them to show proper respect to their elders and betters. They especially reprove

> those servants that profess the truth, which will not be subject in their places, in those things that are wholesome, honest, and just, but take liberty as they will, being stubborn and perverse, not answering the blessed principle of truth, so becoming a stumbling to them without, an ill example to our children and families within, a sore disorder, and grievous burden.

With the Society of Friends undergoing fierce attack from outside, and with the millenarian optimism of the 1640s and 1650s long dead, prophets turned their attention to defensive tactics. By the 1680s, most of the pamphlets published by women consist of lamentations that established Friends are 'falling away', and exhortations to the young to follow faithfully parental guidance.[50] The 'truth' that is being defended, however, changes in nature. Fortitude and gravity become virtues in themselves, and the larger social demands of Quakerism are abandoned. *A Tender and Christian Testimony* is particularly concerned to find Friends dressing with less formality than they earlier had. Mary Forster's

Some Seasonable Considerations to the Young Men and Women, 1684, warns that 'if any of you indulge a loose careless spirit, such make void their suffering, invalidate their testimony, and fall short of the reward and comfort of the upright, and so will not hold out to the end' (p. 5). Geertruyde Dirrecks advises Quakers to strengthen the Society by exercising strict discipline over their offspring, to control their 'stout and stubborn will' (*An Epistle*, 1677, p. 2). Other pamphlets serve as didactic writings, presenting images of exemplary women as role-models for little girls. It is quietness of spirit, constancy and respect for orderliness in Anne Whitehead, Elizabeth Braytwhaite, and Elizabeth Furly that are praised in the testimonials written about them.[51] The power-structure of the patriarchal family, which had been severely strained by the activities of women prophets, was being reasserted.

The transformations that these writings undergo are a clear example of what it means to think of femininity as a negotiated construct. In the early years of the period, while other women were also petitioning parliament and calling for legal reforms, prophets asserted a right to preach and then to publish the fruits of their divine inspiration. These acts were not made possible through an outright rejection of the bonds of femininity. On the contrary, women's identification as 'weak vessels' particularly prone to irrational, hysterical acts, provided the framework which made such behaviour thinkable. Women might in general be enjoined to silence, but if their words could be interpreted, by themselves and others, as issuing from God, they could speak and would be listened to. The wariness of the Inquisition in its dealings with Katherine Evans and Sarah Chevers exemplifies this.

By the late 1660s, such behaviour had become unacceptable as a part of feminine identity. The development of the patriarchal nuclear family was closing off these options. At the same time, the increasing persecution suffered by the Society of Friends led to the growth of its bureaucratic structure, and stress on the importance of the family, as a means of self-protection. The female prophets were exiled to the feminine duties of Women's Meetings, which controlled women in new ways while they also provided a ground where they could regroup and develop other challenges to the limits of femininity. Anne Tobin's (unpublished) study of the minutes of the White Horse Vale Meeting of the early 1680s has revealed, for instance, that the Women's Meeting used its control over charitable funds to continue to support families which were being rebuked by the Men's Meeting. Such activities help to explain why some male Friends resisted so vehemently even the limited powers given to their Sisters' meetings, necessitating Joan Vokins's rapid return home to defend them in about 1680. God called her back to her native Berkshire from New England, she recalled, and blessed her mission with success though Amalek lay in wait by the way, and the opposite spirit did strongly strive; yet our Good Shepherd did visit his handmaids, and (blessed be his name) filled us with his overcoming power, when the mothers in Israel were so dismayed, as we were likely to have lost our Women's Meetings.[52]

The shift to an apparently more tranquil female role after the Restoration also markedly affected the writings. While it is true that Elizabeth Bathurst and Isabel Yeamans were far more apologetic about their works than earlier prophets had been, they still benefited from the tradition of writing which by that time had been established by their Sisters. The books they publish are more evidently crafted than those of their predecessors. Once 'inspired' behaviour was no longer desirable, writing God's words no longer had to appear to be an effortless outpouring. (It had never in fact been effortless, of course, as the careful emending described above of Lady Eleanor's text might illustrate.) A woman could, with apologies, order and structure her final product. Elizabeth Bathurst prefaces her book with a list of its contents, and with remarks which are self-effacing and yet which emphasise the care with which she has constructed her text.

The truth is, though I at first thought to have filled but one sheet of paper, when I set about it, I saw a field before me, which cost me some spiritual travel before I got through. And now, lest any should think the trace too long to follow, I have taken pains to prefix and page contents to every material point, that so they may readily turn to that which they are most desirous to be at.[53]

When Rebeckah Travers, one of the most influential of women Quakers was asked in 1680 to promote the publication of Alice Curwen's autobiography, she refused, 'there not being much prophecy in it'. On reflection, however, she changed her mind. She says that the decision was caused by her belief that Curwen's cheerful acceptance of death as God's will and her refusal to be given medicine were a good example of commendable behaviour.[54] Perhaps this image of Curwen as a truly holy woman was the factor that enabled her text to be published. The main body of the work, however, consists of her own account of her travel in New England and Barbados. If she had died less meekly, the tale of her earlier heroism might never have been made public. Quaker women were not silenced in their retreat, but the price they paid to continue being heard was a high one.

ANNE WENTWORTH: BABYLON AND MALE POWER

At first glance, therefore, it comes as a surprise to find the Baptist Anne Wentworth publishing ecstatic millenarian prophecies as late as 1679.[55] Her *True Account*, *Vindication* and *Revelation* all look forward to an imminent judgement day, a 'great overturning' when her persecutors,

and most specifically her husband, will receive their just punishment
at God's hands. God will take care of her, and her husband's power over
her will cease.

> And he has assured me, that the man of earth shall oppress me no more; no more
> shall I be under the hands of the hard-hearted persecutors, unless he become a
> new man, a changed man, a man sensible of the wrong he has done me, with his
> fierce looks, bitter words, sharp tongue and cruel usage. (*Vindication*, p. 5)

Her other tormentors, named in *The Revelation* as Hickes, Dicks,
Knowles[56] and Philip Barder, are also assured of their specific punishment for orchestrating 'the flood of scorn, contempt, bitter railing, false
accusations, scandalous papers, and lying pamphlets' (*The Revelation*,
p. 9) against her.

By the time *The Revelation* appeared in 1679 (as a preamble to the text
by a woman friend explains), she had been ejected from the marital home
by her furious husband, and he had withdrawn all financial support from
her. It also seems likely that he was trying to divorce her, and she had
been 'rejected by all her friends and relations, and left by them to shift for
herself'. Husband, religious community and family had collaborated to
try to silence her prophetic voice. What was the nature of her prophecy?

The title pages of her *Vindication* and *The Revelation* juxtapose the
fates of 'Babylon' and 'Zion'. Earlier in the century, prophetic writings
had used 'Zion' and 'Babylon' as symbols of good and evil: the longed-
for triumph of the Saints would include the overthrow of 'Babylon', a
state which could be variously interpreted as referring to King Charles,
Cromwell or 'kingly power'. Anne Wentworth uses these same metaphors to describe her own situation. She is a 'daughter of Zion, newly
delivered from the captivity of Babylon' (her husband and his allies)
(*Vindication*, title page). She explains how Christ revealed to her the
truth which she must now pass on to people at large: this is no mere
personal oppression of herself by her husband. The images of Zion and
Babylon are appropriate because what is at issue is a far more general
oppression of good by evil. She communicates to the reader the insight
which freed her, making her able to understand male power as a general
evil, supported by a legal system that must be resisted.

> The Lord showed me why the people did not understand me, nor my work;
> because they will not (saith the Lord) go to the root of the matter, but blind
> themselves with pouring so much upon a man and his wife, and will look no
> further: but continue writing all faults in thy forehead, as delusions and
> disobeying of thy husband, and see none in themselves: they are so stark blind
> that they can see nothing at all of what I the Lord am doing: they will not see,
> how I have placed the two spirits in a man and his wife, to figure out Zion and
> Babylon . . . And then the Lord spake thus in verses:

Full eighteen years in sorrow I did lie,
Then the Lord Jesus came to hear my cry;
In one night's time, he did me heal,
From head to foot he made me well.
With ointment sweet he did me anoint,
And this work he then did me appoint.
A hand in Babylon's ashes I must have,
For that end the Lord took me from the grave,
And said, 'A new body I the Lord will give thee,
To convince thy enemies . . .
I the Lord will openly, and surely avenge thy cause,
Upon all thy enemies, for their unjust laws'.
(*Revelation*, p. 9)

The term 'new body' refers in part to her 'resurrection' into the number of true believers. It also evokes the physical battering she has suffered at her husband's hands. In her *Vindication* she explains that she had fled her husband in literal fear for her life. The eighteen years of sorrow and oppression to which she repeatedly refers is the timespan of her marriage.

He has in his barbarous actions towards me, a many times overdone such things as not only in the *spirit* of them will one day be judged a murdering of, but had long since *really* proved so, if God had not wonderfully supported, and preserved me. (p. 4)

The earlier prophets of revolution had claimed that they were not the originators of their works, but were being used as divine instruments. Anna Trapnel had even recorded her argument with God, asking him not to send her on his mission. Anne Wentworth also presents herself as a reluctant handmaid, who would rather have remained in ignorance, or at least stayed silent. The compulsion to communicate her truths, however, was too strong. She declares that she felt

that I might rather die, than do it. That I was commanded of God to record them. That my own natural temper was so greatly averse to it, that for eleven months together I withstood the Lord, till by an angel from Heaven he threatened to *kill me*, and took away my sleep from me. (*Vindication*, p. 7)

She must endeavour to present herself as properly feminine if she is to have any hope of acceptance. Perhaps, too, she found the burden of seeing the reality of male power very heavy to bear, and would have preferred to have been left in ignorance. But to a battered wife, well-versed in biblical imagery, the grim reality was too clear to be refused. The passage quoted above continues

And indeed, the writings that man was so displeased with, were in themselves very warrantable, if I had not had any command of God, for I only wrote the way he led me in a wilderness of affliction for 18 years . . . And I do further declare, the things I have written are true, and no lie: and that what is so distasteful in them to man, are such things as I could not leave out, without prejudice to truth, and disobedience to God.

Her foes attempted to discredit her, she says, by describing her as an archetypally unfeminine woman taken over by the deplorable 'enthusiasm' that characterised the radical sectaries.

I am reproached as a proud, wicked, deceived, deluded, lying woman, a mad, melancholy, crack-brained, self-willed, conceited fool, and black sinner, led by whimsies, notions and knick-knacks of my own head; one that speaks blasphemy, not fit to take the name of God in her mouth; an heathen and publican, a fortune-teller, an enthusiast, and the like much more. (*Revelation*, p. 19)

The re-establishment of order at the Restoration made such charges dangerous for anyone, and especially for a woman. Her fourth revelation contains an amazonian image of herself equipped for battle, which would have served as ammunition in these accusations. God has given her strength to stand

> Against all my enemies, with His battleaxe in my hand,
> To wound, kill, amaze and put to flight, and cut them down,
> And when they are in their graves, I shall wear a crown.
> (*Revelation*, p. 4)

In leaving her husband, she has also made herself vulnerable to the most damaging accusation: that she is a loose woman. Her publication of her *Revelation* comes partly from the need to deny 'that I keep men company, and have rogues come to me, and live a scandalous life in an almshouse' (p. 20).

Anne Wentworth's mission is to reveal to the world the true identity of 'Zion' and 'Babylon'. If her husband will agree to her doing this, she will return to him

provided I may have my *just* and *necessary* liberty to attend a more than ordinary call and command of God to publish the things which concern the *peace of my own soul*, and *of the whole nation*. (*Vindication*, p. 6)

This is scarcely a likely outcome, of course. She had discovered the same catch that, in the twentieth century, was to cause the creation of the slogan 'the personal is political'. Her revelation is not purely personal, but comes from and is part of the power structure of patriarchy. At one level, her husband might not be personally responsible for oppressing her, and in theory his help could be enlisted to overthrow 'Babylon'. (Though this might be an unnecessarily charitable interpretation of the behaviour of a man who had repeatedly beaten his wife. Such violence lies at the extreme edge of what patriarchy finds permissible.) In fact, he is the personification of male power, created by it. She will not abandon the hope that he might, somehow, be converted. But in the mean time, she is living alone, drawing strength from her God who has shown her the truth, and from her woman friend.

For the moment, she ends her text preparing to write more. She is an isolated woman, unsupported by a wider social movement as the earlier Quakers and Baptists had been. She cannot call on others to take up arms, as Trapnel and Cary had, or change the laws as Barwick had. Her only possible contribution to the great change she sees approaching is to save her own life, and record her message. It is unimaginable that women, divided in their homes, could unite to bring about the apocalypse. Her religion had provided the tools to analyse oppression, and it had also suggested only one solution. Women must be patient and wait for God to intervene.

> From Heaven will I the Lord come to appear,
> For to make them all my own voice to hear:
> And all those, that long to see this thing done,
> Must patiently wait till I the Lord do come.
> (*Revelation*, p. 10)

The earlier revolution of the Saints had failed to bring the New Jerusalem into being. Anne Wentworth had given a new identification to 'Babylon'. Alone in her newly privatised home, a single 'daughter of Zion' could not destroy it.

CHAPTER TWO

RELIGIOUS POETRY, MEDITATIONS AND CONVERSION NARRATIVES

WHILE radical sectaries were out in the streets pamphleteering, proclaiming the social implications of the belief that each person had an individual relationship with God, other women were engaged in its more private anatomising, analysing and recording the development of their spiritual well-being. Such texts fall into two main groups. First, there are three books of poetry and meditations, the authors of which are clearly well to the right of Quakers and Baptists. Second, there is a series of spiritual autobiographies composed by members of Independent congregations, mostly in London. What all these writings have in common is the fact that their authors faithfully promote highly restrictive ideologies about women's duties and necessary passivity, while at the same time finding ways to justify their own unfeminine activities.

*

> My bounded spirits, bounded be in thee,
> For bounded by no other can they be.
> (*Eliza's Babes*, p. 36)

For a woman to write for publication at all in the seventeenth century was to challenge the limits of acceptable feminine behaviour. Between 1652 and 1656, three women published books of religious poetry and meditations, all of them finding ways within their work of making such activity possible. In their texts they construct models of a writing, female Christian who is supposed to be acceptable to the reading public. The ideal female author who appears in these texts is able to enter the public world free from male prefaces, but nonetheless is restricted by the characteristics of this ideal. All these texts, to a lesser or greater extent, are didactic, creating for writer and reader an image of desirable femininity which can embrace the identity of poet.

Much of *Eliza's Babes*, 1652, was produced abroad, possibly at the court of Elizabeth of Bohemia, after the anonymous author had fled England during the 1640s. Her references to the civil war ('To the King, writ, 1644', p. 23) make it clear that she was a royalist who had hoped for some compromise between king and parliament in the mid-1640s. Once in exile, however, she rejoiced in the unexpected delights found in forced exclusion from her country, and in 'To the Queen of Bohemia' celebrates the fact that her exile had made it possible for her 'To see that queen, so much admir'd' (p. 23).

Many of the defeated royalists, of course, had to find some way of making failure and withdrawal from the world palatable. In *Eliza's Babes*, however, we also find an exploration of the specifically female advantages of abandoning the world. The Eliza persona that the poems create demonstrates the freedoms available for women who retire from the public domain and immerse themselves in religious devotions. Not only can women dismiss concerns of state; they can also, to some extent, retire from the family structures which compose it.

The title page of *Eliza's Babes* announces that the author 'only desires to advance the glory of God, and not her own'. This reiterates the point that Eliza makes several times in introductory remarks: the normally reprehensible act of publishing her works is acceptable, even necessary, because of her duty to God. Publishing is a Christian act, she argues, because Christ died a 'public death', compelling her 'to return him public thanks, for such infinite and public favours' (sig. A3). This action should be emulated by all true believers, and not criticised in her.

And if any shall say 'Others may be as thankful as thee, though they talk not so much of it'; let them know that if they did rightly apprehend the infinite mercies of God to them, they could not be silent: and if they do not think the mercies of God worth public thanks, I do. (sig. A3)

Like her more radical sectary sisters, she uses the idea that women should be the most lowly of creatures to argue that, therefore, they are least able to resist being used by God to his greater glory.

And now I dare not say 'I am an ignorant woman, and unfit to write', for if thou will declare thy goodness and thy mercy by weak and contemptible means, who can resist thy will. (p. 75)

Although inhabiting this passive role restricts her subject matter – in one of her poems she exhorts 'Lord let no line be writ by me,/That excludes, or includes not, thee' – it also frees her from fear of human disapproval. Her opening poem exults in this licence.

I glory in the word of God,
 To praise it I accord.
With joy I will declare abroad,
 The goodness of the Lord.

All you that goodness do disdain,
 Go; read not here:
And if you do; I tell you plain,
 I do not care.

For why? above your reach my soul is placed,
And your odd words shall not my mind distaste.
(p. 1)

Eliza has committed herself to Christ – 'He is my spouse', she assures God (p. 21) – and her description of herself as Christ's wife is a highly developed image, drawing on the language and concepts of courtly love poetry. In 'The Flight', for instance, she reworks the conventional notion of a lover dying from grief at his (usually) beloved's death.

Eliza for, ask now not here,
She's gone to heaven, to meet her peer.
For since her Lord, on earth was dead,
What tarry here? she'd not, she said.
And to the heavens, she took her flight,
That she might be still in his sight;
And so to us she bid adieu,
But proved herself a lover true. (p. 11)

As 'a lover true' she delights in praising her beloved, 'his fair sweet lovely face' and 'his pleasing eyes [that] do dart/Their arrows which do pierce my heart' (pp. 24–5).

When it comes to earthly love, however, she asks God to harden her heart 'as hard as steel' (p. 2): 'Great God, thou only worth desiring art,/ And none but thee, then must possess my heart' (p. 12). The comparison between earthly love and divine affection, made repeatedly in the poems' use of love poetry conventions, is clear and consistent. As God's spouse she has peace and freedom. Repeatedly and wittily she dismissed the claims of men to possess her as a limitation, even a slavery.

Since you me ask, why born was I?
I'll tell you; 'twas to heaven to fly,
Not here to live a slavish life,
By being to the world a wife. (p. 31)

If we turn to her poem 'What I Love', we find that what might at first glance be anticipated as a heartfelt declaration of love for some man, in fact mocks the very idea of her deigning to feel affection for any man.

> Give me a soul, give me a spirit,
> That flies from earth, heaven to inherit.
> But those that grovel here below,
> What! I love them? I'll not do so. (p. 36)

The product of this marriage with God is her book of poems, her 'babes'. Her first use of the term 'babes' to describe her work serves to emphasise her purported passivity in its production. Addressing other women as 'my sisters', she urges them

> Look on these babes as none of mine,
> For they were but brought forth by me;
> But look on them, as they are divine,
> Proceeding from Divinity. (sig. A^v)

Publishing her writings, even though she claims divine sanction, was as great a risk to her modest reputation as sexual irregularities would have been. Defining herself on the title page as a 'virgin', and stressing the modesty of her entry into the public domain with these 'babes', she adds: 'I am not ashamed of their birth; for before I knew it, the Prince of eternal glory had affianced me to himself; and that is my glory' (sig. A2). These offspring, the result of an 'irregular union' with God, are a blessing to their 'mother' which makes them far preferable to children of flesh and blood born in wedlock, since 'they immortalise the name' (p. 42; children of the flesh, of course, would only immortalise a husband's name). Addressing 'a Lady that bragged of her children', Eliza delights in the joy and holiness of her own 'babes'.

> If thou hast cause to joy in thine,
> I have cause too to joy in mine.
> Thine did proceed from sinful race,
> Mine from the heavenly dew of grace.
> Thine at their birth did pain thee bring,
> When mine are born, I sit and sing.
> Thine doth delight in nought but sin,
> My babes' work is, to praise heaven's King.
> Thine bring both sorrow, pain and fear,
> Mine banish from me dreadful care. (pp. 54–5)

Some of the later poems in *Eliza's Babes* describe the unavoidability of marriage, and work out a pattern whereby the poet can maintain her autonomy within it. Dutiful to her God and to the male hierarchy of the family, she finds herself 'given away' despite her own gift of her heart to God. The only solace offered in 'The Gift' is to continue to follow God's bidding.

> My Lord, hast thou given me away?
> Did I on earth, for a gift stay?
> Hath he by prayer of thee gained me,
> Who was so strictly knit to thee?

To thee I only gave my heart,
Wouldst thou my Lord from that gift part?
I know thou wouldst deliver me
To none, but one beloved by thee.

But Lord my heart thou dost not give,
Though here on earth, while I do live
My body here he may retain,
My heart in heaven, with thee must reign.

Then as thy gift let him think me,
Since I a donage am from thee.
And let him know thou hast my heart,
He only hath my earthly part.

It was my glory I was free,
And subject here to none but thee,
And still that glory I shall hold
If thou my spirit dost enfold.

It is my bliss, I here serve thee,
'Tis my great joy; thou lovest me. (p. 42)

This fate, however, is exemplary. Making the married Eliza representative of women's rightful role in wedlock, the poet explains 'Not a husband, though never so excelling in goodness to us, must detain our desires from heaven' (p. 45). Even though the new spouse is kind – 'with him I have no annoy' (p. 45) – this is unimportant in comparison with the spiritual freedom that a relationship with God gives her. Representative of all women, Eliza draws out the lesson that true religion frees the female sex from dependence on male approval or concern.

For should our husband's love fixed be
Upon some others, not on thee
Heaven's Prince will never thee forsake,
But still his darling will thee make.
And should he of thee careless be,
Heaven's Prince, He will more careful be.
He from the earth will raise thy heart,
That thou content mayst act that part.

Being married is merely playing a necessary role; her true identity is defined in relation to God.

Producing her 'babes', the fruit of her union with God, Eliza reflects that God must have 'something here remarkable for me to do, before I leave the earth' (p. 102). The relationship between woman and God that the poems represent and define makes her 'capable of as great a dignity as any mortal man'.

Peace! Present now no more to me (to take my spirit from the height of felicity) that I am a creature of a weaker sex, a woman. For my God! If I must live after the example of thy blessed apostle, I must live by faith, and faith makes things to come, as present; and thou hast said by thy servant, that we shall be like thy blessed Son: then thou wilt make all thy people like kings and priests. Kings are men, and men are kings; and souls have no sex. The hidden man of the heart makes us capable of being kings; for I have heard it is that within makes the man. Then are we by election capable of as great a dignity as any mortal man.

It is through withdrawal from the world and in obedience solely to God, these 'virgin's offerings' demonstrate, that women can attain a measure of self-definition and control.

An Collins's *Divine Songs and Meditacions* appeared in 1653. The book, which is almost entirely in verse, is highly experimental in stanza form, and it is possible that some of the songs, at least, were intended to be set to music and performed. In the introductory address 'To the Reader', Collins explains that she has found writing 'so amiable, as that it inflamed my faculties, to put forth themselves in a practice so pleasing'. Writing is described, in other words, as a delightful and empowering activity for the author. Choice of subject-matter, however, was not free. She had found no satisfaction, she asserts, in writing 'profane history'. It was only when committing herself to the exposition of 'divine truth' that she found contentment. Composing poetry on such themes 'reduced my mind to a peaceful temper'. Her 'inflamed faculties', therefore, were at the same time 'peaceful'. The *Songs and Meditacions* proceed to promote tranquillity and contentment as qualities of the highest value, both for the state and for the individual. The author is portrayed in her poetry as a pattern for the reader, a Christian woman who has achieved satisfaction by following the rules promoted in the text.

If women's sphere, according to conventional wisdom and dominant practice, extended no further than the boundaries of her home, An Collins is shown as more especially confined within such limits. The long introductory poem 'The Preface' consists of a fascinating fusion of personal history, commentary on the contemporary religio-political conflicts and a brief history of Christianity, with a series of statements about the role of the author. Collins describes how her confinement to the house was necessitated by chronic ill-health, inactivity lulling her brain to sleep. Writing has revived her. In 'The Preamble' to her first meditation, she also describes writing as a release from crippling despair and misery.

> Amid the ocean of adversity,
> Near whelmed in the waves of sore vexation,
> Tormented with the floods of misery,
> And almost in the guise of desperation,
> Near destitute of comfort, full of woes,
> This was her case that did the same compose.[1]

Writing has empowered her, and it is particularly important that she is writing about divine truth. Since her subject matter is righteous, she is protected by a 'sovereign power' from the malice of her enemies who would wish her to remain silent. People have tried to hinder her, 'Yet this cannot prevail to hinder me/ From publishing those truths I do intend' ('The Preface').

Firm in the duty to publish her truths, she makes no further apology for commenting on affairs of state. Her task is to give voice to God's truth, which entails a duty to pass on to her contemporaries and to future ages the need for moderation, peace and order. The people are 'wrapped in fangles new', corrupted and confused by ill-doers ('Time past we understood by story'). Committed to the position that radical sectaries are merely producing 'new glosses' on 'old heresies' ('The Preface'), she argues for re-establishment of order and authority in church and state, and 'Another Song Exciting to Spiritual Mirth' proposes abandonment of concern over the outcome of human conflict.

> But those that are contented
> However things do fall,
> Much anguish is prevented,
> And they soon freed from all;
> They finish all their labours
> With much felicity.

If the author and reader become singleminded in the pursuit of wholly spiritual concerns, they will find happiness. Only by refusing rebellion and discord can the true Christian find happiness ('Another Song' "Having restrained discontent").

Quite clearly in such passages, the model Christian woman that the poet represents asserts that conflict and dissension are evils, the work of the devil, and so should be rejected in favour of social order and moderation. While calling for retreat from argument she is also, therefore, promoting a particular (and reactionary) political ideology. Arguing that state politics are unimportant, she makes a political statement, and holds up the contented poet persona as evidence that retirement from worldly concerns brings happiness. She looks to God to provide the only possible unity in the families of a nation torn apart by civil war.

> No knot of friendship long can hold
>   Save that which grace hath tied,
> For other causes prove but cold
>   When their effects are tried.
> For God who loveth unity
>   Doth cause the only union
> Which makes them of one family
>   Of one mind and communion.

> This is the cause of home debate,
> And much domestic woes,
> That one may find his household mates
> To be his greatest foes,
> That with the wolf the lamb may bide
> As free from molestation
> As Saints with sinners, who reside
> In the same habitation.
> ('A Song Declaring that a Christian May Find True Love only where True Grace Is')

The championing of withdrawal from the world indeed becomes particularly interesting when applied specifically to the question of family ties: a woman's duty of obedience to her father, and her subsequent absorption within her husband's identity were, after all, supposed to be of paramount importance. The retirement advocated in *Divine Songs and Meditacions*, therefore, is of particular advantage to women, and is certainly an important factor in the presentation of the poet's contentment. The good Christian of these *Songs* is not just singleminded, but also singlehearted. Her only spouse (like Eliza's) is Christ. She must withdraw from duties to men, as well as from conflicts of state.

> Then let them know, that would enjoy
> The firm fruition,
> Of his sweet presence, he will stay
> With single hearts alone,
> Who [but] their former mate,
> Do quite exterminate:
> With all things that defile.
> They that are Christ's truly,
> The flesh do crucify
> With its affections vile.
> The grounds of truth are sought
> New principles are wrought
> Of grace and holiness,
> Which plantings of the heart
> Will spring in every part,
> And so itself express.
> ('A Song Expressing Their Happiness who have Communion with Christ')

In this union with Christ, the female poet can justify her writing as proper feminine employment. 'The Preface' describes the *Songs* as offspring clad in homely dress – fitting products of a virtuous woman. She defends her writing

> Now touching that I hasten to express
> Concerning these, the offspring of my mind,
> Who though they here appear in homely dress
> And as they are my works, I do not find

> But ranked with others, they may go behind,
> Yet for their matter, I suppose they be
> Not worthless quite, whilst they with truth agree.

The fruit of this union with Christ is necessarily good.

> So sorrow served but as springing rain
> To ripen fruits, endowments of the mind,
> Who thereby did ability attain
> To send forth flowers, of so rare a kind,
> Which wither not by force of sun or wind:
> Retaining virtue in their operations,
> Which are the matter of those meditations.

The overriding assertion of the *Songs and Meditacions*, indeed, is that the poet, the Christian woman, having suffered greatly in the world from conflict and physical constraints, has found the wisdom to willingly abandon worldly concerns and fence herself into a narrow domain which allows, in practice, greater freedom. The final expression of this is the *Songs* themselves, 'flowers of so rare a kind,/ Which wither not by force of sun or wind'. The most succinct statement of this conclusion appears in 'Another Song' "The winter of my infancy", which traces the poet's suffering and subsequent attainment of peace. The enclosing of her mind by the strictures of contentment and divine truth has brought with it safety, making it possible for her to write undisturbed and thus attain more than most women ever can. The cottage garden of her mind can grow rare fruits indeed.

> Yet as a garden is my mind enclosed fast
> Being to safety so confined from storm and blast
> Apt to produce a fruit most rare,
> That is not common with every woman
> That fruitful are.

Most women's 'fruitfulness' is shown in their ability to bear sons for their husbands. Her offspring were acquired, the text proclaims, through accepting the need for quiescence and withdrawal from worldly turmoil and family ties in a country split apart by civil war. This alone can bring happiness.

> For in our union with the Lord alone
>   Consists our happiness.
> Certainly such who are with Christ at one
>   He leaves not comfortless.
> ('A Song Expressing Their Happiness who have Communion
> with Christ')

In *Divine Songs and Meditacions* an apparently conventional restatement of a basic Christian tenet – that God alone is the source of secure joy – becomes a justification for female celibacy and a celebration of women's writing.

Elizabeth Major's *Honey on the Rod: Or a comfortable Contemplation for one in Affliction* appeared prefaced by a commendatory note by the censor Joseph Caryl in 1656. Caryl recommends the book to the reader as evidence that 'the Lord gives instruction with correction'. The author's own address to her readers is properly self-deprecating, while making the necessary claim that her writings are both godly and useful.

If you please so far to descend, as to cast an eye upon these poor lines presented to you, you may behold in it a little (but a full) hive. I entreat thee not to be offended, if thou find in it more wax than honey, and more dross than either. The honey (the divine part) I commend to thee, and the wax (the mortal part) being clarified from the dross (that is, the faults and failings through weakness) is useful in its place. (sig. A3ʳ⁻ᵛ)

That which is good in the book comes from the Lord, she asserts, or from the experience he has seen fit to give her (sig. A4). Since it is godly, her uneasiness about 'making it public' (sig. A6ᵛ) has been overcome: 'the subject will be the honour of it' (sig. A7ᵛ). Apologising for her 'lowly' achievements, she makes it clear that the book is all her own work (helped by the Lord), and that it is the best she can do. The book is her child.

And now to you, O my friends, I present these poor and undressed lines, being as they came into the world, I not finding any hand to help me to put it into a better dress than what it brought with it . . . For though I was not ambitious of a beautiful babe, yet I confess I would gladly have had it appear comely; therefore where you find it harsh or uneven, know, it should not have come abroad so, had not my ignorance to find the fault been the cause of it. (sig. h3ᵛ)

As a godly text, *Honey on the Rod* is didactic. The author warns her reader to understand the 'comfortable contemplation' as exemplary, not just revealing the author's condition but also showing the sinner her/ his own true, mortal state.

Come, O come, I beseech you, whoever you are that read these lines, and behold yourselves and me in them, as objects of mortality, like dust before the wind or as stubble before a consuming fire; weak, and not able of ourselves to resist the least assault. (p. 9)

The recurrent simile of *Honey on the Rod* portrays the author as an erring child or poor scholar, God as the father and teacher. The author and reader together are led through a series of lessons in order to achieve their salvation.

The major part of the book – about three quarters of it – consists of a prose dialogue 'A Comfortable Contemplation for One in Affliction'. The main protagonists are 'Consolation' and 'Soul', who discuss how hope and salvation can be found in the midst of affliction. The soul, cast down and repentant, looks to language and specifically to writing as a way to find relief from despair.

I could wish my tongue were as the pen of a ready writer, if there be hopes of ease by imparting; for my sighs are many, and my heart is heavy. I, I am she that hath seen affliction. (p. 2)

Honey on the Rod, then, acts as the site where affliction is made sense of, and a particular understanding and interpretation of suffering is given to the distressed author and reader. In the author's case, the suffering is not solely the conventional penitence of a believer seeking salvation and escape from the bondage of sin, but a particularly acute pain. Major explains to the reader that God 'was pleased in the prime of my years to take me, as it were, from a palace to a prison, from liberty to bondage, where I have served some apprenticeships' (sig. A4ᵛ). This 'prison' is physical confinement brought on by sudden and crippling illness.

No help here is below; alas, I must, I must to prison here: where Lord, thou knowest, some apprenticeships I have close prisoner been: my strength thou were pleased to melt away by secret, unseen ways, leaving me almost as helpless, as when I first entered this vale of tears: and to my debility many other afflictions thy wisdom sees it needful here to add; for scarce doth the day break in upon me, before a new cause of sorrow hath made a breach. (p. 8)

Her weakness and consequent close confinement to the home are presented, however, as having a particular metaphorical significance. She reminds herself repeatedly that her disability is God's judgement on her as a sinner: 'because ye have sinned against the Lord, and have not obeyed his voice, therefore this thing is come upon you' (p. 14). She presents herself to the reader as a particularly clear exemplar of the state of sin; and, as the text proceeds, the sinner saved. Her illness and pain have given her the lesson that *Honey on the Rod* offers to the reader: we must withdraw from the world, and concern ourselves only with Christ who (like the author) suffered for the sake of our salvation.

The passive, chastened self can be useful, and so the sinner calls on God to humble and break her. In the context of constant references to real physical pain, such passages acquire poignancy. Passivity here is not a metaphorical state advocated by a man with real power and control in the world. It is an inescapable fate, based in female powerlessness and the author's chronic illness, which she is trying to present and interpret in a manner which gives it some purpose and her some stature.

> Lord, give an humble heart, that I may yield,
> O get the conquest ere thou quit the field:
> And melt it, Lord, by mercies, if that won't do,
> Break it in pieces, and then make it new.
> O frame it to thy will, to thee 'tis known,
> And not to me, O Lord, though 'tis mine own.
> O bring it to obedience, make't what thou wilt
> So thou wilt own it, help ere my soul be spilt. (p. 185)

The self torn apart and remade by God is one who has a right to write, and who can represent the sinner saved. The final section of the book includes several poems which do, quite literally represent (and re-present) the author in this exalted role. These poems use her name, Elizabeth Major, as a frame to lay out her qualities and aspirations, defining and constructing a self that is both saint and sinner, saved by suffering and God's grace. Elizabeth Major the author, as depicted in these verses, is a blessed and exemplary Saint. The most remarkable of these is 'The Author's Prayer'.

The Author's Prayer: O my blessed Lord and Saviour Jesus Christ, have mercy on thy poor hand-maid, Elizabeth Major.

Oh	gracious God, inhabiting	E ternity
My	blest redeemer, that hast	L ovingly
Blessed	me with hope, a kingdom to	I nherit,
Lord	of this mercy give an humble	S pirit,
And	grant I pray, I may my life	A mend:
Saviour	'tis thou that canst my soul	B efriend.
Jesus	with grace my guilty soul	E ndue
Christ	promised grace, and thou, O Lord art	T rue;
Have	care of me, deal out with thine own	H and
Mercy	to my poor soul, thou canst com-	M and
On	me a shower of grace, sin to	A void,
Thy	praise to sing, my tongue shall be	I mployed;
Poor,	Lord I am, with fear and care	O ppressed,
Handmaid	to thee I am, in thee I'll	R est.

The self thus defined and recommended to the reader is one with strictly limited freedoms. She must behave in acceptable, godly ways — something which would not usually involve writing, for a woman, necessitating her introductory justification of the act, and the didactic concern of the book. In order to explore the range of subject-matter relevant to a discussion of sinfulness, she also has to vindicate making reference to things 'that your blushing sex should want confidence to mention' (sig. h3). When writing 'On Immodesty', therefore, she inevitably reprimands women for not being sufficiently chaste and modest.

> For England sure doth Sodom pass in sins,
> O here's committed unseen, unheard of things
> To former ages, by my own sex are done,
> Things but to name, would taint a modest tongue:
> Therefore myself I'll silence, since tongue nor ear
> Of a chaste soul can it describe, nor hear:
> For certainly, 'tis scarce unknown to any.
> With grief I speak, ill's acted by too many. (p. 175)

She can only make the immodest step of writing and publishing by claiming to silence herself on certain matters, while warning other women against being overbold. Writing allows Major to create and inhabit a contradictory space, where she is both free to write as a sinner saved, and yet still tightly bound by rules of passivity and modesty. She constructs a new self, but a new self broken by suffering and made up only of permissible feminine elements.

'I could not see the need I had of my troubles, nor the end for which they were sent.' (Sarah Davy, *Heaven Realiz'd*, p. 5)

Women's published records of their spiritual lives have roots in the convention of spiritual self-examination recommended by Puritan divines. This practice served in part to replace the earlier Catholic pattern of confession to a priest to obtain absolution: each person had to examine their own soul's health to discover whether s/he would be numbered among the saved. Such a practice was particularly relevant when death seemed imminent, and it is thanks to the desire of the dying to recall evidence that they were included among God's chosen people that accounts survive of the lives of Elizabeth Moore, Mary Simpson[2] and Luce Perrot. The writings of all these women were published posthumously by men. None of them appeared as autonomous texts, but were reworked by their male editors to serve their own ends. Elizabeth Moore's *Evidences for Heaven*, for instance, appears in Calamy's *The Godly Man's Ark* as part of his argument in favour of patient forebearance. Luce Perrot's *Account* was divided into short sections, each one followed by far more lengthy interpretations and observations composed by her husband, Robert. In all three cases, the women's names only appear in print to be used to urge modesty and acceptance of duty.

It was not only when confronted by the fear of their own imminent demise, however, that Puritans assessed their chances of salvation. In the early 1650s, compilations of 'conversion experiences' were published by Henry Walker, Vavasor Power, Samuel Petto and John Rogers. These 'confessions', many of which were made by women, are professions of faith made by individuals seeking to join a specific Independent congregation. For an experience to be accepted as a genuine guarantee of salvation, it would have to fall within a specific pattern: otherwise the conversion might be a false one, and the sinner caught in the hypocrisy of a false confidence in their salvation. As Owen Watkins has demonstrated in *The Puritan Experience*, the conversion narrative rapidly established its own conventions, a particular pattern of false confidence, doubt, and renewed, true confidence coming to be seen as the necessary sequence in achieving genuine salvation, permitting admission to a gathering of Saints. This structure came to be so surely accepted as proof of true deliverance that Elizabeth Moore cited the fact that God had taken her through the same processes as those reported by other converts as evidence of her own Sainthood.[3] It was probably the same conviction of the inevitability of a specific pattern that led the editor of Sarah Davy's posthumous *Heaven Realiz'd* to divide it into sections, the headings of which trace a formal development that bears little relation to the actual content of the text.

The conventions of spiritual autobiography both provided an acceptable reason for women to write about their experiences, and established a framework through which they could order and make sense of disparate elements of their lives. On the whole, however, it was not possible for women themselves to publish their own accounts. These spiritual autobiographies were often published posthumously and they enter the public domain more carefully surrounded by a bevy of masculine praise, exhortation and interpretation than any other body of women's writing in the period. Anne Venn's *A Wise Virgins Lamp Burning*, for instance, although clearly written with a readership of Christians in mind, was not published until her parents found the manuscript in her closet after her death. It is prefaced by a recommendation from her congregation's minister, Thomas Weld, who hopes it will serve as an example of desirable female behaviour, even if 'to thy knowledge it should not add much'.[4]

The writings most excused and qualified by male approval include those by Sarah Wight, Jane Turner and Anne Venn. Sarah Wight had first entered the arena of public scrutiny in 1647 when, at the age of fifteen, she had fallen into a trance. She had arisen from this periodically to quote scripture or to converse with some of the crowds who came to observe her. Henry Jessey's best-selling description of this period of her life, *The Exceeding Riches of Grace*, includes a list of almost thirty ministers and over fifty 'persons of note' who came to visit her.[5] She was the ideal model of the divinely inspired woman, humbly submitting to being used as God's tool, and not presuming to speak on the issues of state politics that should lie beyond her scope. Unlike her fellow seer Anna Trapnel, she represented no threat to the civil authorities. It is consistent with this that her only publication should have found its way into print without her prior knowledge. (Perhaps the bookseller, Richard Moone, was hopeful that *A Wonderful Pleasant and Profitable Letter Written by Mrs Sarah Wight* would sell as well as Jessey's work about her had.) Although her *Letter* is of prodigious length – about fourteen thousand words – it shows no sign of having been written with any audience in mind other than the friend (minister Robert Bragg?) to whom it is addressed.[6] It records the stages of her conversion, and consists mainly of a detailed exposition of Christian doctrine, starting from the premise that 'A Christian's true happiness lies in being emptied of all self, self refined, as well as gross self; and being filled with a full God' (p. 5).

Jane Turner's *Choice Experiences* portray a woman far less hemmed in by male approbation, who nonetheless needs masculine endorsement for publication of her work. For her, a personal relationship with God engendered not passive submission but a new activity and responsibility for vigilance against backsliding. She explains

> In the work of conversion we are passive, I mean as to inward spiritual activity, we can do nothing being dead . . . But after conversion we are active, and therefore commanded to keep ourselves in the love of God. (p. 189)

Even her description of the 'passivity' of conversion itself is only a conventional acceptance of the tenet that it is God who calls the sinner, and decides who is to be saved. This quiescence does not mean that she should make no initial effort to find the truth. Her third 'Note of Experience' relates how she had read and rejected some unnamed book promoting the new theology. When her Presbyterian minister later preached against the text, however, and talked about it in terms which differed from her recollection of its contents, she went to considerable lengths to acquire another copy of this banned text. Finding that the minister had indeed misrepresented the book was a key element in her decision to change her religious allegiances (pp. 49–53).

It has frequently been noted that the ideas of the sects allowed women some measure of autonomy from their husbands. Quite what this could mean becomes apparent when we examine the writings of the women themselves. Jane Turner's husband, in fact, always enters the text as an afterthought. Only once she has pondered an issue and made her decision does it occur to her to discuss it with him. It is quite in accordance with this sense of separateness that she should have been writing her *Choice Experiences* without her husband's knowledge, and that his first sight of the book should have been when it was nearly finished (dedicatory epistle).

Jane Turner writes to be useful. Having found reading helpful in her own soul's growth, she wants the record of her experiences to profit others. Despite her disclaimer in her 'word from the author to the reader' that the thought of publication had never occurred to her, the text exhibits many signs that it was written with a public in mind. Details of her narrative are frequently omitted with the observation that it is fitting only to 'hint' at them, and a thorough attempt is made to order the story, referring the reader back and fore to other passages. This care for her work and attention to a reader's needs might even have extended to following it through the press, as more than one of these directions to the reader refers her/him to specific page numbers.

The lengthy prefaces to *Choice Experiences*, written by John Turner and two ministers, John Spilsbury and John Gardner, indicate the existence of a dispute within their church concerning the role of women. (Spilsbury's congregation were an offshoot of the Jacob group of churches in London. The group's membership ranged from the conservative Henry Jessey, who wrote the account of Sarah Wight's famous trance described above, to the radical Katherine Chidley, who was centrally involved in the pamphleteering by Leveller women in the 1640s.[7]) Jane Turner complains that her greatest discouragements have come from the Saints even while affirming her belief that 'such brethren only whose gifts are approved of by the church, may exercise their gifts publicly, and no other' (p. 7). She is determined that such approval should be given to her, and cautions her fellows 'to take heed of casting stumbling blocks in each other's way', and to leave the final selection of the Chosen to God (p. 8). It is only with the explicit backing of Spilsbury, and her husband's attesting to her modesty and his 'owning' of her work, that publication can be countenanced. The alternative would be to align herself with the more radical Quakers, whose advocacy of Inner Light she examines, and finally rejects as impermissible, in the course of her experiences (pp. 111–30). Having made her way into print, the conclusion of the text (which might well be the section written after her husband had seen and approved the work) contains a general reflection on the meaning of the concept of 'experience' and her recommendations on specific issues, such as the status of the church's younger members (pp. 193–207). Within the confines of her church, she gained the time to write carefully and at length about weighty matters, and was able to negotiate a route into print.

The pattern of the conversion experience could provide a framework to make sense of various crises in the course of a lifetime, and resulted in widely different reminiscences being written. In the case of these women writers, the experiences of falling in love, marrying and childbearing – events commonly regarded as key stages in female existence – were frequent matters of concern. The unifying factor of conversion allowed such issues to be understood and written about, and justified publication. Sarah Davy's reminiscences centre on the terror produced by her falling in love with a minister, another woman. Susannah Bell uses her text to work out the requirements of wifely duty, and Elizabeth White writes to produce a vision of marriage that discounts the relevance of romantic love. In Hannah Allen's account, finally, the usefulness of the written word itself, and of the conversion narrative framework in particular, are brought into doubt, though finally reaffirmed. Since almost all the texts under discussion here were published posthumously, the writers shared the problem that a third party had to be convinced, through the format of the conversion experience, of the potential interest of publishing a woman's work.[8]

Sarah Davy's 'precious relics', *Heaven Realiz'd*, were published by her minister Anthony Palmer, who recommends them as a model to be imitated by 'younger persons (especially young gentlewomen)', in the hope that they will help to stem the rise of atheism.[9]

Davy describes her early life as a period of great loneliness and isolation, during which time her mother and baby brother died and she passed through a crisis of faith. The turning point comes when she meets the person who effects her conversion to an Independent congregation. Her depiction of this, and of her subsequent heartache at being parted from her new-found friend, is in language which conjures up associations of romantic love. Release from misery arrives when she joins the Independent church her friend belonged to. God then addresses her directly, as recorded in one of her meditations.

Did not I first love you? and therefore give you this new commandment, that as I have loved you so you should love one another, with a pure unbounded love . . . to love one another as I have loved you, or to love thy friend, as thou lovest thyself, most willingly to do that which may be for thy friend's good, although it be to some prejudice to thyself, this is love and by this you shall know that you are my disciples. (p. 37)

This divine command gives licence to love 'although it be to some prejudice to thyself', justifying to Davy and her reader a relationship which is taboo, since the friend who gave her so many 'sweet refreshments' (p. 21) was another woman. This female friend first enters *Heaven Realiz'd* in a passage which at first avoids assigning gender, dwelling on the religious significance of the encounter.

One day the Lord was pleased by a strange providence to cast me into the company of one that I never saw before, but of a sweet and free disposition, and whose discourse savoured so much of the gospel, that I could not but at that instant bless God for his goodness in that providence. It pleased the Lord to carry out our hearts towards one another at that time, and a little while after, the Lord was pleased to bring us together again for the space of three days, in which time it pleased God by our much discourse together, to establish and confirm me more in the desires I had to join with the people of God in society, and enjoy communion with them according to the way of the gospel. She was of a society of the Congregational way called Independents . . . Then were our hearts firmly united, and I blessed the Lord from my soul for so glorious and visible an appearance of his love. (pp. 20–1)

Peace, the end of Davy's story, and the beginning of the possibility of writing about it, arrive when, having joined her friend's Independent church, she abandons this forbidden love and marries. She writes no meditations on wedded love.

The other longing that fills Davy's text is the desire to be useful in her life. She learns that this can be achieved by making herself the wholly passive instrument of God's will, and urges him to accept her converted soul: 'make me useful to thee in that way or any way thou shalt be pleased to choose' (p. 29). It is this submission to God's bidding that permits her both to be united with her friend, if only for a while, and to write the meditations which are finally published. By writing about the episode, she is able to make sense of it, and integrate it into an acceptable interpretation of the world. She had begun by puzzling over 'the need I had of my troubles' (p. 5). By accepting the logic of conversion she ends a Saint, a married woman and, once dead, a published author.

Susannah Bell's *Legacy of a Dying Mother* was also published by her church minister, the Independent Thomas Brooks.[10] Bell's account of her experiences was, Brooks tells us, written down by one of her sons as she spoke it on her deathbed. The 'Epistle Dedicatory' by Brooks which prefaces the story in fact fills two thirds of the book (pp. 1–43). He holds Bell up as a model of humility, who faithfully continued to justify the Lord during her suffering. Her acts of charity, earnest desires for the salvation of her friends and family, and loving behaviour to poor miscarrying Christians all gain a mention. She is presented as both virtuous and self-denying, the ideal woman.

The 'conversion experiences' which follow are as much concerned with Bell's conversion to the merits of wifely duty as they are with more mystical matters. She tells how when her husband had first wanted to go to New England she had resisted his will, as she had a small child and was heavily pregnant with another. The Lord reminds her of the command 'Wives submit yourselves unto your own husbands, as unto the Lord', and she submits. She has seen the error of her ways too late, however, and the second child dies. God tells her that this has happened as a punishment for her disobedience. She informs her husband of her decision to accompany him after all, and by the time they set out she is again 'big with child' (pp. 45–7). Most of the rest of the narrative is concerned with her life in New England, while her husband travels back and forth between the two countries. She has become a good wife and Christian, and is soon allowed to join the local church. She sees it as a reward for this godly behaviour that her family are not hurt by an earthquake, and that on their return to England they survive the Plague and the Great Fire (pp. 59–61). The only disturbance to this surface contentment comes during one of her husband's trips back to England. While he is there, war breaks out, and Susannah Bell's neighbours fear that he might have been killed. This, too, she accepts with cheerful resignation, telling them 'If God should take my husband out of the world, I should have a husband in heaven, which was best of all' (pp. 55–6).

The manuscript of Elizabeth White's *The Experiences of Gods*

Gracious Dealing was found after her decease, as Anne Venn's had been, in her closet.[11] The reasons she gives for her writing are the same as those of the authors of meditations and conversion experiences: memory of God's goodness will support her in times of darkness, and prevent her forgetting its details. The text will remind her that 'he only hath wrought my works in me, for of myself I am not able to think a good thought, speak a good word, or do a good action' (pp. 21–2).

Her story follows the usual conversion narrative format of progress from ignorance and self-deception through spiritual torment to the acquisition of true confidence in her salvation. The experiences she describes, however, like those that Bell and Davy depict, are problems caused by love and childbearing. Her first crisis of faith occurs immediately before her marriage, the second about fifteen months later when she is expecting the birth of her first child. The wrongdoing which preoccupies her thoughts at both these times is the fact that she had spent so much time in her youth reading 'histories [i.e. romances], and other foolish books'.[12]

I was a great lover of histories, and other foolish books, and did often spend my sleeping-time in reading of them, and sometimes I should think I did not do well in so doing, but I was so bewitched by them, that I could not forbear; and hearing of a friend of mine, which was esteemed a very holy woman, that did delight in histories, I then concluded it was no sin, and gave myself wholly then to this kind of folly, when I had any spare time, for two or three years. I had sometimes slight thoughts of repentance, but was loath to set about it. (p. 3)

Such reading might seem a venial enough sin, unless we reflect that the subject-matter of these romances which had so obsessed her was a glorification of the joys of love. Perhaps the reality had not matched up to her expectations. Certainly the thought that dominates as her confinement approaches is the fear that she will perish in childbed: 'I was much dejected, having a sense of my approaching danger' (p. 11). After giving birth, she has a vision and then a dream which confirm that she will die. While still convalescing from the birth, she finds release from fear by writing of 'God's Gracious Dealings' with her. As the title page informs the reader, she did then die in childbed, like many of her contemporaries (see Chapter Seven).

The introductory remarks to Hannah Allen's *Satan his Methods and Malice Baffled* seem to be written by a church minister and direct the reader to the expected interpretation of her story: melancholy is physical in its origins, but the devil can use this 'malady' to his own ends. Hannah Allen's experiences are to be understood as the tale of her overcoming, with God's help, Satan's temptations to despair and self-destruction. This interpretation of her story is remarkable in view of the fact that the problem the narrative centres on is the failure of this religious framework to explain or relieve Hannah Allen's state of mind.

Allen's story begins conventionally enough: she records being raised by religious parents, undergoing early doubts about her salvation, and finding relief and new hope when reading a book by Mr Bolton. After her marriage in 1655 or 1656 at the age of seventeen to a merchant, Hannibal Allen, she joined Edmund Calamy's church (pp. 1–6). Eight years later her husband died on one of his many foreign voyages, and she 'began to fall into a deep melancholy' (p. 7). She turned to the established routines of her religion to lift her depression, seeking evidence that she was one of the saved and could look forward to an eternity of bliss. Attempting to relieve her melancholy, Hannah Allen reread her diary, seeking proof that her writing had served some useful purpose and that her belief in her salvation was not 'hypocrisy'.

Then I would repeat several promises to my condition, and read over my former experiences that I had writ down, as is hereafter expressed, and obligations that I had laid upon myself, in the presence of God, and would say, 'Aunt, I hope I write not these things in hypocrisy, I never intended any eye should see them; but the devil suggesteth dreadful things to me against God, and that I am an hypocrite'. (pp. 8–9)

Despite all the comforts her diary offered, her depression deepened. The Bible, too, failed to assuage her misery: 'When I had seen the Bible, I would say, "Oh that blessed book that I so delighted in once!" ' (p. 9). Travelling between friends and relatives, and seeking spiritual counsel, she found no comfort and ceased bothering to keep her record of God's marks of favour to her, and began to despair. As she began to have dreams and visions confirming her doom, and found no relief in writing or in reading the Bible, she forbade her son to read and spurned the written word herself.

Nor could I endure to be present at prayer, or any other part of God's worship, nor to hear the sound of reading, nor the sight of a book or paper; though it were but a letter, or an almanac . . . I would wish I had never seen book, or learned letter; I would say 'It had been happy for me if I had been born blind'; daily repeating my accustomed language, that I was a cursed reprobate, and the monster of the creation. (pp. 58, 59)

Throughout the time of her melancholy, which lasted about three years, she made a series of dramatic suicide attempts, smoking a pipeful of spiders (generally believed to be venomous) to poison herself (p. 33); trying to starve herself to death but losing courage (p. 36); cutting her arm so as to bleed to death (p. 44).

She gives no real explanation for the cessation of these efforts at self-destruction, or how her despair lifted. After about three years the melancholy began to leave her, she records, and then I changed much from my retiredness, and delighted to walk with friends abroad . . . And this spring it pleased God to provide a very suitable match for me, one Mr Charles Hatt, a widower living in Warwickshire; with whom I live very comfortably, both as to my inward and outward man, my husband being one that truly fears God. (p. 71)

Her religion had provided no explanation for the arrival of her melancholy at her first husband's death, and produced no reason for its leaving her at her remarriage. Nonetheless, with the problem gone the experience could be written about, and an attempt made to fit it into the accepted pattern of false confidence, doubt and new, true knowledge of salvation. The text ends by quoting a series of biblical passages selected to make sense of events in such a framework.

Fear not: for I have redeemed thee, I have called thee by thy name; thou art mine. When thou passest through the water, I will be with thee; and through the rivers, they shall not overflow thee: when thou walkest through the fire, thou shalt not be burned; neither shall the flame kindle upon thee. Isaiah 43.1–2.

Behold, we count them happy which endure. Ye have heard of the patience of Job, and have seen the end of the Lord: that the Lord is very pitiful and of tender mercy. James, 5.11.

Ye are of God, little children, and have overcome them: because greater is he that is in you, than he that is in the world. 1 John, 4.4.

With the experience itself removed, the written word can be allowed once again to reinterpret its significance.

These books of religious poetry, meditations and conversion experiences indicate that even such apparently narrow and formulaic genres could be used by women to justify their writing. Also, it is clear that women were able to use the available formats to explore subject-matter that might be taboo, and that they wrote about love, marriage and their relationships with women and men in ways which challenge fundamentally the impressions of female existence that can be gleaned from male texts. The religious poetry, particularly, shows that women were not at all convinced that love and marriage were in their own best interests. Nonetheless, texts had to be publishable, and their female authors found it necessary to negotiate some acceptable way of existing within the constraints of the society in which they lived. The struggle to find a solution provides the dynamic of the texts themselves. Women daring to examine closely the limits of female behaviour are forced in their writing to reaffirm femininity, their texts becoming both an exploration of its constraints and an analysed self-policing which vindicates the fetters of feminine duty. The authorial personae that emerge in the process are model women, held up for admiration and emulation. The contradictions of this position are neatly expressed in *Eliza's Babes* in a couplet addressed by the author both to her God and to her poetry itself: 'My boundless spirits, bounded be in thee,/ For bounded by no other can they be' (p. 36).

CHAPTER THREE

AUTOBIOGRAPHIES AND BIOGRAPHIES OF HUSBANDS

THE marble pillars of Knole in Kent and Wilton in Wiltshire were to me oftentimes but the gay harbours of anguish, insomuch as a wise man, that knew the inside of my fortune would often say that I lived in those my Lords' great families as the river of Rhone or Rhodanus runs through the Lake of Geneva, without mingling any part of its streams with that lake. For I gave myself wholly to retiredness, as much as I could, in both those great families, and made good books and virtuous thoughts my companions which have never deserved afflictions, nor been daunted when it unjustly happeneth. And by a happy genius I overcame all those troubles, the prayers of my blessed mother helping me herein.[1]

So wrote Anne Clifford, recording in widowhood the circumstances of her two very unhappy marriages. Since much of her life had been spent fighting for the inheritance which her father had illegally willed away from her, it would be surprising if she was unfamiliar with T.E.'s guidebook for women on legal problems, *The Lawes Resolution of Womens Rights*. In the Introduction, I quote T.E.'s description of the state of wedlock, in which the married woman is compared with the little rivulet that loses its name and identity once joined to the might of the Humber, Rhone (Rhodanus) or Thames. Clifford's depiction of herself as the great river, refraining from mingling itself with the lake it enters is a woman's answer to this. Despite her annihilation in law, she could find ways to maintain her separateness.

A good few diaries and autobiographies written in the period survived in manuscript form, and have been published in more recent times. This is not the place to undertake an extended discussion of such writings, since the focus of interest here is published works. It is well to note, though, that the picture these autobiographies give of women's lives differs radically from the stories told us by modern history books. The change in marriage patterns in the period, as more people began to marry for love, did not necessarily result in happier relationships. Mary Rich, the Countess of Warwick, for instance, refused to accept the husband her father had arranged for her, eloping with Charles Rich for 'passion'. Her diary and autobiography show how quickly the word 'passion' came to stand instead for 'anger' – his. Her only escape from his pervasive control over her life was through meditation and prayer, retreating to 'the wilderness' in the grounds of their house, Leighs Priory. In response, he had the trees in her retreat cut down.[2]

This is not to say that a change back to older methods of matchmaking would have been preferable for women. However the marriage partner was chosen, or by whom, the end result was significantly similar: men held all power and authority, women were to be subservient. Alice Thornton also married for love. Her husband, William, turned out to be 'much addicted to a melancholic humour', and seems to have been of little practical use to her.[3] Before she married him, she had been through three more traditional, and more repugnant, courtships, as she describes in the three parallel versions of her autobiography. The first of these suitors was Captain Inns, who talked his way into being quartered at her family's house in Ireland in 1643. He took a fancy to the sixteen-year-old Alice, and offered her aunt £3000 or £4000 if she would help his suit. The young woman, as her aunt suggested would be the case, had no desire to be sold off in this manner, and when Lord Adare arrived to press his friend's suit she ran away and hid in another house. She seems to have received her mother's support in the resistance (her father had died three years previously), since she remembers

This villain captain did study to be revenged of my dear mother, and threatened cruelly what he would do to her because she hid me, though that was not true, for I hid myself. (p. 45)

The second man to express an interest in Alice Thornton was more brutal in his approach, but fortunately equally unsuccessful. In one of the accounts of her young womanhood she gives thanks to God for delivering her from Jerimy Smithson, whose plot to kidnap and rape her was revealed just in time by another man.

A great deliverance from the violence of a rape from Jerimy Smithson, Sir Heugh's son, who had solicited me in marriage by his father and uncle Smithson, who would have settled on him two hundred pounds a year if I would have married him; but I would not, but avoided his company because he was debauched. And he hired some of his company to have stolen me away from Lowes, but Tom Binks discovered it, I bless God. (p. 47n.)

Once her virginity had been lost, she would have had little option but to marry the man who sought to assault her so savagely.

The third courtship she describes actually predated the other two. When she was fifteen years old, her brother's property was sequestered by parliament. In an attempt to have the order lifted, her uncle tried to win the assistance of one of his relatives by offering Alice in marriage in return for anticipated favours. Neither Alice nor her mother was informed of these negotiations until they were well advanced. Once again, the two women united to resist the proposal. In the account which the Surtees Society prints in the main body of the text, Thornton attests to her willingness to be governed by the general family interest, 'deeming their judgement above mine'. In her later retelling of the episode, however, a far more ironic grimace is apparent. What choice did she have? she asks.

Which manner of persuasion to a marriage, with a sword in one hand, and a compliment in another, I did not understand, when a free choice was denied me. (p. 62n.)

The autobiography and biography are generally regarded as seventeenth-century inventions, as this period saw the first great outpouring of such works. A brief survey of standard texts on the subject could give the impression this was a predominantly or purely male phenomenon.[4] In fact, as the preceding chapters have illustrated, many female writers described or analysed their experiences. In the case of Quakers, some also contributed to deathbed testimonials that delineated the lives and characters of their deceased Sisters and Brothers. Hannah Wolley and Elizabeth Cellier (see Chapter Seven and the Introduction) also gave more lengthy summaries of their experiences. In addition, some women undertook the more daunting task of assessing and recording in detail their own lives, or those of their husbands.

Since once women were married they legally became a part of their husband, it is not surprising that the projects of writing their autobiographies and writing the biographies of their husbands were intimately connected. Lady Ann Fanshawe, for instance, describes her memoirs, written for her son as 'the most remarkable actions and accidents of your family as well as those more eminent ones of your father and my life'.[5] Her life and her husband's were one and the same. As they wrote, such women set out and bumped against the circumscription of their lives in marriage.

In reading these memoirs, it is important to bear in mind that autobiographies are not a clear glass through which we can view the 'real lives' of their authors and the people around them. The picture we derive of someone's experiences from a biography or autobiography is just as much an artificial construction as any other kind of writing. The image produced through writing is a partial one, and 'partial' in more than one sense. Everything cannot be recorded – what is written down is only part of the whole, both because some things are omitted, and because language cannot, by its very nature, represent the fullness of experience.

In addition, these writings are undertaken with an audience in mind: an audience that has to be convinced or persuaded, and this is also a determining factor in the version of a 'personality' constructed in the text. I mention above that there are three parallel accounts of Alice Thornton's life, all written by herself over a period of some years. Each presents us with a different version of the central character, 'Alice Thornton'. There is also more than one 'Mary Rich': it is from her diary that we learn of her husband's 'passion', and of his destruction of 'the wilderness'. The autobiography, by contrast, celebrates the fact that her marriage brought her 'into a noble and, which is much more, a religious family' (p. 13). If we turn to Lucy Hutchinson's celebrated *Memoirs of the Life of Colonel Hutchinson* we find there are two 'Lucy Hutchinsons' in the *Life*: a 'she' who is a devoted wife, dutiful to her husband in all things and pleased to be so; and an 'I' who is the author, the creating artist who stands outside the relationship. In an extensive passage, the author stands back and describes this 'she'.

She only reflected his own glories upon him: all that she was, was *him*, while he was here, and all that she is now is at best but his pale shade . . . She was a very faithful mirror, reflecting truly, though but dimly, his own glories upon him, so long as he was present; but she, that was nothing before his inspection gave her a fair figure, when he was removed, was only filled with a dark mist, and never could again take in any delightful object, nor return any shining representation . . . 'Twas not her face he loved, her honour and her virtue were his mistresses, and these (like Pygmalion's) images of his own making, for he polished and gave form to what he found with all the roughness of the quarry about it; but meeting with a compliant subject for his own wise government, he found as much satisfaction as he gave, and never had occasion to number his marriage among his infelicities.[6]

It is important to remember, then, that while these autobiographical writings give us information that qualifies or contradicts the impressions of women's lives, and of the 'companionate marriage', given in male texts past and present, they still do not give us an uncomplicated access to the 'truth'. It was necessary for women to interpret and present their lives in ways consistent with desired models of femininity. If, as seems likely, more autobiographical accounts by women come to light, we must be self-conscious about the sense we make of what we find.

Since women were supposed to have no autonomous lives, but were deemed to be absorbed into their husbands' identities, it was peculiarly difficult and dangerous for a woman to compose her autobiography. Only two women in the period, Margaret Cavendish the Duchess of Newcastle and Theodosia Alleine, managed to combine such an act with having their writings published.

Theodosia Alleine's biography of her husband Joseph was published in 1672 as a small part of a larger work compiled in his honour by his male friends, and it passed through many subsequent editions. The dedicatory epistle sees fit to justify the inclusion of something written by a woman, explaining that Alleine had sent her account 'to a worthy divine, by him to be published in his own style, she not imagining it should be put forth in her own words'. He, however, had judged it worthy to appear uncorrected.

The modesty exemplified by Alleine's suggestion that her text would need redrafting, after she had taken the bold step of writing for publication, is characteristic of the conflicting images of herself that occasionally filter into the biography. Her story is mostly taken up with a depiction of her husband's sufferings, terms of imprisonment and eventual death, after he had resigned his ministry at the time of the Act of Uniformity. She describes her devoted submission to his decisions, and her careful nursing of him during his sickness. Through emphasising her wifely devotion, the text also draws attention to her strength and endurance, and reveals his unthinking egotism without having to complain about it. Through one long winter he was ailing, and she had to rise as often as forty times a night, we are told, to help the various women who rallied round to share his nursing. In the daytime, she was given no peace.

> Neither would he suffer anyone all the day to touch him but me, or to give him anything that he did receive: by which I discerned it was most grateful to him, and therefore so to me.[7]

It is only after his death that the narrative shifts back to the earlier days of their married life. The marriage took place after fourteen months of courtship, and Theodosia Alleine clearly hoped for loving companionship. What she got was a man whose work came first, and who blithely assumed that his wife would fit in with his plans.

> When I have pleaded with him for more of his time with myself, and family, he would answer me: his ministerial work would not permit him to be so constant as he would . . . He was a holy, heavenly, tenderly-affectionate husband, and I know nothing I could complain of, but that he was so taken up, that I could have but very little converse with him. (p. 92)

She claims to 'have been convinced and silenced' (p. 96) by his remarks, but she was not quite silenced. Instead she wrote about his life, thereby giving her side of the story, as she bursts periodically into the text. It is finally, though, *his* life that she writes about, and her own absorption into it. The story of her own work could also have made interesting reading: she mentions in passing that she ran a school from their house, sometimes having as many as sixty students, some thirty of whom were boarders (p. 91). These affairs, though, were not allowed the importance that writing about them would have accorded them. Only by being her husband's recorder could she be an author. Her description of her taking down his words for him when he was too sick to write himself, is a kind of emblem for this process.

> His next work was to send letters to all his relations, and intimate friends, in most of which he urged them to observe his counsels, for they were like to be his last to them. I always wrote for him, for he could not by reason of his weakness write a line. (p. 87)

Her room for manoeuvre as the devoted wife of a great man was small indeed, but by arranging her narrative in her own way she was able to make public something of the life of a woman in her position. By appearing to be wholly subsumed by her husband, she could write her own character.

Margaret Cavendish, the Duchess of Newcastle, was born into the largest landowning family in Colchester. Two of her brothers fought on the king's side in the civil war, and she joined the court at Oxford as a lady-in-waiting, accompanying the queen on her escape to France. There she met William Cavendish, the Marquis (later Duke) of Newcastle, who had fled England after the defeat of the royalist troops he had been commanding. When she returned to England briefly in 1653, she arranged for the publication of her first two books, *Poems and Fancies* and *Philosophical Fancies*. Between then and 1668 she published in all twelve separate works, some of which went through more than one edition, ranging from natural philosophy to plays, poems, stories, her autobiography, a biography of her husband and a collection of semifictional letters.

She is best known as the biographer of her husband. Wherever her name appears, the merits and failings of the *Life of the Duke of Newcastle* are seriously discussed. It is the only one of her works which has been reprinted several times, and in various editions, this century. Most of these modern editions also include her autobiography.

Long before the *Life of the Duke* appeared in 1668, however, Cavendish had written her autobiography. It was published in 1656 as 'the true story at the latter end' of a book of stories entitled *Natures Pictures Drawn by Fancies Pencil to the Life*. In writing explicitly about her life for publication, Cavendish goes further than any of her female contemporaries in breaking into the male, public world. Her work is indeed both produced by this male/female, public/private divide, and extraordinarily self-conscious about its existence. She does not want to be confined and defined wholly by female 'honour', or sexual chastity, but desires 'fame' which can only come from publication. All her books open with a series of epistles to the reader. One of those prefacing *Natures Pictures* reads

I confess my ambition is restless, and not ordinary; because it would have an extraordinary fame. And since all heroic actions, public employments, powerful governments, and eloquent pleadings are denied our sex in this age, or at least would be condemned for want of custom, is the cause I write so much.

The final paragraph of Cavendish's autobiography explains that she has written it to establish – or, we might say, to construct – her individuality and identity separately from the husband whose name she bears. This passage is also delightfully typical of her writings, as she compares herself assertively to Caesar and Ovid.

But I hope my readers will not think me vain for writing my life, since there have been many that have done the like, as Caesar, Ovid, and many more, both men and women, and I know no reason I may not do it as well as they. But I verily believe some censuring readers will scornfully say 'Why hath this Lady writ her own life? Since none cares to know whose daughter she was, or whose wife she is, or how she was bred, or what fortunes she had, or how she lived, or what humour or disposition she was of?' I answer that it is true, that 'tis of no purpose, to the readers, but it is to the authoress, because I write it for my own sake, not theirs. Neither did I intend this piece to delight, but to divulge, not to please the fancy, but to tell the truth, lest after-ages should mistake, in not knowing I was daughter to one Master Lucas of St Johns, near Colchester, in Essex, second wife to the Lord Marquis of Newcastle, for my Lord having had two wives, I might easily have been mistaken, especially if I should die, and my Lord marry again. (pp. 390–1)[8]

There is irony in the fact that when Cavendish comes to define explicitly who she is, the only criteria she has available are the names of her father and husband. Her actual practice, however, both in her writing and in her daily life, serves to distinguish her from others. She appears in Pepys's diary (entries for 11 and 26 April 1667) as a slightly crazy, eccentrically dressed woman. Her own explanation for her idiosyncratic choice of clothes is made in her autobiography.

I took great delight in attiring, fine dressing, and fashions, especially such as I did invent myself, not taking that pleasure in such fashions as was invented by others. Also I did dislike any should follow my fashions, for I always took delight in a singularity, even in accoutrements of habits. (p. 387)

Although in law Cavendish might have 'lost her stream' by marrying, in her practice she could still distinguish herself from her husband. At one level, she might have been subsumed by him. *Natures Pictures* includes some passages identified in the text as written by the Duke; they are unacknowledged on the title page, however, and incorporated into the text as part of the body of Cavendish's work.

Making a bid for fame in the public world could cause Cavendish's reputation for feminine modesty, and hence her reputation for chastity, to be brought into doubt. The conflicting demands of 'fame' and 'honour' combine to produce the autobiography. This is why, although it deals with the publication of her early works, it is overwhelmingly concerned with constructing a picture of her as a virtuous, truly feminine woman. She says,

> But whatsoever I was addicted to, either in fashion of clothes, contemplation of thoughts, actions of life, they were lawful, honest, honourable, and modest, of which I can avouch to the world with a great confidence, because it is a pure truth. (p. 387)

She twice says of her childhood 'we were bred virtuously, modestly, civilly, honourably, and on honest principles' (pp. 369, 371). Her modern biographer, Douglas Grant, has accepted at face value her depiction of herself as blushing and retiring when at the queen's court.

The fact that the autobiography was written in part to defend her against being thought unfeminine comes out as well in her description of her behaviour during her visit to London in 1653.

> Nor seldom did I dress myself, as taking no delight to adorn myself, since he I only desired to please was absent, although report did dress me in a hundred several fashions. (p. 382)

If we compare this remark with that quoted earlier, where Cavendish proclaims her delight in using fashion to make herself 'a singularity', the directly contradictory demands of 'fame' and 'honour' are made clear.

Cavendish's depiction of her inferiority and obedience to her husband could have been copied straight from the conduct books of the day. She says that her husband married her because she was so shy that he could mould her to his desire. This prolific writer also claims to be silent in his company, hanging on his every word.

> Not that I speak much, because I am addicted to contemplation, unless I am with my Lord, yet then I rather attentively listen to what he says, than impertinently speak. (p. 384)

I am not questioning whether Cavendish actually *was* subservient to her husband, or self-conscious in company. The point is that she should repeatedly assert her subservience and shyness in her autobiography. It is in keeping with this highly repressive image of her own femininity that she should attack other women who might dare to speak publicly, entering the male sphere, and counsel them to attend to their reputations.

> The truth is, our sex doth nothing but jostle for pre-eminence of words, I mean not for speaking well, but speaking much, as they do for the pre-eminence of place . . . but if our sex would but well consider, and rationally ponder, they will

perceive and find, that it is neither words nor place that can advance them, but worth and merit: nor can words or place disgrace them, but inconstancy and boldness: for an honest heart, a noble soul, a chaste life, and a true speaking tongue, is the throne, sceptre, crown, and footstool, that advances them to an honourable renown. (p. 380)

I mentioned earlier that the bulk of Cavendish's writing has been ignored by literary critics, who are mainly interested in her biography of her husband. Interestingly enough, she actually wrote nothing new after her presentation of herself in the *Life of the Duke* as an entirely submissive wife. In this book, she is not present as the controlling author figure in the same way that she is in her other works, and when she narrates her journey to England to plead for a share of Newcastle's sequestered estate, she does not even mention her writing and publishing when there, which she does describe in the parallel account in her autobiography. She also presents herself as writing not for fame, and from her own inspiration, but firmly directed by her husband. He had dictated what should be included and what omitted, she says in the preface, describing her 'submission to his Lordship's desire, from whom I have learned patience to overcome my passions, and discretion to yield to his prudence'. The contradictions between fame and honour had become so great that silence resulted, and she is absorbed into the non-identity of the *femme covert*, the married woman.

The particularly overt assault on the male world represented by her publishing separate accounts of her own life and her husband's had also to be rejected: the implicit public announcement of her autonomy, however carefully guarded by assertions of modesty, had to be silently withdrawn. The autobiography was omitted from the second edition of *Natures Pictures*, 1671, and the title page altered which disguised its exclusion. After publishing the *Life of the Duke* in 1668, this prolific author wrote nothing new. Even she was finally silenced by the threat to her femininity involved in this essentially aggressive attempt on the public world.

This is particularly ironic since she, like Rich and Thornton, depicts herself as having married for love even though she would rationally have preferred to remain single.

Though I did dread marriage, and shunned men's company as much as I could, yet I could not, nor had the power to refuse him, by reason my affections were fixed on him, and he was the only person I ever was in love with. (p. 375)

CHAPTER FOUR

ROMANTIC LOVE – PROSE FICTION

ONE of the perennial preoccupations of male writing has been the relationship between the sexes, and men's poetry, especially, is full of coy and scornful mistresses and aching male desire. The next three chapters will examine female prose fiction, plays and poetry in which the relationship between women and men is a primary focus.

During the 1640s and 1650s, large numbers of women challenged the orthodoxy that they should be passive and silent. They petitioned parliament, agitated for social reforms and travelled the country spreading their message. Even those who stayed at home found a new voice, and were able to publish texts making a case for some kind of female autonomy. With the Restoration in 1660, all this began to change. One sign of this development was the appearance of a series of mock 'Women's Complaints', all of which shared a central feature: women's only dissatisfaction, according to these scurrilous (male) pamphleteers, was that they were sexually frustrated.[1] One of the most unpleasant of these pamphlets is *The Young-womans Complaint*. It describes in rollicking verse a fifteen-year-old woman being married off to a man of seventy-two, who beats and reviles her. The situation is presented as one of light humour. In 'The she-Anchoret', Margaret Cavendish's female philosopher had warned men not to beat their wives, and advised women to desert a husband who would not reform.[2] No such solution is offered by the ballad-writer of 1680. The 'remedy' adopted by the young woman is to find another man in secret, and cuckold her husband, leaving the power-structure unchanged and her ill-treatment unrelieved. The only moral drawn is that women should be more careful about which men they marry, or they will be forced to look elsewhere for sex.

Even today, the court of Charles II is best known for its profligacy and overt sexuality. This is variously presented as a joyous rejection of the repressiveness of Puritan morality, or an anxious rebellion against the superego or father-figure that the Puritan patriarch could be seen to represent.[3] What both these explanations discount is the essentially misogynous character of this court and the ideology that it propagated. It could be argued that the central issue for Charles II himself, and the only one on which he was immovable, was the patriarchal line of descent. Despite all his apparent cheeriness and willingness to compromise on other matters, he refused steadfastly to allow anyone other than his brother to lay claim to the throne. After years of fairly peaceful co-existence with parliament, he repeatedly adjourned them whenever the question of the succession was raised, ending his reign without a parliament. Whether or not a stubborn commitment to the male line is considered sufficient explanation for this behaviour, other aspects of his court's life certainly show an overwhelming male dominance. Charles's many mistresses were subjected to an endless barrage of anonymous ballads and pamphlets, portraying them as libidinous, diseased and immoral, and while the king's illegitimate sons regularly received noble titles, his daughters by the same women were left in unsupported obscurity.[4] So fashionable was it to follow the king's example and 'keep a whore' that Francis North was counselled to acquire one forthwith if he wished to maintain his political credibility.[5] This cynical exploitation of women as sexual objects was an essential part of a gentleman's calling.

It would be a mistake to imagine that the increased promotion of an ideal that men should use women as sexual objects, and that women were longing to be abused, was caused by the royal household itself in any simple way. The king's behaviour is however the most visible evidence of a far-reaching male backlash against female liberty. The most striking feature of this period of English history, in fact, is that it marks the beginnings of home-grown pornography.[6] The only extended study of this material is Roger Thompson's *Not for Modest Ears*. He shows that pornographic works escalated in volume and obscenity in the second half of the seventeenth century, reaching two peaks around 1660 and again after 1680. His extensive reading of these texts leads him to conclude that the relatively small number of obscene texts published before 1660 'turn out to be very thin gruel indeed by Restoration standards'. He notes that the peaks of production thereafter coincide with moments of acute political tension, and suggests that pornography can therefore best be understood as connected with an Oedipal anxiety about, and rebellion against, father-figures. While this reading might serve as a partial explanation, what Thompson fails to explore is the fundamentally misogynous nature of this pornography. Perhaps men were anxious; their anxiety, however, could have been channelled in various directions. The fact that women were made the targets of their aggression is crucial. In moments of uncertainty, we can argue, men returned to the one thing they needed to be sure of: their right to use, abuse and dominate women. All of the texts Thompson cites share an overwhelming contempt for women, presenting them as the two sides of that most hideous of male fantasies: reduced merely to 'sex', women become ravenous or ravished, sexually predatory or victims of rape. Often, women are described actively inviting and encouraging brutal assaults on themselves. Women, these texts proclaim, are essentially masochistic. They are portrayed eagerly agreeing to be whipped. Their flesh is torn, their blood is spilt. Even today, when we are once again witnessing a vicious male backlash against uppity females, these works make terrifying reading.

Such attitudes as these also appear with great frequency in post-Restoration popular ballads, a few examples of which will be more than sufficient. *The Swimming Lady: Or, a Wanton Discovery* describes with voyeuristic fascination a 'coy lady' undressing before taking a swim in a lake. Her care to ensure that she is not observed is gleefully detailed before the ballad proceeds to laughingly depict her rape by a man whose advances she has repeatedly refused.

> She shrieks, she strives, and down she dives,
>   he brings her up again,
> He got her o'er, upon the shore,
>   and then, and then, and then,
> As Adam did old Eve enjoy,
>   you may guess what I mean;
> Because she all uncovered lay,
>   he covered her again.

No compassion for her plight, for the trauma that rape entails, is allowed to sully the rollicking male delight. She has no choice but to agree to wed her rapist, who returns to assaulting her until morning dawns, when his ownership of her will be complete.

The Dumb Lady tells a similarly light-hearted account of a rape. In this version, the woman is shown stubbornly responding to male overtures with the constant refrain 'No, not I'. The man turns this to his own ends, framing his questions differently until her response has come to be an undertaking not to struggle if she is forced to have intercourse. The ballad ends with the clever fellow raping her triumphantly, having won her 'consent'. As is so often the case with pornographic works, the woman is described as co-operating lasciviously once forced to acquiesce.[7]

In European cultures at least, men have always raped and battered women.[8] This most extreme expression of male power was not invented in the seventeenth century. What is particular to this period, however, is the first upsurge of home-grown pornography. In her article 'Pornography and Grief', Andrea Dworkin has expressed the significance of such growth.

Pornography is not a genre of expression separate and different from the rest of life; it is genre of expression fully in harmony with any culture in which it flourishes . . . Pornography exists because men despise women, and men despise women in part because pornography exists. (p. 289)

Before the return of the monarchy, women had fought for a different world for themselves and their sisters. After 1660, they had to be put firmly back in their place. Pornography presented the relationship between the sexes as a bitter war, one that would always be won by men. This was the dominant framework within which any woman writing about love, sex or romance would have to position herself. In the next few chapters, I want to explore the different ways in which women negotiated spaces within this skeleton.

Since the novel was to become the great literary genre for the exploration of human relations, perhaps it makes sense to examine first works which have been identified as precursors of the novel form. The romance, with its concern with love and adventure, was one of the few places where women could confidently expect to appear in works by men, and it is not surprising to find some early women turning to this genre themselves, when they came to write.

From the mid-seventeenth century on, increasing numbers of translations of foreign romances were published in England. Particularly popular were Cervantes' influential *Don Quixote*, Boccaccio's novels, and the *romans* and *nouvelles* written by prominent Frenchwomen such as Madeleine de Scudéry, Marie-Catherine La Mothe (Mme D'Aulnoy), and Marie-Catherine Desjardins.[9] These were much read by English women. Several of the female autobiographers of the period castigate themselves for their early delight in such frivolities, and Dorothy Osborne and Katherine Philips both refer to romances frequently in their letters. Romance-reading was frowned on by contemporary authors of conduct books, many of them agreeing with George Hickes that having read about 'those imaginary princesses', 'a poor raw girl' would find it hard 'to descend from this heroical state, down to the meanest parts and offices of housewifery'.[10]

Several English women, like their French counterparts, tried their hand at writing their own romances. Anna Weamys undertook a *Continuation* of one of the most popular English romances, *The Countess of Pembroke's Arcadia*. Margaret Cavendish, who experimented with most contemporary genres, composed the short fictions of *Natures Pictures*. Both these authors published before the Restoration. After 1660, Mary Carleton's semi-fictional autobiography, which draws heavily on romance conventions, appeared, and Aphra Behn composed her 'histories and novels', many of which were not published until after her death.

In 1657, Anna Weamys's *Continuation of Sir Philip Sydney's Arcadia* was published. *Arcadia* itself was much read in the period, running through thirteen editions in the century after its original appearance in 1593. The publication of Weamys's *Continuation* coincided with one of these reprints, and it is possible that making it public was at least partly the idea of the bookseller, Thomas Heath.

Arcadia is dedicated to the Countess of Pembroke, and it was popular with generations of ladies: Suzanne Hull records that for two centuries this romance was referred to as favourite female reading matter. It is not altogether surprising, then, to find that Anna Weamys was not the first woman to imitate this famous pastoral text: in 1621, Lady Mary Wroth, Sidney's niece, had published *Urania*, a work modelled on the style of *Arcadia*.[11] Weamys's book is related even more closely than this to *Arcadia*: a thorough acquaintance with the preceding plot is assumed, and the rather fragmentary incidents Weamys describes would make little sense to the uninitiated reader. She was writing, indeed, for devotees of romance. The *Continuation* even follows the convention of looking to virtuous ladies for its protection: it is dedicated 'To the two unparalleled sisters, and patterns of virtue, the Lady Anne and the Lady Grace Per-point' (sig. 3). Weamys had originally written, she says (echoing Sidney's dedication of *Arcadia*), for the private entertainment of these ladies. Only at their insistence has she allowed the work to be made public.

The stationer's preface to the *Continuation* anticipates that the reader might 'disrelish the shrillness of the note' of this female extension of Sidney's story, and reassures us that the *Continuation* should not really be seen as a product of women's writing. 'No other than the lively ghost of Sidney, by a happy transmigration, speaks through the organs of this inspired Minerva' (sig. 4). The lengthy male praises that preface the book expand on this theme, describing Weamys's text as 'pretty stories' (sig. 5^v), and affirming that Sidney, not Weamys (nor, we might add, Mary Pembroke[12]) is the real genius behind the tale. Her role is merely that of passive vehicle for his inspiration. 'He breathes through female organs, yet retains/ His masculine vigour in heroic strains' (sig. 6^v).

Weamys's continuation of the unfinished stories of Amphialus and Helena, Plangus and Erona, Claius, Strephon and Urania could hardly have been more self-effacing. She hides her name, merely identifying herself as 'a young gentlewoman, Mrs. A.W.', and seeks only to give some shape to an extension of a man's work, using his characters solely. *Arcadia* was famed for its extended use of rhetorical conventions, especially a stylistic technique known as periphrasis, so anyone under-taking its continuation was liable to unfavourable comparisons with the original[13]: a woman especially so, since her education was unlikely to include training in these conventions. Weamys modestly decries her ability to do justice to her pattern, for instance remarking of 'King Evarchus', 'A large and rare theme might be chronicled of his wisely governed passions; but that is too pregnant a virtue for my dull capacity to go on with' (p. 30). She does not always shy away from descriptions, however, even if the resultant passages are less extended and flowery than comparable scenes in *Arcadia*. The deaths of the evil Plaxirtus and Anaxius are told with relish.

> Then entered they into so fierce a fight, that it goes beyond my memories to declare all the passages thereof: but both parties showed such magnanimity of courage, that for a long time none could discern who should be victor; till at length Musidorus gave a fatal thrust to Plaxirtus, who being before faint with loss of blood, fell from his steed, and in the fall clashed his armour in pieces; and then his steed, for joy that he was eased of such a wicked burden, pranced over his disgraced master, and not suffering him to die such an honourable death as by Musidorus' sword, trampled out his guts, while Plaxirtus, with curses in his mouth, ended his hateful life.
> Then Pyrocles redoubled his blows so eagerly upon Anaxius, that he could no longer withstand them, but gnashing his teeth for anger, he fell at Pyrocles' feet and died. Thus pride and treachery received their just reward. (pp. 104–5)

It was because women were supposed to love romance that Weamys was able to write at all. Her identity as an author, however, was almost entirely eclipsed, and she does not appear to have attempted another work.

Margaret Cavendish repeatedly stresses in her books her overwhelming desire to be an originator. It comes as no surprise, therefore, to find that she was the only woman before the Restoration to publish romances spun from her own conceptions.[14] In 1656, while still in exile in Antwerp with her husband and other royalists, she published *Natures Pictures Drawn by Fancies Pencil to the Life*, a collection of stories divided into eleven sections: the last one being her autobiography. The majority of these stories feature romance characters of fair ladies and noble knights. The debt to the popular genre is evident, but Cavendish is quick to deny any simple relationship with it, stating 'Neither do I know the rule or method of romancy writing; for I never read a romancy book throughout in all my life' ('To the Reader', 1656). A closer acquaintance with her stories confirms her own assessment of them. She was doing something very strange, and peculiarly female, with the elements of romance.

The first section of *Natures Pictures* is written in verse, and has its heritage in the *Canterbury Tales*. Its series of stories is told by a group of women and men of various ages and dispositions, gathered around a winter fire. As their narratives unfold they argue with one another, drawing out new tales for ammunition in their dispute. The centre of their controversy lies in the nature of love and the possibility of constancy. The divisions are clear enough: the women's stories give a female perspective, and are mostly told in sisterly solidarity; the men's tales argue for a male view of the subject, requiring ladies to die for their lovers and reviling any woman not sufficiently constant to do so. (Eventually Cavendish seems to have grown bored with the dispute, or to have run out of ideas, since the final part of this section is composed instead of stories about civil war.) Having established that the nature of romantic love is a point of dispute between the sexes, the remainder of Cavendish's book is devoted to exploring the question from a female perspective. In doing so, she produces heroines who by being either sexless or androgynous seek to avoid the traps of romance.[15]

There are too many tales in the fictional books of *Natures Pictures* to be able to describe them all here, and a few typical examples will have to serve. 'The Discreet Virgin', for instance, consists of a discussion between a 'grave matron' and a 'young virgin' concerning the latter's refusal to marry. The virgin's essential proposition is that 'Men in this age are far worse than women' (p. 110). She draws a humorous picture of masculine habitual drunkenness, their vanity and idleness, and their condemnation of women 'for gossiping once in a quarter of a year, at a labour, or a christening, or at the upsitting of a childbed woman' (p. 112). Men are quarrelsome, and more prone to lie and flatter than women are, she continues. Her closing summary of the divide between the sexes is allowed to rest unchallenged by her interlocutor. Men are useless creatures, she says

like flies bred out of a dunghill, buzzing idly about, and then die; when women are like industrious ants, and prudent bees, always employed to the benefit of their families. (p. 113)

This tale is more a moral discourse than a story, as is the one that follows it, 'Ambition Preferred Before Love'. Here, too, a woman refuses marriage, explaining that she wishes to remain single so as to be free to climb 'fame's high tower'. This is impossible for wives, she shows. 'Husbands will never suffer them to climb, but keep them fast locked in their arms, or tie them to household employments' (p. 120).

Neither of these tales has a plot. The later stories in the book, however, do contain many elements of romance, with the protagonists going to war, falling in love and finally marrying. The most gripping of these is 'Assaulted and Pursued Chastity', where the central character leads an army into battle, is declared monarch and then marries. What is most remarkable is the fact that this hero is actually a heroine, Affectionata-Travelia, a woman disguised as a man. (In *Arcadia*, by contrast, the mighty 'amazon' who challenges and beats Prince Plangus in a fight turns out to be a man disguised as a woman.) The man Affectionata-Travelia marries is a prince from whom she fled in the early scenes of the narrative, after he tried repeatedly to rape her and she finally drew a pistol to defend herself.

> He for a time stood in amaze to see her in that posture, and to hear her high defiance, but considering with himself that her words might be more than her intentions, and that it was a shame to be out-dared by a woman, with a smiling countenance, said he 'You threatened more evil than you dare perform; besides, in the grave honour will be buried with you, when by your life you may build palaces of pleasure and felicity'; with that he went towards her to take the pistol from her . . . and in the midst of these words she shot him. (p. 223)

She leaves him for dead, but he recovers.[16]

Halfway across the world, she comes to lead an army into battle in defence of a queen who has been forced into war by a neighbouring king who wants to marry her and so rule her nation as well as his own. The king's army, by coincidence, is commanded by the erstwhile wounded prince. Only once the army of the king and prince is thoroughly beaten do Travelia and the queen agree to marry their men, drawing up as they do so contracts to preserve their own independence. The plot is actually far more complex than such a brief summary can indicate, and includes the fleeting possibility of a lesbian conclusion when the queen falls in love with the disguised Travelia. What is clear is that Cavendish recombined the elements of romance in such a way as to undercut an ideology that would define women as passively virtuous and preoccupied solely with their lovers' prowess, leaving all the fun, and all the power, to men.

Mary Carleton's writings boldly straddle a divide between autobiography and romance. In her texts, as in her life, she freely exploited the conventions of romance to make her feats acceptable to her audience. She inventively combined fiction and fact to produce the romantic motif of a disguised foreign lady fleeing from male pursuit, creating her persona of the German princess who captivated the hearts and won the credence of many contemporary men, including Samuel Pepys who hotly defended her 'wit and spirit' against the censorious Lady Batten.[17] Her pamphlets, and Francis Kirkman's semifictional biography of her, are among the earliest examples of the 'criminal romances' on which Defoe was to draw when writing *Moll Flanders*, and Carleton's place in literary history ought to be secure. Her *Historicall Narrative* was the first criminal autobiography published in England, being predated only by fictional accounts of lives of crime. By the time of her execution, in 1673, more texts had been published concerning her misdeeds than were issued about any contemporary criminal, and the popularity of her story continued well into the eighteenth century.[18]

Despite this vast reservoir of print concerning her, the known facts of

Carleton's life are few. They are, nonetheless, extraordinary. In 1663, at the instigation of her father-in-law, she was arrested, and tried for bigamy. She protested her innocence, and was found not guilty. While in Newgate prison awaiting a hearing, she was visited by various notables, and the claims and counterclaims of the parties involved seem to have been public knowledge even before the trial took place. At least two anonymous pamphlets, *The Man in the Moon* and *The Lawyer's Clarke Trappan'd by the Crafty Whore of Canterbury* appeared within a few days of her arrest. *The Lawyer's Clarke* assumes her guilt, stating that Mary had been making her living for some time through tricking unsuspecting men. Mary Carleton immediately replied with *A Vindication of a Distressed Lady*, which was rebutted by her husband in his *Replication*. After her release, many accounts of the trial appeared, including one by Mary Carleton herself, and she printed her own more expanded *Historicall Narrative* just six days after her acquittal. Within a matter of weeks, John had again replied with his *Ultimum Vale*. The whole affair also prompted stationers keen for a quick profit to bring out lampoons embroidering upon the series of events.[19]

A second group of texts concerning Mary Carleton appeared ten years later. These claim accurately to relate her exploits in the intervening decade, which apparently included appearing on stage in a play relating her life history during the 1660s, and being deported to Jamaica for theft in 1671. They also describe a second trial, for theft, and her execution in January 1673.[20] Finally, Francis Kirkman published *The Counterfeit Lady Unveiled*, a semifictional treatment of her story, which combines some sections of his writing with passages copied verbatim from various earlier texts.

C.F. Main suggests that whereas her husband wrote to 'set the record straight', Mary Carleton's drive was to advertise herself ('The German Princess' p. 174). She treats the incidents of her life as so much material out of which to spin stories. If she did in fact act in *A Witty Combat*, the comedy by Thomas Parker dramatising the events of her life (Main, p. 176), this would be quite in keeping with the way in which her narratives work and rework her story as she attempts to win the reader's sympathy. It would also be consistent with the fantastic way in which she first became involved with John Carleton.

Both Mary and John agree that they first met after she arrived at his sister's inn in London.[21] She claims to have been fleeing a lover from her native Germany. He contradicts this, maintaining that the whole story of her earlier experiences was a trick. Both sides agree that she was being subjected to the unwelcome advances of a parson who accompanied her, and that she sought refuge at the inn. She was dressed as a lady, and quickly convinced her hostess and host that she was a rich catch. The landlady, Mrs King, thought to trick her into marriage with her brother, hoping to make a useful alliance in the match. According to Mary, John was presented to her as a wealthy Lord, and the marriage hurried through. Shortly after this, once she had spent a lot of his money, the mutual deception became clear. Neither had the financial resources to maintain their lifestyle, and John Carleton's father, apparently, decided to rid his family of this unexpected encumbrance. Perhaps the bigamy charge was invented solely for this purpose: the evidence presented for it in court was singularly thin, as Mary delighted in pointing out. In her eloquent speech to the court, she remarked, 'Instead of this defamation that I am loaded with, my Lord, my crime is, that I have not an estate, or at least such a one as they imagined it to be' (Mary Carleton, *Historicall Narrative*, p. 17).

Carleton was careful in her books to leave ambiguous the question of whether she really was wealthy. Her strategy, both in court and in her narratives afterwards, was to win the sympathy of her audience by convincing them that John Carleton and his family had intended to cheat her. So great was her skill that she could confidently remark, with an ironic smile, in *The Case of Madam Mary Carleton*

Let the world now judge, whether being prompted by such plain and public signs of a design upon me, to counterplot them, I have done more than what the rule and a received principle of justice, directs: to deceive the deceiver, is no deceit.[22]

Carleton depended for her success, in court and in her writings, on her ability to skilfully manipulate the stereotypes of romantic femininity to her own advantage, and the author of the *Great Tryall* attributed her acquittal to her ladylike bearing. In the long speech that she made at the trial, and records (and perhaps polishes) in her *Historicall Narrative*, she refutes the idea that a woman of her gentility would ever have married a shoemaker or a bricklayer, as has been alleged. She draws on the language of romance, presenting herself as the defamed Lady of virtue: 'My soul abhorreth such a thought, and never was accommodated with such condescension, to move in so low an orb' (p. 18). This is the key moment of a defence which had already made extensive use of romantic clichés.

In *The Case*, these romantic allusions are expanded, and made more explicit. Mary Carleton reminisces about a childhood delight in romances, especially the novels of Boccaccio. She describes being left an orphan at the age of three, and being taken in by a nunnery and designed by them for a religious life. Wearying of these restrictions, she had developed the wanderlust that had finally brought her to England (pp. 12–17).

The details of this narrative conform so closely to fictional conventions that it seems a highly unlikely account of her life. Its interest lies in the way in which she uses these set ideas to save her reputation and, through sales of her books, to earn her living. Whatever the truth of her childhood, she seems to have realised early in life that the only career open to her was to use men to her own advantage. The observation she makes in *The Case* about her intended life as a nun could be extended as a description of the more general limitations of contemporary femininity.

> I blindly wished I were (what my inclinations prompted me to) a man, and exempt from that tedious life, which yet was so much the worse, because it was altogether passive and sedentary. (p. 18)

She makes her way out into the world, unconcerned 'to learn anything for use or ornament of a woman', desiring only to make a 'better fortune' (p. 40). On meeting John Carleton, she was fooled into believing that she had succeeded.

What she had not counted on, it seems, was the vast bias of the law in her husband's favour. Had she been found guilty of bigamy, as the judge at her trial pointed out, she would have been executed (*The Arraignment*, p. 15). Even with the verdict of not guilty, she was left in sorry straits. As a *femme covert* she had no material possessions. When she asked the court to force her father-in-law to return her jewels to her, she was sternly told that only her husband could press such a claim (Mary Carleton, *The Case*, p. 126). According to the biographies of Mary published after her execution for theft, the remaining ten years of her life were spent moving from one man to another, tricking them out of money and valuables. She did not marry again, but used feminine wiles to maintain her shaky independence. In a society which would have given other openings for her eloquence and wit, she might have achieved memorable acts. As it was, her only appearance to posterity is as a tricker of men, and the author of her books.

Mary Carleton's great skill with words is attested even in hostile accounts of her trial, and is demonstrated by her ability to talk her way out of a conviction for bigamy. One of her identifying features, according to both defenders and detractors, was her ability to speak several languages. Despite this, her claim to authorship has been dismissed. The first person to deny that she could have written so fluently was John Carleton, her great enemy. He claims that she employed hack writers to do her work, and both Ernest Bernbaum and C.F. Main have believed his assertion, saying that she was too ill-educated to have written them. John, however, vacillated in his opinion of the matter, claiming at times that 'she owns it [her writing] and it is like her' (John Carleton, *Ultimum Vale*, p. 13). Modern critics have also neglected to notice John's remark that, after the trial, Mary Carleton went to live at the Inns of Court, to study law and astrology (ibid., p. 37). This gratuitous information cannot have helped his case, so there is no reason to doubt its veracity. All the evidence indicates, in fact, that she was unusually well educated for a woman of the day, however she might have acquired her learning. It is therefore unnecessary to conspire with her husband to rob her of the title of author.[23] She could more justly be assessed as a great manipulator of romance, both in her life, and in the works in which she embroidered upon her exploits.

Aphra Behn's stories map out a world of female possibilities and limits: a bleak world, since the options open to her heroines are shown to be few indeed.[24] It is rescued from despair only by the sparkling courage and daring of her women protagonists, who with great determination negotiate their way through a universe where men have all the power.

Her most well-known story, *Oroonoko*, sits uneasily in my account of female romance in other respects, but it nonetheless exhibits some central features of the genre. The tale's two main protagonists are startlingly beautiful, and they maintain an undying love despite opposition from a tyrannical parent. The heroine's bravery in battle and her subjection to the ever-present threat of rape also bear the hallmarks of Behn's special vision of femininity. Nonetheless, my attempt to reduce the novel to such factors distorts it. Its central characters, Oroonoko and Imoinda, are Black slaves, and Behn's presentation of a slave rebellion and white racism introduces a further set of issues which cannot be fitted into my argument. Both I and others need to rethink our work on white women's writing to take account of these concerns.[25]

Behn's novels show that male control of women has two main sources, economic and ideological: to begin with, men have money; in addition, they set the terms of sexual relationships, deeming female desire repellent while callously exploiting their own capacity to rape when it suits their purposes. In such circumstances, women repeatedly discover, although arranged property matches might be repulsive, a liaison based on love or passion is also no guarantee of happiness.

Nearly all the novels have as their central figures strong young women who are trying to make their way through the maze of male intrigue that surrounds them.[26] These female characters bear the names of romance: Philadelphia, Alcidiana and Belvideera are no more likely inhabitants of seventeenth-century England than of the twentieth century. It is some-times argued that such romance figures are two-dimensional, lacking the character-development that typifies the novel. The use of this naming convention, however, does not prevent Behn's protagonists being vividly individual. Although the primary focus of each tale is the situation the heroine confronts, rather than her individual personality, the women are not at all interchangeable with one another. The accepted wisdom of dating the rise of the novel to the appearance of Daniel Defoe's *Robinson Crusoe*, 1719, some forty years after Behn was writing, and a full sixty-five years after Carleton, seems a singularly arbitrary act if we once pay serious attention to the romances that preceded it. Maureen Duffy's research on one of Behn's best-known stories, *The Fair Jilt*, has shown that the most 'unlikely' incident in this romance, the abortive execution of Prince Tarquin, in fact closely accords with contemporary newspaper accounts of the affair. Novel critics have been too quick to dismiss these romances as 'fantastic'.[27]

The opening paragraph of *The Adventure of the Black Lady* shows how Behn's writings reverberate with echoes from the timelessness of romance, while firmly particularising the story with details from the contemporary scene (a combination that is supposed only to characterise the novel). The heroine's name, and apparently her situation, are pure romance: her setting, however, is London, and her identity, it is claimed, personally known to the narrator.

> About the beginning of last June (as near as I can remember) Bellamora came to town from Hampshire, and was obliged to lodge the first night at the same inn where the stage coach set up. The next day she took coach for Covent Garden, where she thought to find Madam Brightly, a relation of hers. (p. 3)[28]

It quickly becomes apparent that the generality of this novel comes from elements of Bellamora's circumstances that are indeed timeless: she is unintentionally pregnant. The way in which a solution to this problem is worked out, however, is quite particular to Aphra Behn's society. Bellamora's pregnancy is due to Fondlove having 'urged his passion with such violence' that eventually she had been forced to give in to his desires (p. 6). This experience was quite sufficient to warn her that a man's love was not reliable, and she had run away to the city to bear her child alone, refusing Fondlove's proposal of marriage. Since the rape, she has 'abhorred the sight of him' (p. 7). She would rather risk the ignominy of raising her child alone, in the relative anonymity of London, than place her hopes in the chanciness of such a marriage.

In late seventeenth-century England, single parenthood was not supposed to be available to women. The bailiffs of the parish are alerted to Bellamora's presence, and rush to send her to a House of Correction and her child to a parish nurse. The Black Lady does the only thing she can: she marries the child's father in the nick of time. The bailiffs arrive to be directed mockingly to the only unmarried mother in the household: a black cat that had just had kittens.

The landlady showed 'em all the rooms in her house but no such lady could be found. At last she bethought herself, and let 'em into her parlour, where she opened a little closet door, and showed 'em a black cat that had just kittened: assuring 'em, that she should never trouble the parish as long as she had rats or mice in the house; and so dismissed 'em like the loggerheads as they came. (p. 10)

As this quotation indicates, the novel portrays a spirited solidarity between its female characters: something also true, for instance, of *Agnes de Castro*. *The Black Lady* seems, indeed, to twist from its initial trajectory at the appearance of this theme. In the opening scene, the novel sets out as a tale about a country bumpkin who arrives in the big city only to lose her luggage. The landlady is initially implicated in a suspicion of theft. This narrative is swiftly abandoned in favour of another story altogether, and male characters are banished to its edges. Fondlove, though mentioned early in the story, never appears, and the landlady's husband is sent on his way with little ceremony.

The gentleman, her husband, just saw her within doors, and ordered the coach to drive to some of his bottle-companions; which gave the women the better opportunity of entertaining one another. (p. 5)

Although the framework of the society is man-made, men are kept to this skeletal periphery. The question of interest is the shape of the spaces inhabited by women.

Whereas female friendship is shown as an enduring value in such stories, men's commitments to one another are seen as far more fitful. Time and again, central male characters perish having turned automatically to the sword on discovering that they love the same woman. In *The Nun; or, the Perjur'd Beauty*, for instance, Henrique and Antonio send the beauteous Ardelia off to a nunnery for a few hours, while they fight out their rival claims over her. By the end of the novel, all the major protagonists have been killed. There are comparable episodes of irrational male violence in *The Unfortunate Bride* and *The Dumb Virgin*.

Nunneries feature frequently in Behn's stories, and several of her heroines start out as nuns who, in their assertive expression of desire, become the viragos of Restoration men's nightmares. (It is important to remember what we are only too inclined to forget in this post-Victorian age: before about 1700, women were seen as the more lustful sex, with a larger carnal appetite than men.) Perhaps the most interesting of Aphra Behn's nuns is Miranda, *The Fair Jilt*, the perfect romance heroine, a rich young orphan who retires to a nunnery to await the advent of a suitable husband. She is supremely desirable, unflawed in body, soul and mind. All the young men who pass through the city come to court her, and 'thousands of people were dying by her eyes' (p. 7).

She continues to play the game of the desired lady until she falls desperately in love with a young friar, Prince Henrick. The tables are turned, and she is forced into a traditional male role, courting him with promises of wealth if he will only agree to leave the church and marry her. When he refuses, she wreaks a male revenge on him. A man could rape his reluctant beloved, and force her to wed him. Miranda essays a female version of this by falsely charging Henrick with rape, and he is imprisoned.

The second man of her choice is Prince Tarquin, and this one she marries. Her delight in high living leads her to misappropriate her sister Alcidiana's trust fund, however, and she nearly loses her husband when he is arrested for attempting to murder the sister. At the end of the story, she is nevertheless triumphant. She and Tarquin flee the country and live happily till his death. All in all, Miranda has done the best she can.

They say Miranda has been very penitent for her life past, and gives Heaven the glory for having given her these afflictions, that have reclaimed her, and brought her to as perfect a state of happiness as this troublesome world can afford. (p. 178)

Isabella of *The Fair Vow-Breaker*, by contrast, discovers that abandoning celibacy for reasons of passionate love (or to seek social advancement) is no recipe for fulfilment. Having been raised in a nunnery she decides aged thirteen to take a vow of chastity. When subsequently she falls in love with Henault, she immediately experiences her passion as oppressive and a loss of autonomy, but marries him nonetheless.

He has done that in one fatal hour, that the persuasions of all my relations and friends, glory, honour, pleasure, and all that can tempt, could not perform in years; I resisted all but Henault's eyes, and they were ordained to make me truly wretched. (p. 42)

Her life with Henault indeed turns out to be miserable. The marriage is disapproved of by his family, and their only financial support comes from Isabella's aunt. In quick succession, the aunt dies and Henault is lost in battle. It happens that Villenoys, who comes to bring news of the tragedy, is an old suitor of Isabella's. She decides, pragmatically, to marry him for material security. When Henault returns some years later, she realises that both men have to be disposed of. She smothers Henault, and tells Villenoys that he has died a natural death. Persuading Villenoys to dispose of this friend's body by carrying it up to a nearby bridge and throwing it into the river, she sews together the coats of the two men once Villenoys has Henault on his back. In the light of Villenoys's consequent drowning by being pulled into the water after the corpse, her anxious directions to him to make a good job of it take on a macabre humour.

When you come to the bridge, (said she) and that you are throwing him over the rail, (which is not above breast high) be sure you give him a good swing, lest the sack should hang on anything at the side of the bridge, and not fall into the stream. (p. 136)

Even when she goes to identify the corpses of her erstwhile lovers Isabella's nerve does not crack, and she does not confess until directly accused. The narrative voice nowhere suggests, however, that her murder of two unsatisfactory husbands was wrong. Her crime lies in not having stayed faithful to her initial vow, true to herself, as her closing scaffold speech explains (p. 147).

The fault lies not with her, but with a society which has given her such dire choices in life. Behn suggests the existence of a female subculture that has its own values, one superior to the dominant, male imperatives, but which gradually becomes sullied and eroded. It is important to note that these higher ethics, according to Behn, would cause women to be so faithful to their lovers that they 'like Indian wives, would leap alive into the graves of their deceased lovers, and be buried quick with 'em' (p. 3). This is not a liberating vision. Nonetheless, her consistent premise is that the world would be a more loving and supportive place if it were run according to these 'female' beliefs. Her grim conclusion is that such a revolutionary change is impossible. All women can do is to make the best they can out of the status quo.

Since I cannot alter custom, nor shall ever be allowed to make new laws, or rectify the old ones, I must leave the young nuns enclosed to their best endeavours, of making a virtue of necessity; and the young wives, to make the best of a bad market. (p. 7)

This blunt assumption of female impotence in the public world of law-making contrasts sharply with the committed lobbying of the 1650s women. This new generation of women writers, who engage in far more 'literary' pursuits than their predecessors, are also more quietist or reactionary in their relation to national politics. Many of them were outspoken royalists: Behn even worked as a pamphleteer for the Tories. As women were beaten back into the home, moulded into companions for the Enlightenment man, they engaged in a detailed analysis of love which had been unnecessary in earlier decades, when women's lives had been filled with so many larger concerns. Once women are confined to a sphere of romantic love, they must, as Behn argues, turn their energies to designing strategies to win as much space as possible.

Since men, she demonstrates, are violent and dangerous to women, such an endeavour is far from easy. The most striking feature of Behn's novels, in fact, is a characteristic they share with her plays. She starkly portrays the connections between masculine desire and male violence, and makes it clear through the actions of her heroines that female choices were few and nasty.

Love, romance and courtship as viewed by these female authors of prose fiction were not at all a stylised game. Living in a world where they were men's prized or despised possessions, women's explorations of these issues unfailingly involved an examination of the power relations between the sexes. The fictions they construct out of their female view of male conventions show plotting and daring as necessary to a woman if she is to escape domination and abuse from her 'lovers'. They might all say with Mary Carleton, in her vindication of her exploits,

Let the world now judge, whether being prompted by such plain and public signs of a design upon me, to counterplot them, I have done any more than what the rule, and a received principle of justice directs. (Mary Carleton, *The Case*, p. 45)

CHAPTER FIVE

ROMANTIC LOVE – PLAYS

IN 1633 the Puritan William Prynne lost his ears to the public hangman, in part at least for denouncing 'women-actors, notorious whores' (*Histriomastix*), a reference that was interpreted as an attack on Henrietta Maria and her ladies for acting plays at court.[1] In 1642, the London theatres were closed down by parliament and remained shut until the Restoration, although performances of plays did not entirely cease between 1642 and 1660. It seems certain, for example, that the 'private' presentations of plays and masques so loved by the queen's court continued in the houses of some aristocrats. Elizabeth Brackley and Jane Cavendish (the step-daughters of Margaret Cavendish whose plays are discussed later), for instance, wrote and probably performed their play *The Concealed Fanseys* some time in the mid-1640s. The text, which survives only in two manuscript copies, is full of references to the sadness of being parted from family and loved ones, and I think it highly probable that it was written with the women's father, the exiled Marquis of Newcastle, very much in mind.[2]

Keeping the drama alive was a royalist preoccupation during the interregnum. The importance of the theatres as a royalist cultural symbol and meeting place is further demonstrated by the fact that one of the first acts of the returned monarch was to issue patents to Henry Killigrew and William Davenant to establish two London playhouses, and the fate of the theatre continued to be closely tied to court patronage throughout Charles II's reign. Performance runs were very short indeed by modern standards, and this was largely due to the tiny size of the available audience. Seats were very expensive, costing anything from one shilling to four shillings for a normal performance (more on special occasions), and the audience consisted largely of minor state officials and members of the court.[3] For a show to run for more than a few nights, an appreciable number of people would have to have attended more than once.[4] With the right patronage – and here court influence was especially important

– a full house could be recruited for the third night, the takings from which went to the playwright, giving her or him a very healthy income.[5]

The close relationship between the tastes of the reinstated royalists and success or failure for playwrights is also demonstrated in the ecstatic reception given to a translation by Katherine Philips of Corneille's *Pompée*. Today Philips is better known as a poet than a playwright, but the success of *Pompey* in the new theatre in Dublin in 1663 was a crucial step in establishing her reputation as an author among her contemporaries. At its subsequent performance later that year in London, *Pompey* became the first play written by a woman to appear on the public stage in England after the Restoration. After circulating widely in manuscript, it was brought out in a printed edition in Dublin, and Henry Herringman, the prestigious London bookseller, approached the author for permission to publish it in England.[6]

Corneille's plays, with their themes of loyalty to the monarch and pursuit of *gloire*, had been very popular with royalist exiles in France.[7] It is in some ways not surprising, therefore, that this innovative translation should have been the first major success of the new Dublin theatre.[8] This first Restoration translation of a French play was sure to appeal to the wealthy coterie that surrounded Philips in Ormonde, who included Sir Maurice Eustace (the Lord Chancellor), Dr Pett (the Advocate-General), Sir Nicholas Armourer (the head of the king's guard), Sir Edward Dering, Viscount and Lady Dungannon, Richard Boyle the Earl of Cork, Anne and Elizabeth Boyle, the Earl of Roscommon and Lord William and Lady Mary Cavendish.[9] The play's themes, of women holding true to a higher sense of honour regardless of the pressures of personal affection, and of achieving true glory by learning to live within necessarily narrow limits, were also of obvious appeal to Philips, whose poetry is frequently preoccupied with such questions (see Chapter Six).

The playhouses were a major social centre for the court and its supporters. In the early 1660s, the royalists' appetite for entertainment was fed largely by revivals of Elizabethan and Jacobean plays and adaptations or translations (like Philips's) from French sources. The major playwrights were William Davenant, Roger Boyle, Robert Howard and John Dryden. By the end of the decade, Davenant was dead and Boyle and Howard had stopped writing.[10] Briefly, therefore, with the theatre's popularity growing fast it was a writer's market, and several women – Frances Boothby, Elizabeth Polwhele and Aphra Behn – were among the aspiring authors who began to write. Like their male contemporaries, they addressed themselves to the questions of love, courtship, marriage and adultery that were the ubiquitous concerns of Restoration comedy.

There is today what might best be described as a 'free love' school of Restoration drama critics. These authors interpret the appearance of explicit sexuality in Restoration comedies as the bubbling up of a natural, exuberant sensuality repressed by the Puritans in the Common-wealth period. The Restoration rake, in plays and at court, is celebrated by such critics for his self-knowledge, his ability to place himself above or outside society, his commitment to 'put[ting] the animal vitality back into the male–female relationships'. He is even seen as epitomising ideal gentlemanly conduct.[11]

Advocacy of 'free love' and championing of the rake might well be predominant characteristics of male Restoration comedies as well as of modern critics' responses to the period. For men, a woman's 'obsession' with her reputation for chastity could well be interpreted as yet another example of a central theme in the drama of the period: the difference between 'appearance' (the chaste reputation) and 'reality' (women's alleged libidinous nature). From a male standpoint, all that is at stake is an abstract principle.[12] In *The Country Wife*, for instance, the play's action is dependent upon the 'truth' of Horner's assertion 'your women of honour, as you call 'em, are only chary of their reputations, not their persons' (I i). In this play, as in Etherege's *She Wou'd If She Cou'd*, almost all the female characters are wild for sex, and their whimsical insistence on maintaining their modest reputations is a major source of the play's humour. Horner's power resides in the 'fact' that while women are revolted by male impotence, they delight in virility. The 'woman of honour' (IV iii) in *The Country Wife* is Lady Fidget, who is praised by Horner for faithfully keeping an adulterous liaison with him. By contrast Alithea's assertion of the need for women to defend their reputation is cool and abstract (IV i), lacking the passion of comparable declamations in Cavendish, Boothby or Behn. Likewise, Harriet in *The Man of Mode* is portrayed as witty and delightful, experiencing no fear of exposure or of loss of reputation as she collaborates with Young Bellair. She is the charming playmate that the refined, clever courtier would like to create, a woman made to a male fantasy image. The power imbalances between women and men, the rigorous restrictions on female choices, are denied by these plays, just as their existence is refused by modern literary critics. 'Proviso scenes', where men and women sketch out their models of a satisfactory relationship, are read as 'an almost complete equality of the sexes engaged in a duel of wits'.[13] 'The heroine, not the hero, subjugates all, and indulges every caprice.'[14] Female writers knew that such 'liberation' was illusory, invented and promulgated by men, since for women, chastity and a modest reputation were deadly serious matters: their thriving in the world depended on them.

This chapter will discuss plays written by four women: Margaret Cavendish, Frances Boothby, Elizabeth Polwhele and Aphra Behn. Cavendish's plays, which appeared in two volumes in 1662 and 1668, really stand in a category of their own, since they were written during the 1650s when the public theatres were closed, and were not intended for performance. The other three women discussed here all began work in the late 1660s or early 1670s, and, in rather different ways, take up the dominant motifs of male Restoration comedy and show that the choices presented to women by this framework are both few and dire.

Margaret Cavendish's first book of plays, published in 1662, appears to have been finished before her return to England at the Restoration.[15] The timing of the composition of these plays is significant, since it confirms what one of the dedicatory epistles asserts: they were written while the theatres were closed, with no view to being acted or, indeed, to being actable; written for readers who 'may read as short or as long a time as they please . . . I shall never desire they should be acted' (sig. A3/2ᵛ). Cavendish has never been allowed, however, to make new rules for the drama. The plays have been universally condemned as 'extremely dull', 'dull plays', 'without an atom of dramatic power'. 'They are perhaps the worst plays ever published.'[16]

If they are not designed for acting, what kind of compositions are these works? They are a kind of closet drama, intended to be recited aloud by a reader in the privacy of her (or his) own home, and they consist of a series of possible roles to try out for size. Using the play format, Cavendish is freed from the need to commit herself to an authorial stance, and experiments more freely than in any of her works with outrageous and remarkable female characters. Writing drama when the theatres are closed, she can also reject the genre's rules and conventions when they do not suit her needs.

Indeed, in a period when men's debates around the niceties of dramatic form were to become increasingly heated, Cavendish refuses as 'un-natural' the most basic premises of such conventions. She rejects the rule that all characters should know one another, or be in some way connected, and with this the common pattern of the final scene ending with everyone on stage together. It is improbable, she says, that the full diversity of humankind could be found in a small group of acquaint-ances, and 'I would have my plays to be like the natural course of all things in the world'.[17] Like her female contemporaries, Cavendish could not help being aware that her education had been very different from men's, and that it excluded her from dominant male literary traditions and sources. With typical wit, she tries to turn this handicap into an advantage. She could not be accused of plagiarism in such circumstances, and her originality, a characteristic that was gaining new status in this period, must be respected.

> But noble readers, do not think my plays
> Are such as have been writ in former days;
> As Jonson, Shakespeare, Beaumont, Fletcher writ;
> Mine want their learning, reading, language, wit:
> The Latin phrases I could never tell,
> But Jonson could, which made him write so well.
> Greek, Latin poets, I could never read,
> Nor their historians, but our English Speed;
> I could not steal their wit, nor plots out take;
> All my plays' plots, my own poor brain did make.
> (sig. A7/2^{r-v})

The numerous dedicatory epistles she composed to preface her *Playes* constitute Cavendish's most extended discussion of literary conventions, and her position is both clear and defiant. She refuses either to regret the fact that she had not been educated in male literary laws, or to respect rules that seem senseless. It is significant in this regard that her defence of 'originality' includes a vindication of her 'misuse' of the genders of abstract qualities.[18]

I know there are many scholastical and pedantical persons that will condemn my writings, because I do not keep strictly to the masculine and feminine genders, as they call them . . . but I know no reason but that I may as well make them hes for my use, as others did shes . . . As for the niceties of rules, forms, and terms, I recognise, and profess, that if I did understand and know them strictly, as I do not, I would not follow them: and if any dislike my writings for want of those rules, forms, and terms, let them not read them; for I had rather my writings should be unread than be read by such pedantical scholastical persons. (sig. A4/2^v)

She refuses to bow to the judgement of the three gentlemen whose discussion of female writers introduces her plays. These men know that if they admit that women have wit and reason enough to write plays 'we shall lose our pre-eminency'.[19]

For some reason, Cavendish's *Playes* were not published until 1662, by which time the London theatres had reopened, and the relevance of a new dramatic genre invented for reading, not watching, was no longer evident. Her second collection of dramatic pieces, *Plays, Never before Printed*, 1668, shows some signs of being influenced by theatrical conventions – there is more coherence, and more linking together of scenes and characters in these later works than is found in most of her earlier plays. In addition, she makes use of song and dance, popular elements in Restoration stage entertainment that are entirely absent from the 1662 *Playes*, and includes fewer long, philosophical declamations. The author's introductory remarks suggest that such alterations in her format were made in part as a response to ridicule from the critics, the 'scholastical and pedantical persons' whose judgement she had refused in

1662. She does not, however, back down very far. The rules she is violating are man-made and temporary, she says, and refuses to accept that they will be good for all time.

I regard not so much the present as future ages, for which I intend all my books . . . When I call this new one 'plays' I do not believe to have given it a very proper title: for it would be too great a fondness to my works to think such plays as these suitable to ancient rules, in which I pretend no skill; or agreeable to the modern humour, to which I dare acknowledge my aversion: but having pleased my fancy in writing many dialogues upon several subjects, and having afterwards ordered them into acts and scenes, I will venture, in spite of the critics, to call them plays. (sig. A2ʳ⁻ᵛ)

The alterations she makes to her earlier practices are indeed not performed with any great conviction. The clearest example of this is the case of *The Presence*. Having bowed to convention and removed twenty-nine of the original scenes of the play, saying they make it too long, she then prints them immediately following the play they relate to, with an explanatory note.

Broadly speaking, Cavendish's plays fall into two types. Roughly half of them incorporate two or, more usually, three completely separate plots. Generally, the characters in the different plots do not know of one another's existence, and they are not linked in any simple way by theme or circumstance. In plays of this type, Cavendish simply rotates her attention from one set of characters to the next, following a scene about one group by a scene about the second, and then the third, before returning to the first one. Many of these plays are in two parts, divided halfway through with apparent disregard for plot or character development. Her second type of play is structurally simpler, although this does not necessarily mean that they have fewer characters. In these, the characters are a group of young women (and, usually, their suitors), who discuss love, marriage, politics, education and other matters of social significance. All the plays take place in an imaginary world, with little scenery or background. The characters are there to be performed, brought to life, by the reader her/himself.[20]

The staple preoccupation of *Playes* and *Plays, Never before Printed* is the question of how a woman can find happiness or fulfilment. This is not abstract philosophising. Some of these dramas consist almost entirely of gossip: of women meeting together to debate the difficulties of living their lives with men when male power is so all-pervasive. In such plays, gossip is shown creating solidarity among women, providing a forum for them to share their experiences and work out their ideas. The women of *The Several Wits* and *Wits Cabal*, for instance, know only too well that courteous wooers can become tyrannical husbands (*Playes*). Caprisia in *The Several Wits* is not fooled by the illusion of gallantry: 'I have heard that gallant men are civil to our sex, but I have met with none, but rough, rugged natures, more cruel than wild tigers' (p. 97). A similar group of gossips meets in *The Unnatural Tragedie*, where their discussions are set off against the other two plots of the play. While the Sociable Virgins remark that 'most husbands think, when their wives are good and obedient, that they are simple' (p. 330), the scenes concerned with Madam Bonit show a gentle, acquiescent wife being literally bullied to death by her husband. She is avenged by one of the Sociable Virgins, who marries the widowed Monsieur Malateste, dominates and cuckolds him, and drives him into an early grave. This is characteristically outrageous behaviour by one of a group of women whose gossip sessions include the musing that it might be quite easy to replace male dominance in the world by female government.

Second Virgin: . . . Good statesmen are bred in courts, camps and cities, and not in schools and closets, at bars and in pulpits; and women are bred in courts and cities, and only want the camp to give them the perfect state breeding.
Third Virgin: Certainly, if we had that breeding, and did govern, we should govern the world better than it is.
Fourth Virgin: Yes, for it cannot be governed worse than it is: for the whole world is together by the ears, all up in wars and blood, which shows there is a general defect in the rulers and governors thereof. (p. 332)

The third plot in this play, the 'Unnatural Tragedy' of the title, demonstrates that even a happy marriage cannot keep a woman safe from the cruelty of male power. Madam Soeur's brother tries to persuade her to become his mistress and, when she refuses, he rapes and murders her, reflecting in satisfaction 'Now she is dead, my mind is at rest, since I know none can enjoy her after me.' (p. 362)[21]

The dominant theme of these plays, indeed, is that virtue (chastity) is not in itself sufficient to make a woman happy, or even to keep her safe. There are many shy, modest women in the dramas, each of whom in her different way either suffers from being trapped in a virtuous role, or finds a way of escaping its limitations. Lady Innocence in *Youths Glory and Deaths Banquet* has been raised with such modesty that she does not even know the mechanics of human reproduction when she marries Lord de l'Amour. Uneducated and pure, she is completely unsuspecting of her husband's relationship with his mistress, Lady Incontinent. All she has is her 'honesty', and when this is brought into question by Lady Incontinent and doubted by Lord de l'Amour she is driven to suicide.[22]

By no means all Cavendish's bashful and modest heroines are destroyed. Lady Disagree and Lady Poverty in *The Matrimoniall Trouble* both leave their bullying, profligate husbands and embark on a life alone. The more frequently presented resolution, however, is for the modest woman to persuade her man to accept and live according to her values, as is achieved by Lady Ward in *Lady Contemplation*. Lady Bashful in *Love's Adventures*, another such modest heroine, is so shy that she cannot help blushing when in company. She has the courage, however, to take her fate into her own hands, and to choose her own mate, Sir Serious Dumb. (Like many of Cavendish's heroines, the play opens with her conveniently orphaned and left in charge of her own destiny.) She settles on him having taken his sword and saved his life in a duel he fights with Sir Humphrey Bold. In acquiescing to her unfeminine behaviour, he places himself in the submissive, female role. She offers to marry him since he 'delivered up his life and honour into my hand, when he gave me his sword'.[23] She finds a marriage in which she can hope to retain some of the independence that had initially inclined her to remain single.

I am now mistress of myself, and fortune, and have a free liberty; and who that is free, if they be wise, will make themselves slaves, subjecting themselves to another's humour, unless they were fools, or mad, and knew not how to choose the best and happiest life. (p. 78)

Nonetheless, she refuses to agree to a public celebration of her wedding, insisting on a quiet ceremony with the question 'Do you call that a triumphant day, that enslaves a woman all her life after? No, I will make no triumph on that day' (p. 66). She takes her man on her own terms, for her own reasons.

The common feature of all these characters is their diffidence and chastity. Another possible role for the reader to play while reciting aloud these dramas is that of the warrior, and the vivid fantasies of Lady Contemplation in the play of that name, for instance, include not only lovers who die from their desperate passion for her, but also portray her dressed as a general leading her troops into battle, killing the enemy's leader with her own hands. Although her amazonian exploits are all imaginary, Lady Victoria of *Bell in Campo* is so angered by male derision about women's capabilities that she raises her own, female army. Once trained it is these Amazons who save their country, and the male troops, from defeat. Lady Victoria's constant assertion is that women are not naturally inferior to men, but are made so by their education. The reward she exacts for her army's victories is a wide-ranging change in women's peacetime role. Entering her home town in a masculine-style triumph, she ensures that laws are passed to secure women's autonomy and financial independence in the family, their freedom of movement in public places, and that Victoria's achievements are recorded in history, to serve as a model for other women (p. 631, misnumbered 625). Lady Victoria's congratulatory speech to her soldiers emphasises that women can do anything, if they can only escape their conditioning long enough to have faith in themselves.

Gallant heroickesses, by this you may perceive we were as ignorant of ourselves as men were of us, thinking ourselves shiftless, weak, and unprofitable creatures, but by our actions of war we have proved ourselves to be every way equal with men; for what we want of strength, we have supplied by industry, and had we not done, we should have lived in ignorance and slavery. (p. 617)

These plays are a series of fantasy sketches, consisting largely of idealised role-models, women whose mighty exploits and lengthy disquisitions allow the lone female reader access to a series of fantastic strategies for negotiating with patriarchal limitations. The most eloquent of these role-models are lady philosophers, who give public lectures analysing the world and women's place within it. Lady Sanspareille in *Youths Glory and Deaths Banquet* and Mademoiselle Grand Esprit in *Natures Three Daughters* both make public orations which women and men flock to hear and admire. Both early decide to remain single throughout their lives, since a husband might seek to sabotage their intellectual endeavours to prevent themselves being outshone by their wives. Even the most ideal marriage is not as desirable as the single state to these thinking women.

Even those marriages that are pefectest, purest, lovingest, and most equallest, and sympathetically joined, yet at the best marriage is the womb of trouble, which cannot be avoided, also marriage is the grave or tomb of wit. (p. 525)

These women, who decide that their own fulfilment and development must take priority over other social expectations, win themselves public acclaim in their lifetimes, and the promise of eternal fame after their deaths. They, like the women warriors, are set side by side in the plays with the quiet, modest souls who try their best to make good wives. The appeal of glamour and glory is obvious enough, but it is left to the reader to try out the different personae, and to decide for herself whether Lady Sanspareille is right in her first public oration, as she reads it out to herself.

It is not against nature and reason, but that women may discourse of several subjects as well as men, and that they may have as probable opinions, and as profitable inventions, as fresh fancies, as quick wits, and as easy expressions, as men; if their education be answerable to their natural capacities and ingenuities. (pp. 136–7)

As always in Cavendish's works, the choice for women is between two broad types of solution. Again and again in these plays, attention is rotated from one kind of choice to another. Is she to stay within the bounds of private honour and chastity, risking ill-treatment but possibly finding an acceptable compromise? Or is she to sally forth and seek public acclaim and fame? Within the framework of these dramas, character types can be sketched, and the consequences of their choices explored. Freed from the authorial voice of lyric poetry or narrative, the texts can be left open-ended, if not unweighted. In the private space of her own home, far from the public spectacle of a Restoration playhouse, the reader is left to spell out to herself the patterns formed in alternatives lived by the characters. Cavendish, unhampered by the danger of herself appearing immodest in endorsing through a narrative voice the amazonian Lady Victoria or the learned Lady Sanspareille, can develop with more daring than anywhere else in her works a range of visions, of imaginable female roles. Verisimilitude, for Cavendish, need not preclude such flights of fancy. In the framework of her *Playes*, she can provide for women a function traditionally performed by the drama for young men: she can give them a medium through which to learn about the world.[24]

For poets teach them more in one play, both of the nature of the world and mankind, by which they learn not only to know other men, but their own selves, than they can learn in any school, or in any country or kingdom in a year. (sig. A4/2)

In the late 1660s the playhouses were booming, but with the death of Davenant and with Boyle and Howard no longer writing, there was a shortage of new material, and two women, Frances Boothby and Elizabeth Polwhele, tried their hands as playwrights. In about May 1669, Elizabeth Cottington wrote to Herbert Aston,

We are in expectation still of Mr Dryden's play. There is a bold woman hath offered one: my cousin Aston can give you a better account of her than I can. Some verses I have seen which are not ill; that is commendation enough: she will think so too, I believe, when it comes upon the stage. I tremble for the poor woman exposed among the critics.[25]

The play in question could well be Frances Boothby's *Marcelia: or, the Treacherous Friend*, which was licensed for publication in October 1669, having had what might have been its premiere performance by the King's Company in August of that year.[26] The play is dedicated to the author's kinswoman, a Lady Yate of Harvington, Worcestershire, to whom she looks for protection from expected social censure for 'this uncommon action in my sex' (sig. A2).

The prologue to *Marcelia* centres on the playwright's gender, anticipating in hyperbolical terms the scorn that male critics will vent on it. Her venture into the theatre is presented explicitly in terms of a daring female invasion of male territory, and Boothby calls on women to rally to her support in public, even if they might have some private reservations about the play.

> But still she hopes the ladies out of pride
> And honour, will not quit their sex's side:
> Though they in private do her faults reprove
> They'll neither public scorn nor laughter move.
> (sig. A3ᵛ)

This is a significant redefinition of female 'pride' and 'honour', which conventionally were used solely with reference to women's behaviour in courtship and their chastity. It prefaces a play in which courtship practices are presented from a female perspective, and where women's solidarity with one another reveals their superiority to men when questions of 'pride' and 'honour' are concerned.

The pivotal character in *Marcelia* is Melynet, the new king's favourite, who schemes to obtain his cousin Marcelia's hand for the king in order to increase his own influence at court. To do so, he has to lie, slander, manipulate and betray his friends. In the end, his plotting is discovered, he is banished, Marcelia is reunited with her beloved Lotharicus, and King Sigismund is shamed into returning to his betrayed mistress Calinda, whom he marries. If Melynet is the chief villain of the play, none of the male characters is admirable. They are hot-headed, self-seeking, irrational and inconstant, even while making grandiose speeches about honour and pride. Marcelia's brother Euryalus, for example, jumps automatically to the conclusion that she is dishonest, and vows to seek Marcelia out and kill her (sig. G3ᵛ). Lotharicus, too, is only too quick to believe that Marcelia has been false to him, and to charge her with being inconstant and ambitious.

> Woman! what art thou but man's tempting shame,
> That didst at first his soul with weakness stain:
> And still that power keep, and still betray?
> Oh that some plague had took you all away!
> False sex! that neither truth nor love does know,
> But what ambitious pride can overthrow. (sig. F4ᵛ)

The play shows, however, that these are male characteristics, not female ones. The king's deserted mistress, Calinda, is able to turn to her friend Ericina for unstinting support, and is gently reproved by her for briefly doubting her constancy and fearing that she, too, would abandon her.

> *Ericina*: You can no trouble have but what is mine,
> My love does make my share as great as thine.
> Unkind Calinda, what is't you intend?
> To punish your false lover in your friend.
> Can this inconstancy make you despise
> That friendship which you once so much did prize? . . .
> *Calinda*: Dear Ericina, can y'a pardon give,
> To an offence makes me unfit to live?

Ericina: I can forgive much more than you can do.
         Love, in that kind, ne'er yet a limit knew. (sig. I1^{r-v})

Elsewhere in the play, Perilla and Arcasia mock male courtship rituals. They know that all this sighing and dying for love is insincere. Their choices, however, are few. The best the play offers its women is the possibility of laying bare male scheming, whether in the form of Melynet's careerism, the king's debauchery, or Lotharicus's suspicion and aggression, and then accepting them nonetheless. Closing the play is left to Calinda's cynical matter-of-factness. The king has not been true to his high-sounding moral principles, but she must nevertheless marry him.

Calinda: Had you been still, sir, to that maxim true,
         I had not then been scorned, nor left by you:
         When you the life did take of all my joy,
         You showed not the least pity to destroy.
         But you would have, I find, a woman's breast
         With more compassion and more love possessed.
         (sig. M3^{v})

If the marriages finally contracted in *Marcelia* are dire arrangements, so are those that end a play by another woman which was acted by the rival Duke's Company in 1670. Elizabeth Polwhele's *The Frolicks, or The Lawyer Cheated* was not printed after its performance by the Duke's Company, but more than one manuscript version of it has survived. Its modern editors have demonstrated that it exhibits sound dramatic technique and a clear sense of the coming fashions of the theatre.[27] Characterising herself as 'an unfortunate young woman . . . haunted by poetic devils' (p. 57), Polwhele dedicates *The Frolicks* to Prince Rupert.[28] She cannot help knowing that women are supposed not to have sufficient wit to be playwrights, and so, while deftly drawing attention to the fact that this is her third play, she ascribes her competence to 'nature', not learning or intellectual ability.

Those that have ever seen my *Faithful Virgins* and my *Elysium* will justify me a little for writing this. I am young, no scholar, and what I write I write by nature, not by art. (p. 58)

The play is indeed 'a frolic', full of trickery and disguise worked into a light, rapidly moving plot. The main action concerns the courting and eventual matching of Clarabell and Rightwit, despite conventional obstacles of parental opposition, her initial desire to remain single and his history of profligacy. (At one point, he staggers onto the stage with his bastard children on his back.) Clarabell and Rightwit are lively and quick-witted, and he wins her admiration by outdoing even her in extravagant flights of fancy. When he has the comic butts of the play, Sir Gregory and Zany, arrested as prostitutes when they are disguised as women, she is impressed: 'Oh, how I love this Rightwit and his wicked wit! He has gone beyond me in this frolic, clearly' (p. 106). Despite all this frivolity, the conventional outcome of the play, where all the young central characters end married, is nothing to celebrate. Rightwit's treatment of his earlier mistresses, and his self-centredness in relation to Clarabell, suggest that she would have been wiser to stay true to her initial resolution.

There's witchcraft in everything this fellow does. My soul is ready to run out at my eyes after him. I fear I shall be fool enough, and madwoman together, to fall in love with him. But I will resist it with an Amazonian courage. Love is but a swinish thing at best. (p. 81)

When she finally accepts him, it is in a scene where he also cynically sells off his sister, Leonora, to the ridiculous Zany. Despite Leonora's forthright assertion earlier in the play that she will not marry 'witless puppies' at her brother's whim, she is shown, in fact, to be powerless. Much of the play's humour comes from women's clear recognition that the inflated language of male courtship is absurd. Their laughter does not, however, alter the power balance one jot.

We do not know why Elizabeth Polwhele, having had three plays professionally produced, ceased to write after the performance of *The Frolicks*. Since none of her plays was ever published, perhaps it is a fair guess that she was not sufficiently successful. (If she did not have a private income, success would have been financially necessary.) If she is the Polwhele identified by her modern editors Milhous and Hume, maybe she married about this time and this caused her to fall silent.[29] Whatever the reason, it was not she, but Aphra Behn, who also began to write for the Duke's Company at about this time, who was to go on to be a prolific and highly successful dramatist.

It was after her release from debtors' prison that Aphra Behn, presumably recently widowed, turned to writing to make a living. Contrary to popular belief, she was not the first woman playwright, nor was she the first woman to earn her living by her pen. Sarah Jinner and Hannah Wolley, to name two contenders for that title, used their writing to earn money and to advertise their businesses (see Chapter Seven), and we do not know whether Elizabeth Polwhele or Frances Boothby might have hoped to make enough money to support themselves. To object to claims of origination being made for Behn is not, however, to deny how unusual and difficult her chosen path was.

It was during the period that the Duke of York's theatre was being managed by William Davenant's widow that Behn, like Polwhele, began to write for it.[30] Somewhere she must have learnt her trade, since from the very beginning her plays exhibit technical competence and a clear sense of the possibilities of the stage.[31] Her first play, *The Forc'd Marriage*, opened with a run of six days, a very creditable achievement in a period when Samuel Tuke's *Adventures of Five Hours*, 1663, probably held the record, at thirteen consecutive nights, for many years.[32]

The theatres were closely connected with the court, the audience consisting largely of courtiers and minor state officials. Also, seats were expensive, so potential playgoers were few. An author's financial survival (unless s/he had a private income), therefore, was tied to her/his ability to please or interest a small clique that had pronounced political allegiances. While this does not altogether explain Aphra Behn's unmistakeable alliance with the dominant faction at court, the Tories, it is true to say that had her politics been different or less publicly avowed, it is unlikely that she would have been able to make a living. In the closed world of the Restoration theatre, the audience's tastes were crucially important in determining what sold, and therefore, in the case of a professional writer like Behn, in determining whether the author lived comfortably or starved. The playgoers' approval of an author became particularly vital from the late 1670s, when political tensions over the Succession Crisis and scares and machinations over the Popish Plot caused people to stay away from the theatres in large numbers, and the prologues and epilogues to *The Feign'd Curtizans*, 1679, and *The Emperor of the Moon*, 1687, comment on the consequent problems of playwrights.[33]

Aphra Behn's political allegiances did not begin with the troubles of the late 1670s, but had been clear early in her writing career. *The Dutch Lover*, 1673, for instance, includes the first of her many satirical, dashing Cavaliers, and uses dull Puritans as a butt for its humour.[34] Her first play, *The Forc'd Marriage*, indeed, opens with a metaphor describing the author as a scout or spy for a new party (women). It is possible that the audience understood this as a reference to Behn's spying activities in Holland on behalf of the government, whereby she had already demonstrated her loyalty to the Crown (and had been imprisoned for debt for her pains).[35] Once the Popish Plot hysteria had started, however, an open alliance with the Whig or Tory faction became essential for playwrights. Although it might not have been her sole motive in the decision, Behn certainly chose the commercially viable path in aligning herself with the Tories, since Whig playwrights were subjected to direct interference and censorship.[36] It was in these circumstances that Behn wrote her plays that most explicitly espouse a position on state politics: *The Roundheads* and *The City-Heiress*. She also revised an early play (*The Young King*), and wrote into it explicit contemporary political references, presumably with a view to ensuring its commercial success.[37]

The Roundheads is dedicated to the Duke of Grafton (Charles II's second son by Barbara Villiers, the Countess of Castlemaine). Where Behn's early plays appear without named sponsors, these later ones frequently bear a dedication, presumably partly to make an express political statement and partly to raise some extra money. Her dedicatees included the Duke of York (*The Second Part Of The Rover*), Nell Gwyn (*The Feign'd Curtizans*), Lord Mowbray (*The City-Heiress*), Lord Rochester (*The Luckey Chance*), and the Marquis of Worcester (*The Emperor of the Moon*). *The Roundheads* is set in 1659, at the moment when London was in the hands of Lambert, shortly before Monck and his troops took over and offered the crown to the exiled Charles. The storyline centres on affairs developing between two Cavaliers, Freeman and Loveless, and the wives of two leading Puritans, Desborough and Lambert. Scenes depicting key state officials, such as Warriston and Fleetwood, caricature them and their politics. Elizabeth Cromwell is presented as an absurd, vain creature, and Lambert's political progress attributed to Lady Lambert's willingness to prostitute herself on his behalf. In V ii, the mythical 'Council of Ladies' that male royalist propagandists so enjoyed inventing is shown in session, and petitioning gentlewomen and the Council made ridiculous. The play ends with the Cavaliers saving their mistresses from rioting apprentices, having converted Lady Lambert to their own political opinions (Lady Desborough is shown as having long been a secret royalist). In short, the play is blatant political propaganda that was no doubt warmly received by the royalists of 1682, proving highly successful. The bitter partisanship of the play has generally been found shocking by modern critics, although for its period it is relatively tame, and is certainly less vitriolic than contemporary political satires.[38]

Quite apart from the particular political crisis of the Succession, however, the problems facing an author whose sole source of income was writing plays were considerable. With the small potential audience and consequent short runs of plays, playwrights had to be prolific in order to make a living. Speed of composition was probably one reason why many of Behn's plays, like those of her contemporaries, are adaptations of other works. Of the twenty plays generally regarded as hers, only five can be shown to be predominantly original in their material, and two of these are her first plays, *The Forc'd Marriage* and *The Amorous Prince*, which nonetheless borrow heavily if generally from the Beaumont and Fletcher school.[39] Behn's relationship to her sources, though, is far from passive or imitative. She makes her borrowings her own, cutting and altering to increase pace and humour and to make dialogue more lively, and her stagecraft and sense of spectacle are almost always original.[40] The best example of this is her most strikingly successful play, *The Rover*, which took many of its characters and plot elements from Thomas Killigrew's long and rambling romance *Thomaso*. When the play proved hugely popular, charges of plagiarism were swiftly brought against her, to which she replied with tired irony in a postscript to the printed play. Nobody would have been bothered about its borrowings, she claims, if it had been less well received. In the third issue of the first edition, she takes the opportunity of adding the phrase 'especially of our sex' to her defence of the play, making it thereby a more general attack on male responses to female writers.

> I will only say the plot and business (not to boast on't) is my own: as for the words and characters, I leave that to the reader to judge and compare 'em with *Thomaso*, to whom I recommend the great entertainment of reading it, though had this succeeded ill, I should have had no need of imploring that justice from the critics, who are naturally so kind to any that pretend to usurp their dominion, especially of our sex, they would doubtless have given me the whole honour on't.[41]

Behn's ability to assess the tastes of her audience and provide entertaining spectacle using a variety of techniques is particularly evident in her farces. *The False Count*, a *pot pourri* of accidents, mistakes and confusions, was a huge success and continued to be regularly revived for twenty years.[42] *The Emperor of the Moon* was likewise long a favourite in repertory. It is liberally spotted with impressive visual effects, ridiculous mock fights and parodies of male courting practices and friendship rituals (Scaramouch, for example, resolves to tickle himself to death on hearing that his mistress is false). Popular farcical scenes also appeared in other plays by her in the period.[43]

Restoration comedy is known not only for its delight in spectacle and song and dance (in the use of which Behn was skilled[44]), but also for its bawdiness. Pope's attack on Behn has often been quoted: 'The stage how loosely does Astrea tread,/ Who fairly puts all characters to bed!'[45] In fact, not only were her plays considerably less bawdy than those written by her popular male contemporaries, but one of the principal characteristics of her rewriting of her sources was the reduction of sexual explicitness. This continued to be true of her writing in a period when the trend (and, presumably, the popular taste) was away from a concern with romance and satire towards increasingly overt sexual jokes.[46] Her real indecency was to be a woman writing successfully for money.

I shall return below to discuss the appearance of prostitutes and 'fallen women' in Behn's plays, and to examine the role of sexual licentiousness in them. In her preface to *Sir Patient Fancy*, Behn makes her own case against those who condemn her. The argument is a complex one. She agrees that there are immodest elements in her plays, but argues firstly that they are not as lewd or as blatant as popular men's writing, and secondly that if she were a man, these elements in her work would not be thought noteworthy. Her crime is that she is a *woman* making use of this material, and that she is a successful woman, too. What rankles is that her fellow-women have not understood this, and do not realise that she has to write to the popular taste to earn her living. She argues, therefore, both that she has to write in a particular (licentious) way to be successful with her audience, and that there are limits to how far she will go to this end: unlike male hack writers, she implies, who write pure pornography. She turns the women's criticisms back on them, discreetly pointing out to them that she is faced with the same kind of compromises with male values as they are themselves. If the women criticising her were really chaste and blushing in the way men would have them be, they would not, after all, understand the risqué elements of her plays, or anyone else's. In fact, the theatre is popular with women. Let us admit that women know about these things, she says; then we can begin to talk about them in our own way.

I printed this play with all the impatient haste one ought to do, who would be vindicated from the most unjust and silly aspersion, woman could invent to cast on woman; and which only being a woman has procured me; *that it was bawdy*, the least and most excusable fault in the men writers, to whose plays they all crowd, as if they came to no other end than to hear what they condemn in this: *but from a woman it was unnatural* . . . The play had no other misfortune but that of coming out for a woman: had it been owned by a man, though the most dull unthinking rascally scribbler in town, it had been an admirable play. Nor does its loss of fame with the ladies do it much hurt, though they ought to have had good nature and justice enough to have attributed all its faults to the author's unhappiness, who is forced to write for bread and not ashamed to own it, and consequently ought to write to please (if she can) an age which has given several proofs it was by this way of writing to be obliged, though it is a way [i.e. writing scurrilous ballads or other deliberately obscene texts?] too cheap for men of wit to pursue, who write for glory, and a way which even I despise as much below me. (*Sir Patient Fancy*, sig. A^{r-v})

Such attacks on her must have become routine. By the time she came to write the preface to *The Luckey Chance*, 1687, the tone is positively weary as she catalogues the elements of 'the old never failing scandal – that 'tis not fit for the ladies' (*The Luckey Chance*, sig. A3^v). In the interim, her name has been commonly associated with all the most smutty anonymous plays, and she is tired of it. If she had a day or two to spare, she says, she would analyse for the reader all the indecencies printed by male playwrights, whose morality is never questioned. Faced with these criticisms, and safe in the knowledge of her own success despite the cavillers, she takes the 'unnatural' step of making a claim for fame. If being identified as a woman means that she will be condemned, she demands to be assessed simply as a 'poet', as part of a long male tradition.

And this one thing I will venture to say, though against my nature, because it has a vanity in it: that had the plays I have writ come forth under any man's name, and never known to have been mine; I appeal to all unbiased judges of sense, if they had not said that person had made as good comedies, as any one man that has writ in our age; but a devil on't the woman damns the poet . . . All I ask, is the privilege for my masculine part the poet in me, (if any such you will allow me) to tread in those successful paths my predecessors have so long thrived in . . . If I must not, because of my sex, have this freedom, but that you will usurp all to yourselves; I lay down my quill, and you shall hear no more of me . . . for I am not content to write for a third day only. I value fame as much as if I had been born a hero. (sig. A4^v–a1^r)

This is probably the clearest and most uncompromising statement made in the period about the way in which a woman's gender excluded her from acceptance as a writer. Aphra Behn reaches this clarity through her public success. As a popular playwright, making her living by her pen, she had to confront head-on the ideologies and fashions of patriarchy and its relationship to writing. To become successful, she had to make use of male sources, and of techniques and themes popular in the dominant tradition. Through the charges of impropriety consequently brought against her, she was able to analyse the factors both of her success and of the condemnation this had provoked. She was forced to define, for herself and her reader, where she stood. If she was to eat, she also had to continue to write, and to reap success.

Despite her bid for fame, Behn had made it clear from the very beginning that she (like Cavendish) did not belong to the male traditions of playwriting, and that she could not do so. An important clique within the audience were the critics, who fell into two competing groups centred on Dryden and Shadwell. Male writers lined up on one side or the other, using evidence from their classical education to argue a case, forming alliances that helped to promote their careers.[47] As a woman, Behn was effectively excluded both from the networks and from the education that might gain her access to them. She quickly fell foul of the critics, in part perhaps because of her refusal to take their debates seriously. In the preface to *The Dutch Lover*, 1673, for example, she rejects the (Jonsonian) principles of the Shadwell clique, but is quick to add that she is not thereby aligning herself with the opposing faction.

In short, I think a play the best divertisement that wise men have; but I do also think them nothing so, who do discourse as formally about the rules of it, as if 'twere the grand affair of human life. This being my opinion of plays, I studied only to make this as entertaining as I could. (sig. A4)

In her rejection of the debate she continues by explaining that the drama is one kind of writing where male education gives men no real advantage over women. Both Shakespeare and Jonson, after all, had little schooling, she says. The critics are introducing irrelevancies with their 'musty rules of unity' (the favourite of the Dryden circle). She will not allow men to define what drama is, or how it should be written. They would be better employed working out their rule-making obsessions by arguing about the conventions of children's games, she suggests (sig. A1). Like Isabella in *Sir Patient Fancy*, she has no great awe of male learning.

If they can find any of our sex fuller of words, and to so little purpose as some of their gownmen, I'll be content to change my petticoats for pantaloons and go to a grammar school. (*Sir Patient Fancy*, p. 3)

From the opening lines of her first play, Behn presents herself primarily as a *woman* writer, venturing out into male territory on women's behalf. The first lines of the prologue to *The Forc'd Marriage* are spoken by a man, and they characterise the author as a spy in language taken from courtly love conventions. Women are 'charming victors', whose victories through their eyes' darts are to be consolidated by the achievements of the playwright's wit. The second section of the prologue, spoken by a woman,[48] coyly reassures men that all women seek is 'constancy in love': they need not be alarmed (sig. A2^{r-v}). The act of a woman taking up the pen is simply a new feminine wile, and her play is merely a new kind of offspring, bade on the title page '*Va mon enfant! prend ta fortune!*' Having played with female stereotypes and courtly love metaphors in its prologue, the play itself initiates what was to be the dominant theme in Behn's plays: the actual meaning of courtship and marriage for women, and the fact that male power is an inescapable component in such relationships and has to be negotiated with.

The theme of familial control over marriage contracts is omnipresent in Behn's plays. The 'forced marriage' in the play of that title is between the king's favourite, Alcippus, and Erminia, who is given to him by King Sigismund as a reward for his success in battle. She is already in love with and secretly betrothed to the king's son, Philander. Alcippus reveals that in keeping with strict courtly love convention, she has long known that Alcippus has been 'conquered' by her, but, an 'ingrate', has only given him 'scorn' (*The Forc'd Marriage*, p. 7). Meanwhile, the king's daughter, Gallatea, is also stricken at the arranged match, since she secretly longs for Alcippus herself.

The men of the play respond to the enforced marriage between Alcippus and Erminia with courtly love logic. Philander immediately assumes when Erminia marries Alcippus that she has broken her vows to him (in fact, she refuses to sleep with her new husband), and serenades outside her bedroom window with a conventional ditty lamenting his 'Silvia's' inconstancy. He does not really like Erminia or respect her, and as she tries to balance the rights of ownership her husband has over her with her commitment to her beloved, he maligns her to her face as 'a woman, a vain, peevish creature'. The other man in her life, her husband Alcippus, portrays himself as a helpless slave of love, bemoaning his 'fetters', but nonetheless has the power to strangle her, leaving her for dead and celebrating her murder as the ultimate act of possession of a coy mistress.

> If she be dead the fitter she's for me,
> She'll now be coy no more,
> Nor cry 'I cannot love',
> And frown and blush, when I but kiss her hand. (p. 63)

When she returns as a 'ghost' to haunt him, she tells him he has 'deified' her in this final act of worship.

What is at issue in this play is not jealousy as an abstract human trait (its subtitle is *The Jealous Bridegroom*), but male jealousy which has so much control over a woman's freedom and can destroy her reputation or even take away her life. This, and not generalised questions of love and freedom, is the focus of the play, and is also the key to *The Amorous Prince*, where Clarina laments the 'unapprehensive madness' of her unwanted lover's jealousy (p. 32). What is sobering is that by the end of the play, when the 'true lovers' of Erminia and Philander, Galatea and Alcippus are united, Alcippus has not changed one iota of his courtly love ideology, according to which he had every right to kill Erminia. On realising that Erminia was bound by precontract to Prince Philander he surrenders his claim over her, but does not hesitate to reassert his rectitude.

> Yes, fair Erminia:
> Hadst thou been mine, I would i'th'face of Heaven,
> Proclaim I'd just and brave revenge:
> But, madam, you were wife unto my prince,
> And that was all my sin.
> Alas, in vain I hoped for some return,
> And grew impatient of th'unkind delay,
> And frantically I then outrun my happiness. (p. 87)

It is doubtful, with male power so all-pervasive, that women are any better off at the end of the play for being matched to their chosen partners by the repentant Sigismund, grand patriarch, king and father.

Many of Behn's other plays, including *The Rover*, *The Younger Brother*, *Sir Patient Fancy* and *The False Count*, also address the problem of arranged marriages and marriage for money, and Lady Fulbank of *The Luckey Chance* is an extended study of the unhappiness of a woman married to a man she has not chosen. The unacceptability of forced marriages is in fact a presupposition in the plays, as it is in plays by

Behn's male contemporaries. The matter of concern for Behn, however, is the character of the *chosen* lover, and the problems involved in forming such a relationship. One of the most extended expositions of this issue in Behn's plays is her most popular work, *The Rover*.

Commonly, Behn's plays feature at least two pairs of young lovers, whose attitudes to love and marriage serve as contrasting strategies in courtship. A common pattern is that of the 'constant couple', who remain true to one another, and finally marry, despite parental opposition and, usually, confusions over one another's true identity and conduct. These lovers are not, however, idyllically well matched or perfectly happy. In *The Rover*, Florinda and Belvile are just such a constant couple. From the beginning they are in love with one another, and resolved to accept no other partner. Except for her stubbornness on this one issue, Florinda is all quiet obedience, failing to argue her case against an arranged marriage. Her passivity is no ideal. Twice in the course of the play she narrowly escapes being raped by the friends of her beloved, and on each occasion is only saved because her obvious high social class causes her attackers to hesitate, fearing retribution from her relatives. The second of these incidents is a nightmare scene where, seeking refuge in Blunt's house, she is regarded by him as the perfect target for his revenge against all women (and Lucetta in particular) for making fun of him. When Frederick, the play's great upholder of patriarchal morality arrives, the two men agree to rape her.

> Blunt: We'll both lie with her, and then let me alone to bang her.
> Fred.: I'm ready to serve you in matters of revenge that has a double pleasure in't. (*The Rover*, p. 65)

In a world where men can choose to rape a woman, any woman, for spite, there is no safety for the romantic heroine. In Behn's plays, as in her novels, rape or the threat of it is shown to be an almost routine masculine strategy to bully and manipulate women. In *The Amorous Prince*, Frederick threatens to rape Laura at knifepoint to humble her for scorning him, and in the same play Silvio threatens to rape his 'sister' Cleonte. Sir Timothy Tawdrey in *The Town-Fopp*, when threatening to rape Phillis tells her that old patriarchal lie: that all women want to be forcibly taken. Phillis's fate is the most terrible of all. Having no economic choices (like Philadelphia in Behn's novel *The Unfortunate Happy Lady*), she has no option but to marry her would-be rapist.

Setting out with a theme of courtship and marriage, Behn writes about rape and prostitution, constructing scenarios that show how closely connected these fates are for women. Where Florinda's reliance on 'true love' for her salvation twice brings her to the brink of being raped, the courtesan Angellica Bianca in the same play is betrayed by her final inability to escape from the tempting lies of romance. Early in the play, she makes a cool assessment of women's position, explaining that she had opted to sell her body for the solid return of financial reward, rather than trusting to illusory male fidelity: 'Nothing but gold shall charm my heart' (p. 20). She knows, too, that marriage for money is a no less mercenary affair than prostitution. Disaster arrives, however, because she has seriously misjudged the power structure of her society. She arrives in town hoping to captivate either the viceroy's son Don Antonio, or Don Pedro, the nephew of her deceased 'protector'. Had she been married to her old lover, Don Pedro would have been her kin, and had some social duty to support her. As it is, she is left to live on her wits and her transitory physical charms. When Willmore, the 'rover' of the title, finally rejects her in favour of the wealthy virgin Hellena, she is forced to recognise that her chosen independence was illusory. In a world where men make the rules, her only saleable item is her virginity. Having sold that in the wrong market, she is damned.

When Angellica falls hopelessly for the feckless Willmore, she wants to believe that love and romance can be dissociated from social and economic structures, that 'true love' in her world can be above financial considerations. She calls on him to see things her way and, blinded by this desire, does not recognise that he is using her for his pleasure.

> *Angellica*: Thou'rt a brave fellow! put up thy gold, and know
> That were thy fortune large as is thy soul
> Thou shouldst not buy my love.
> Couldst thou forget these mean effects of vanity
> Which set me out to sale, and, as a lover, prize my yielding joys?
> Canst thou believe they'll be entirely thine,
> Without considering they were mercenary? (p. 27)

In the course of the play, Willmore's repeated answer to this is a resounding 'No'. Having worshipped her beauty, tasted the pleasures of her body and spent her money to attract a wealthier woman, he leaves her for a better catch.

Angellica is a troubling and uncomfortable figure in the play, disrupting the wit and airiness of scenes between Hellena and Willmore and under-cutting the conventional 'happy ending' of true lovers united. Realising she has been betrayed by Willmore despite giving him 'My virgin heart ... Oh! 'tis gone!' (p. 53), she plots her revenge 'for the public safety of our sex' (p. 76). Trapping him at gunpoint she decides, however, to let him live: he is not worth the trouble of an execution: 'But now to show my utmost of contempt,/ I give thee life' (p. 77). Through Willmore, she has learnt that male protestations of devotion, and all their courtly love rhetoric, are for them just a game. There is no true power, no safety, for women.[49]

> Had I remained in innocent security,
> I should have thought all men were born my slaves,
> And worn my power like lightning in my eyes,
> To have destroyed at pleasure when offended.
> – But when love held the mirror, the undeceiving glass
> Reflected all the weakness of my soul, and made me know
> My richest treasure being lost, my honour,
> All the remaining spoil could not be worth
> The conqueror's care or value.
> – Oh how I fell like a long worshipped idol
> Discovering all the cheat. (pp. 75–6)

Angellica is one of many 'fallen women' in Behn's plays. Cloris in *The Amorous Prince* is also debauched by a man, Prince Frederick, having been raised in country innocence and so not realising that men's protestations of love and fidelity are not to be trusted. She is saved from ignominy by marrriage to Frederick when it is discovered that she is nobly born. Other women keep their wits about them, and are able to trick, persuade or bully their seducers into marrying them. Hyppolyta in *The Dutch Lover* learns that Antonio has debauched her as part of a cynical plan of revenge against her brother. Dressed as a man, she challenges and fights him, winning his respect and his hand. Charlot of *The City-Heiress* loses her reputation when she elopes with Wilding, only to find him in love with Lady Galliard, and has to use all her inventiveness to finally secure him as husband. These are fairytale endings, made necessary and possible by the heroines' wealth and social class.

Angellica Bianca, on the other hand, disturbs literary critics, who feel that the way in which her situation is left unresolved at the end of the play mars its unity.[50] In fact, Angellica's situation, and the questions that it raises, cannot be resolved within the terms allowed by Behn's world. The lack of completion in her story, and the uneasiness this creates, are necessary parts of a vision which shows the connections between romance, prostitution and economics. She is a character of tragic status, carefully embedded into the breezy comedy of *The Rover*, just like Lady Galliard in *The City-Heiress* and Julia Fulbank in *The Luckey Chance*.

Lady Galliard is a rich widow courted by many of the male characters in *The City-Heiress*, who finds herself irresistibly attracted to the rakish Wilding. She refuses to think or behave as a stereotypical lusty widow, and repulses Wilding furiously when he presumes that he can bed her simply because she is attracted to him, even though he is already contracted to Charlot. As she wavers between consent and refusal of his advances, she remains clear in her understanding that men's lust is no guarantee of their liking or respect for women. In truth, men who seduce women in a world where this brings down calumny upon them despise them.

> And have I promised then to be
> A whore? A whore! Oh let me think of that!
> A man's convenience, his leisure hours, his bed of ease,
> To loll and tumble on at his idle times;
> The slave, the hackney of his lawless lust!
> A loathed extinguisher of filthy flames,
> Made use of, and thrown by. — Oh infamous! (p. 41)

When she yields, she is indeed made use of and thrown off by Wilding, only to have her body immediately occupied by another of her suitors, who had decided on rape as a means of claiming her. Forced to marry her rapist, she is cursed for inconstancy by Wilding.

Julia Fulbank in *The Luckey Chance* is another woman who refuses to yield to the advances of the man she loves because of her commitment to autonomy. When all his courtly advances to her fail, Gayman gambles with her husband, using the price of a night in her bed as a stake. Having bought her, he tricks his way into her body with her husband's collusion, raping her while allowing her to think that she is with Sir Cautious Fulbank. On discovering the deception, distraught, she sends him away and vows never to share a bed with her husband again.

Julia: Oh! You unkind — what have you made me do?
  Unhand me false deceiver — let me loose—
Sir Cautious: Made her do? — so, so — 'tis done — I'm glad of that —
                                                    [Aside, peeping
Gayman: Can you be angry, Julia?
  Because I only seized my right of love.
Julia: And must my honour be the price of it?
  —What make me a base prostitute, a foul adulteress,
  Oh — be gone, be gone — dear robber of my quiet.
                                                    [Weeping (p. 65)[51]

Both Gayman and Wilding, like Willmore in *The Rover*, show themselves wholly incapable of understanding the viewpoint of the women they have sex with. Bound within their own desires, but untrammelled by the social restrictions that hedge women in, they cannot hear what is said to them, but this does not stop them getting what they want. Willmore is shown flirting with women at every opportunity, Wilding plays three women off against one another, Gayman is an irrepressible philanderer, and Alonzo, in *The Dutch Lover*, takes the opportunity when it arises to make overtures to both Cleonte and Clarinda, while planning to capture Euphemia. These men's tireless pursuit of women's bodies does not mean, however, that they either like or understand them. Willmore's opportunistic attitude to the 'fair sex' leads him to attempt to rape Florinda, or buy sex from her, refusing to believe that she is serious in her rebuffing of him.

Florinda: I'll cry murder! rape! or anything! if you do not instantly let me go.
Willmore: A rape! Come, come, you lie you baggage, you lie, what, I'll warrant
  you would fain have the world believe now that you are not so forward as I.
  (p. 42)

In his dealings with Angellica, his fixation on the dynamics and language
of courtly love makes him unable to hear what she is saying, or to
recognise the differences between their assumptions. Trying to talk his
way into her bed, he promises undying devotion.

Angellica: And will you pay me then the price I ask?
Willmore: Oh why dost thou draw me from an awful worship,
  By showing thou art no divinity?
  Conceal the fiend, and show me all the angel!
  Keep me but ignorant, and I'll be devout
  And pay my vows for ever at this shrine.

                                                    [Kneels and kisses her hand
Angellica: The pay I mean is but thy love for mine.
  – Can you give that?
Willmore: Entirely – Come, let's withdraw! Where I'll renew my vows
  – And breathe 'em with such ardour thou shalt not doubt my zeal. (p. 28)

Delighting in his conquest of her, he can wax eloquent to his friends
about the 'darts' her eyes have shot him with (p. 32), but he can only
respond to her rage at his treachery with jests and flirtations, offering to
'oblige thee with a kindness, had I but opportunity' (p. 74).

In many of Behn's plays, men's obsessions with their courtship conventions prevent them from understanding the women they address.
Romance is a male invention, and women are jeopardised and often
betrayed if they believe such declarations of undying passion. The task
for the witty heroine who is at the centre of many of Behn's plays, as
Hellena is in *The Rover*, is to discover as much as possible about her
man's true intentions, beneath his courtly façade. Willmore refers to both
Angellica and to Hellena as his 'angel' in highflown rhetoric, but where
Angellica is briefly fooled by this worship, Hellena is quite clear-sighted
about the limit of his commitment. As far as possible, she takes control of
her situation, disguising herself and playing parts, testing out and then
capturing the man she has chosen. Disguised, she watches him court and
promise fidelity to Angellica, and in a bitter but witty scene mocks him,
throwing back at him the overblown promises she has heard him make
(p. 36). She has no interest in traditional courtship rituals, thinking them
'a very pretty, idle, silly kind of pleasure to pass one's time with' (p. 31),
but she is not deceived by Willmore's forthright arguments in favour
of unfettered sensuality. She knows already what Angellica shows the
audience: marriage is a necessity for women, otherwise, as she challenges
Willmore, 'What shall I get? a cradle full of noise and mischief, with a
pack of repentance at my back?' (p. 80).

She gets her man, but it is a tawdry victory and the audience knows it, with Angellica there to remind them. Willmore has shown himself to be insensitive, capricious and dangerous to women, and there is no reason to imagine that he will be faithful to Hellena for longer than the month that he originally resolves to sacrifice to gain her. In *The Second Part of the Rover*, where Willmore again chooses between two women (and this time chooses the prostitute), it is revealed in passing that Hellena had died at sea within three months of the marriage (p. 3).

The world of courtship and marriage depicted by Behn in these plays is a bleak one. Bright, witty women like Hellena use daring and imagination in a desperate attempt to evade the arranged marriages or confinements to nunneries destined them by their families. They race against time, trying their best to negotiate when all power lies in others' hands. None of the dashing young blades they choose and test out are admirable characters, but they seem preferable to a fool like Haunce van Ezel (in *The Dutch Lover*) or an odious tyrant like Octavio (in *The Feign'd Curtizans*). Woven in with the wit and humour, music and spectacle, are hard, sober women's truths about the debauchery of the Restoration court and its acolytes. Armed with wit and driven by necessity, like her heroines, Aphra Behn succeeded in dramatising in marketable form the dilemmas that faced her and her sisters.

CHAPTER SIX

ROMANTIC LOVE – POETRY

ORINDA AND FEMALE INTIMACY

KATHERINE Philips, 'the Matchless Orinda', the author of a book of poetry, two play translations and some published correspondence, has long been perceived as a model lady poetess, dabbling in versification in a rural Welsh backwater, confining her attention solely to the proper feminine concerns of love and friendship. It is generally agreed that she was modestly alarmed at the prospect of any public attention for her work. By briefly examining her *Letters from Orinda to Poliarchus* (her correspondence with the Master of Ceremonies at Charles II's court, Charles Cotterell) and the images of constraint and retirement found in her poetry, I will suggest that the 'Orinda' persona who appears in modern critical accounts is a creation made necessary by the particular circumstances confronting this seventeenth-century woman poet. Through 'Orinda', Philips gained acceptance in her own period, and has a reputation that has survived into our own. I will then go on to examine more closely Philips's best-known work, her poetry celebrating women's friendship, and how it engages with the conventions of the courtly love tradition to produce an image of female solidarity (and, perhaps, of lesbian love) that could be sustained within the tight constraints of marriage.[1]

Since her death in 1664, Katherine Philips's writings have never dropped entirely from the public eye.[2] There is a certain significant irony in this, since she is remembered as the archetypal blushing poetess, who shied away from any public recognition of her works. She never desired publication, and was horrified when a surreptitious edition of her poetry appeared in 1664, the story goes. The figure who appears in her poetry and her *Letters to Poliarchus* is 'the matchless Orinda', the self-effacing lady poet who thoroughly understands that she is inferior to the male sex. As such, she has been allowed a tiny and peripheral place in the literary canon.

In part, the image of Orinda that has come down to us is dependent on the belief that her writing was really a secret and private affair, her poems passed around only in manuscript form to a few trusted friends. This is an anachronistic distortion of the method of 'publication' that she used: circulation of manuscripts was the normal way to make writing public before the widespread use of printed books, and was a method that continued to be popular in court circles throughout the reign of Charles II, at least.[3] Such a description also fails to consider the fact that, as a royalist poet married to a leading parliamentarian, she had positive reasons for avoiding too much public attention during the 1650s, which was when she did most of her writing. Bearing these factors in mind, we find that the evidence suggests that she was actually a well-known writer.

As early as 1651, when she was nineteen years old, Philips's writing was sufficiently well thought of for a poem of hers to be prefaced to the posthumous edition of William Cartwright's plays, and a poem written in praise of Philips by Henry Vaughan was included by him in his collected works in that same year. She must already have been circulating some of her writings. In 1655, a song of hers was printed by Henry Lawes in his *Second Book of Ayres*. Although Katherine Philips's identity was not revealed in Cartwright's text, both Vaughan and Lawes printed her full name. It is clear that her achievements were well known, at least among prestigious royalists. She addressed poems to Francis Finch, John Birkenhead and Sir Edward Dering, and the fact that they were also involved with the publication of Cartwright's plays and the *Second Book of Ayres* could indicate that her acquaintance with them dated from 1651 or even earlier. It is not surprising to find that by 1657, when Jeremy Taylor answered in print Katherine Philips's enquiries about the nature of friendship, his complimentary address to her should have heralded her as someone known to be 'so eminent in friendships'.[4] And after the Restoration, she sought out recognition from aristocracy and royalty, sending poems to the Duchess of York, the Archbishop of Canterbury, and to King Charles himself, and dedicating her translation *Pompey* to the Countess of Cork. Her skill as a translator had a sufficiently high public profile for John Davies to praise her by name when dedicating his 1659 translation of *Cléopatre* to her in 1662, and for Lord Roscommon to claim to have undertaken a translation from French purely in compliment to her.[5] Any assessment of Philips's writing that suggests that she was of a shy and retiring spirit, forced into the public eye in 1664 against her strongest inclinations, is choosing to ignore her involvement with this then more traditional form of public recognition. The 'public' she was interested in reaching was the coterie of court and leading poets, not the wider world.

The assertion that Philips did not wish her works published is based on the letters she wrote to Sir Charles Cotterell between 1661 and 1664, published in 1705 after his death as *Letters from Orinda to Poliarchus*. The correspondence deals in part with her preparing a translation of Corneille's *Pompée*, and seeing it onto the stage and through the press in 1663, and her attempts to suppress an unofficial edition of her poems in 1664. The established judgement of these letters' significance is that they demonstrate Katherine Philips's blushing horror at the thought of her works and name becoming public property. They are used to reconfirm the image of her that has come down to us from posterity. The fact that *Pompey* was published without identifying the translator is seen as proof that Philips held a suitably modest assessment of her own abilities. What is not noticed is that the prologue to the play, written by the Earl of Roscommon, and its epilogue by Sir Edward Dering, both identify the author as female.[6] Given Philips's reputation as a translator, and the fact that she was living in Dublin during the play's much-acclaimed performance there, it is likely that her identity was common knowledge, at least among those whose opinion of her she valued. In the copy that she sent to the Countess of Roscommon she certainly made no attempt to hide her name, and the stationer Henry Herringman knew whom to contact when he wanted to bring out a London edition of *Pompey* (see Chapter Five).

The *Letters to Poliarchus* have been read as if they give straight-forward access to 'the real Katherine Philips', her personal doubts and fears, and that they can therefore tell us the 'truth' about her identity as an author.[7] Such a reading discounts the fact that all writing is governed by specific conventions, and that in the case of a mid seventeenth-century woman these conventions included the requirement that she apologise for daring to take up the pen, and find ways to excuse her boldness. We would therefore expect to find, as we do, that the *Letters*, written to her important political ally and sponsor Charles Cotterell, are preoccupied largely with finding ways to justify writing as a 'female' activity. The *Letters to Poliarchus* indeed provide material for a fascinating study of the process through which 'Orinda' is constructed and refined through-out the correspondence, making it possible for Philips to write and gain wide public acclaim while disavowing any desire to do either. Orinda can also humbly request advice and guidance from Cotterell with her trans-lation of *Pompée*, whilst blithely continuing to follow her own judge-ment when he disagrees with her.

There are many examples of this in the *Letters*. The most extended is found in a long-drawn-out discussion of one word in her translation: the word 'effort', at that time seen as a French term not an English one. Cotterell counselled her to omit the word, and the subsequent correspondence continued for some months. There was every reason for Philips to take Cotterell's advice and change her text. He was, after all, a recognised linguist and translator. However, although she finally asks Cotterell to change the text himself, the word appears unaltered in the published version. Part of the justification for her consistency, which might have been seen as unfeminine stubbornness, is that she is leaving the word alone at the insistence of another eminent man and writer, Roger Boyle. She tells Cotterell,

I would fain have made use of your correction, and thrown away 'effort', but my Lord Orrery would absolutely have it continued; and so it is, to please his humour, though against my will and judgement too. (*Letters*, p. 123)

There is no need to assert her own opinion against Cotterell's. She can cite another male authority instead.

Translation, as defined by Philips in the *Letters*, was a suitably modest undertaking for a woman, the task being to produce a text that kept well within the specific and narrow bounds of the original. This restrictive format could then be used, however, to vindicate her own expertise, and to criticise judiciously the work of others. This is demonstrated strikingly in Philips's detailed analysis of 'what chiefly disgusts me' (p. 179) in a rival translation of *Pompée* undertaken by a group of men. Her comments become so scathing as to strain the limits of self-effacement, and her letter criticising the men's translation ends with the necessary retraction: 'I really think the worst of their lines equal to the best in my translation' (p. 180).

One of the 'wits' involved with the male *Pompey* translation was William Waller, and he and Philips became rivals again shortly after the publication of her play when both sent poems to the king celebrating the queen's recovery from a serious illness. Charles, apparently, far preferred Philips's poem (p. 205), a victory not without its costs, since as Philips knew, Waller could be a dangerous enemy to a woman poet. In her letter to Cotterell delighting in the king's praise of her poem, she recalls Waller's public insult to her contemporary, Margaret Cavendish the Duchess of Newcastle.

Mr Waller has, it may be, contributed not a little to encourage me in this vanity, by writing on the same subject the worst verses that ever fell from his pen. I could be an outrageous critic upon them, if I were not restrained, by other considerations . . . I remember I have been told that he once said, he would have given all his own poems to have been the author of that which my Lady Newcastle writ of a stag: and that being taxed for this insincerity by one of his friends, he answered, that he could do no less in gallantry than be willing to save the reputation of a lady, and keep her from the disgrace of having written anything so ill. Some such repartee I expect he would make on this occasion. (p. 205)[8]

The best-known of Philips's *Letters to Poliarchus* is the one most centrally concerned in producing the image of the poetess that has come down to us. It appears as part of the preface to the posthumous, 1667 edition of the poems, having been written after Richard Marriot had brought out a surreptitious edition from an imperfect manuscript early in 1664. Cotterell hurried to suppress the edition, and Philips's letter refers to this with gratitude. The letter has been read, as the editor of the posthumous edition no doubt designed, as clear proof of the poet's diffidence.[9] In the 1667 edition of *Poems* the letter lies framed by his assertion of her bashfulness and self-effacement, directing the reader how to interpret it. Much is made of her description of herself as someone 'who never writ any line in my life with an intention to have it printed'. Printing Philips might have been nervous about: it could in no way be construed as a feminine act. She was not, however, averse to having her writings published in a more traditional way. This letter, which finally was printed, was not the 'private' communication it is presented as, but was designed for a public audience. In a covering note, which is not included in the 1667 preface, Philips urges Cotterell to 'show it to anybody that suspects my ignorance and innocence of that false edition of my verses' (p. 34).[10] The greatest danger, indeed, was that she might be suspected of the same kind of scheming that many male authors practised: of having arranged the appearance of this incomplete edition as a way of testing how it would be received, before fully committing herself to it in public. Those with long memories would know, after all, that some of her works had already appeared in print, in 1651 and 1657. If her identity as the acclaimed translator of *Pompey* was also known or suspected despite its anonymous publication, such a consequence was likely, and would do irreparable damage to her carefully sculpted public image.

It is worth noting that Katherine Philips had other objections to the surreptitious printing of her poems, which she also mentions in the published letter. Since she died before the 1667 *Poems* appeared, it is impossible to know how she would have re-edited the text, but it is clear that there are many variants between the editions. The most obvious change is that the 1667 edition contains some fifty-five poems, and the two play translations, not found in the earlier text. Many of the omitted poems were written in Ireland, which suggests that the manuscript used by Marriot was an early one, perhaps an early draft, since some verses also scan badly. In addition, the absence of some lines and inclusion of nonsense verses suggests that it was illegible in places. The reader of the surreptitious edition would get an impression of the poet's skill far inferior to that provided by the amended text.[11]

So what kind of poetry was written under the name of Orinda? Katherine Philips was a royalist and High Church Anglican whose immediate family included many important parliamentarians and Independents. Having been born and educated in London, the daughter of a wealthy merchant, John Fowler, she had moved to Wales to join her mother by the time she was fifteen. Her father had died, and her mother was remarried to a prominent parliamentarian, Richard Phillipps. In August 1648, at the age of sixteen, Katherine was wedded to a fifty-four-year-old relative of Sir Richard's, James Philips of Tregibby and The Priory, Cardigan.[12] James was called to the Barebones Parliament in 1653, and served locally as a commissioner for sequestration.

During the 1650s, the political differences between husband and wife seem to have become known, and Colonel John Jones apparently attempted to discredit James Philips by publishing some writing of Katherine's. Her poem addressed to her husband on this occasion is fascinating. While expressing remorse and admitting she had undermined her spouse's reputation, she in no way promises to alter her opinions. Indeed, the poem is in fact a statement of her separateness from him, and a call for her to be assessed as an independent being, not as a part of her husband. At one level, there is nothing indecorous in these lines, as she is asking that her husband be considered free from her guilt. At another, she asserts that from the first, from the time of Adam and Eve, women and men should be regarded as autonomous, each responsible for their own actions. Even her enemy's wife, she maintains, need not be treated as though she agreed with Colonel Jones's opinions (Jones's wife indeed differed from him politically).[13] Under a legal system where the husband and wife were assumed to be one person, the husband, this is a quietly radical statement.

> *To Antenor, on a Paper of mine which J.J.*
> *threatens to publish to prejudice him.*
> Must then my crimes become thy scandal too?
> Why, sure the devil hath not much to do.
> The weakness of the other charge is clear,
> When such a trifle must bring up the rear.
> But this is mad design, for who before
> Lost his repute upon another's score?
> My love and life I must confess are thine,
> But not my errors, they are only mine.
> And if my faults must be for thine allowed,
> It will be hard to dissipate the cloud:
> For Eve's rebellion did not Adam blast,
> Until himself forbidden fruit did taste.
> 'Tis possible this magazine of hell
> (Whose name would turn a verse into a spell,
> Whose mischief is congenial to his life)

> May yet enjoy an honourable wife.
> Nor let his ill be reckoned as her blame,
> Nor yet my follies blast Antenor's name.
> (*Poems*, 1667, p. 47)

This poem to Antenor was not the only one Philips wrote on this occasion. She also addressed one to her close friend, Anne Owen, 'the truly competent judge of honour, Lucasia', asking her to believe in her untainted honesty. This appeal to Lucasia's support is unsurprising. Philips's solution to finding herself surrounded by those whose political and religious beliefs contrasted sharply with her own had been to establish her Society of Friendship. The friends admitted to this select band were all royalists, and their correspondence and companionship must have done much to offset her isolation. Naming herself 'Orinda', she gave similar pastoral-sounding names to her friends, and addressed poetry to them which uses the language and imagery of courtly love conventions.[14] Some of the Society's members have not been identified, but their number seems to have included Anne Owen (Lucasia), Mary Aubrey (Rosania), Francis Finch (Palaemon) the brother of the philosopher Anne Conway, John Birkenhead (Cratander), Sir Edward Dering (Silvander), Lady Mary Cavendish (Policrite), James Philips (Antenor) and Sir Charles Cotterell (Poliarchus). (Those added after the Restoration, when the Society of Friendship presumably changed somewhat, included Anne Boyle – Valeria – and Elizabeth Boyle – Celimena – relatives of the diarist and autobiographer Mary Rich.)

In general, the extant poems that she addresses to these friends make few overt comments on state politics. (Almost all her explicitly royalist poems were written after the Restoration.) During the 1650s, addressing issues of state politics was far more common among women sectaries than their more conservative sisters. Affairs of government were supposed to be beyond the realm of proper female concern, and in her lines deploring the execution of Charles I Philips found it necessary to assert that, in general, women should leave public issues well alone. Only with the whole world order upset by the 'murder' of the monarch, she asserts in 'Upon the Double Murther', could the unfeminine act of commenting on affairs of state be excused.

Philips's poems on solitude, retreat and the country life, however, also reveal her royalism. Maren-Sofie Røstvig has shown how the defeated royalists in their rural exiles took up classical images of contentment and virtue in the countryside.[15] The controlled and balanced happy man, contemptuous of the fervent battles of the political world, was their answer to the Puritan image of the committed Christian warrior. Henry Vaughan and Abraham Cowley both wrote in this vein, and both men were known by Philips. The writings of Saint-Amant were also incorporated into this tradition in England, and Philips was familiar with his work, translating his 'La Solitude'.

Her poetry shows many signs of commitment to this philosophy of retirement, wherein submission and acceptance of limitations are heralded as positive and necessary virtues. Many of the poems which in other respects are widely different from one another are characterised by advocacy of contentment or confinement or restriction, and the assertion that true freedom and choice can be found through this. (These include, for instance, 'A Sea-Voyage from Tenby to Bristol', 'To my dear Sister Mrs C.P. on her Marriage', 'Happiness' and 'Upon the Graving of her Name Upon a Tree in Barnelmes Walk'.) These sentiments would have been deeply familiar to Philips's royalist contemporaries.

There is, however, a radical difference between Katherine Philips's situation and that of her fellow-poets. They were men, and their retirement from affairs of state was a recent change in circumstances, and in some cases self-imposed. Philips was a woman. Her residence in the countryside was due to the fact that she had to be with her husband. She had no choice in the matter, and no hope that this apparently natural state of affairs had ever been different, or could ever be changed. This is most poignantly apparent in the many poems written on parting from one of her close women friends. Orinda recommends a stoical acceptance of separation, claiming that only through such a resignation of will can true self-determination be found. The way in which the parting is experienced, she argues, is something that friends do have control over, and this is where their freedom lies. This gives a very special inflexion to the traditional courtly love motif of separation from a beloved. Only by giving this particular extension to notions of self-control and contentment under compulsion could Katherine Philips find a way to maintain some autonomy, living as she was surrounded by her political enemies, people who had legal control over her existence. In 'Parting with Lucasia: A Song' this theme is especially interesting because Philips suggests that through resignation women can become 'conquerors at home'. The double meaning in this phrase – it can be read both as 'conquerors of ourselves' and 'conquerors in the house' – shows how, for this woman poet, a measure of self-determination could be achieved. If women can control their grief at being separated from one another, she argues, any task is slight by comparison, and can be performed. The poem ends

> Nay then to meet we may conclude,
> And all obstructions overthrow,
> Since we our passion have subdued,
> Which is the strongest thing I know. (pp. 65–6)

About half of Philips's poems are concerned with love and friendship. The great majority of these address the theme of intimacy between women, exploring its delights and problems. This anatomisation and celebration of female closeness is made in direct defiance of the accepted view of women. Although from its earliest days the language and themes of courtly love poetry had been used to glorify friendships between men, women's relationships with one another had never been treated to such serious consideration in print.[16] Orinda's response to this nonsense is unequivocal.

> If souls no sexes have, for men t'exclude
>   Women from friendship's vast capacity,
> Is a design injurious or rude,
>   Only maintained by partial tyranny.
> Love is allowed to us and innocence,
> And noblest friendships do proceed from thence. (p. 95)

It is entirely characteristic that she should argue that qualities normally attributed to women are the very features that most fit them to move outside the conventional requirements.

The courtly love conventions are an important and frequent feature of Orinda's poetry. In some poems, she adopts wholesale the stance and language of the frustrated lover, wooing a merciless mistress. An integral part of this tradition was the poem renouncing love, and Philips's works include a wholly conventional example of this kind, 'Against Love'. Addressed to Cupid, the poem includes stock references to lovers burning and raving and the 'killing frown' of the mistress who provides only diseased joys. What is unusual is for such a renunciation of love to be made by a woman. By writing from the position usually reserved for the male lover, the woman poet gains access for herself to the power and freedom that were usually enjoyed only by men in love relationships. Traditionally, this poetry, while lamenting the control wielded by the mistress over her lover through her 'killing frown', nonetheless gives voice only to the lover, who explores and revels in his (usual) 'subjuga-tion' to the mistress's gentle charms. The price that Philips pays for this access to male speech in at least some of her poems is that she is limited thereby to the kinds of relationship allowed by this essentially male tradition. Some of the poems addressed to Mary Aubrey include a great deal of this conventional language, and are restricted to situations taken directly from the courtly love tradition. Since one of the fundamental assumptions of this poetry is that the beloved object is an exception to the general run of womankind and infinitely superior to other females, this can have the result of deprecating other women. Such is the case in 'Rosania shadowed whilst Mrs Mary Aubrey'.

> Unlike those gallants which take far less care
> To have their souls, than make their bodies fair;
> Who (sick with too much leisure) time do pass

With these two books, pride and a looking-glass:
Plot to surprise men's hearts, their power to try,
And call that love, which is mere vanity.
But she, although the greatest murtherer,
(For every glance commits a massacre)
Yet glories not that slaves her power confess,
But wishes that her monarchy were less. (pp. 48–9)

Many of Orinda's poems, however, rigorously rework these conventions, giving them new meanings that express a particularly female perspective. In 'A Dialogue betwixt Lucasia, and Rosania, Imitating that of Gentle Thyrsis', Lucasia is a shepherdess and Rosania the wooer who tries to persuade her to leave the flocks and go away with her (pp. 126–7). Lucasia explains that she would much rather leave with Rosania, given the choice, but must stay where her duty lies. The poem presents loving friendship between women as the part of their lives that is characterised by choice and freedom, but prevented from blossoming by the duties of female existence: 'Lucasia: Such are thy charms, I'd dwell within thine arms/ Could I my station choose.' The poem, like many in the tradition from which it springs, looks forward to a final union after death.

Rosania: Then whilst we live, this joy let's take and give,
  Since death us soon will sever.
Lucasia: But I trust, when crumbled into dust,
  We shall meet and love for ever.

These lines echo another dialogue, 'A Dialogue of Absence 'Twixt Lucasia and Orinda, set by Mr Henry Lawes', which ends in a chorus anticipating a future where women will no longer be forced to part by other concerns: 'But we shall come where no rude hand shall sever,/ And there we'll meet and part no more for ever' (p. 26).

Some of the most interesting of Katherine Philips's poems take particular images from the received patterns and rework them. In doing so, Philips both shows that relationships between women are different from those between men and women, and implicitly criticises her male poetic sources. A notable instance of this is her reworking of John Donne's famous 'compasses' image in his 'A Valediction: forbidding Mourning'.

If they be two, they are two so
  As stiff twin compasses are two,
Thy soul the fixed foot, makes no show
  To move, but doth, if th'other do.

And though it in the centre sit,
  Yet when the other far doth roam,

It leans, and hearkens after it,
    And grows erect, as that comes home.

Such wilt thou be to me, who must
    Like th'other foot, obliquely run;
Thy firmness makes my circle just,
    And makes me end, where I begun.

This has been praised as the expression of all-transcendent love. A quick and simple feminist reading, however, would point out how the compasses actually celebrate woman's immobility and fixity in 'the centre', and man's freedom to move and still be loved. It is the male 'foot' that roams: the female can only lean in sympathy with it. Katherine Philips's response to these lines seems to involve the same analysis. 'To my dearest Lucasia' celebrates love between women. It describes an emblem that could be used to represent the relationship, and uses an image of compasses to describe equal freedom and equal control.

The compasses that stand above
Express this great immortal love:
For friends, like them, can prove this true,
They are, and yet they are not, two.

And in their posture is expressed
Friendship's exalted interest:
Each follows where the other leans,
And what each does, this other means.

And as when one foot does stand fast,
And t'other circles seeks to cast,
The steady part does regulate
And make the wanderer's motion straight:

So friends are only two in this,
T'reclaim each other when they miss:
For whosoe'er will grossly fall,
Can never be a friend at all.

Katherine Philips's poetry provides a developing definition of female friendship. One of its most fundamental characteristics – and one which by implication must exclude men from this greatest intimacy with women – is that women friends are so alike that they mirror one another. This idea appears explicitly, for instance, in 'A Friend'.

Thick waters show no images of things;
    Friends are each other's mirrors, and should be
Clearer than crystal or the mountain springs,
    And free from clouds, design or flattery,
For vulgar souls no part of friendship share:
Poets and friends are born to what they are. (p. 94)

A comparison with a poem addressed to her husband, 'To my dearest

Antenor, on his Parting', illustrates how very different this essentially equal relationship is from marriage. Philips-as-wife is her husband's image, passively reflecting him. There is no equal mirroring here.

> And besides this thou shalt in me survey
> Thyself reflected while thou art away . . .
> So in my breast thy picture drawn shall be.
> My guide, life, object, friend, and destiny:
> And none shall know, though they employ their wit,
> Which is the right Antenor, thou, or it. (pp. 76–7)

Even though she calls Antenor her friend, the relationship defined here is quite different from the one she celebrates with women who are close to her.

Orinda's most extended exposition of the argument that women's friendship has a special and superior quality is the poem 'To my Excellent Lucasia, on our Friendship'. This moves from the opening 'I' of the first stanzas to the exultant, united 'we' of the final one. The friendship, through mirroring and recognition of similarity, gives joy and peace that is found in no other relationship – certainly not in the 'bridegroom's mirth'.

> I did not live until this time
>   Crowned my felicity,
> When I could say without a crime,
>   I am not thine, but thee.
>
> This carcase breathed, and walked, and slept,
>   So that the world believed
> There was a soul the motions kept:
>   But they were all deceived.
>
> For as a watch by art is wound
>   To motion, such was mine:
> But never had Orinda found
>   A soul till she found thine;
>
> Which now inspires, cures and supplies,
>   And guides my darkened breast:
> For thou art all that I can prize,
>   My joy, my life, my rest.
>
> No bridegroom's nor crown-conqueror's mirth
>   To mine compared can be:
> They have but pieces of this earth,
>   I've all the world in thee.
>
> Then let our flames still light and shine,
>   And no false fear control,
> As innocent as our design,
>   Immortal as our soul. (pp. 51–2)

Marriage contains elements of duty and compulsion. Struggling to resolve the conflict between wifely submission and passionate friendship, and accept that she cannot change her situation, Katherine Philips asks her dearest friend to be patient with her imperfections. She reflects on the divine essence of friendship, claiming that in its origins the relationship is superhuman. True friendship should consist of harmony and freedom, and she laments that, in her human imperfection, she is seeking to control and possess her friend. In a world where so many imperative demands were made of them, women seek, she says, to allow perfect liberty to one another in this most perfect of relationships. Having described the state she aspires to, she sighs,

> But what's all this to me, who live to be
> Disprover of my own morality?
> And he that knew my unimproved soul,
> Would say I meant all friendship to control
> But bodies move in time, and so must minds;
> And though th'attempt no easy progress finds,
> Yet quit me not, lest I should desperate grow,
> And to such friendship add some patience now. (pp. 58–9)

The range and themes of Katherine Philips's poetry show the ways in which a woman whose religious and political allegiances placed her outside the sisterhood of the radical sects could negotiate a space of autonomy for herself and her female friends. She was a tremendously important reference point for contemporary High Church women. Her translation *Pompey* was greeted with overwhelming joy by an Irishwoman who signs herself simply 'Philo-Philippa'. The terms of this praise illustrate the fact that Orinda's spirited defence of women's friendship was not lost on the women of her times.

> Let the male poets their male Phoebus choose,
> Thee I invoke, Orinda, for my muse;
> He could but force a branch, Daphne her tree
> Most freely offers to her sex and thee,
> And says to verse, so unconstrained as yours,
> Her laurel freely comes, your fame secures:
> And men no longer shall with ravished bays
> Crown their forced poems by as forced a praise.
>   Thou glory of our sex, envy of men,
> Who are both pleased and vexed with thy bright pen:
> Its lustre doth entice their eyes to gaze,
> But men's sore eyes cannot endure its rays;
> It dazzles and surprises so with light,
> To find a noon where they expected night:
> A woman translate *Pompey*! which the famed
> Corneille with such art and labour framed!
> To whose close version the wits club their sense,

And a new lay poetic SMEC springs thence!
Yes, that bold work a woman dares translate,
Not to provoke, nor yet to fear men's hate.
Nature doth find that she hath erred too long,
And now resolves to recompense that wrong.
Phoebus to Cynthia must his beams resign,
The rule of day and wit's now feminine.

That sex, which heretofore was not allowed
To understand more than a beast, or crowd;
Of which problems were made, whether or no
Women had souls; but to be damned, if so;
Whose highest contemplation could not pass,
In men's esteem, no higher than the glass;
And all the painful labours of their brain,
Was only how to dress and entertain:
Or, if they ventured to speak sense, the wise
Made that, and speaking ox, like prodigies.
From these thy more than masculine pen hath reared
Our sex; first to be praised, next to be feared.
And by the same pen forced, men now confess,
To keep their greatness, was to make us less . . .
Ask me not then, why jealous men debar
Our sex from books in peace, from arms in war;
It is because our parts will soon demand
Tribunals for our persons, and command.

Shall it be our reproach, that we are weak,
And cannot fight, nor as the schoolmen speak?
Even men themselves are neither strong not wise,
If limbs and parts they do not exercise.

Trained up to arms, we Amazons have been,
And Spartan virgins strong as Spartan men:
Breed women but as men, and they are these;
Whilst Sybarite men are women by their ease . . .

That noble friendship brought thee to our coast,
We thank Lucasia, and thy courage boast.
Death in each wave could not Orinda fright,
Fearless she acts that friendship she did write:
Which manly virtue to their sex confined,
Thou rescuest to confirm our softer mind;
For there's required (to do that virtue right)
Courage, as much in friendship as in fight.
The dangers we despise, doth this truth prove,
Though boldly we not fight, we boldly love . . .
Thus, as the sun, you in your course shine on,
Unmoved with all our admiration:

Flying above the praise you shun, we see
Wit is still higher by humility.[17]

Philips's poetry was also an essential reference point for women poets who followed her. Many of those writing later in the seventeenth century, including Aphra Behn, Anne Killigrew, Ephelia and Jane Barker, refer to her as their guide. In the post-Restoration world, where acceptable female behaviour was again being narrowly defined, she was an important example that it was possible for a woman to be praised for her writing, as long as she was sufficiently modest in her claims. While helping to open a pathway into print for women, therefore, she also staked it out as a strait and narrow way. Through the critics' appraisals, 'the matchless Orinda' became the scourge of such followers as the 'incomparable Astrea', Aphra Behn.

COURTLY LOVE CONVENTIONS

The writers who followed Katherine Philips, although they made frequent reference to her name, did not share her emphasis on women's friendship. Their poems, by contrast, addressed the vagaries of romantic love between men and women as it was described (or constructed) by courtly love conventions. In taking this as their subject-matter, they were at one level pursuing a quite acceptable course. A woman's main task, according to this male poetic orthodoxy, was to love and be lovable. A woman writing about love, therefore, was addressing herself to the issue that should be central to her existence. Composing such poetry, especially if it were to be set to music, was a sufficiently respectable female occupation for several examples of songs by otherwise unknown women writers to be included in Aphra Behn's collections of airs and lyrics in 1685 and 1692.[18] The 'several hands' whom she chose to include in her 1685 *Miscellany* included a Mrs Taylor, author of three songs, and at least one 'lady of quality' who wrote a song and made a translation of some verses by Sappho. The *Miscellany Poems* collected in 1692 include one poem 'made by a fair lady who is since dead'.[19] All of these are love poems in some sense, rejoicing in or lamenting the lot of women in love.

Male love poetry, in a combination of courtly love and neo-Platonic conventions, assumed that the prime or even sole function of a woman was, through her virtue or yielding beauty, to act as a link to heaven for the man, or at least to provide heavenly delights. (The Restoration court rakes and ballad-writers frequently equated this with purely physical pleasures.) Traditionally, women were also divided into two categories, the angelic and desirable mistress (beloved) being contrasted favourably with the rest of her sex. The convention included fear that the beloved would lapse into the more usual female pattern, and prove unyielding or unfaithful. A sorrowful plaint and angry railing against the mistress who has not played the role assigned to her was therefore a common subject of such poetry.

The close relationship between this reproof of an individual fickle mistress and a bitter hatred of all women is shown extremely clearly in Robert Gould's poem *Love Given O're*, 1682. The occasion for this poem is said in its opening lines to be the infidelity of 'Silvia' (a conventional name for the beloved). It opens lamenting her desertion of him, but swiftly becomes a diatribe against womankind. The memory of Eve is evoked as proof of women's evil, hell is said to be full of the female sex (who, Lucifer is warned, are no doubt plotting revolution), and femininity equated with lasciviousness.[20]

The writings of contemporary female poets show that women who were subjected to such glorifying addresses from men were not blind to the limitations and implications of these male conventions. Sarah Fige takes issue directly with Robert Gould, making an overt challenge to the ideas promoted in *Love Given O're*. Ephelia both inverts the conventions and shows how miserable they actually are. In writing songs for her plays, Aphra Behn composes poems which, when taken out of their dramatic contexts, appear wholly bound by male thought structures; elsewhere, however, she exposes and rejects the whole framework. Anne Killigrew abjures love altogether, repelled by male misogyny, and retreats into an avowal of virtue. Jane Barker also prefers singleness to marriage, recommending that women acquire practical skills to make themselves socially useful in their independence.

In her later *Collected Poems* in 1706, Sarah Fige Egerton recalls her writing of *The Female Advocate*, and her father's response to it.

> But ah! my poetry did fatal prove,
> And robbed me of a tender father's love;
> (I thought that only men, who writ for fame,
> Or sung lewd stories, to unlawful flame,
> Were punished for their proud or wanton crime.
> But children, too, must suffer if they'll rhyme.)[21]

Her judgement is acute. While it was permissible for a man to twist poetic love conventions to produce the savagely anti-woman sentiments expressed by Gould and others, it was extraordinarily shocking for a woman to be so bold as to dispute with such men in print. Perhaps if she had been older than her fourteen years in 1686 Sarah Fige would have already learnt this lesson thoroughly enough to have not been so audacious. As it is, her text boldly declares in its title page that it is 'written by a lady in vindication of her sex'. This twenty-four-page pamphlet appears free from any apologetic male assessment, and is addressed by its author 'to the reader'.

I might enlarge this preface with the common excuse of writers for the
publication of their books, viz. the importunities of her obliging friends: but what
it was put me upon the publication of this, I am not bound to give the reader an
account of; but I think the debauchery which I now answer, is a sufficient
warrant for this appearing of mine. (1686 edn)

It is clear that she has deliberately submitted her rebuttal of Gould and
his ilk to the press.

By the following year, however, when Fige brought out her second
edition of this work, her account of the circumstances of its initial
appearance had changed significantly. The response to her boldness had
been sufficiently sharp for her to revise the text, in some cases making
more than cosmetic changes. One of the most significant of these is the
fact that she denied having been so unfeminine as to have had the text
published by her own volition. In 1687 the passage quoted above was
omitted, and in its place a more apologetic piece inserted.

I might, if I pleased, make an excuse for the publication of my book, as many
others do; but then, perhaps, the world might think 'twas only a feigned
unwillingness: but when I found I could not hinder the publication, I set a
resolution to bear patiently the censures of the world, for I expected its severity,
the first copy being so ill writ, and so much blotted, that it could scarce be read;
and they that had the charge of it, in the room of blots, writ what they pleased,
and much different from my intention. (1687 edn)

She did not wholly withdraw her charges against Gould in this new
preface. But she did reflect that it was not proper for her to have made
public opinions she might reasonably have expressed in private. For this
reason, she says, she has amended the first edition to omit things which
'though they might pass well enough in private, they were not fit to be
exposed to every eye'.

It is interesting, therefore, to see what changes Fige had in fact made in
her second edition. Certainly her complaints about the standard of printing in the first edition seem justified, as the poetry of the 1687 version is
in many cases superior. Either her printer had misread her text in 1686,
as she claimed, or she had in the meantime redrafted whole passages. In
other respects, however, Fige had to make more radical changes to her
poem. These did not wholly change her general argument: she still
disputes Gould's key assertions, saying that women cannot be damned
for all time because of events in the Garden of Eden, pointing out that, if
anything, Adam was more guilty than Eve, and that it was a woman,
Mary, who brought salvation into the world. Fige also compares men's
cursing of women for inconstancy with devils' complaints against hell:
men debauch women and then blame them for it, just as devils created
the hell that they lament. It is the masculine sex, she says, that delights in
unfettered sensuality, for all their charges about women's lust. Women

find no delight in such behaviour, but would naturally require marriage first. (We need to remember that in a society where the ignominy of an illegitimate birth was carried by the woman, this position made perfect sense.) The world is changing, she continues, and true virtue is no longer valued. Women are the losers, now no longer permitted to live in a moral fashion, since certain reprehensible kinds of behaviour have become a mark of 'good breeding'.

> But now the scene is altered, and those who
> Were esteemed modest by a blush or two,
> Are represented quite another way,
> Worse than mock-verse doth the most solid play.
> She that takes pious precepts for her rule,
> Is thought, by some, a kind of ill-bred fool;
> They would have all bred up in Venus' school.
> (1686 and 1687 edns, p. 7)

She continues by detailing cases of women in history and in myth who saved their husbands' lives, or who committed suicide rather than risk rape and dishonour. She immediately adds, in the light of this grim recital, that she does not think that all women need be married. The single state, for some at least, is best.

> And I would praise them more, only I fear,
> If I should do it, 'twould make me appear
> Unto the world much fonder than I be
> Of that same state, for I love liberty.
> Nor do I think there's a necessity
> For all to enter beds, like Noah's beast
> Into his ark. I would have some released
> From the dear cares of that same lawful state;
> But I'll not dictate, I'll leave all that to fate.

This is a most careful and modest rejection of marriage, but is nonetheless a rejection of it in favour of 'liberty'.

Fige's poem ends with an attack on the very basis of Gould's arguments. There are disturbances in the land, she says, and men are trying to blame women for them. In these troubled years of the mid-1680s, when it looked as if revolution might once more break out, it is curious to reflect on the full import of these lines. I have argued that the belittling of women undertaken by the Restoration court, reducing them just to 'sex', came in part from a desire to obliterate the public presence won by female radical sectaries. Women's 'natural' evil, bringing chaos into the world (like Eve), could be pointed to as the cause of rebellion. Fige seems to be making an observation on the general state of affairs in the country when she says 'Nay, woman now is made the scapegoat, and/ 'Tis she must bear the sins of all the land' (1686 and 1687 edns, p. 23). An earlier generation of women had confronted evil in the world by going out to change society. By 1686, female writers were angrily advocating a retreat from the public world into higher feminine values. Some women might err, Fige says, but as a sex they are superior to men.

> There's not a history which doth not show
> Man's pride, ambition and his falsehood too . . .
> But I believe there's not a priest that can
> Make an atonement for one single man,
> Nay, it is well if he himself can bring
> An humble, pious heart for th'offering.[22]

If Fige's general argument survives intact into the second edition, some sections are toned down, or even omitted, to make the text less shockingly unfeminine. Several passages are cut from the 1687 version: passages which make pointed reference to specific instances of male profligacy. It is unseemly enough for a woman to comment on history and biblical events. To make sharp judgements on the behaviour of contemporary men was altogether too much. Key lines occur when she writes about women who have bravely defied their male seducers or rapists. Her recital of past women's courage in this respect is, in the 1686 edition, followed by a quatrain that states that such attacks are continuing, but this is omitted in 1687. A single year of public responses, and of her father's rage, had been sufficient to teach Sarah Fige that she could only go so far in her defence of virtue. Such references to the contemporary world had to be omitted if an image of higher feminine honour was to be maintained.

We do not know who Ephelia was. Halkett and Laing in their dictionary of anonymous and pseudonymous works quote a manuscript suggestion by Henry Wheatley that she might be one 'Joan Philips'.[23] That is all the information given on this score, and for the moment the trail ends there. Until a more confident identification of the author is made, it seems wisest to call her by the name she used herself: Ephelia. Some kind of connection with the court, if a tenuous one, is indicated by the poems themselves. The book is dedicated to Mary Stuart, the Duchess of Richmond and Lennox, who was appointed a Lady of the Bedchamber to the Queen in 1662, and the first poem is addressed to the king 'presented to His Sacred Majesty, on the discovery of the plot'. This poem had already been published the previous year as an anonymous broadside 'written by a gentlewoman', and it presumably helped prepare the ground for acceptance of the *Female Poems*.[24] Her explicit alliance with Charles's policies is evidenced here, as it is in her elegy lamenting the death of Gilbert Sheldon, the Archbishop of Canterbury until his decease in 1677, and in her later broadside 'Advice to his Grace'. Published in

1681, this urges the Duke of Monmouth to disentangle himself from plots against his royal father.[25]

Ephelia several times refers to herself as young and single. Her poems addressed to her various friends suggest the existence of a circle conceived to be similar to that established by Katherine Philips, and her choice of a pseudonym with a pastoral ring to it adds to this impression. In her poem to Eugenia she laments her inability to rhyme as sweetly as Orinda, and one of her verses to J.G. welcomes his appointment as steward to a club known as 'The Society' (pp. 87–8; 14). A particular debt to Jeremy Taylor's reflections on friendship, which were dedicated to Katherine Philips, is also indicated in 'To Phylocles, inviting him to Friendship' (p. 86).

Female Poems appeared in 1679, and what purports to be a second edition, 'with large additions', came out in 1682. This 'second edition' is in fact a reissue of the first with new title page, which suggests that the stationer might have had difficulty selling the book.[26] His solution to this was the additional material: none of it, in all probability, by Ephelia, despite the title page claims. The 1679 edition, including its dedicatory verse, is made up of sixty-five poems. In 1682, the final page is cancelled and a new gathering added, making a further thirty-six poems in all. These are all songs, and most of them can be traced to plays or songbooks published in the few years before 1682 (or found in later collections attributed to other authors). This is true in a sufficiently high number of cases to make it highly probable that the stationer, James Courtney, took them at will from such sources to bolster his sales.[27] One of his major sources was the 1680 editions of the poems of John Wilmot, Earl of Rochester. Scholarship on these poems has shown that, although the first thirty-eight poems in Rochester's collection are his work, or closely concern him, the remainder are a miscellany. David Vieth's researches indicate that such wrongful attribution of poems was commonplace at that time: the point was to find a market, and the wishes of an author were of little significance in a society where copyright belonged to the stationer. James Courtney does at least make a minimal attempt to fit his extra poems into the mould established by Ephelia. The most offensive poems from the Rochester canon are omitted, and those adopted are sometimes changed to make them rather more ladylike, or less overtly woman-hating.[28]

The poems in the 1679 edition delight in experimenting with the formal possibilities of verse. Ephelia writes many songs with varied rhyme-schemes and line lengths, and her attention to the fine detail of the possibilities of patterning language is also suggested by the inclusion of four acrostic poems in her book, all apparently written around the names of women friends.[29] It is possible that she also wrote a play, *The Pair-*

Royal of Coxcombs, since *Female Poems* includes the prologue, epilogue and two songs she composed for its performance (pp. 16–21).

It has been suggested that *Female Poems* traces a purely personal story of the poet's unrequited love for her Strephon.[30] This man, identified as 'J.G.' in her poems addressed to him, proves to be unfaithful to her, marrying for money during a trip to Africa. The fact that she had a particular man in mind, and that his initials were indeed 'J.G.', is indicated in one of her laments. She has been in love for four years, she says, and still cannot find either happiness or mental quiet. She cannot even distract herself from her obsession for a brief period.

> Sometimes with books I would divert my mind,
> But nothing there but Js and Gs I find:
> Sometimes to ease my grief, my pen I take,
> But it no letters but JG will make. (p. 29)

She also describes his physical appearance, castigating herself for being so devoted to a plain-looking, ill-mannered creature who is twice her age, and certainly in no sense her superior.

> And yet I love this false, this worthless man,
> With all the passion that a woman can;
> Dote on his imperfections, though I spy
> Nothing to love; I love, and know not why. (p. 58)[31]

To read this poetry simply as an innocent outpouring of feminine grief, however, is to overlook that artistry Ephelia employs. In fact, she uses her particular experiences as a source for poetry that explores and reveals the more general implications for women of the whole courtly love motif. Even in her choice of 'Strephon' as the name for her beloved, she gives a certain universality to her writings. This name seems to be a male counterpart to the commonplace 'Phillis' or 'Silvia'. David Vieth records the fact that Rochester was often referred to as 'Strephon', and mentions with some surprise finding the same name being applied to Carr Scroop. Aphra Behn, Mrs Taylor, Anne Killigrew and Jane Barker all use the same label for their poetic lovers, and other examples could no doubt be found.

A consistent ironic distance is kept between the poet Ephelia and the figure Ephelia who plays a part in these songs. 'Beneath a Spreading Willow's Shade' opens with a description of Ephelia, who sits making a garland for Strephon's hair, unaware that he is off gallivanting with another woman. Unwittingly, he approaches the willow where Ephelia is seated, while 'boasting of the favours she [Ephelia] bestowed'. The poem ends with its heroine wondering on behalf of all women whether love must always involve being treated with scorn.

> The angry nymph did rudely tear
> Her garland first, and then her hair,
> To hear herself abused:
> Oh Love! she said, is it the fate
> Of all that love, to meet with hate,
> And be like me, unkindly used? (p. 33)

This third-person description of Ephelia's dilemma, in imagery that exploits the conventional pastoral setting of such poetry, induces the reader to reflect on the general situation, rather than to concentrate solely on the personal circumstances of the poet. In another song, 'Ephelia while her flocks were far', the shepherdess is shown neglecting her work through her obsession with Strephon. Her sheep stray and are eaten by wolves, and her earlier proud economic independence is lost.[32]

These love poems, therefore, are not simply descriptive of a particular personal experience, but are symbolic reworkings of such a relationship into language that gives her own affairs a more general application. The pastoral figure Ephelia represents all women involved in the courtly love mystique. The book is justly entitled *Female Poems*: the poet speaks from a quintessentially female position, addressing herself to a problem – love – that is perceived by her society to be her most proper concern. Exactly because she writes from a female viewpoint, rather than a male one, however, Ephelia challenges the accepted evaluation of this convention.

The images and patterns of thought of the courtly love tradition, as changed by the more specifically lascivious interests of Restoration male poets, were common currency in the circles Ephelia moved in. Many of her poems make what at first appears to be a simple reversal of male and female roles usual in such verses. In 'Love's First Approach' she describes herself exhibiting all the physical symptoms of blushing, trembling, panting and giddiness that normally characterise a man who is falling in love. This is followed by 'The Change or Miracle' (pp. 8–9), which finds her longing for a kind look or kiss, and him playing the part of the cruel refuser. When she writes 'To J.G. in Absence' (p. 15), she refers to the fact that she has refused 'preferment' in order to be faithful to her vows to him. In 'To J.G.' (pp. 32–3) and 'A Lover's State' (pp. 62–4) it is men, not women, who are characterised as inconstant in their love. As each of these poems develops, however, it casts new light on the emotions or characteristics described. The bodily symptoms described at love's first approach, it transpires, are not the result of becoming hopelessly besotted, as they are in custom. On self-examination, Ephelia finds that her 'change' is due to the fact that, despite herself, her eyes have betrayed to Strephon her love for him. Once he is armed with this knowledge – and it is just such information as this that the male poets sue for – he has her in his power, and she becomes his 'willing victim'.

Virtue of Necessity

From the very beginning of her presentation of this theme, Ephelia shows that for a woman, falling in love entails loss of freedom and rationality. When first falling for Strephon, she resigns herself to submission.

> Great Love, I yield; send no more darts in vain,
> I am already fond of my soft chain;
> Proud of my fetters, so pleased with my state
> That I the very thoughts of freedom hate. (p. 7)

The next stage in the story, recorded in 'The Change or Miracle', might be expected to be an alteration in the beloved. In the conventional pattern, the poet longs for a kind look, a miraculous transition being made when the loved-one agrees. Ephelia's poem of that name, while wooing for a kiss, is actually centred on a different concern. After opening with the remark 'What miracles this childish god has wrought!/ Things strange beyond belief!', she explains the cause of her astonishment. By falling in love she has lost her dignity and self-respect. A man could lament the cruelty of his mistress but still have power and freedom in the world and the alternative sources of fulfilment that his maleness gave him. Perhaps this is why, finally, male poetic complaints about unyielding mistresses are so easily converted to scornful railing against the worthlessness of womankind. A woman's life's meaning, and her identity, were supposed to come through her commitment to the right man. If she failed to attract him, she had nowhere to turn. Suing for what is, at best, an 'empty bliss', she is responded to with disdain and disrespect.

> For my proud victor does my tears neglect,
> Smiles at my sighs, treats me with disrespect,
> And if I do complain, with frowns I'm checked.
>
> Though all I sue for, be the empty bliss
> Of a kind look, or at the most a kiss,
> Yet he's so cruel to deny me this.
>
> Before my passion struck my reason blind,
> Such generosity dwelt in my mind,
> I cared for none, and yet to all was kind.
>
> But now I tamely bend, and sue in vain,
> To one that takes delight t'increase my pain,
> And proudly does me and my love disdain. (pp. 8–9)

Her verses, in fact, are not a simple inversion of standard male complaints and yearnings, but a specifically female transformation of such themes. A man could bemoan his mistress's inconstancy, but the truly unfaithful woman would meet with scorn and calumny in a society where so much was invested in female sexual virtue. The Restoration court had a reputation for lechery, but the 'freedom' involved was not really the right of women. The sexually 'free' woman would be mocked and insulted by court satirists, and might be confined to the house or banished to the countryside by an outraged husband or father.[33] The court rake might accuse a woman of inconstancy, but the real choice in matters of sexual mores was his, not hers, for all the male poems to the contrary. Ephelia explains that her fear of abandonment by her lover is typical, not peculiar to her alone.

> Men are inconstant, and delight to range,
> Not to gain freedom, but their fetters change:
> And, what a year they did with passion seek,
> Grows troublesome, and nauseous in a week:
> And the poor lady, newly taught to love,
> With grief and horror, sees her man remove. (p. 63)

Ephelia raises the question of where, in such a world, a woman can find a source of pride. At first, she tells Strephon, this came from being loved by him. She found there a proper, womanly pride, the correct counterpart of male delight in warlike pursuits.

> No conquering hero e'er did foes pursue
> With half the pleasure that I took in you;
> No youthful monarch of a glittering crown,
> Or prating coxcomb of a scarlet gown
> Was half so proud, as I was of your love;
> Nor could great Juno's state my envy move,
> While in your heart I thought I reigned in chief (pp. 42–3).

The comparisons made here are clearly heavily ironic, but nonetheless they raise a question: what can replace the delights of being loved by a man? One answer Ephelia proposes is her pride in being a poet. As well as praising 'sweet Orinda's happy strain' (p. 87), she pays more extended homage to Aphra Behn, heralding her command of language and poetic convention (pp. 72–3). As a poet herself, she counsels a 'proud beauty', her own 'acquired parts' offer more security than a mistress's 'fine face'. Do not despise me, she warns.

> Since then my fame's as great as yours is, why
> Should you behold me with a loathing eye?
> If you at me cast a disdainful eye,
> In biting satire I will rage so high,
> Thunder shall pleasant be to what I'll write,
> And you shall tremble at my very sight;
> Warned by your danger, none shall dare again,
> Provoke my pen to write in such a strain. (pp. 54–5)

There is another figure in *Female Poems* who relies entirely on relationships with men. She is Mopsa, Ephelia's dread rival for her Strephon's attention. Ephelia's progress to rejecting an assessment of her own worth based solely on Strephon's estimation of her is made in relation to 'servile Mopsa', 'that ill-looked hag' (p. 42), 'that ugly witch' (p. 80). If a woman like this can interest Strephon, the reasoning goes, then his declared passion for Ephelia is no dependable recommendation. No woman in particular may be signified by 'Mopsa', but it is nonetheless true that Ephelia's attempt to establish her own independence from male esteem is based in part on a manlike defamation of another woman.

Working through the conventions of courtly love, Ephelia leads her female reader to a position where she can understand the misery and degradation of love. She seeks the re-establishment of wise reason in her heart, now that she has regained it from Strephon's grasp.

> Now 'tis my own again, with care and art
> I'll guard each passage that leads to my heart;
> Love shall resign, and reason shall command,
> And care and wisdom sentinels shall stand.[34]

The love poems which occupy the last pages of her book are addressed variously to Coridon and Clovis: they are not the angry, aching laments of the episode with Strephon. Love has become less important than self-respect. Her rebuff to Coridon when he refuses to see her is firm.

> but yet so much my pride
> Surmounts my passion, that now were I tried,
> And th'heart so long I've wished for, prostrate lay
> Before my feet, I'd spurn the toy away. (pp. 93–4)

Female Poems traces a woman's path through the maze of male courtship rituals, presenting to the reader a final alternative, higher set of values.

Aphra Behn was the most prolific woman writer of her age, and her love poems make up only a small part of her oeuvre, which also includes verses on affairs of state, and praises addressed to her patrons and fellow-writers. Her love poetry is built around the common ideas of the day, and the text liberally sprinkled with sighing shepherds and shepherdesses who weepingly lament the cruel effects of Cupid's darts. Some of these, such as 'The Reflection' (*Poems*, 1684), describe a woman's languishings. Others, like the song 'While, Iris, I at distance gaze' (*Miscellany*, 1685), present a conventional male lament on hopeless love. The masculine perspective is so thoroughly worked through in 'The Complaint' (*Poems*, 1684) that the lover's charge that his mistress is his rightful possession appears unmodified by any female demurrer.

> Those smiles and kisses which you give
> Remember Silvia are my due;

> And all the joys my rival does receive
> He ravishes from me not you.

Writing as a dramatist, she presents various points of view. A great many of the poems, however, concentrate on the infidelity of men, and argue inconstancy to be an integral part of masculinity. Like Ephelia, she shows that for a woman, falling in love entails loss of freedom and, crucially, of self-esteem. Repeatedly, the woman who has rejoiced in her immunity to love's charms is forced to succumb. 'Celinda who did love disdain' is one such victim. She goes to cry out against love, only to find that, though she still feels shame, her pride has gone.

> She would have spoke, but shame denied,
> And bid her first consult her pride;
> But soon she found that aid was gone;
> For love alas had left her none:
> Oh how she burns, but 'tis too late,
> For in her eyes she reads her fate.
> (*Poems*, pp. 122–3)

Behn repeatedly declares and enlarges upon the joys of sensuality in a world where men take the initiative and women yield gladly. This view of female sexuality, especially when the idea that women are secretly lustful is added, is quite consistent with the dominant ideology of the day. To travel from this state to the assertion that, if truth were told, women long to be raped is a short and logical step. If a woman's resistance is really sweet coquetry, which can be overcome by using sufficient force to arouse her hidden, lascivious drives, then a world where men rape women is justified and seen as 'natural'. Trapped inside this structure, Aphra Behn can indeed present women as silently welcoming rape. This is the dark fantasy of male power, where men's control of women's lives and very bodies is excused, and even made into an heroic act.

> Had daring Sextus had thy lovely shape,
> The fairest woman living had not died,
> But blest the darkness that secured the rape,
> Suffering her pleasure to have debauched her pride.
> ('To Amyntas', *Lycidus*, pp. 161–3)

The myth that a woman could enjoy being raped is one of the most outrageous and most pervasive lies imposed by patriarchal ideologies. It seems that Aphra Behn could only perceive and write about sexual desire in her poetry within this framework.

She was, however, quite capable of using these themes in a convincingly pro-woman manner. One of her best-known poems is 'The Disappointment' (*Poems*, 1684). Here, too, the woman is described as panting and swooning with longing, as her lover teases, cajoles and forces her into acquiescence. He advances 'without respect or fear' towards the altar 'where rage is calmed, and anger pleased'. The poem builds steadily to a glorious anticlimax, where the gallant proves to be impotent and his mistress far more shocked by this than by any of his 'liberties'. The whole piece is a joke against men's absurd conceit about the male member 'the fabulous Priapus,/ That potent god, as poets feign'.

In some of her poetry, however, Behn could reject the entire pattern and role-play of romantic love. In her poem addressed 'To Alexis, in Answer to his Poem against Fruition', Behn shows how, in the logic of love poetry, woman is damned if she concedes to male desire and damned if she refuses. She speaks on behalf of womankind, calling on her sisters to reject the whole set-up.

> Since man with that inconstancy was born,
> To love the absent, and the present scorn
>   Why do we deck, why do we dress
>   For such a short-lived happiness?
>   Why do we put attraction on,
> Since either way 'tis we must be undone?
>
>   They fly if honour take our part,
>   Our virtue drives 'em o'er the field.
>   We love 'em by too much desert,
>   And oh! they fly us if we yield.
> Ye gods! is there no charm in all the fair
> To fix this wild, this faithless wanderer?
> (*Lycidus*, pp. 129–30)

If women have to be faithful to their lovers or risk being social outcasts or worse, it is only reasonable to require fidelity from men, she argues. She writes 'To Lysander, on some Verses he writ, and asking more for his Heart than 'twas worth' (*Poems*, pp. 109–12), reproving him for wanting to keep a mistress when denying her the right to another lover.

> Be just, my lovely swain, and do not take
>   Freedoms you'll not to me allow;
> Or give Amynta so much freedom back
>   That she may rove as well as you.
>
> Let us then love upon the honest square,
>   Since interest neither have designed.
> For the sly gamester, who ne'er plays me fair,
>   Must trick for trick expect to find.

Aphra Behn's most radical poetic statement on romantic love, however, appears in the work that opens her *Poems* in 1684. 'The Golden Age' is a translation from a French source, but its appearance here shows that Behn considered its thoughts her own.[35] The poem takes as its central concept the idea of 'honour', the stress on female chastity which was so pivotal in contemporary assessments of, and injunctions to, the female sex. With the loss of the innocence of the Golden Age, the poem argues, women have been confined to the narrow restraints of 'honour', which forces them to play the part of wounding lovers with their eyes while withholding the cure; and causes them to flush and tremble not with desire, but with shame. The poet calls for a return to the first happy state, a world without kings or religions, and without such false distortions of desire.

> Oh cursed honour! thou who first didst damn
> A woman to the sin of shame;
> Honour! that robst us of our gust,
> Honour! that hindered mankind first,
> At love's eternal spring to squench his amorous thirst.

The poem calls for the abandonment of this whole framework, so that people can fulfil themselves in a manner conceived of as consistent with their basic nature. The poet wants an end to dissembling, an end to denial of physical passion.

> Be gone! and let the Golden Age again
> Assume its glorious reign;
> Let the young wishing maid confess
> What all your arts would keep concealed:
> The mystery will be revealed,
> And she in vain denies, what we can guess,
> She only shows the jilt to teach man how,
> To turn the false artillery on the cunning foe.

The poem ends with a warning to women, in the person of Silvia, not to be duped into depending on their physical beauty to provide them with the power that male love poetry protests about. Such power is fleeting. It is in women's best interests to abandon such relationships altogether.

Anne Killigrew's *Poems* were brought out by her father shortly after her death. Since the book was advertised in *The Observator* on 2 November 1685, it seems likely that it actually appeared earlier than the title page date of 1686.[36] Some of the poetry, at least, had earlier circulated in manuscript. A poem she addresses 'To my Lord Colrane' records her gratitude at his complimentary reaction to her verses (p. 49). This must have been particularly welcome to her. 'Upon the saying that my Verses were made by Another' reveals that her authorship had been questioned, due to the fact, she says, that she had rejected 'gold' for 'purer fame': that is, had opted for manuscript circulation rather than selling her works for publication.

Her self-portrait is prefixed to the book, and her skill as a painter is mentioned by John Dryden in his laudatory poem which prefaces her book. The general argument of his verses, however, presents her not as a conscious artist, but as the passive recipient of her father's abilities: she is informed 'Thy father was transfused into thy blood'. In Dryden's 'complimentary' assessment, the products of her mind were not truly hers, but the work of 'nature' in her, not her art. His poem does, however, draw attention to the central problem addressed by Killigrew. The dissoluteness of the Restoration court was producing a lifestyle and a poetry that was lurid and offensive. In an interesting and significant turn of phrase, he accuses himself and his male associates of having prostituted the muse.

> O gracious God! How far have we
> Prophaned thy heavenly gift of poesy
> Made prostitute and profligate the muse,
> Debased to each obscene and impious use,
> Whose harmony was first ordained above
> For tongues of angels, and for hymns of love?

Anne Killigrew was a Maid of Honour to Mary of Modena, the Duchess of York. She was therefore part of a household identified as opposing the profligacy of King Charles and his court. Killigrew responded to the disparagement of women that this reduction of her sex to a mere tool for men's physical pleasure involved, by abjuring sensuality altogether. In some respects this can be regarded as a defeat, a retreat from a right to involvement in such concerns, into a feminine purity wholly dominated by concern for chastity. On the other hand, though, it could be perceived as a rebellion against male baseness. Anne Killigrew was not concerned to preserve her reputation for her husband's sake – she had none – nor for her father's, but for herself.

The structure of the opening of her *Poems* can be seen to act out just such a withdrawal. The first poem, 'Alexandreis', is a fragment, left unfinished, Killigrew's editor (her father?) tells us, because 'this young lady' was not yet 'equal to so great a work' (*Poems*, p. 5). It is certainly the case that 'Alexandreis' has a noble theme, and that its apparent subject-matter, the conquests of Alexander the Great, would normally be considered beyond the scope of a gentle poetess. However, although the poem opens by praising Alexander as 'the man that never equal knew' (implicitly, thereby, denying notions of general male superiority), the reader's attention is swiftly deflected to women. These enter the text surreptitiously, as what at first glance appears to be a depiction of Alexander's troops turns into something different.

> Dire scarlet plumes adorned their haughty crests,
> And crescent shields did shade their shining breasts,
> A bow and quiver rattle by their side;
> Their hands a knotty well-tried spear did bear,

Jocund they seemed, and quite devoid of fear.
These warlike virgins were. (pp. 3–4)

The poem breaks off at the point that the Amazons' leader, Thalestris, steps forward to address Alexander. It is as if Anne Killigrew could not break through any further social bounds.

In her next poem, 'To the Queen' (pp. 6–8), Killigrew says she has turned her attention to a much greater subject than the warfare that was the ostensible theme of 'Alexandreis': 'Victories, laurels, conquered kings/ Took place among inferior things' (p. 7). She accepts and welcomes the idea of withdrawing from the world to concern herself solely with more feminine matters. More can be achieved through virtuous womanly influence than through warfare, she says.

No, give me prowess, that with charms
Of grace and goodness, not with harms,
Erects a throne i'th'inward parts,
And rules men's wills, but with their hearts. (pp. 7–8)

In the context of the recent upheavals of the revolution, it is easy to read these remarks as being addressed as much to the likes of Hester Biddle and Anna Trapnel (see Chapter One) as they are concerned with Amazons. Women cannot and should not interfere with such matters, in the view of the Restoration courtier. Her rejection of Alexander and Thalestris as a theme is also a refusal of Cromwell and his more radical allies.

No more I'll praise on thee bestow,
Who to ill deeds their glories owe;
Who build their Babels of renown,
Upon the poor oppressed crown. (p. 7)

As a royalist, she is wholly opposed to the overthrow of the monarchy that was wrought by an earlier generation. Michael Heyd has shown how the concept of 'enthusiasm' was used against all radical, and even liberal, thought after the Restoration to disaffect people from earlier alliances. The egalitarian prophets of rebellion were dismissed as crazy 'enthusiasts', whose ideas and lifestyles must be rejected if a stable and happy kingdom were to be re-established.[37] This idea occurs in key passages in Killigrew's poetry, as she commits herself to the calm and even rule of reason. 'The Miseries of Man', for instance, ends with an appeal to reason to take control of her emotions, using language that might also be applied to the management of the state.

For shame then raise thyself as from a sleep,
The long neglected reins let Reason keep,
The chariot mount, and use both lash and bit,
Nobly resolve, and thou wilt firmly sit:

> Fierce Anger, boggling Fear, Pride prancing still,
> Bounds-hating Hope, Desire which nought can fill
> Are stubborn all, but thou mayst give them law;
> Th'are hard-mouthed horses, but they well can draw.
> Lash on, and the well governed chariot drive,
> Till thou a victor at the goal arrive,
> Where the free soul does all her burden leave,
> And joys commensurate to herself receive. (p. 42)

Personal happiness and salvation have become synonymous with abandonment of the passions of both love and rebellion.

'The Miseries of Man' is also of interest because its narrator is a young nymph who at the beginning of the poem retreats into a grotto. This imagery originates in the courtly love tradition. The important change, however, is that in Killigrew's poem the nymph speaks of wide-ranging matters of life and death, rather than withdrawing there to lament some lost love. The retreat, for Killigrew, is one that is away from the uncertainties of civil war, and also from the thing that replaced it: the vice of Charles II's court. Her poem 'To the Queen' describes Mary as the firm proponent of virtue's cause, valiantly surviving despite the attacks made on her. Although this clearly has particular contemporary referents – she mentions attempts being made to banish Mary for her Catholicism – there is also a more general revulsion at immorality at stake. Her references to masks and ulcerous faces conjure up images of the ravages wrought by venereal disease.

> How dare bold vice unmasked walk,
> And like a giant proudly stalk?
> When virtue's so exalted seen,
> Armed and triumphant in the queen?
> How does its ulcerous face appear
> When heavenly beauty is so near?

She conceives herself as the dove confined in Noah's ark, sheltering from the deluge, awaiting the day when the floods will recede, as God has promised. This is the image that is echoed in her last printed poem, which is unfinished, where she calls on her soul to leave behind the dross of daily life.

> Arise my dove, from midst of pots arise,
> Thy sullied habitation leave,
> To dust no longer cleave,
> Unworthy they of heaven that will not view the skies.
> Thy native beauty reassume.
> Prune each neglected plume,
> Till more than silver white.
> Than burnished gold more bright,
> Thus ever ready stand to take thy eternal flight.

For Anne Killigrew, writing poetry is an escape from the confines of sexual exploitation. Her three 'Pastoral Dialogues' all use this form which is usually preoccupied with love and wooing to address quite different questions. The first of these consists of Dorinda's attempt to wean her beloved Alexis from his devotion to Lycoris (whose name, of course, signifies 'lust'). She offers to write poetry for him if he will devote himself to her virgin purity and abandon his obsession with a woman who is unchaste (p. 8). In the second 'Pastoral Dialogue' the courtship is performed by a man, Amintor. His shepherdess at first listens tolerantly while he assures her that he loves her for her piety, and will not desert her as other men have left their beloveds. She firmly refuses him, however, and sends him on his way: 'Shepherd, no more: enough it is that I/ Thus long to love, have listened patiently' (p. 62). The last of these dialogues has a sage as its main speaker, who sets out in no uncertain terms that women are more endangered by love than men are. Once she is in love, she loses power over herself and falls under a man's sway. Far better to abandon passion altogether, and to keep herself constrained by the gentle bands of reason.

> Remember when you love, from that same hour
> Your peace you put into your lover's power:
> From that same hour from him you laws receive,
> And as he shall ordain, you joy, or grieve,
> Hope, fear, laugh, weep; Reason aloof does stand,
> Disabled both to act, and to command.
> Oh cruel fetters! rather wish to feel
> On your soft limbs, the galling weight of steel;
> Rather to bloody wounds oppose your breast.
> No ill, by which the body can be pressed
> You will so sensible a torment find
> As shackles on your captived mind.
> The mind from heaven its high descent did draw,
> And brooks uneasily any other law
> Than what from Reason dictated shall be.
> Reason, a kind of inmate deity,
> Which only can adapt to ev'ry soul
> A yoke so fit and light, that the control
> All liberty excells; so sweet a sway,
> The same 'tis to be happy, and obey;
> Commands so wise, and with rewards so dressed,
> That the according soul replies 'I'm blessed'. (pp. 69–70)

Jane Barker was a Catholic spinster who, in the eighteenth century, went on to become a popular novelist, earning just sufficient money to support herself.[38] Like Anne Killigrew (and like the *Eliza's Babes* poet before them), she celebrates in her poetry the freedom entailed in singleness. In her *Poetical Recreations*, 1688, in a poem ostensibly decrying the 'charms of poetry', it is the practices of male misogynous writers that preoccupy her. Like Dryden, she abhors the muses 'now they're all grown prostitutes'. The poets responsible for this

> make their verse imbibe the crimes
> And the lewd follies too o'th'times;
> Who think all wit consists in ranting,
> And virtuous love in wise gallanting:
> And thousand sorts of fools, like these,
> Make love and virtue what they please:
> And yet as silly as they show,
> Are favourites o'th'muses now. (pp. 95–6)

In one of several poems against marriage, she portrays spinsterhood as a nearly angelic state, permitting virtue and moderation in all things. This is not its only advantage, however. It also denotes liberation from 'men's almost omnipotent amours' (p. 12): a choice of phrasing which indicates that men are the beneficiaries of the disarming qualities of Cupid's dart. Elsewhere, in 'To my Friend Exillus, on his Persuading me to Marry Old Damon', she shows that the real power-structure of romantic love makes marriage too great a risk to take. The growth of love brings trouble with it. The necessary corollary of male love is jealousy, and a man's resultant control over a woman's life will remove all other social contact.

> Now round his neck my willing arms I'd twine,
> And swear upon his lips 'My dear, I'm thine',
> But that his kindness then would grow, I fear,
> Too weighty for my weak desert to bear.
> I fear 'twould even to extremes improve,
> And jealousy, they say, 's th'extreme of love . . .
> Not only he-friends innocent as thou,
> But he'll mistrust she-friends and heaven too. (pp. 14–15)

Examining the works of the great love-poet Ovid, she laments the fate of his heroines, who gave up all dignity and virtue for the sake of men, and finally were wrecked by despair.

> Bright shes, what glories had your names acquired,
> Had you consumed those whom your beauties fired,
> Had laughed to see them burn, and so retired. (p. 28)

These classical figures, she says, are now used as the model of female behaviour, and all women are required to succumb to male lust.

The single woman is not lonely and despised, for all the mockery heaped upon her as an 'old maid' (p. 12). A spinster with a private income is released to pursue female friendships, to study her books and help the poor and needy. It becomes her duty to 'Be's good a subject as the stoutest man'.

> And when she any treats or visits make,
> 'Tis not for tattle, but for friendship's sake;
> Her neighbouring poor she does adopt her heirs,
> And less she cares for her own good than theirs;
> And by obedience testifies she can
> Be's a good a subject as the stoutest man.
> She to her church such filial duty pays,
> That one would think she'd lived i'th'pristine days.
> Her closet, where she does much time bestow,
> Is both her library and chapel too,
> Where she enjoys society alone,
> I'th'great Three-One –
> She drives her whole life's business to these ends,
> To serve her God, enjoy her books and friends. (p. 13)

Barker uses the pastoral pseudonym 'Galaecia' in some of her poems, and her sense of writing in a tradition established by 'the matchless Orinda' is evident in many of the *Poetical Recreations*. Addressing her own friends, she makes passing reference to Orinda (p. 95), and the dedicatory verses written by one of them, 'Philaster', asserts that Barker is using Orinda's 'seraphic pen' ('To Madam Jane Barker, on her Incomparable Poems'). The debt to Philips is not superficial. One of her most moving works is 'On the Death of my Dear Friend and Play-Fellow, Mrs E.D., Having Dreamed the Night Before I Heard Thereof, that I Had Lost a Pearl'.

> Friendship's a gem, whose lustre does outshine
> All that's below the heavenly crystalline:
> Friendship is that mysterious thing alone,
> Which can unite, and make two hearts but one;
> It purifies our love, and makes it flow
> I'th'dearest stream that's found in love below. (p. 18)

Barker's major preoccupation, however, is women's exclusion from the male world, and from male education. The *Poetical Recreations* actually form only half of the book in which they appear. The second half of the text consists of poems by young men, the friends whom she addresses in her verses; and whose praises of her introduce her work to the reader. They are all Cambridge University men, and it is their writing, not Barker's, that is praised by the bookseller in his preface as exciting and innovative: 'They've trod new paths to others' feet unknown,/ And bravely ventured to lead others on'. Jane Barker presents her own case to the reader, explaining that, like other women, she is confined to the 'desert' of the countryside, far from the 'tree of knowledge'. The lines she writes on this subject are fascinating for the way they invert the usual reverie of the conventional 'Invitation to the Countryside'. 'An Invitation to my Friends at Cambridge' is anti-pastoral, explaining that the 'tree of knowledge' will not grow in this rural setting. By alluding in this way to the biblical story of the Fall, she suggests by implication women's desire to leave the 'Garden' of their confinement by, like Eve, tasting the forbidden fruit and recognising their own nakedness and ignorance. Women, having eaten the fruit first, are now denied access to it. The tree of knowledge, the poem continues, does not belong in the university, either: it has been 'transplanted' there, and the men who have access to it gorge themselves on its fruit, not truly appreciating its dainty flavour. Men versify on the pleasures of rural retirement, but they do not have the most elementary understanding of what it entails: they believe the countryside to be a place of innocence, and use it as an escape from the avarice, pride and ambition of the world.

> I should conclude that such it really were,
> But that the Tree of Knowledge won't grow here:
> Though in its culture I have spent some time.
> Yet it disdains to grow in our cold clime,
> Where it can neither fruit nor leaves produce
> Good for its owner, or the public use.
> How can we hope our minds then to adorn
> With anything with which they were not born;
> Since we're denied to make this small advance,
> To know their nakedness and ignorance?
> For in our Maker's laws we've made a breach,
> And gathered all that was within our reach,
> Which since we ne'er could touch; although our eyes
> Do serve our longing souls to tantalise,
> Whilst kinder fate for you does constitute
> Luxurious banquets of this dainty fruit.
> Whose tree most fresh and flourishing does grow,
> E'er since it was transplanted amongst you;
> And you in wit grow as its branches high,
> Deep as its root too in philosophy;
> Large as its spreading arms your reasons grow,
> Close as its umbrage does your judgements show;
> Fresh as its leaves your sprouting fancies are,
> Your virtues as its fruits are bright and fair. (pp. 3–4)

What reasonable man could be offended by such charming compliments on his attainments?

A key concept in Barker's 'An Invitation' is that in their 'cold clime' women are refused access to matters of 'public use'. Her *Poetical Recreations* tend inevitably to one conclusion: women want access to learning so as to lead useful lives. Several of her poems make medical references, and her closing 'Farewell to Poetry' embraces the study of medicine as a replacement for less practical female pursuits (pp. 100–7). In 'On the Apothecary, Filling my Bills amongst the Doctors' she vindicates healing as a proper womanly activity, comparing it with other roles available to women. She would rather cure than kill like the lustful Queen Semiramis did, and would much prefer to exercise solid skill and ease real suffering than play the petty romantic role of the adored lady, relieving men's 'pain' by yielding to their wooing. Women's much-praised softness makes them more suitable physicians than men.

> The sturdy gout, which all male power withstands,
> Is overcome by my soft female hands:
> Not Deb'ra, Judith, or Semiramis
> Could boast of conquests half so great as this;
> More than they slew, I save in this disease.
> Mankind our sex for cures do celebrate,
> Of pains, which fancy only doth create:
> Now more we shall be magnified sure,
> Who for this real torment find a cure.
> Some women-haters may be so uncivil,
> To say the devil's cast out by the devil;
> But so the good are pleased, no matter for the evil.
> Such ease to statesmen this our skill imparts,
> I hope they'll force all women to learn arts. (pp. 31–2)

The way out of the desert, for women, is through study and the acquisition of practical skills.

By the 1680s, it would seem, women were turning their eyes to the power of well-trained reason, rather than to religion, to find a way of developing independence and self-respect. It is important to note, however, that the writers discussed here are a quite different group from those who were active in the radical sects. The sectaries were losing ground with the defeat of the revolution, and indeed were being silenced by the friends and families of these court poets. The sects themselves, most notably the Society of Friends, were also closing down the kinds of activities permissible to women, and women who earlier had shouted and argued for changes in the world were now preoccupied with caring for orphans and the sick. Under the developing bourgeois-aristocratic alliance of the later seventeenth century, it was only royalist and more wealthy women, on the whole, who had the chance to write.[39] It is not surprising that they challenged the restrictions of femininity in ways quite different from their predecessors of another class and political allegiance. They strove to support monarchy and male power in the state, while arguing for the right to develop their own intellectual abilities. In this, they had far more in common with the exiled royalist Margaret Cavendish than they ever could have with a Mary Cary or even a Lady Eleanor. Although they wrote explicitly on behalf of women, their vision of 'womanhood' did not extend very far down the social scale. Anne Killigrew's recoil from her sympathetic description of poverty presents this state as something unknown to anyone: anyone who was anyone, of course.

> What shall I say of poverty, whence it flows
> To miserable man so many woes?
> Ridiculous evil which too oft we prove
> Does laughter cause, where it should pity move;
> Solitary ill, into which no eye,
> Though ne'er so curious, ever cares to pry. (*Poems*, p. 35)

The remainder of her poem changes direction, to discuss the danger of passions and enthusiasm, and recommend substituting the rule of firm reason. Both Ephelia and Aphra Behn lament the evils of wealth, but in both cases they seem more concerned wih the demeaning effects of commercialism on the 'higher' values of a pre-bourgeois society, than with the insufficiencies allowed to the poor.[40] Ephelia describes the effects of the discovery of gold as a loss of meritocracy.

> How happy was the world before man found
> Those metals, Nature hid beneath the ground! . . .
> No man did needless merit now regard,
> None virtue sought, none valour would reward,
> None learning valued, none poor wit did mind,
> None honoured age, few were to beauty kind;
> All gold adored, all riches did admire,
> Beyond being rich, no man did now aspire.
> (*Female Poems* pp. 23–5)

These poets belonged to a class where their role was being ever further reduced, to make them mere ornaments of men, proof of their husbands' social status. Their lives became circumscribed by the conflicting ideologies that make up the courtly love conventions, where woman is both virgin and whore, both a lusty creature of the devil, and man's surest way to heaven, in a world where she exists in him and for him. In other sectors of society, meanwhile, women were faced with the problem of how to earn their living as the number of commercial roles open to them narrowed. As some women turned to write about education and virginal virtue, others turned their attention to the acquisition of practical skills with monetary value.

CHAPTER SEVEN

SKILLS BOOKS – HOUSEWIFERY, MEDICINE, MIDWIFERY

ALICE Clark, Christina Hole, Doris Stenton and others have shown that in the course of the seventeenth century the traditional tasks involved in running a household were slowly being reduced in scope, as brewing, food-production, weaving, medical care and other skills began to be taken over by waged men.[1] I shall discuss here the ways in which some women turned this contraction of the female sphere into opportunities for themselves to make a living by writing about and teaching such skills.

It might seem reasonable to assume that the first subject-matter to attract a female author would be the traditional womanly occupations of running a home, making medicines and aiding one another in childbirth. In fact, the reverse was the case. I have shown that published texts by women in this period frequently addressed the male world of state politics, government and religion. It would seem that the impetus needed to launch women into print initially led to them taking up manly issues, even as they did this in feminine ways. Suzanne Hull, in her extensive study of works written for a woman audience in the period 1475–1640, has also demonstrated that although household 'how-to-do-it' books addressed a female readership, they were written almost exclusively by men.[2] One such book, known as 'the Countess of Kent's *Choice Manuall*' because its editor, William Jarvis, claimed that the Countess had collected its medical recipes, was quickly taken up in its second edition by the highly successful bookseller William Shears, and had run through at least thirteen editions by the time of Shears's death in 1662.

Many of the cookery and medical-remedy books of the mid seventeenth century were addressed to a leisured audience, who were at least as concerned with elegance as with practicalities.[3] *The Queens Closet Opened*, for instance, describes its contents as the 'more private recreations' of the queen, Henrietta Maria. The remedies included are generally attributed to male and female members of the nobility, and there are

many variations on candying and preserving, and on innumerable fanciful desserts made with expensive ingredients. Perhaps their interest for
a wider audience lay partly in the glimpse of extravagant living they
offered, as well as in the many more generally useful therapies for
ailments that they contained.[4]

The first woman known to have broken into this lucrative market was
Hannah Wolley. She was the highly successful author of *The Ladies
Directory* (1661 and 1662), *The Cooks Guide* (1664), *The Queen-like
Closet* (1670, 1672, 1675–6, 1681, 1684), *The Ladies Delight* (1672)
and *A Supplement To The Queen-like Closet* (1674, 1681, 1684). *The
Queen-like Closet* was also translated into German, first appearing in
1674. Three other texts, *The Gentlewomans Companion* (1673), *The
Compleat Servant-Maid* (1677) and *The Accomplish'd Ladies Delight*
(1675), have in addition been falsely attributed to her, and I shall return
below to discuss these erroneous attributions. *The Gentlewomans
Companion* contains a spurious biography of Wolley which, interspersed
(despite the contradictions) with the account of her life given in *A
Supplement To The Queen-like Closet*, has been used in modern descriptions of her; an outline of the known facts of her life will therefore be
useful.[5]

Writing *A Supplement To The Queen-like Closet*, which was first
advertised in the *Term Catalogues* on 6 July 1674, Wolley mentions
(p. 16) that she is then in her fifty-second year. The spurious text she
seeks to refute, *The Gentlewomans Companion*, was advertised in
November 1672, which makes it likely that she was writing during
1673.[6] This would give her year of birth as 1622 and that of her marriage
at the age of twenty-four to Benjamin Wolley, the master of Newport
Grammar School, as 1646.[7] For seven years before 1646 she had lived as
a servant in the house of a 'noble Lady', and learnt the medicinal skills
that she exercised in her local community and in treating the pupils of her
husband's schools. In 1652 she and her husband moved from Newport
Pond near Saffron Walden to Hackney, where they kept another school,
with up to sixty boarders. The *Victoria County History* of Essex gives
August 1661 as the date of Benjamin Wolley's death. Since Hannah's first
book, *The Ladies Directory*, was entered in the *Stationers' Register* on 16
July 1661, it is tempting to speculate that his death had been foreseen,
perhaps at the end of an illness, and that she had set about finding herself
this alternative source of income. In 1666 she married Francis Chaloner.
It is likely that she was quickly widowed again, since her will, registered
in 1669, was made under the name of Wolley, and she was described as a
widow.[8] Presumably Francis Chaloner had in any case died by 1674, when
she was living with one of her four sons, Richard Wolley, at his house 'in
the Old Bailey in Golden Cup Court; he is Master of Arts, and Reader at St

Martin's Ludgate'.[9] We do not know the date of her death, but since she raised no public protest at T.P.'s making free with her work in 1675 in *The Accomplish'd Ladies Delight*, it is possible that she did not live to see it appear.

By 1661 Hannah Wolley had been a domestic servant, and had earned a reputation for her medical proficiency. She had worked alongside her husband in two schools, but, being a woman, presumably did not have the training, or the status, to take over the management of the Hackney establishment. Instead, she set about making money her own way. From the very first, she used her books as an advertisement for her prowess, both preparing the way for her forthcoming publications and inviting her readers to consult her in person if they required further instruction. Her first title page also warns the reader to beware of counterfeits.[10] It describes the book as printed 'for the authoress', which might indicate that she undertook the publication as her own financial venture, not receiving payment for her writings from the bookseller Peter Dring until she had established herself.

Part of the book's sales' promotion is the title page proclamation that Wolley had cooked for Charles I, 'his late Majesty, as well as for the nobility'.[11] It contains many recipes attractive to these refined palates, such as one for candying flowers. Typical both of Wolley's style and of other cookery books of the day, this recipe consists of a single sentence. No precise quantities are given, much being left to the cook's discretion.

Take roses, violets, cowslips, or gillyflowers, and pick them from the white parts, then having sugar boiled to a candy height, with a little fair water, put in as many flowers as your sugar will receive, and continually stir them with the back of a spoon; and when you see the sugar harden on the sides of the skillet, and on the spoon, take them off the fire, and keep them with stirring in the warm skillet till you see them part, and the sugar lie as if it were sifted upon them, then pour them on a paper while they are warm, and rub them gently, and sift them thorough a colander as clean as may be; then pour them upon a clean cloth, and shake them up and down till there be hardly any sugar left hanging about them.[12]

This first book is made up of many such fanciful instructions for candying and for creating court perfumes. Even her medical remedies verge on the fantastic, in keeping with Tudor and Stuart cookery book tradition, calling for the use of 'seven grains of unicorn's horns', or directing women, in a proven cure for consumption, to 'Take a red cock, pluck him alive, then slit him down the back, and take out all his entrails' (*The Ladies Directory*, p. 21).

Her second book, *The Cooks Guide*, centres on recipes for 'Flesh, Fowls and Fish', but in her address to the reader she remarks that she has now 'joined both the books in one that they may pass as one', so she intended it to be sold with *The Ladies Directory*. In the intervening two years, she also seems to have learnt other tricks of the trade. She dedicates this book to Lady Anne Wroth and her daughter, Mary, and explains that her earlier failure to evoke noble protection was due only to modesty.[13] In addition, she has realised that a little more womanly self-effacement about the act of writing is in order. She justifies her publication as a way of preserving her reputation after her death, and in the meantime of showing that she uses her time well and so can encourage other women to be usefully employed. All these explanations have their parallels in the prefaces written by her female contemporaries, especially in those by Margaret Cavendish, and they indicate the beginnings of her transformation from 'a cook who writes' into a professional writer.

With *The Queen-like Closet* in 1670, Wolley turned explicitly to addressing a wider female audience. The title page characterises the book as 'Very Pleasant and Beneficial to all Ingenious Persons of the Female Sex', and her introductory epistle is addressed 'To all Ladies, gentlewomen, and to all other of the female sex who do delight in, or be desirous of good accomplishments'. Although her books were not cheap – she tells us (*A Supplement*, p. 131) that *The Ladies Directory* sold for one shilling, and *The Queen-like Closet* is advertised at two shillings bound – they were less expensive than many other cookery books that appeared in the *Term Catalogues*. Becoming more conscious of the rights and duties of authors, she invokes her readers' professed or assumed desire to have more from her pen after her six years' silence.

Methinks, I hear some of you say, 'I wish Mrs Wolley would put forth some new experiments'; and to say the truth, I have been importuned by divers of my friends and acquaintance to do so. ('To all Ladies, Gentlewomen, and to all others of the Female Sex')

The first 350 pages of this book are loosely based on her two earlier publications. It is in two sections, the first concerned with preserving and candying, the second with meat and fish cookery, and many of the recipes are taken from *The Ladies Directory* and *The Cooks Guide*. Her presentation of her material, however, shows her confidence in the act of writing, and her sense of the role of author, to be expanding. She firmly claims her earlier texts as part of her oeuvre – 'I am not ashamed, nor do I disown what I have already printed' – and proceeds with the bolder attempt of addressing her reader in verse. Contrasting a lady's life of idle riches with her own more industrial activities, she draws attention to the difference between self-indulgent party food and the necessities of life.

I sit here sad while you are merry,
Eating dainties, drinking perry;
But I'm content you should so feed,
So I may have to serve my need.

She is not seeking to upset the social order: it is the tradition of aristocratic and genteel hospitality that provides some of the market for her more fanciful recipes. If she is to reach her maximum market, however, she also needs to sell to servants: at least to those who might afford to pay two shillings for a book, and the third section of the book is preoccupied with servants' duties. She is most particular in her recommendations, advising the kitchenmaid to be humble and willing, if she is to avoid blows from the cook (p. 371), and telling servants at table to watch the eyes of visitors to deduce whether they might want something, to save them the embarrassment of having to make demands in front of their host (p. 315). Her sympathy and understanding for the poor and workless is made clear in her careful instructions concerning the treatment of those seeking alms.

If any poor body comes to ask an alms, do not shut the door against them rudely, but be modest and civil to them, and see if you can procure somewhat for them, and think with yourselves, that though you are now full fed, and well clothed, and free from care, yet you know not what may be your condition another day. (p. 377)

She expresses a similar concern for servants' well-being in *A Supplement To The Queen-like Closet*, where she conjures gentlewomen to be kind to any maid who leaves their service to get married, 'for then her husband will be apt to be the more kind to her' (*A Supplement*, p. 103).

If *The Queen-like Closet* is divided over the problem of which class it is addressing, it is quite certain as to the gender of its audience: 'All Ingenious Persons of the Female Sex'. Since it is nonetheless concerned with the profession or trade of cookery its choice of a wholly female readership is significant. One of Hannah Wolley's arch-rivals as an author was Robert May, whose book *The Accomplisht Cook* ran through five editions between 1660 and 1685. May makes much of his fifty-five years' experience as a professional cook, claiming to have worked at one time or another for Lord Castlehaven, Lord Lumley, Lord Montague in Sussex, the Countess of Kent, and many others.[14] He is also unequivocal about his readership: he is writing for professional cooks, and to him this must mean that he is writing for men: 'To all honest well intending men of our profession, or others, this book cannot but be acceptable, as it plainly and profitably discovers the mystery of the whole art' (sig. A4ʳ). *The Accomplisht Cook* is the most expensive cookery book of the period, being listed in the *Term Catalogues* at five shillings. May seeks to raise the status of the profession by making it more exclusive, by turning it into a 'science', and explains that he is inventing new terminology to this end.

It hath been my task to denote some new faculty or science, that others have not yet discovered; this the reader will quickly discern by those new terms of art which he shall meet withal throughout this whole volume. (sig. A5ʳ)

Hannah Wolley, in her desire to make her skills accessible, at a price, to 'all Ingenious Persons of the Female Sex', responds to such ambitions with contempt.

Here is to be noted, that in divers of these receipts [recipes] there are directions for two or three several things in one, not confounding the brains with multitudes of words to little or no purpose, or vain expressions of things which are altogether unknown to the learned as well as the ignorant; this is really imparted for the good of all the female sex. (*The Queen-like Closet*, p. 181)

This concern with the good of her sex also manifests itself in some carefully ungendered expressions. In answer to May and his ilk she remarks that the skills should be the same regardless of the gender of the worker.

The cook, whether man or woman, ought to be very well skilled in all manner of things . . . they ought to have a very good fancy, such an one, whether man or woman, deserves the title of a fit cook (pp. 370–1)[15]

It is with the appearance of Hannah Wolley's last work, *A Supplement To The Queen-like Closet*, that the final significant development in her writing is made. It is first advertised in the *Term Catalogues* on 6 July 1674, price bound one shilling. The book opens in verse, Wolley addressing her woman reader by referring to her own earlier writings. She combines several conventional defences for publication. It is her duty as a good Christian, she says, not to hide her 'talent', which has been given her to impart for her country's good. She also gives a new twist to the romance conceit of suing for a beloved's commands by offering to 'wait' on ladies as their 'servant'. As a good citizen, a good Christian, a good servant, it is her duty to write.

> 'Tis twelve years past since first in print I came
> More for my country's good, than to get fame.
> My study was to impart to others free,
> What God and Nature hath informed me.
> I must not hide that talent God me gave,
> Content I am others a share should have
> To practise what I teach; if pains they'll take,
> Amends for all my care they will me make.
> Servant to ingenuity I'll be,
> Such ladies shall command all arts from me.
> Nothing from them I'll hide, that's in my heart,
> To wait on them I think it is my part.
> And to confirm to them what I have writ,
> Fearing no censures, 'mongst they that have wit. (sig. A3)

She explains in more detail later that part of her point in publishing this *Supplement* is to clear her name, to explain who she is and how and where she gained the experience from which she writes her recipes and remedies. Among the case histories she recalls is her cure of a woman who had been 'kicked by a churlish husband on her leg, so that a vein was burst, whereby she lost at the least a pottle [= four pints] of blood; I stayed the blood and cured the leg' (p. 12).

In the years since she first went into print, Wolley seems to have established herself firmly in the business of teaching her art, and in placing her trainees in service. In this book, she several times breaks off in the midst of her directions to suggest that the reader should consult her for personal instruction: 'Be pleased to afford me some of your money; And I will repay you with my pains and skill. That I judge to be fair on both sides' (p. 61). She is offering a quite specific contract. Her more likely pupils, of course, are not servants themselves, but their mistresses who, in becoming more leisured, might be losing the traditional female skills of running a household. She seeks, indeed, to professionalise house-work, or to turn it into a recognised trade, offering a seven-year training in some ways comparable to the seven-year apprenticeship that Robert May and other men took to become cooks.

It is more commendable a great deal to wear one's own work, than to be made fine with the art of others . . . and besides it argues that person not to be idle, but rather a good housewife . . . The world is grown very fine of late years . . . Some will plead ignorance, not knowing how to do these things, but that's a bare excuse; for if they know not already, they may learn . . . Likewise if any gentlewoman would learn to preserve, if she please to give me forty shillings in hand, she shall have the liberty to come so oft as she pleases, and bring her materials with her; and at any time if there be any new thing to be learned, at any time, for seven years, I will direct her.[16]

This book includes advice on some areas of housewifely activity that were omitted from her earlier writings. As well as the needlework men-tioned in the passage quoted above, she also dissects for women the art of letter-writing. She reflects on the fact that female education concentrates more on mere prettiness, on 'learning a good hand', than it does on the order and content of composition (p. 148). Before providing examples of the correct and rational way to write, she first includes two letters whose impropriety is 'to be abhorred, and shunned' (p. 148). It is interesting to see how these compositions reveal the contemporary judgement of correctness: some of the jokes come from mis-spelling and poor punctua-tion, others from ambiguity of syntax. They also show Wolley's attain-ment of the self-perceived status of 'writer': she can show others how to write well.

Dear Mother,
My duty remembered unto you hopping that you are in good helth as i am at the

Riting hereof prased be God, this is to let you understand that i have receved the things you sent to me by Tomas Frenge and he had a grot of me for the bringing them, i pray do not forget my Come i left in the Kichen windo and my Aporn in the Chamber, pray send them al to me, i hop my Father is wel and my brother Ned and my suster Joice and i hop godie welsh is wel, thus with my love and duty to you i rest

Your dutiful dafter
Ann Blackwell. (p. 150)

She has progressed a long way from her initial recipe books made up of long, rambling sentences, to being able to advise and adjudicate about the correct language to use for various purposes. Her model-letters include one 'from a wife to her husband, craving his pardon for her long absence from him' (p. 160), a sample asking financial assistance, written 'from a widow to her friend' (p. 163), and one 'from a woman in prison to her friend, to help her' (p. 165). These passages weave varying stories around the possible events in a woman's life, and include the inevitable illustration of how to rebuff an unwelcome suitor.

Hannah Wolley turned her hard-won housewifely competence into a source of income for herself, both by advertising her willingness to teach, and by being paid as a writer. Her fury at Dorman Newman for publishing in 1673 a book loosely based on her writings, but which had been reworked by a hack, still using her name on the title page, is therefore quite understandable. In her dedicatory poem to *A Supplement*, she refers to this text, objecting to the false biography it gives of her, and taking offence at the fact that her style had been tampered with. She invites women to visit her in her home, to let her

vindication bring
Unto myself, who have been much abused
By a late printed book, my name there used:
I was far distant when they printed it,
Therefore that book to own I think not fit.
To boast, to brag, tell stories in my praise,
That's not the way (I know) my fame to raise;
Nor shall I borrow any pen or wit
(Innocence will hide what faults I do commit).

Later in the book, she explains that she had intended to enlarge *The Ladies Directory* herself, but had discovered that the bookseller, Dorman Newman, had employed someone else to do it, 'who hath so transformed the book, that it is nothing like what I had written'. One of her particular complaints is that Newman was selling the text for two shillings and sixpence, when the original had been a much cheaper affair, only one shilling. She says that after she had argued with Newman he had allowed her to remove from his book the parts that were 'scandalous, ridiculous, and impertinent', but that he had then refused to pay her their

· 172 ·

agreed rate for her trouble, offering her only half her due. There is an awful irony in the fact that the false book that so enraged her is the one that has been so frequently quoted as an example of her work. The later editions of *The Gentlewomans Companion*, sold by Edward Thomas, even included a counterfeit portrait of Hannah Wolley, one which has been shown to be a picture of Sarah Gilly.[17]

Even the simplest description of *The Gentlewomans Companion* suggests that it indeed is the book Wolley protests about. It appears in the right year, 1673, and is her only book sold by Dorman Newman. It is advertised in the *Term Catalogues* on 21 November 1672, the author unnamed, for sale at two shillings and sixpence. A closer examination of the book also reveals its style to be quite different from Wolley's, and the biography it gives of her to be inconsistent with her own description of her life.

The Gentlewomans Companion has often been quoted in more recent accounts of seventeenth-century women's lives because of the defence it contains of female education.

The right education of the female sex, as it is in a manner everywhere neglected, so it ought to be generally lamented. Most in this depraved latter age think a woman learned and wise enough if she can distinguish her husband's bed from another. Certainly man's soul cannot boast of a more sublime original than ours, they had equally their efflux from the same eternal Immensity, and therefore capable of the same improvement, by good education. Vain man is apt to think we were merely intended for the world's propagation, and to keep its human inhabitants sweet and clean; but, by their leaves, had we the same literature, he would find our brains as fruitful as our bodies. Hence I am induced to believe, we are debarred from the knowledge of human learning, lest our pregnant wits should rival the towering conceits of our insulting lords and masters.[18]

The book is indeed progressive in its call for women to receive a proper education. Like other male defences of the excellence of women (see Chapter Eight) it cites the existence of earlier learned females, and also makes mention of Anna Maria van Schurman and Katherine Philips (pp. 29–30). In the course of his argument, however, the writer begins to refer to women as 'you', counselling them, for instance, to espouse the 'moving rhetoric' of silence, and restrict themselves to 'the sphere of your proper concern' (p. 43). He is not unreserved in his promotion of equality. The education he would give women is, like the male one, modelled on the classics. He remarks,

Our English tongue is of late very much refined, by borrowing many words from the Latin, only altering the termination; these you will never perfectly understand without the knowledge of the Latin, but rather misapply or displace them to your discredit. (p. 31)

The author's language reveals the fact that his education has concentrated on such matters. His phrases are elaborate, often verging on the preposterous, as is instanced in the passage quoted above, with its 'efflux from the same eternal Immensity'.

The description this work gives of Hannah Wolley's education is very different from her own account of her early life in service. In *The Gentlewomans Companion* she appears as a schoolmistress from the ages of fifteen to seventeen, having somehow acquired already a knowledge of 'smooth Italian', and learnt to sing, dance and play various musical instruments. Being such a cultivated creature, she is taken as governess in the household of a 'noble lady', where she becomes acquainted with the court. The succeeding years find her working in another household as governess, stewardess, scribe and secretary, and reading aloud romances in fluent French. Picking up her knowledge of cookery and medicine along the way, she is saved from her growing acclaim by marriage to her own shining knight. Her story ends with the sad reflection that everyone she loves, including her husband, friends and children are dead (pp. 10–14).

This silly account turns Hannah Wolley into a romance heroine, discounting the problems created by her imperfect education and the financial insecurity of her existence.[19] It also serves the useful function of providing her with a French education, which could compete with the description of Robert May's fluent French in *The Accomplisht Cook*. The French influence on English recipes was growing, May said, and some knowledge of the language might be deemed necessary for a successful author of cookery books (sig. A5–A6).

If we ignore the presence of Hannah Wolley's name on the title page, *The Gentlewomans Companion* is in fact exactly what its dedicatory epistle describes it as: a compilation based on Wolley's books, May's *Accomplisht Cook*, *The Queens Closet Opened*, Francis Hawkins's *Youths Behaviour*, and other popular contemporary skills and conduct books. It also contains an advertisement for Dorman Newman's other publications: the reader is recommended to study Swinnock's *Christian Calling*, Firmin's *Real Christian* and Janeway's *A Token for Children*, among others.

In more recent times, two other books have mistakenly been attributed to Wolley. Since these errors were not made by her contemporaries, they will receive only brief treatment here. Donald Wing's *Short-Title Catalogue* and the Bodleian Library Catalogue list *The Compleat Servant-Maid* as Wolley's work. (The British Library catalogues it as an anonymous work, under 'Servant-Maid'.) This was brought out by the bookseller Thomas Passinger in 1677, reaching its fourth edition by 1685. An anonymous work, it is addressed in condescending tone to

servantmaids who aspire to upward mobility, taking recipes (unacknowledged) from diverse sources, including *The Queen-like Closet* and *The
Accomplish'd Ladies Delight*, to teach them the necessary skills. It was
clearly put together either by or for Thomas Passinger, as a successful
commercial venture.

The Accomplish'd Ladies Delight first appeared two years earlier, sold
by Benjamin Harris. It is easy to see how the attribution of this book to
Wolley might have occurred. Its title is similar to her *The Ladies Delight*,
and some of its recipes and remedies are taken from her books.[20] There
are two major differences. The first is the fact that *The Accomplish'd
Ladies Delight* contains a section on angling, a section that sits uneasily
in the book since it is not addressed to women and does not discuss the
question of the suitability of fishing as a feminine occupation. The second
difference lies in the make-up of the text itself. Hannah Wolley never
developed an orderly or systematic structure in her books. They switch
from subject to subject, often including more than one recipe for the
same dish, and never making any internal cross-references. *The Accomplish'd Ladies Delight* is a very much more polished affair, divided into
discrete sections that are thoroughly, systematically indexed, interleaved
with many illustrations.

Hannah Wolley was the first woman known to have made her living by
writing this kind of book. She was followed into print by others. In 1678,
Mary Tillinghast printed a small cookery book of *Rare and Excellent
Receipts*. Although no biographical information is given, she appears,
like Wolley, to have used her book to advertise herself as a teacher of
such skills: the title page proclaims that it is 'Printed for the Use of her
Scholars only'.[21] The second edition came out in 1690, the year that also
saw the second edition of M.H.'s *The Young Cooks Monitor*, first published in 1683. Either this author is a third woman who also taught her
skills, or the M.H. of the title page is Mary Tillinghast with a new
surname. It, too, is described as 'Made Public for the Use and Benefit of
my Scholars' and the author was sufficiently impressed by the usefulness
of her book to bring out the second edition herself, which was 'Printed
for the Author, at her House in Lime Street'. After a short dedicatory
epistle 'To All Ladies and Gentlewomen, Especially those that are my
Scholars', the book consists entirely of cookery recipes. The second
edition of *The Young Cooks Monitor* adds some extra recipes and
corrects some spellings – 'cabbadge' is changed to 'cabbage', 'lorrel' to
'laurel', and so on – but in other respects is unaltered. The main purpose
of both Mary Tillinghast and M.H. seems to have been to follow in
Hannah Wolley's footsteps, within the limits of their own accomplishments, and make a living by using their writings to publicise their
teaching.

It is possible that the imminent prospect of widowhood prompted Hannah Wolley to go into print and make money out of her skills. The anonymous author of *Advice to the Women and Maidens of London*, 1678, urges women to learn a more unconventional art: accountancy. This is a less risky accomplishment than needlework or lace-making, her title page proclaims,

> whereby, either single, or married, they may know their estates, carry on their trades, and avoid the danger of a helpless and forlorn condition, incident to widows.

She counsels women not to be deterred from this by a command to 'meddle with our distaff', and cites the fact that some foreign women do the bookkeeping for their husbands' businesses (p. 1). (It is an indication of the speed with which the lives of earlier women are forgotten by their descendants that she could not refer to the recent past of her own country, where women had also worked alongside their spouses, or run their own premises, as Alice Clark has shown.[22]) It is important for women to undertake such work, she says, if a widow is not to be wholly helpless.

> For there is not that danger of a family's overthrow by the sauce wanting its right relish, or the table or stools misplaced, as by a widow's ignorance of her concern as to her estate.

Such male skills may be more important than the work conventionally undertaken by women, she continues, but her readers need not fear that they are beyond them.

> Having in some measure practised both needlework and accounts I can aver, that I never found this masculine art harder or more difficult than the effeminate achievements of lace-making, gum-work or the like. (p. 2)

She explains that her own parents had encouraged her to learn arithmetic, and then set her to keep the household accounts to practise what she had learnt. The short book that follows consists of examples of how to manage and record income and expenditure, and how to plan a monthly or annual budget. She also suggests that a woman could use this expertise to go into trade alone (p. 19).

The book ends by recommending Mr Randolph, schoolmaster in Mugwell Street, as a possible tutor. It might therefore be the case that the text was written by him as a way of attracting female pupils. There is nothing in the text itself to reveal whether he or the 'one of that [female] sex' of the title page is the true author: the biographical sketch of the author contains no details that could be checked against other sources, so it is unlikely that the question can be finally settled. Either way, the text remains a useful source for the history of women's education and women's work.

Some of Hannah Wolley's recipes are for medicines. The preparation of such 'folk remedies' was a traditional part of a woman's task in running a household. If she dared to treat others, however, she ran the risk of prosecution for witchcraft, or harassment as an 'empiric' from the College of Physicians. Although Hannah Wolley seems not to have met with such problems, other women did. In 1652, Joan Peterson was found to be 'the witch of Wapping', and executed for her crimes. The report of her trial records that she was arrested for having

conspired with another gentlewoman to administer a potion, or posset, to the Lady Powel (living at Chelsea) who soon after the drinking thereof died, etc. But many conjecture she died a natural death, being aged 80 years.[23]

Lady Powel's ill-health and advanced age were not considered sufficient explanation for her decease, and Joan Peterson was condemned for being 'what is vulgarly called both a good witch and a bad', since other medicines she made had cured many people over the years.[24]

There are records dating back to at least the early fifteenth century of men trying to bar women from the healing professions. Muriel Hughes quotes a petition to parliament from male physicians dated 1421, calling for uneducated men and all women to be barred from 'the practice of physic'. In 1518, Thomas Linacre obtained a Royal Charter to found the College of Physicians in order more effectively to combat the presumption of 'smiths, weavers and women who boldly take upon themselves great cures'. The College also engaged in controlling the activities of barber-surgeons and apothecaries, limiting membership of the College to those men who possessed a medical degree and had had four years' practice.[25] In 1684, Charles Goodall wrote an account of the regulatory activities pursued by the College, prompted, he claimed, by the growing impudence of 'empirics and unlicensed practisers'. These included Margaret Kennix, who in 1581 was providing medications for the local poor, supporting her family with the little money she made; and Tomazine Scarlet, an illiterate woman much sought after by her neighbours, who despite repeated prosecutions, imprisonments and fines, refused to give up her practice.[26] The absurdity of this pursuit of unlicensed medical women and men has been pointed out by Jane Donegan. Without the help of their rivals, the College could not have hoped to treat all sick members of the population. In the early eighteenth century, the membership of the College of Physicians amounted to only 114 men, eighty of whom lived in London.[27] The British Library possesses two collections of advertising broadsides produced by medical women and men in the second half of the seventeenth century, and these give some indication of the widespread existence of such practitioners, at least in London. Some of these broadsides advertise women's businesses and others, although referring mainly to the healing abilities of a man, offer female patients the alternative of consulting his wife. It might have been common practice for widows to take over their husband's businesses: Margaret Searl, 'wife of the late Samuel Searl, famous for relieving and curing deafness' did so, as did Mary Clark, who continued to produce her spouse's scurvy cure after his death.[28]

Some of these women physicians apparently combined healing with other money-making ventures. One unnamed woman who advertised her medicines stating that she would require no payment until her cures proved effective apparently also sold coats to supplement her income.[29] A 'gentlewoman' medicine-seller living 'the next door to the Castle Tavern' also undertook to resolve

these questions following:
life, whether it may be long or short, happy or unhappy?; a person absent, whether dead or alive? if alive, when return?; in what part of the world it is best to live?; whether one shall be rich or poor?[30]

Anne Laverent, 'a German gentlewoman' had frequent broadsheets printed to advertise her treatments for women's ailments: the British Library collections include at least three different texts proclaiming her abilities, as well as a good half-dozen referring to an anonymous woman who seems to have moved her premises repeatedly and wanted to keep in touch with her patients.[31] Many more of such ephemera must have been produced than have survived, and their existence indicates that the College of Physicians was far from successful at repressing unlicensed practitioners.

The differences between physicians and empirics were not simply to do with education or the membership of a particular society. Their treatments for the ill were based on different philosophies of the human body, leading physicians to advocate bleeding as almost a panacea, while the 'chemists' relied in part on old herbal remedies, the effectiveness of which had been tried and proven by generations of experience. In 1665, some of the 'charlatans' so despised by the College of Physicians organised the establishment of a short-lived 'Society of Chemical Physicians', designed explicitly to challenge the physicians' monopoly.[32] The Society had several influential supporters, including the Archbishop of Canterbury and the king. The *Advertisement* they published in 1665 explained their intention to prevent the spread of the plague by using special drugs. It was signed by eight men, including Thomas O'Dowde, the author of *The Poor Man's Physician*.

Ten years later, O'Dowde's daughter, Mary Trye, published her vindication of the Chemical Physicians as *Medicatrix, Or, The Woman-Physician*. She was writing partly in rebuttal of Henry Stubbe, a member of the College of Physicians who had published an attack on the chemists' methods, and partly, therefore, in defence of her father's memory. She explains that she had come across Stubbe's tract while visiting London, and decided immediately that she herself should answer him. In her dedicatory epistle to Lady Fisher (Jane Lane, the woman who helped the future Charles II to escape after the civil war), she opens with a remark that would have astounded women twenty-five years before.

Since it is little of novelty to see a woman in print, I conceive no such vain ideas as to imagine I shall now entertain you with any rare or more than ordinary divertisement. (p. 1)

Aware as she is that she is not original in going into print, she nonetheless uses her 'feminine hand' as a counter in the argument she develops against Stubbe. Having assured the reader that 'there is ability enough in my sex, both to discourse his envy, and equal the arguments of his pen' (p. 2), she is able to make an ironic swipe at his extensive education in the classics – which of course was the subject-matter of most university training – by saying that she can only manage

a reasonable measure of sense, which I believe is as much, and more, than he expects from a woman: he will be so kind as to excuse me for the vacancy of those masculine capacities he himself glories in: and the rather, because he well understands, that such fine things, as are prettily termed philosophical in him, will scarce be thought rational in me. (p. 5)

In the section of her book entitled 'The Author's Opinion of Learning', she is careful to explain that it is not book-learning in itself that she rejects, but the failure of medical education to include practical and experimental knowledge. She proceeds by drawing parallels between chemical physicians and a well-known group of empiricists, the recently founded Royal Society, deciding however that 'they are able to defend themselves without my help, and no doubt have' (p. 83). She contrasts her 'royal' allies with Henry Stubbe, casting doubt on his dependability by questioning the sincerity of his allegiance to the crown during the civil war, and critically examining his own glowing account of his life. Her dead father, by contrast, she establishes as a sincere and unwavering Cavalier (pp. 24–47). To her Restoration audience, these details themselves would have helped vindicate her father's memory.

Mary Trye describes the events of the Plague, which culminated in the deaths of her father and mother, and her own serious sickness. Stubbe made much of O'Dowde's death, using it as proof of the ineffectiveness of chemical remedies. Trye justly retorts that her father died because he had stayed behind in London to treat the sick, while Stubbe and his fellow Physicians had fled to the safer countryside (pp. 45–64).

In her analysis of the shortcomings of a university education and the description of the circumstances of her parents' deaths', Mary Trye went a good way to fulfilling her father's dying wish that she must not let his skills die, or leave the poor to suffer. She also continued to practise the healing methods he taught her, and to make medicines to his formulae. In part, therefore, her book is her own defence, a defence of 'The Woman-Physician' and her livelihood.

I received a medicinal talent from my father, which by the instruction and assistance of so excellent a tutor, as he was to me, and my constant preparation and observation of medicines, together with my daily experience, by reason of his very great practice; as also being mistress of a reasonable share of that knowledge and discretion other women attain; I made myself capable of disposing such noble and successful medicines, and managing so weighty and great a concern. (p. 2)

The book ends with a list of the medicines she can make, and a description of the illnesses each is suitable to treat. It would take more than Henry Stubbe and his College of Physicians to silence the woman-physician.

Almanacs were a common vehicle for the distribution of medical remedies and the popularisation of astrological medicine in opposition to the monopoly of the College of Physicians. In his extensive study *English Almanacs 1500–1800*, Bernard Capp has shown that many almanac-makers were also practising astrological physicians. Almanacs and prognostications numbered among the best-selling books of the mid and late seventeenth century, sales in the 1660s averaging about four hundred thousand copies annually, each costing between two and four pence. They had many mundane uses quite apart from their prophecies on the state of the nation, the weather and international affairs, as they listed the hours of sunrise and sunset, the times of the tides, and the dates of holidays, court sessions, fairs and market days. They were often written by men as a commercial venture, more to advertise their trade as astrologers and physicians than to receive the average fee of forty shillings that was paid by booksellers to 'sorts' writers. Many of the authors were young men, making their first almanac to gain acceptance from more established astrologers. Having this recognition was important as a protection against suspicion of witchcraft, a charge that was occasionally brought against them. Since almanacs were part of the lucrative English Stock, their production was tightly controlled by the Company of Stationers, which had a keen eye to their market, realising that it was not infinitely expandable, so restricting the number of copies and titles printed. By no means every almanac submitted by a writer was accepted for publication, and authors were sometimes paid no royalty at all for their first year, until their reputation was established.

In the light of these restrictions, it is particularly surprising to find two women almanac-makers in the period: Sarah Jinner and Mary Holden.[33] Only a fragment exists of Sarah Jinner's first almanac and prognostication, published in 1658: the medical recipes which were part of it, according to her comments in 1659, are missing from the only extant copy. In 1659, her address to the reader reflects on the happy reception and proven accuracy of her first attempt. She says that her cures have been found efficacious, and that she will provide more. Her remedies concentrate on women's difficulties with conception and pregnancy and with various infections, and on male hernias and ruptures.

She is aware, she says, that such an explicit discussion of these matters might be thought immodest, even though she is merely describing things that really happen. This is not sufficient to deter her from a necessary task: 'It is not fit the world should be deprived of such helps to nature; for want of which, many, by their modesty, suffer much' (sig. B1ʳ). Her aim is educational, and particularly to teach her own sex. She makes a case for women's need and ability to be educated while defending this in terms that the later seventeenth century would further promote: there is nothing to fear from schooling women, since it will only serve to make them more virtuous.

The reason why I commend this piece [Lemnius' treatise on reproduction], is, that our sex may be furnished with knowledge: if they knew better, they would do better. It is better that they should exercise their parts, in that which appertaineth to a virtuous life, and be made a useful adornment to the age wherein they live; which is the only design of S.J. (sig. B1ᵛ).

Her prophecies for the coming year include the likelihood of much adultery and fornication, and advice to seamen on their courting. Her most shocking observation is her forecast that 'breeding' – by which she means heterosexual intercourse – will be painful in February, causing her to recommend to her women readers to 'make much of yourselves, let your husbands pay for it' (sig. C1ʳ).

Perhaps Sarah Jinner decided that in writing about sexuality she would be thought immodest whatever she said, and threw caution to the winds at this point. Inevitably, she provided an easy target for the author of *The Womans Almanack*, who disguises his name under a pun on Jinner's: Ginnor. (Wing wrongly treats this as a variant spelling, and the text is listed in the *Short-Title Catalogue* with those actually by Jinner. It is more surprising to find Capp, who has clearly read the text, repeating this error, and quoting it as though it were a serious almanac, Capp, op. cit., p. 87.) This pamphlet opens with an apparent defence of women's education, embroidering on the passage from Jinner quoted above. The language becomes ever more ambiguous, however, sliding rapidly into sexual puns, undercutting the call for women's education, and casting doubt on the efficacy of women healers.

During the civil war, almanac-makers came to be politically partisan, and Sarah Jinner is no exception to this: Capp, in fact, lists her as one of the most radical of the period. She makes pointed comments on the evils of arbitrary rulers, and asserts that the people are not bound to obey bad masters. She is no sectary, however, characterising the radicals as babbling 'novice lay pulpetiers' (sig. B2ᵛ), reflecting grimly that women are all too often responsible for civil unrest (sig. B3ᵛ). The final section of Jinner's almanacs consists of medical remedies, and in 1664 her remedies extended from those enabling conception to a method of restraining young women's sexual appetites.

To take away the desire of a woman to the act of venery. Take of a red bull's pizzle [penis] and powder it, and put in wine or broth, the quantity of a crown weight of silver, and she will abhor the desire of lying with a man: this may be a good medicine for the preventing of young girls throwing themselves away upon madcap fellows. (sig. K2ᵛ)

Since Jinner continued to publish her almanacs until at least 1664, we can assume she made her living from her writing and the skills it advertised. She therefore replaces Aphra Behn as, possibly, the first woman to make money by her pen.

More than twenty years later, in 1688, Mary Holden 'Student in Phys. and Astrol.' also had her almanac published. She, too, included medical remedies in her books,

for all women troubled with vapours, rising of the mother, convulsion fits, also the canker in the mouth, with so much ease, that the patient will hardly feel it; and all other diseases incident to my own sex. (sig. B4)

In the following year, the title page of her *The Womans Almanack* includes the explanation that she is 'midwife in Sudbury, and student in physic and astrology'. Her prognostication for the year is more closely tailored to the need to sell her skills than her first almanac had been, consisting largely of the expectation that people will be ill, and her book ends with an advertisement for 'that most noble and incomparable medicine known by the name of Clark's Compound Spirit of Scurvy-Grass'; by this time being produced, in all likelihood, by his widow, Mary (see broadsheet advertisements above). It is possible that further research into medical women of the period would reveal more links between them.

Before the establishment of the College of Physicians, and the subsequent founding of the United Company of Barber-Surgeons and the Worshipful Society of the Art and Mistery of Apothecaries, licensing of medicine had all been under the control of the bishops.[34] Bishops continued to license midwives throughout the seventeenth century (except, of course, during the inter-regnum), despite two attempts that the women made, in 1616 and 1634, to have themselves recognised as a separate society, governed by their own regulations.

The licences that were issued, however, demonstrate the existence of an informal training given to aspiring midwives by their experienced sisters. The midwives' oath specifically mentions the existence of 'deputies', requiring certified midwives not to leave their assistants alone at a birth. It seems that in London, at least, women would sometimes train for up to seven years, the standard length of a craft apprenticeship, before applying to a bishop for a licence. Applicants had to be accompanied by witnesses who could testify to their proficiency in the 'science or art or calling' of midwifery.[35] Midwives were required to swear an oath which bound them to ensure that no false charges of paternity were brought, no babies swapped, hidden or killed and not to assist at secret confinements (provisions designed to protect primogeniture, dower rights and the life of the infant); to make sure that babies were properly baptised according to Anglican ceremonies, and not to use witchcraft or other devilish arts themselves; and to provide their expertise equally for rich and poor, not using a woman's pain in childbirth to extort money from her that she would not have given freely. A list of questions to be asked on episcopal visits in Elizabethan times suggests that in that period, at least, the most significant part of the oath was thought to be the provisions against witchcraft.[36]

It is difficult to disentangle the history of the struggle for control of midwifery in the seventeenth century, because standard accounts of the events side firmly with the College of Physicians, dismissing the 'ignorance' of generations of women's acquired experience, and presenting the midwives' resistance to a male takeover as a stubborn refusal of progress.[37] The major advantage physicians had was their superior knowledge of anatomy, gained from the two compulsory dissections they had to attend before receiving a medical degree. On the other hand, as the midwives pointed out when opposing Peter Chamberlen's attempt to take control of their training and licensing, men's experience of the events of a normal labour – and the great majority of labours *were* normal – was slight, since they were only called for in cases of extremity (Jane Donegan, *Women and Men Midwives*, pp. 13–14).

There were two major confrontations between midwives and men who wished to control them. In 1616, midwives, supported by the family who invented the secret obstetrical forceps, the Chamberlen brothers, petitioned the king to allow them to form a society. The matter was referred to the College of Physicians, who suggested instead that midwives should be trained and licensed by the physicians. Neither plan was instituted. In 1634, the Chamberlens made an overt attempt to gain control of midwifery. This time, the midwives dreamt up the ingenious scheme of turning immediately to the College of Physicians as their allies, presenting the Chamberlens' plan as an attempt to gain a monopoly which would be equally damaging to midwives and physicians. The physicians were persuaded to request the bishops to reject the Chamberlens' petition, and Peter Chamberlen himself was prosecuted for not having episcopal licence to practise.[38]

Much bitterness developed between midwives and the Chamberlen men. The Chamberlens kept the exact description of their forceps a strictly guarded secret until shortly before the death of the last male family member, a grandson of Peter Chamberlen the elder, in 1728. In their petition to the College of Physicians, the midwives accuse this family of refusing to help the poor, in direct contravention of their oath. When Hugh Chamberlen translated Mauriceau's treatise of midwifery, he seems to have been rather embarrassed about the family policy of not revealing the construction of their 'crotchets', which they claimed could save the lives of women otherwise doomed to die in labour. The clan has to care first for its profits, he says.

I will now take leave to offer an apology for not publishing the secret I mention we have to extract children without hooks, where other artists use them, which is, that there being my father and two brothers living, that practise this art, I cannot esteem it my own to dispose of, nor publish it without injury to them.[39]

No account of mid seventeenth-century medicine would be complete without some mention of Nicholas Culpeper, herbalist, empiric and astrological physician, who argued fiercely in his many published works against the monopolistic designs of the College of Physicians. In 1651 he printed *A Dictionary for Midwives*. Dedicating the text to the midwives themselves, he promised that if they followed his directions they would be able to ward off the incursion of men into their profession. His book is full of political observations on the state of medicine, reflecting, for instance, on the fact that the much-vaunted remedies sold by physicians were expensive, beyond the means of ordinary people, whereas traditional herbal concoctions could be made free from the plants growing in their gardens. He is also incisive in his criticisms of the advice customarily given to pregnant women to eat well and plentifully, suggesting that nutritional supplements be given free to poor women.

I think 'tis needless to forewarn women of such things as cause miscarriage, or to tell weak women they must eat good victuals, for out of question they will do it if they can get it, I never knew any behindhand in that; I wish from my heart, our state would but be so happy to take such a course, that women in that case might not want, which they might easily do, and it would make them dear in the eyes of God, and the nation.[40]

When Jane Sharp was undertaking her wide reading preparatory to writing *The Midwives Book*, this passage seems to have caught her eye. She echoes it, calling for money wasted by the rich on high living to be spent on improving the health of the needy (p. 92).

Pregnancy was especially frightening for the poor, but it was a life-threatening event for all women. Diaries and other writings by women of the time are scattered with references to this grim fact. Mary Rich, the Countess of Warwick, describes visiting a friend in labour afraid for her life. Alice Thornton records how, at the age of eighteen, she watched her sister, who had already had six still-born children, give birth to her sixteenth baby: she also describes her own narrow escape from death on bearing a child. John Evelyn's biography of Margaret Godolphin narrates her terror of marriage and pregnancy and her eventual death in childbed, and the *Eliza's Babes* poet asks God to spare her the terrors of physical offspring. Lady Elizabeth Brackley, one of the authors of the play *The Concealed Fanseys*, died in childbirth in 1663, and Sarah Goodhue 'died suddenly (as she presaged she should) July 23, 1681, three days after she had been delivered of two hopeful children, leaving ten in all surviving'.[41] Many other examples could be found. It is likely, therefore, that as more books on midwifery began to appear after 1650, they met an audience eager for advice on how to survive. These books frequently drew on one another for information and advice, and used strikingly similar illustrations and examples as they explained reproductive anatomy, the processes of conception, pregnancy and birth, and described treatments for various infections, womb prolapses, and abnormal presentations in labour.[42] One series of such books, *The Complete Midwives Practice*, also contained a translation of the writings of the famous early seventeenth-century French midwife, Louise Bourgeois who worked for the French royal family.

The subject-matter and instructions of *The Midwives Book* by Jane Sharp (1671) bear close similarity to contemporary texts, many passages running parallel to those found elsewhere. She says that she has read all other books on the subject that she could obtain, and paid to have translations made of writings in French, Dutch and Italian. She makes no claim to originality in subject-matter. What is important to her is to teach her fellow-midwives anatomy, a knowledge which has been denied them because they cannot attend the universities or register for apprenticeships to be taught it. Dedicating her book 'To the Midwives of England', she addresses them as 'Sisters', and calls them to the project of keeping midwifery in women's hands by combining their 'practical' knowledge with 'speculative' book-learning (p. 2). Midwifery is one of the few women's trades that appear in the bible, so she is able to appeal to this source as an authority: biblical midwives are all women, indicating that there is a 'natural propriety' for the art to be left in female hands. Theories about 'natural deficiencies' have often been used against women. Sharp could turn such claims to make a case for feminine superiority, while not limiting her case to nature alone. Working together, midwives can develop and pass on their abilities to one another.

And though nature be not alone sufficient to the perfection of it, yet farther knowledge may be gained by a long and diligent practice, and be communicated to others of our sex. (p. 3)

Language itself reveals that midwifery properly belongs to women, she says. Male practitioners are forced to identify themselves by adding 'men' to the title, calling themselves 'men midwives' (p. 3). This is not her only reflection on language. Characteristically, medical books are written by and for men with classical education, and are littered with Latin terminology. Even the radical Nicholas Culpeper uses such vocabulary, inserting a glossary at the end of his text. This irritates Sharp. Book-learning has its place, she says, but 'hard words' serve as a barrier in texts like these.

I have as briefly and as plainly as I could, laid down a description of the parts of generation of both sexes, purposely omitting hard names, that I might have no cause to enlarge my work, by giving you the meaning of them when there is no need, unless it be for such persons who desire rather to know words than things. (p. 80)

Awareness of being a woman with a mission has many intricate effects on Jane Sharp's writings. Conventionally, a description of male anatomy always preceded that of female sexual organs in the textbook. Bowing to tradition in her ordering of *The Midwives Book*, Sharp nevertheless draws attention to the demeaning of women implied by this second place, which has been assigned

because it is commonly maintained that the masculine gender is more worthy than the feminine, though perhaps when men have need of us they will yield the priority to us. (p. 4)

The overt identification of herself as part of 'us', a community of womanhood, runs through her book, providing the structure for many passing jokes that are always made at men's expense. Discussing the male foreskin, for instance, she remarks that its purpose is to protect the glans from pain, but that all cultures have not followed this design.

The Jews indeed were commanded to be circumcised, but now circumcision avails not and is forbidden by the apostle. I hope no man shall be so void of reason and religion, as to be circumcised to make trial which of these two opinions is the best; but the world was never without some mad men, who will do anything to be singular. (pp. 31–2)

When she comes to describe the elastic properties of the vagina, she recalls a man who complained that over the years his wife's vagina had become slack, reducing his pleasure. She is quick to turn the implied derogation against the man: 'Perhaps the fault was not the woman's but his own, his weapon shrunk and was grown too little for the scabbard' (p. 53). Her sense of the ridiculous grows to grotesque proportions when listing possible symptoms of pregnancy. A woman might experience various changes, she says. For instance, 'she hath a preternatural desire for something not fit to eat nor drink, as some women with child have longed to bite off a piece of their husband's buttocks' (p. 103).

Many examples could be drawn from *The Midwives Book* to illustrate the way that Jane Sharp continually re-establishes her allegiance to other women, and their need to identify with one another. Her training in humoral medicine forces her to conclude and state that women are 'less perfect' than men, having less heat, and that some women are lascivious, unchaste creatures. She also follows her sources in condemning lesbians (p. 45) and in describing infibulation (female circumcision) as necessary for physiological reasons for some women (p. 46). Nonetheless, the text is peppered with rebellions against other accepted anti-woman senti-ments. Responding to masculine defamation of the female sexual organs, for instance, she firmly asserts

we women have no more cause to be angry, or be ashamed of what nature hath given us than men have, we cannot be without ours no more than they can want theirs. (p. 33)

She also completely forbids the performance of a caesarian section unless the mother has died, since it is inevitably fatal to a woman, whatever surgeons may assert to the contrary (pp. 195–6); and warns women not to allow their marriage to be consummated during their menstrual period, since the extra vaginal lubrication of the flow might cause their virginity to be doubted (pp. 50–1). As she describes how to turn babies in cases of bad presentation, how to expel growths or dead foetuses from the womb, or ways of treating the ravages of venereal disease, her language remains clear and compassionate. She is determined to share her book-learning, having 'often sat down sad in the consideration of the many miseries women endure in the hands of unskilful midwives' (sig. A2).

Elizabeth Cellier's analysis of the solution to midwives' educational shortcomings was not published in her lifetime, but it must have cir-culated widely enough in manuscript to have provoked public discussion, since in 1688 she went into print claiming a need to answer the objections of a surgeon who opposed her ideas.[43]

During the controversies surrounding the Popish Plot and the Meal-Tub Plot, Cellier had established her loyalty to the Catholic cause and James II, suffering fining, imprisonment and stoning in the pillory for her pains (see Introduction). She was later installed as royal midwife, and delighted in proving wrong the physicians who had predicted that the queen would never bear live offspring.[44] In 1687 she addressed the king directly with a request to provide funds to establish training for midwives and care for poor and abandoned children at a royal hospital. Quoting the mortality rates of women in childbed and of newborn infants over the previous twenty years, she argues that there is a clear need to provide midwives with more formal training. The hospital could serve as a college for this purpose, as well as ending the practices of 'wicked and cruel mothers' who she says overlay and suffocate babies they cannot afford or do not want. She proceeds to describe the financing and workings of such an institution, to be run under the government of a group of experienced and 'matron-like' women. Presumably she expected herself to be one of these governors.[45] The college was not to be solely under the control of women. She assumes that suitable physicians will be appointed, who will have the right to inspect and examine the midwives.

Even this was too radical for some. Cellier's second pamphlet on the subject was published in the form of a reply to an objecting doctor. Perhaps she had a particular opponent in mind: on the other hand, the major points of *An Answer to Dr* —— might have been to advertise James II's consent to the scheme, and to establish a firm biblical precedent for the idea.[46] Cellier's proposal comes at the end of seventy years of agitation around the question of male incursion into midwifery, a period in which midwives had learnt a great deal about the history of their profession. She retells the story in Exodus about the midwives' refusal to execute newborn infants, pointing out that physicians had accepted the command to do so. In recognition of their goodness, God had built them a house, the proto-type, she argues, of her college. She also uses classical sources, citing the case of the Athenian Agnodicea who had disguised herself as a man to gain training as a doctor and midwife when women were banned from the profession. When Agnodicea's deception is discovered and she is prose-cuted, Cellier shows Athenian women uniting to storm the court.

The house being encompassed by most women of the city, the ladies entered before the judges, and told them they could no longer account them for husbands or friends, but for cruel enemies, that condemned her to death, who restored them to their healths; protesting they would all die with her if she were put to death. (p. 4)

The men are forced to change the law, making it legal for women to practise medicine on their own sex.

This image of women's collective action achieving change must owe much to Cellier's experience of the unity among her own profession in more recent times. She also gained from this a knowledge of the recent history of women in her own country, and is able to cite and explain the various changes in licensing procedures for midwives since the 1640s. Calling on doctors to recognise that their abstract book-learning is no substitute for the midwives' acquired practical experience, she threatens a rebellion of women in her own time if physicians try to block the establishment of her college.

I hope, doctor, these considerations will deter any of you from pretending to teach us midwifery, especially such as confess they never delivered women in their lives, and being asked what they would do in such a case, reply they have not yet studied it, but will when occasion serves; this is something to the purpose I must confess, doctor: but I doubt it will not satisfy the women of this age, who are so sensible and impatient of their pain, that few of them will be prevailed with to bear it, in compliment to the doctor, while he fetches his book, studies the case, and teaches the midwife to perform her work, which she hopes may be done before he comes. I protest, doctor, I have not power enough with the women to prevail with them to be patient in this case. (pp. 6–7)

In the end, no college was established: but midwifery did remain a predominantly female profession until the nineteenth century.[47]

The years after the Restoration saw several women writing to teach one another skills which had once been assumed female by right, and a necessary part of housewifely duties. In doing so, they also sought to make a living for themselves, advertising their arts, and offering them for sale. Two of them, Sarah Jinner and Hannah Wolley, predate by several years Aphra Behn's decision to use her pen to make a living. On the one hand, their writing can be interpreted as an upgrading of traditional feminine activities, claiming them as suitable subjects for women to write about and study. On the other hand, this also marks a loss: it could no longer be assumed that these fields of endeavour belonged to women, as hack-writers, professional male cooks, the College of Physicians and men-midwives made inroads into the 'female' crafts. Instead of arguing that women should be allowed access to the 'male' concerns of govern-ment, or admitted to the schools and universities that gave men their socially valued classical grounding, these writers mostly concentrated on fighting a rearguard action, struggling to prevent their complete exclusion from all remunerative fields of endeavour. Faced with the imminent danger of losing the little they had had, who could hope to gain more?

CHAPTER EIGHT

EDUCATION

WE are become like worms that only live in the dull earth of ignorance, winding ourselves sometimes out by the help of some refreshing rain of good educations, which seldom is given us; for we are kept like birds in cages to hop up and down in our houses, not suffered to fly abroad to see the several changes of fortune, and the various humours, ordained and created by nature; thus wanting the experiences of nature, we must needs want the understanding and knowledge and so consequently prudence, and invention of men: thus by an opinion, which I hope is but an erroneous one in men, we are shut out of all power and authority, by reason we are never employed either in civil or martial affairs, our counsels are despised, and laughed at, the best of our actions are trodden down with scorn, by the overweening conceit men have of themselves and through despisement of us. (Margaret Cavendish, *Philosophical and Physical Opinions*, 1655, sig. B2ᵛ)

Margaret Cavendish addressed these remarks on behalf of women to the two English universities when she was living abroad with her exiled royalist husband in 1655. She shows women's limited education and inferior social position to be tightly linked in the ideas and practices of patriarchy: women are excluded both from the schooling and from the experiences which would allow them to achieve great things. In attributing male superiority to education and arrogance rather than to natural ability, she is directly contradicting her own statement published only a few months earlier, where in page after dreary page she had catalogued women's slight achievements in the world (*The Worlds Olio*, sig A4ʳ–A5ᵛ). On that occasion, she had been forced to conclude that women were naturally inferior to men in both mind and body, an assertion consistent with her belief there that 'thoughts are free, those can never be enslaved'. To change her angle of approach to the problem in this way permits an analysis of the hierarchy between the sexes as a system made by men, not a structure inevitably ordained by God or nature.

The question of female inferiority certainly had to be addressed. The abolition of all 'kingly power' was being urged by radical groups like the Diggers, who explained that the aims of the revolution were not attained by the single act of cutting off the king's head: all power structures related to this system of government must also be destroyed.[1] Although it was not inevitable that such arguments would also raise the question of men's power over women, the activism of women in the radical sects, and the defence of castles and pleading for money that wives of absent royalists undertook, do seem to have raised the issue as a matter of hot public debate in the period. Cavendish's catalogue of female failure in *The Worlds Olio* is prefaced by a summary of contemporary female objections against male supremacy. She is explicit that these arguments are being made by women, and by many of them.

True it is, our sex make great complaints, that men from their first creation usurped a supremacy to themselves, although we were made equal by nature, which tyrannical government they have kept ever since, so that we could never come to be free, but rather more and more enslaved, using us either like children, fools, or subjects, that is, to flatter or threaten us, to allure or force us to obey, and will not let us divide the world equally with them . . .; whereas in nature we have as clear an understanding as men, if we were bred in schools to mature our brains, and to mature our understandings, that we might bring forth the fruits of knowledge. (sig. A4)

The reality of female low status in the world was obvious: the problem was how to account for it, and what could be done about it.

The educational opportunities available to women in this period were certainly slighter than those reserved for men. Little information is available concerning the teaching given to the majority of the population, but Margaret Spufford and David Cressy have pointed to the existence of short-lived schools in rural communities, where the poor could probably acquire basic literacy, if they were not taught this at home.[2] Richard Brathwait, at least, was unimpressed by country schoolmistresses, whom he characterised as 'ladies cashiered gentlewomen' who he said moved to the countryside only if they were unable to make a living teaching in the cities (*The English Gentlewoman*, 1631, pp. 74–5). Since details about such schools are sparse – we know of their existence mostly through statements from witnesses at trials in church courts – little is known about what they taught, or how commonly their pupils included girls. Theodosia Alleine mentions setting up a school where she taught local children and took in boarders, after her husband resigned as a church minister in 1662, but she does not describe what or whom she actually taught (*The Life and Death*, p. 91). Few women writers of the period comment explicitly on their class origins, and it will not be possible to judge how much education was commonly available to which class until further research has been undertaken. Such evidence as we do possess does not all suggest the same picture. To take two examples, Anna Trapnel, the daughter of a shipwright, was able to write her autobiography and records that she was 'trained up to my book and writings' (*The Cry of a Stone*, p. 3). We can assume, however, that her fellow-prophet Elinor Channel, whose husband was 'a very poor man', was unable to write, necessitating her journey from Cranley in Surrey to London to find someone to write down her message (*A Message from God*, p. 2). Nonetheless Cressy has shown that in all classes during this period men were considerably more likely than women to be able to at least sign their names. Whatever degree of education was available to the poor, boys were more likely than girls to receive it.

Where sons of the gentry and aristocracy were taught by private tutors or attended grammar schools, graduating then to the universities, inns of court or dissenting academies, the daughters of the same families had narrower choices. Among the aristocracy, Margaret Cavendish and Ann Fanshawe both recall in their autobiographies being educated at home by their mothers. Unless the mothers had received a thorough education themselves, such an arrangement could not be expected to produce highly literate students. I have quoted above from Cavendish's conclusion that it is 'against nature for a woman to spell right', and the Victorian editor of Rachel Wriothesley Lady Russell's letters describes the originals as being full of orthographic errors. Daughters of gentry could be sent out to study. Sarah Davy, for example, mentions being sent away to school (*Heaven Realiz'd*, pp. 7, 15), and Katherine Philips, who was educated at home by a relative until the age of eight, was then transferred to Mrs Salmon's school in Hackney. Little information concerning what was taught at such establishments survives, but passing references in various works suggest that they were more concerned with training girls in 'accomplishments' – singing, dancing, needlework and French – than with the study of classical authors that was central to male middle-class schooling. Dorothy Dury, recalling the emphasis in her own education on 'dancing and unnecessary works', proposed the introduction of a more useful course of study for girls of this class. It is not surprising, then, to find that Mary Carleton's evidence that she is a foreign princess, not an English gentlewoman, rests in part on her declared familiarity with Latin, Greek and oriental languages: attainments generally beyond the ken of Englishwomen.[3]

The primary task of the grammar school[4] was to instruct its boy pupils in a knowledge of the classics, especially Latin. The ability to speak Latin gave men access to all that was considered important in their own culture and that of the past, and armed them with the language of international communication. Those men and women who knew no Latin were thereby excluded from the most mundane points of reference of learned dispute. Grammar school pupils were taught to translate, and were drilled in the 'imitation' of classical models: that is, to select and adapt appropriate phrases and sentiments from the Ancients in their own compositions. Useful passages were stored in commonplace books, for future reference, and disputations (a means of testing and displaying this knowledge) were employed in classroom and public orations. Boys were also sometimes taught some Greek and Hebrew. University education assumed familiarity with basic Latin grammar and vocabulary, and entrance to the legal and medical professions, and to the church, required a ready knowledge of classical languages. Foster Watson was more accurate than he perhaps realised when he described this general use of Latin as leading to 'the "freemasonry" of learned men'. Those inside the secret society knew its codes and culture and could profit from membership. Those outside – most men and almost all women – were excluded from a wide range of social activities and employments.[5] I have quoted (Chapter Seven) Jane Sharp's anger over the exclusive language used by medical men. Mary Trye, defending the theories and methods of alchemists, has no option but to mention that, although she has some familiarity with the classics, she has read them in translation, not in the original, and to say that she would raise her children to book-learning, given the opportunity (*Medicatrix*, p. 73).

One of the few seventeenth-century women to learn both Greek and Latin was Anne Finch, Viscountess Conway. Her brother went to Oxford and studied under the philosopher Henry More. She stayed at home, taught herself Latin and Greek, studied mathematics, and wrote a philosophical treatise which was not published until she was dead, and even then appeared anonymously. Her letters, edited in 1930 by Marjorie Nicholson, build a picture of the narrowness of the constraints that kept this woman confined to her home while she corresponded with Leibnitz, van Helmont and Henry More, and served as the recipient of More's mocking dismissals of Margaret Cavendish's published philosophy. The fact that she suffered acutely from migraine is no surprise in the light of recent feminist research linking the condition to repressed female anger and frustration. Her only access to the academic disputes that filled her daily life was through private correspondence with these men. Those of her letters that More describes as long and interesting, and which presumably dealt with philosophical matters, have not survived. What we do have are More's constant attempts to silence her, and to persuade her to abandon studying.

Madam, your disease not permitting you to think very anxiously of anything, you would do well to forbear wholly from any the least labour of the brain, and pass

away the time with the greatest ease and content you can contrive . . . Madam,
I desire your ladyship not to read Descartes with over much curiosity and
solicitude at first, but carefully remembering your headache . . . Madam, I had
like to have forgot one principal thing I thought of which is to desire your
ladyship to forbear reading anything that has any considerable difficulty in
it, though your head permit it, but husband your strength as much as possibly
you can.[6]

Even so distant a connection with university learning was to be
discouraged. The fact that Conway persevered and wrote a book on
philosophy, when confronted by such obstacles, is an extraordinary
achievement.

The most radical voices of the interregnum, clearly perceiving the links
between the established educational system and the ideological indoc-
trination and domination of the church and state, wanted to abolish the
universities.[7] They called for an abandonment of Latin, and of book-
learning in general. The right to write, and to express opinions on the
state of the world, were to come from a grasp of truth, not from books.
With the Second Coming imminently expected, and God's servants and
handmaids inspired by the Holy Spirit, no teaching was necessary: 'Then
shall the Saints be of one mind, and one heart, and shall not need to teach
one another' (Anna Trapnel, *A Legacy for Saints*, p. 23). The universities,
as the training-ground of the clergy, were the particular target of the
Saints. Quakers and other sectaries turned away from books, even from
the Bible, and looked to the Inner Light, their own consciences, as a
source of understanding. Again and again, they called on people to deny
priests, and on priests to abandon book-learning.

Therefore know you, that you may be, and are ignorant, though you think
yourselves wise: silly men and women may see more into the mystery of Christ
Jesus, than you: for the apostles, that the scribes called illiterate, and Mary and
Susanna (silly women, as you would be ready to call them, if they were here now)
these knew more of the Messiah, than all the learned Priests and Rabbis . . .
Would you hearken to Jesus Christ, and obey his light in your consciences, you
would come down to humility and fear of the Lord, to the true wisdom and
understanding, that you would not need so many authors, and books, you would
not need to rent your heads with studying, but you would come to see your
Teacher in you. (Cotton and Cole, *To the Priests and People of England*, p. 4)

Knowledge is to be freely available, not given at the price of tithes by
hireling church ministers. The women's petition against tithing (*These
Several Papers*) included a proposal to abolish the universities altogether.
God was thought to be on his way, and the universities and book-
learning could and should be abandoned in favour of the Inner Light.[8]

The radical edge of the revolution was blunted, and the universities
were not abolished. Discussions about their status, and of the role of

education in society, continued throughout the 1650s, however, and during the early years of the Commonwealth period a number of texts by men critical of the established educational practices were published. Hartlib, Dury and Comenius argued the need to establish a school in every town and village in the country. The young of both sexes in all classes were to be educated, to familiarise them with God's Will for His chosen people. Latin, it was argued, should hold a less all-pervasive place in the timetable, and should be replaced by practical divinity and study of the empirical sciences. These proposals were not intended, however, to abolish social distinctions between classes or genders. Improved education was expected to fit each group for its necessary role in society, and close attention was to be paid to manners and religious beliefs.

The impact of these suggested reforms was slight, since after an initial flurry of interest in educational reform in the late 1640s and early 1650s, parliament turned its attention to other matters.[9] Some of the individuals connected with Hartlib, Dury and Comenius, however, were involved in the establishment of the Royal Society, a body which sought to establish empirical observations as the new basis of human knowledge, eschewing the Ancients and classical languages, and arguing for texts to be written in clearer, more colloquial language. Margaret Cavendish at first assumed these reformers to be her natural allies in her quest to establish her reputation as an original philosopher. If Latin and Greek and familiarity with ancient authority was no longer required, her philosophical system might find acceptance.

The most ubiquitous concern of Cavendish's writings is her attempts to ensure her acceptance and fame as an author, and above all as a philosopher. In a world where respected male philosophers were mostly ensconced at universities, she was quick to point out the limited usefulness of the education such figures actually received. The rigorous drilling of grammar school pupils and university students in the rules of classical grammar made their thought pedestrian and unoriginal, she argues in *The Worlds Olio*, sig. O3^v, and the heroine of the *New Blazing World* scolds her empire's philosophers for their pedantry.

I have had enough, said she, of your chopped logic, and will hear no more of your syllogisms; your formal argumentations are able to spoil all natural wit.[10]

Cavendish is able, by dint of the kind of doublethink so typical of her female contemporaries, to turn an acknowledged handicap – her lack of education – into a space where she could negotiate acceptance of herself as a writer. She is a greater thinker because of her independence from men's schooling in the classics; she is not a scholar but a philosopher.

A scholar is to be learned in other men's opinions and actions, and a philosopher is to teach other men his opinions of nature, and to demonstrate the works of nature, so that a scholar is to learn, a philosopher to teach, and if they say there is no distinction between a professed scholar, and a professed philosopher, I am not of their opinion. (*Philosophical and Physical Opinions*, sig. B1ᵛ)

A similar case for women's superiority in some activities because they are not trammelled by the conventions of the male curriculum is argued by Dorothy Osborne, mocking the language of one of her relatives, who displays his learning in an inflated style. For letters, she argues, a woman's simpler style is more appropriate (*Letters*, p. 45). Aphra Behn is equally witty in her attack on men's education, and her assertion that a lack of it is irrelevant to her skills as a playwright.

I have heard that most of that which bears the name of learning, and which has abused such quantities of ink and paper, and continually employs so many ignorant, unhappy souls for ten, twelve, twenty years in the university (who yet poor wretches think they are doing something all the while) as logic, etc. and several other things (that shall be nameless lest I misspell them) are much more absolutely nothing than the errantest lay that e'er was writ . . . Plays have no great room for that which is men's great advantage over women, that is learning. (*The Dutch Lover*, Epistle to the Reader)

Cavendish establishes herself as an unlearned author, and at first she dismisses the significance of the classics whose students she expects to reject her. She has no Latin and no training in logic or disputations, and cannot develop or justify her propositions in the manner conventionally accepted. She aligns herself with new science, the adherents of which also rebelled against the tyranny of the Ancients, and in 1666 actually made a visit to the Royal Society to watch some experiments. The Minutes of the occasion betray the patronising forbearance with which the duchess was received: she was to find no allies among these learned men.[11] The two arenas of male intellectual endeavour, the universities and the Royal Society, might be divided on many things,[12] but they were united in their opposition to educational changes which might alter women's subordinate position.

Cavendish turned her attention back to the universities, to which she dedicated her last two philosophical works, *Observations Upon Experimental Philosophy* and *Grounds of Natural Philosophy*. Whatever the shortcomings of male academics, she must win acceptance there if her future fame is to be secured. After her visit to the Royal Society she rejects their experimental equipment, and defends the superiority of classical learning. The new scientists are just so many little boys, playing entertaining games and maligning their elders.

As boys that play with watery bubbles[1] [marg: glass-tubes], or fling dust[2] [marg: atoms] into each other's eyes, or make a hobby-horse[3] [marg: exterior figures of snow], are worthy of reproof rather than praise, for wasting their time with useless sports; so those that addict themselves to unprofitable arts, spend more time than they reap thereby. (*Observations*, pp. 10–11)

In the event, neither the disciples of the Ancients nor the Moderns welcomed an ill-educated woman into their ranks. Cavendish's class position, and the support of her husband, provided her with the leisure time to write, and the finances to have her works published. Dedicating them to the universities, she sent copies to individual colleges and they have survived, never having brought her the fame she sought.[13]

Arguments about education were intimately bound up with their authors' more general hopes and beliefs about society's structure and purpose. It is not surprising, therefore, to find that when men turned their attention to female education, they advanced schemes that reflected or promoted their various conceptions of female essence, and of women's place in the family and nation. The same figures from the Ancients and from recent world history were evoked to demonstrate women's essential goodness, or chastity, their susceptibility to temptation or their willingness to learn: Semiramis and the Amazons, Eve and Martha, Queen Elizabeth, Coke's daughters and the ubiquitous Anna Maria van Schurman are repeatedly cited, as was the feminine gender of the arts, graces, muses, virtues and four continents. For all the differences between these works, what unites them is their confident tone when holding forth on woman's place in the world, and their ransacking of classical sources for cases possibly saved from the authors' grammar school commonplace books. The purest example of this mode of argument is Henry Care's translation of Agrippa von Nettesheim's treatise *Female Pre-eminence*. The title page quotes from the Book of Esdras the proposition 'Women are strongest' (a thesis overruled in the Scriptures by 'Truth triumphs over all'), and the preface to the reader recommends the text as an ingenious logic exercise that proves by implication that all the arts and sciences are mere vanity. What is really important in the treatise is not the issue under discussion: female ability. What is at stake is the status of a mode of argumentation. If any case, even this one of female pre-eminence, can be proved from authority, then the status of disputation as a mode of education is brought into doubt. The central question, in fact, is not women's education at all, but the best method of educating men. It would be a mistake to reduce all male writings on female education to this kind of trivialising logic exercise. Some of the authors, most notably Charles Gerbier in his *Elogium Heroinum*, 1651, make a coherent case for women's potential, reproving men for excluding the sex from education. What unites these authors, however, is their clear and confident tone. They have a right to hold forth on this matter, and their training in disputations arms them with the conventions that produce the logical ordering of their works.[14]

The attainments of Anna Maria van Schurman of Utrecht were frequently cited by those seventeenth-century men who wrote in defence of female excellence, so it was highly appropriate for her treatise on women's education *The Learned Maid; or, Whether a Maid may be a Scholar?* to be translated into English in 1659.[15] Her 'logic exercise' has much in common with those of her male contemporaries. Being an exceptionally highly educated woman, she was able, like the men, to cite Greek and Latin sources for her opinions, as she advanced a case carefully faithful to the syllogistic conventions of contemporary logic.[16] Following these rules, she proves exhaustively women's need of, and right to, an education in grammar, logic and rhetoric on lines identical to those of the male grammar schools and universities. Like Comenius and his fellow educationalists, she also argues that a close acquaintance with classical sources will serve to make the Scriptures, and therefore Christian virtue, more accessible to them.

As the logic exercise advances, it becomes apparent that the education here promoted is intended only for selected women. To study, a woman must be 'endued at least with an indifferent good wit', must be someone 'not oppressed with want' (schooling is expensive), someone who is leisured enough to have 'spare hours from her general and special calling, that is, from the exercises of piety and household affairs' (p. 3). The student should preferably be single, since a married woman's household cares would prevent her having the leisure time to study. The title page of *The Learned Maid* and its dedicatory epistle by Spanheim are quick to point out Schurman's own virgin status. The case argued is, in fact, almost as conservative as its mode of argumentation. Only those women who can be spared without disrupting the existing social hierarchies can have access to schooling.

Within the bounds of this structure, and firmly inside the rules of feminine duty and the sphere of the home, however, van Schurman makes a case for leisured women to be educated. The tedious idleness of those whose main task in life is to be decorative is centrally what she seeks to save women from. Accepting that women belong in the home, she is then able to argue that this very fact makes study most suitable for them. The woman reading quietly at home will not be able to wander outside it, interfering with concerns not properly hers.

The study of Letters is convenient for them, for whom it is more decent to find themselves both business and recreation at home and in private, than abroad among others. (p. 13)

Women can study quietly in their parents' houses, and such an arrangement will be right and proper. It is consistent with this that, though she
defends a woman's right to study the 'masculine' fields of politics and
religion, it is beyond question to her that feminine action should not
extend to such matters (p. 15).

By using a respected male convention for argumentation, and by not
challenging the accepted role limitations of women, she is able to demonstrate her own learning and virtuous self-effacement simultaneously, and
to argue for some improvement in the lot of some women. It is significant
that even the revered van Schurman, a woman famous in several European countries, was unable to have her writings published without
rehearsing her unworthiness and asserting her virtue. The treatise is
followed by a collection of her letters to various European notables,
including one to Frederick Spanheim which names him as the originator
of the plan to publish her works. Without such urging she would not
have risked overstepping the bounds of modesty, the inclusion of this
letter implies.

As to the edition of my trifles, which you still persuade me to yield unto: though
I have been hitherto irresolute, yet now because it is your pleasure, I cannot any
longer resist your counsels, proceeding from so much candour and friendship.
(p. 51)

The pivotal problem for van Schurman, and for her fellow-female
promoters of women's worth, was indeed how to maintain a reputation
for modesty and feminine virtue while promoting the abilities and
achievements of their sex. For men this was easy: an ingenious case could
be argued, and to defend women could be interpreted as a charming piece
of gallantry. Several male authors use the necessity to defend helpless
females as the justification for their writing. Henry Care, the translator of
Agrippa's *Female Pre-eminence*, for instance, characterises Agrippa as a
man akin to the chivalrous knights of old, quick to defend ladies' slighted
reputations, 'obliging all to succour oppressed innocency' (sig. A2).

How could a woman argue for female worth without appearing immodest? After the Restoration, as women were ushered back into more
passive and home-bound roles, this question became one of pressing
urgency. A new approach to this subject was made by an acquaintance of
van Schurman's, Bathsua Makin.[17] The author of *An Essay to Revive the
Antient Education of Gentlewomen*, 1673, she had been tutor to the
daughter of Charles I, Princess Elizabeth, and dedicated her pamphlet to
Princess Mary (later Mary II). Her brother-in-law was John Pell, a noted
mathematician.[18] Even the possessor of this impressive array of contacts anticipates that to propose female education is a bold step that will meet with

opposition: she sees a need to contradict the accepted belief that learned women, like comets, bode mischief wherever they appear (p. 3). At first glance this caution might seem surprising, since, like Anna Maria van Schurman, the education she proposes and the statements she makes about female ability are less radical than the suggestions made by contemporary male authors. She constantly reiterates that if the plan she proposes were adopted, it would make women better wives and daughters, and would encourage boys to achieve more so as not to be outdone by their sisters (p. 4). The modesty of the proposal is indeed its central identifying feature. Makin is unimpressed by the hyperbolical claims and praises made by men of female excellence. She is not engaged in making an ingenious case, but in specific and possibly attainable improvements in some women's lot.

Let not your ladyships be offended, that I do not (as some have wittily done) plead for female pre-eminence. To ask too much is the way to be denied all. (p. 4)

She presents the power structure of patriarchy, where men have the right to philosophise on women's abilities, to 'quibble and droll upon a subject of this nature', and finally to permit or forbid their education. She knows that effective opposition to her proposal could come from men, and turns to her female reader to support her claims.

I have bespoken, and do expect your patronage; because it is your cause I plead against an ill custom, prejudicial to you, which men will not willingly suffer to be broken. (p. 5)

An Essay to Revive the Antient Education of Gentlewomen has been accepted as the composition of Bathsua Makin, despite the fact that the voice of the text is male, and the author states 'I am a man myself'. Without the discovery of a manuscript, or some other collaborative evidence, it is impossible to decide certainly whether Makin wrote this text, which acts in part as an advertisement for her school for young gentlewomen, or whether she merely commissioned a co-operative man to write it. Its argumentation clearly suggests, however, that it is indeed the work of a woman. The keen sense of solidarity with women and, more importantly, the particular understanding of the power structure of patriarchy present in the pamphlet, both indicate that the problem is approached from a female perspective, the position of the oppressed and marginalised. The adoption of a male persona allows her the freedom of a male voice: she can be judicious, expansive, judgmental without apology or proviso. A virtuous, modest female voice would be hard put to argue for women's equality with their masters. A male author-figure has the requisite authority, and Makin has access to such a persona through her training in the classics and in the rhetorical mode of argumentation that characterises the text. The price paid for this desexing, of course, is to remove her value as a role-model for other women. Only a man – or a male persona – can write with such assurance on such a matter. Only those in power have the right to make extensive pronouncements on the fate of the powerless.

The author has obviously read widely in books such as Gerbier's *Elogium Heroinum*, 1651, Heywood's *The Generall History of Women*, 1657, and Agrippa's *Female Pre-eminence* (translated 1670), the texts that make up the male debate on female excellence. She cites many of the instances listed by these writers, cataloguing extensively women's achievements in classical times, and mentioning the feminine gender of the continents, muses, virtues, arts and so on. The text is not particularly orderly – it reads as though it has been constructed from scattered notes of various sources, pausing in the middle of her remarks on poetry, for instance, to add, 'I had almost forgot the Sybils'.[19]

Makin negotiates a case for women's education through a maze of male obstructive assumptions. Taking the case of Eve's eating the apple that gave knowledge to humankind, and thereby lost them paradise, a story so often cited by detractors of women, she argues that the incident indicates the need for education. Everyone agrees that 'men, by liberal education, are much bettered, as to intellectuals and morals'. If women were educated equally, it would prevent them being tempted by evil (p. 7). Other elements of her argument show a similar juggling of truisms. Those seeking to restrict women's sphere of activity commonly cited Solomon's description of a virtuous woman (Proverbs, 31.10–31). Makin analyses the parts of this picture, and uses it to argue the need for a widely ranging curriculum.

To buy wool and flax, to dye scarlet and purple, requires skill in natural philosophy. To consider a field, the quantity and quality, requires knowledge in geometry. To plant a vineyard, requires understanding in husbandry. She could not merchandize, without knowledge in arithmetic. She could not govern so great a family well, without knowledge in politics and economics. She could not look well to the ways of her household, except she understood physic and surgery. She could not open her mouth with wisdom, and have in her tongue the law of kindness, unless she understood grammar, rhetoric and logic. This seems to be the description of an honest, well-bred, ingenious industrious Dutchwoman. I desire our women (whose condition calls them to business) should have no other breeding, but what will enable them to do those things performed by this woman. (p. 35)

If turning to carefully qualified arguments for women's education represents a retreat, a loss of the visionary potential of the revolutionary years – and I think that it does – this is nonetheless a retreat that is armed with the knowledge of the recent past. The reference in this quotation to the 'industrious Dutchwoman', and other mentions of Holland in the pamphlet (pp. 27–8), suggest that Makin may have corresponded with van Schurman on the relative position of women in their two countries. The *Essay* is also liberally dotted with references to the abilities and achievements of contemporary women: Ann Bradstreet, Katherine Philips, the Countess of Huntingdon, Mrs Thorold, Lady Mildmay and the Duchess of Newcastle are all named and their learning detailed (pp. 10, 12, 20). Like van Schurman, she wishes the curriculum to include details of women's history, to give young females something to aspire to. Her recognition of what has been attempted in the recent past is acute. Women have achieved remarkable things during the revolutionary years, and she does not want this breaking of role constraints to be forgotten. Women's education, it is implied, should enable future similar occurrences.

> In these late times there are several instances of women, when their husbands were serving their king and country, defended their houses, and did all things, as soldiers, with prudence and valour, like men. They appeared before committees, and pleaded their own causes with good success. (p. 25)

This is, of course, a very partial picture of female activism in the Commonwealth. No mention is made of the antics of Makin's class enemies, the radical sectaries. It is in these times, with the return of a frivolous and licentious court, where women's place was to be decorative and biddable, that the case for women's education, and her need to be considered as able and intelligent, is made. The alternative to spending time on book-learning is to idly squander it in dicing, flirting and card-playing. The timeliness of the attempt to save some channels of useful and interesting activity is paramount.

> I am very sensible it is an ill time to set on foot this design: wherein not only learning but virtue itself is scorned and neglected, as pedantic things, fit only for the vulgar. I know no better way to reform these exorbitancies, than to persuade women to scorn those toys and trifles they now spend their time about, and to attempt higher things here offered.[20]

For all its similarity to male defences of female education, therefore, *An Essay* is also radically different from those. It is written from a female understanding of the dangers to women of changes in contemporary society, and with the tactical aim of saving what is salvageable. This is not the only respect in which it is a far more pragmatic text than *Elogium Heroinum* or *Female Pre-eminence*. The pamphlet works in part as an advertisement for Bathsua Makin's school for young gentlewomen, and the direction of its argument is formed in part by the need to persuade the reader to buy the education described. The case made for female education therefore has to be general enough to sell. Too radical an argument, by the 1670s at least, is unlikely to be considered seriously, and so is unlikely to create a market for the school. Makin needs her reader not only to be interested or entertained by her argument, but be sufficiently convinced to take action upon it. It is by running a school that she is making her living. The pamphlet also, therefore, discusses in detail contemporary theories of education, to justify the curriculum offered at the school. Since the timetable includes study of the classics – the area of knowledge most closed to women – Makin also makes her case that, using Comenius's *Orbis Pictus* and *Janua Linguarum*, a girl is capable of learning these languages (p. 37). Lilly's grammar, she explains, is much inferior (pp. 38–9). The *Essay* ends with listing the curriculum offered at Makin's school.

The *Essay* negotiates some space for some women, but it is a negotiation made in retreat. A close ally of the returned monarchists, Makin in no way supports or identifies with the rebellious women who had fought for the ending of hierarchy and kingly power, and called for the abolition of the universities and book-learning. In the post-Restoration world, she is bound to state: 'My intention is not to equalize women to men, much less to make them superior. They are the weaker sex' (p. 29). In describing the limits of her plans she, like van Schurman, is clear that the recipients of education must necessarily be the rich: the poor are too busy with other matters (p. 22). Education is justified as a rarefied adornment of women's leisure time, something to relieve tedium and idleness (p. 33). Women are still to be raised to their distaff, and she makes it clear that she does not intend 'to hinder good housewifery, neither have I called any from their necessary labour to their book' (p. 38). It is to the established order that she appeals, and she calls on women to believe that education will make them better pleased with their subordinate position in life.

God hath made man the head, if you be educated and instructed, as I propose, I am sure you will acknowledge it, and be satisfied that you are helps, that your husbands do consult and advise with you (which if you be wise they will be glad of) and that your husbands have the casting-voice, in whose determinations you will acquiesce. (p. 4)

An Essay to Revive the Antient Education of Gentlewomen marks a retreat to quiescence, a retreat to the home and the schoolroom: but a retreat armed with Latin and Greek, the keys to male knowledge, and therefore the hope of not being defeated entirely.

BEGINNING AGAIN

ANYONE who has spent a long time working on one project knows that a major feeling when you near its end is that you would do it differently if you started again. That is in part how I feel about this book. So instead of making some grand summarising statements, I would like to spend these last few pages sketching out what I think are the major gaps here, in material and approach, and how I think they have come about.

I argue in the Introduction that the study of 'history' is the study of the present as well as the past. In many ways, we find in the past what we look for: by and large, we only come up with answers to the questions we think to ask. So the present creates the past – or creates our perception of it, which is all we have. When I started this project, in 1979, I 'simply' wanted to find out about forgotten women writers, because studying English literature had meant almost solely studying men's writing. I just wanted to know what was there, and wanted to share what I discovered with other women. That desire in me was created by my involvement with the Women's Liberation Movement, and the initial stages of my research made possible through the existence of pioneering collections of early women writers made by other feminists, such as Jean Goulianos, Cora Kaplan and Louise Bernikow (and, long before all of us, Myra Reynolds's *The Learned Lady in England 1650 – 1760*).

As the work continued, my perspective shifted. A Conservative government, elected at the time I began my research, began to implement a systematic programme reducing the income, rights and employment chances of us all. Alongside these economic and legal changes, shifts in people's perception of our society also began to take place. Like many of my friends, I became increasingly alarmed at seeing the terms of debate changing: everything began to be argued about in terms of 'value for money', all other kinds of value being scorned or ignored. And at the same time, too, there came the experience of 'friends falling away from the truth': sisters and comrades from years past settling down, giving up, giving in. The parallels between these developments and the changes that took place after the Restoration of the Monarchy made it possible for me both to perceive the ideological shifts that happened, I believe, in Restoration England, and made me more uneasy about some of the changes I see underway in the women's movement. Quite a lot of recent feminist debate, it seems to me, presents both violence and sexual desire as quintessentially male; women, by contrast, are seen as peace-loving and as more interested in gentle cuddling than in energetic lovemaking. Since dominant ideas about 'women's nature' also define us as nurturing, sexually passive beings, I am not convinced that anti-sex, anti-violence feminist positions are really that radical at all. The parallels with seventeenth-century women's retreat into virtue seem only too painfully clear. No doubt my allegiances in the present on such issues 'distort' how I understand the past, and my work on the past 'distorts' how I perceive the contemporary debates. I am sure that as the political circumstances of the here and now change, how I see the there and then will change again.

When I began this study, I was working on 'forgotten women'. By the time it was finished, I was concerned with the problem of what happens to subordinate groups living under reactionary regimes; and what happens to radicals when they lose their vision, their sense of purpose. How would this book be different if I were beginning again now? Firstly, I would try not to make it such a white woman's book. The increasing prominence and anger of Black people have finally made me aware that to say of my work that I *would* talk about race, but that there *were* no Black writers then, is not good enough. Just as feminists are becoming tired of explaining to men that studies of writing or history must include an exploration of the problem of gender, whether the people studied are male or female, Black people (I believe) are weary of trying to make white people think through the implications of race in the work that we do. I cannot pretend that I know yet how this change in my consciousness will affect my future work.

I am also beginning again my work on Katherine Philips, as part of a new project around seventeenth-century sexuality, and especially homosexuality, and I doubt if my statements on romantic love will look the same once this thinking has gone further.

Changes I would make come not only from the here and now, but also from the texts themselves. When I first came across a single-sheet broadside by Damaris Strong, I didn't know what to do with it. For about three years my notes on it sat in a file by themselves. When I finally came to try to write about it, the ideas it raised made me aware of a fundamental distortion in this study.

When Damaris Strong made a brief foray into print in 1655, it was not her own status as an author that was at stake in her text, but her husband's. He, William Strong, had been a well-known Independent preacher and author before his death the previous year, his congregation including many MPs. His writings might be expected to sell well, and Damaris Strong seems to have hoped to have the use of them herself. She had even gone to the lengths of learning her husband's cypher from him on his deathbed, so as to be able to read his manuscripts.[1] Instead, a spurious edition of his works, entitled *The Saints Communion with God*, was brought out, claiming to contain all of the surviving writings of the minister. To make matters worse, this book was then attacked in print by someone assuming it to be William Strong's work. This was the spur to Damaris Strong's pamphlet that opens 'Having seen a paper printed', repudiating *The Saints Communion* and assuring the reader that William Strong's sermons 'will all (in God's due time) come out, word for word as himself wrote them, if I may be allowed to have the dispose thereof'. The indignation the text contains appeals to the public's sense that (despite the fact that there was no author's copyright at that time) it would be only right and proper for her, as William's widow, to have control over his writings. Since many works by him, edited by his fellow-ministers, subsequently appeared, we can assume his widow won her point.

We know about Damaris Strong's text because it was printed as a separate work, and so catalogued under her name. The existence of this writing, and the assumption it makes about a widow's right to her husband's work, alerts us to the existence of what might turn out to be a huge number of neglected texts by women: those prefacing works by men, especially their husbands. This is likely to apply to collections of sermons and books about church ministers – the book usually catalogued as the work of Theodosia Alleine, *The Life and Death of . . . Joseph Alleine*, is in fact only partly by her: the majority of it is the work of his fellow-ministers. By some quirk of cataloguing history, it is her name that is remembered. It is also probable that women in other walks of life edited men's works: Culpeper's posthumous texts, for instance, were brought out by his wife, Alice, and contain introductory remarks by her; some of James Nayler's prophecies are prefaced by the otherwise-unknown Mary Booth.

I believe that a systematic search of posthumous works by men would reveal much forgotten women's writing. Other uncatalogued names are likely to appear in song collections (we meet Mary Knight and many anonymous 'ladies' this way), and in poetic miscellanies. Quaker deathbed testimonials, such as Anne Whitehead's *Piety Promoted*, also bring to light many unknown names. Most of these are women, since it was women who tended the sick and dying, and felt drawn to write about their departed Friends.

When we reflect on the problems confronting a woman who dared to go into print in her own name, it becomes clear that this back door into the public world might be particularly attractive: editing a man's work for his greater glory, or describing the dying words of godly people, might be understood as suitable feminine activities. Similarly, to have a few songs or poems appear anonymously or under a pseudonym in a miscellany carried minimal risk to a woman's modest reputation. Something as apparently non-ideological as the practice of cataloguing books under the name of the major author, therefore, might turn out to be a contributory factor in erasing women's names from public record. Special collections, like the Quaker books held in Friends' Library, are sometimes indexed in card catalogues by 'minor' authors or contributors as well, and this would therefore be a good place to start the search for embedded writings.

If my speculation is correct, and it turns out that many more women wrote and published in this fragmentary way than ever set their names to an entire book or pamphlet, our understanding of the significance of the writings discussed in this book will greatly change. I look forward to research being done to make this possible. In the meantime, I am also beginning again myself.

NOTES

The place of publication, unless otherwise indicated, is London. Where anything other than a first edition of a secondary source has been used, the date of the first edition and the edition used have both been given.

Introduction: Making a Virtue of Necessity

1. Patricia Crawford, 'Attitudes to Menstruation in Seventeenth-Century England', *Past and Present*, 91, 1981; Jean Gagen, 'Honor and Fame in the Works of the Duchess of Newcastle', *Studies in Philology*, 56, 1959; Margaret George, 'From "Goodwife" to "Mistress": the Transformation of the Female in Bourgeois Culture', *Science and Society*, 1973; Angeline Goreau, *Reconstructing Aphra: a Social Biography of Aphra Behn*, New York, 1980; Roberta Hamilton, *The Liberation of Women: A Study of Patriarchy and Capitalism*, 1975; Ian MacLean, *The Renaissance Conception of Woman*, 1980.

2. Eli Zaretsky, *Capitalism, the Family and Personal Life*, 1976; Miranda Chaytor, 'Household and Kinship: Ryton in the late sixteenth and early seventeenth centuries', *History Workshop Journal*, 10, 1980, argues that since 'family' meant all members of a household (including servants and apprentices), it was a less private space than has been suggested.

3. See also Carole Shammas, 'The Domestic Environment in Early-Modern England and America', *Journal of Social History*, 14, 1980.

4. For criticisms of Stone's thesis, see Christopher Hill, 'Sex, Marriage and the Family in England', *Economic History Review*, 31, 1978; Joseph Kett, 'Review of *The Family, Sex and Marriage*', *Chronicle of Higher Education*, 1978; Alan MacFarlane, 'Lawrence Stone, *The Family, Sex and Marriage in England*: Review Essay', *History and Theory*, 18, 1979; J. Plumb, 'Review of *The Family, Sex and Marriage*', *New York Review of Books*, November 24, 1977; Joan Thirsk, '*The Family, Sex and Marriage in England*: Review', *Past and Present*, 27, 1978; Keith Thomas, 'Review of Lawrence Stone, *The Family, Sex and Marriage*', *Times Literary Supplement*, 21 October 1977; E.P. Thompson, 'Happy Families', *New Society*, 8 September 1977.

5. Leonore Glanz, 'The Legal Position of English Women under Early Stuart Kings and the Interregnum, 1603–1660', unpublished PhD thesis, Loyola University, 1973.

6. *Katherine Pettus, Plaintiffe, Margaret Bancroft, Defendant, in Chancery 1654*, [1654], p. 1.

7. *The Case of Anne Smyth*, [1650]. *Calendar of State Papers (Domestic) (CSPD)* lists a licence issued to her on 18 May 1650 to come to town. It seems unlikely that parliament would have heeded her claim, since the Danvers complained of was

probably Sir John Danvers the regicide (1588?–1655), who from 1649 to 1653 was a member of the Council of State (*DNB*).

8. Mary Alexander published a broadside *To the Right Honourable, the Parliament* in 1654, and in the same year a fuller account of the case in an eight-page pamphlet *To the Supream Authority*. This second pamphlet is made up of two different petitions, and also includes a reply to one from Levingston, referred to as 'a printed paper; entitled, Some Considerations Humbly Proposed'. This might or might not be the same as *The State of the Case in Brief*, also 1654, which is wrongly ascribed to Alexander in Donald Wing's *Short Title Catalogue* (S5685). *The State of the Case in Brief* gives Levingston's version of events. There are references to the case in the *Commons' Journals* and *CSPD*. Further information about Mary Alexander in *The Victoria County History of England* (*Wiltshire*), volume 10; *The Scots Peerage*; *The Complete Peerage*. See also the execution of Joan Peterson for her murder (p. 177).

9. David Cressy, *Literacy and the Social Order*, 1980; Margaret Spufford, *Contrasting Communities: English Villagers in the Sixteenth and Seventeenth Centuries*, 1974, and *Small Books and Pleasant Histories*, 1981.

10. British Library manuscript.

11. Estimated by comparing my figures for women's writing with Wilmer Mason, 'The Annual Output of Wing-Listed Titles 1649–1684', *Library*, 29, 1974. For the purposes of this comparison I normalised my figures to Mason's principles.

12. This argument draws broadly on the work of the Centre for Contemporary Cultural Studies, Birmingham, and especially on Stuart Hall, et al, *On Ideology*, 1977; and John Clarke, et al, *Resistance Through Rituals*, 1975.

13. See especially the dedicatory epistles to her *Poems and Fancies*.

14. *Death's Master-Peece*, p. 6.

15. A useful analysis of historians' differences is given in Barry Coward, *The Stuart Age*, 1980.

16. *To the Parliament of the Commonwealth of England, Scotland, and Ireland. The humble Petition of Margaret Countess of Worcester*; *To the Parliament of the Common-wealth of England, Scotland and Ireland. The Humble Petition of Anne Henshaw*; *To the High Court of Parliament, of the Common-wealth of England, Scotland, & Ireland. The Humble petition of Katherine Stone*. There are references to Stone's and Henshaw's cases in *CSPD*.

17. *To the Supreme Authority of this Commonwealth . . . The humble petition of severall Wives and Children of such Delinquents.*

18. There are many references to Bastwick's petitions in the *Commons' Journals* between 1640 and 1659.

19. Ellen MacArthur, 'Women Petitioners and the Long Parliament', *English Historical Review*, 24, 1909; Patricia Higgins, 'The Reactions of Women', in Brian Manning, (ed.), *Politics, Religion and the English Civil War*, 1973.

20. *Unto every individual Member of Parliament: the humble Representation of divers afflicted Women-Petitioners.*

21. *To the Parliament of the Common-wealth of England. The humble Petition of divers afflicted Women.*

22. *To the Supreme Authority of England the Commons . . . the Humble Petition of Divers Well-Affected Women.*

23. A. Woodhouse, *Puritanism and Liberty*, 1950, p. 367n. See also H.N. Brailsford, *The Levellers and the English Revolution*, ed. Christopher Hill, 1961.

24. Christopher Hill, *The World Turned Upside Down*, 1975.

25. Susan Staves, *Players' Scepters: Fictions of Authority in the Restoration*, Nebraska, 1978, p. 26.

26. Many mock-petitions with the words 'maid', 'woman', 'lady' in the title have a similarly offensive content, e.g. *The Good Women's Cryes, The Parliament of Ladies, The Ladyes Vindication.* See also *The Midwives Petition,* 1643 and 1646.
27. Roger Thompson, *Unfit for Modest Ears: A Study of Pornographic, Obscene and Bawdy Works Written or Published in England in the Second Half of the Seventeenth Century,* 1979.
28. *Exultationis Carmen to the Kings Most Excellent Majesty,* translated into Latin as *Carmen ΘPIAMBEYTIKON Regiae Majestati Caroli II.*
29. *CSPD* May? 1662. Charlotte Brégy, *The Royal Standard* also welcomes the king, as does Anne Clayton, *A Letter to the King.*
30. For Wyndham's story, see Alan Fea, *The Flight of the King,* 1897. I do not believe *Claustrum Regale Reseratum* was written by Anne Wyndham, despite its attribution to her in Wing, because the text is Latinate in syntax and vocabulary, and contains many anti-woman sentiments. Its editor is also self-confident about the right to print it once the king's permission has been granted.
31. *To the Honourable . . . The humble petition of Dame Mary Hewytt widow.* Other published female petitions include *The Case of Lady Maria Wentworth.*
32. *The case of the Lady Wandesford* [*c.* 1660?], a broadside in the Folger Library omitted from Wing.
33. The story sketched here is mostly gleaned from *Malice Defeated.* See also *The Triall of Elizabeth Cellier;* John Kenyon, *The Popish Plot,* 1974.
34. *Malice Defeated,* p. 43; *CSPD,* 16 August 1680.
35. Comments on Cellier's case (most of them savagely attacking her) include *Answers to queries; The Complaint of Mrs Celiers;* Thomas Dangerfield, *The case of, Mr. Tho. Dangerfeilds Particular Narrative* and *Mr. Thos. Dangerfeilds Second Narrative; The Devil Pursued; A Letter from the Lady Cresswell; Madam Celliers answer; The midwife unmask'd; Mistris Celliers Lamentation; Modesty triumphing over Impudence; Newgate Salutation;* Thomas Osborne, *The New Popish Sham-Plot; The Popes Letter; Reflections Upon the Murder; To the Praise of Mrs Cellier; The Triall of Elizabeth Cellier; A True Copy of a Letter; The Tryal and Sentence; The Tryal of Elizabeth Cellier.*

One: Prophets and Prophecies

1. Christopher Hill's work provides a survey of radical groups. See also G.E. Aylmer, *The Levellers in the English Revolution,* 1975; Joseph Besse, *A Collection of the Sufferings of the People called Quakers,* 1753; William Braithwaite, *The Beginnings of Quakerism,* 1912; Louise Brown, *The Political Activities of the Baptists and Fifth Monarchy Men,* Oxford, 1912; Champlin Burrage, 'Anna Trapnel's Prophecies', *English Historical Review,* 26, 1911; Kenneth Carroll, 'Early Quakers and "Going Naked as a Sign" ', *Quaker History,* 67, 1978, and 'Martha Simmonds, a Quaker Enigma', *Journal of the Friends' Historical Society,* 53, 1972; Alfred Cohen, 'The Fifth Monarchy Mind: Mary Cary and the Origins of Totalitarianism', *Social Research,* 31, 1964; Norman Cohn, *The Pursuit of the Millenium, Revolutionary Millenarians and Mystical Anarchists of the Middle Ages,* 1959, 1970; Gerald Cragg, *Puritanism in the Period of the Great Persecution,* 1957; Emily Manners, *Elizabeth Hooton, First Quaker Woman Preacher (1600–1672),* 1914; Arthur Morton, (ed.), *Freedom in Arms; A Selection of Leveller Writings,* 1975, and *The World of the Ranters,* 1970; Barry Reay, 'The Quakers, 1659, and the Restoration of the Monarchy', *History,* 63, 1978; Keith Thomas, 'Women and the Civil War Sects', *Past and*

Present, 13, 1955; Michael Walzer, *Revolution of the Saints: a Study in the Origins of Radical Politics*, Cambridge, Mass., 1965; Michael Watts, *The Dissenters*, Oxford, 1978; Charles Whiting, *Studies in English Puritanism from the Restoration to the Revolution, 1660–1688*, 1931; Ethyn Williams, 'Women Preachers of the Civil War', *Journal of Modern History*, 1, 1929; and other sources cited in notes to this chapter. Little research has yet been undertaken on women's activities in these groups, and some of the works here cited appear because of their attention to this issue, despite being out of date in other respects.

2. Thomas O'Malley, ' "Defying the Powers and Tempering the Spirit": A Review of Quaker Control over their Publications 1672–1689', *The Journal of Ecclesiastical History*, 33, 1982.

3. Thomas, op. cit.; Christopher Hill, *Milton and the English Revolution*, 1979, p. 118.

4. Christopher Hindle, *A Bibliography of the Printed Pamphlets and Broadsides of Lady Eleanor Douglas*, Second Edition, 1936, is a good if incomplete source. A more recent, unsatisfactory study is Christine Berg and Philippa Berry, 'Spiritual Whoredom: An Essay on Female Prophets in the Seventeenth Century', in Francis Barker, (ed.), *1642: Literature and Power in the Seventeenth Century*, Essex, 1981. See also Theodore Spencer, 'The History of an Unfortunate Lady', *Harvard Studies and Notes in Philology and Literature*, 20, 1938. The best study is Kate Pahl's (forthcoming), which is sensitive to the ways in which Lady Eleanor's language, like those of other prophets, is rich in biblical resonances.

5. I have compared copies held at the British Library, Houghton Library and Folger Shakespeare Library.

6. *The Appearance or Presence*, pp. 7–8. This, the most fascinating of Lady Eleanor's prophecies, appears to have survived in only one copy, now at the Folger Shakespeare Library. The text is merely a fragment, breaking off in mid-sentence.

7. Pendaves is not named in the pamphlet, but this identification, made in Richard Greaves and Robert Zaller (eds.), *Biographical Dictionary of English Radicals*, 1982, seems convincing. Paul Hardacre has alternatively suggested that T.P. might have been the wife of George Payne, Abingdon's governor.

8. Elizabeth Poole, *An Alarum of War*, 1649, p. 9. T. P.'s defence of Poole does not appear in the earlier, 1648/9, edition.

9. Mary Cary, *The Little Horns Doom and Downfall*, 'To the Reader'. The title page describes the text as 'printed for the author'.

10. See also Rebeckah Travers, *A Testimony*, p. 2.

11. The prophecy of the four beasts appears in Daniel 7.

12. Bernard Capp, *The Fifth Monarchy Men: A Study in Seventeenth-Century Millenarianism*, New York, 1972.

13. *Report and Plea*, pp. 19–45. Dorothy Ludlow, ' "Arise and Be Doing": English "Preaching" Women, 1640–1660', unpublished PhD thesis, Indiana University, 1978, p. 292, says that all newssheets of the period reported Trapnel's movements. See also *Calendar of State Papers (Domestic) (CSPD)*, 1654, and Philip Rogers, *The Fifth Monarchy Men*, 1966.

14. There is a further, untitled book of verse by Trapnel in the Bodleian Library, which I have not seen.

15. Capp, op. cit., p. 174.

16. Capp assumes that Trapnel and Adman were related, giving, I believe, too narrow an interpretation of the term 'sister', which Trapnel frequently uses to refer to her fellow-believers.

17. *Report and Plea*, p. 26. This pamphlet appears to have had more than one printer. The

first 26 pages are in a standard-sized print, but pages 27 and 28 are in a very small typeface. The next page returns to the larger typeface but the pagination starts again at 25. This passage is taken from the first page 26.

18. Diary entry for 21 April 1657. Many of Dorothy White's prophecies also slip into verse. See also Anne Wentworth.

19. p. 22. Studies of seventeenth-century witchcraft beliefs include Keith Thomas, *Religion and the Decline of Magic. Studies in Popular Beliefs in Sixteenth- and Seventeenth-Century England*, 1978; Brian Easlea, *Witch-Hunting, Magic and the New Philosophies*, 1980; see also Mary Douglas, (ed.), *Witchcraft, Confessions and Accusations*, 1970; Barbara Ehrenreich and Deidre English, *Witches, Midwives and Nurses: A History of Women Healers*, 1973; Christina Larner, *Enemies of God: The Witch-hunt in Scotland*, New York, 1981; Brian Levack, 'The Great Scottish Witch Hunt of 1661–62', *Journal of British Studies*, 3, 1975; Edward Monter, 'Pedestal and Stake: Courtly Love and Witchcraft', in Rosa Brindenthal, (ed.), *Becoming Visible: Women in European History*, 1977; Wallace Notestein, *A History of Witchcraft in England from 1558 to 1718*, Washington, 1911.

20. Luella Wright, *The Literary Life of the Early Friends, 1650–1725*, New York, 1966, p. 80.

21. Mabel Brailsford, *Quaker Women 1650–1690*, 1915, p. 13; Elaine Huber, 'A Woman Must Not Speak', in Rosemary Ruether and Eleanor McLaughlin, (eds.), *Women of Spirit: Female Leadership in the Jewish and Christian Traditions*, New York, 1979, p. 131.

22. Richard Vann, *The Social Development of English Quakerism*, Cambridge, Mass., 1969. See also Margaret Spufford, *Contrasting Communities: English Villagers in the Sixteenth and Seventeenth Centuries*, 1974. Blackborow's account appears in *The Just and Equal Balance*, p. 8. For Hooton's early activities, see Huber, op. cit, p. 165, and M. Brailsford, op. cit.

23. Margret Braidley, *Certain Papers*, pp. 9–10.

24. Rebeckah Travers, *A Testimony for God's Everlasting Truth*, p. 30; Anne Travers and Elizabeth Coleman *Unto which is added A brief Answer*.

25. Alice Curwen, *A Relation*, p. 3. One of the Quaker women suffering in New England was Mary Dyer, who was finally executed. See Marmaduke Stephenson and William Robinson, *A Call from Death to Life*, 1660, p. 26.

26. Vokins, p. 71. The description of Jane Whitehead appears in Theophila Townsend's *Testimony* to her, pp. 6, 16. The Brooksop passage is from *An Invitation of Love*, p. 12.

27. Katherine Evans and Sarah Chevers, *This is a short Relation*, 1662. Wing wrongly attributes this to Baker. The second, expanded edition appeared in 1663, entitled *A True Account of the Great Tryals* (not in Wing).

28. Such pamphlets include Elizabeth Hooton, et al, *False Prophets*; Margret Braidley, et al, *Certain Papers*; Priscilla Cotton and Mary Cole, *To the Priests*; Anne Audland and Jane Waugh, *A True Declaration*; Anne Audland, et al, *The Saints Testimony*. See also Margaret Fell, *A Declaration*; Huber, op. cit.

29. These include Margaret Killin and Barbara Patison, *A Warning from the Lord*; Martha Simmonds, *A Lamentation* and *When the Lord Jesus came*; Hester Biddle, *Wo . . . Oxford* and *Wo . . . Cambridge*; Martha Simmonds, et al, *O England*; Ann Gargill, *A Warning* and *A Brief Discovery*; Mary Howgill, *A Remarkable Letter*; Susanna Bateman, *I matter not*; Jeane Bettris, *A Lamentation*; Sarah Blackborow, *A Visit*.

30. *These several Papers was sent to the Parliament*, 1659; Wing enters this as Mary Forster's work.

31. Reay, op. cit.; W. Alan Cole, 'The Quakers and the English Revolution', in T. Aston, (ed.), *Crisis in Europe 1560–1660*, 1970. Texts by women published in these years include some by Mary Anderson, Grace Barwick, Hester Biddle, Sarah Blackborow, Joan Brooksop, Katherine Evans and Sarah Chevers, Susanna Fairman, Margaret Fell, Anne Gilman, Ann Gould, Mary Howgill, Margret Lynam, Rebeckah Travers, Mary Webb, Dorothy White.

32. These include Alice Curwen, et al, *A Relation*; Mary Forster, *A Declaration*; Elizabeth Hendericks, *An Epistle*; Theophila Townsend, *A Word of Councel*; Theophila Townsend, et al, *An Epistle of Love*, *A Testimony*; Mary Waite, *A Warning*; Margaret Waters, *A Warning*; Anne Whitehead, *An Epistle*; Joan Whitrow, et al, *The Work of God*; Isabel Yeamans, et al, *A Lively Testimony*.

33. Other collectively-written prophecies include Anne Audland and Jane Waugh, *A True Declaration*; Margret Braidley, et al, *Certain Papers*; Priscilla Cotton and Mary Cole, *To the Priests*; Elizabeth Hooton, et al, *False Prophets*; Margaret Killin and Barbara Patison, *A Warning*; Martha Simmons, et al, *O England*.

34. Hester Biddle, *Wo to thee City of Oxford*. Wing suggests a date for *Cambridge* that is post-1660, but this is highly improbable. The two texts appear to have been printed on the same press one after the other. The only differences are the replacing of 'Oxford' by 'Cambridge' and 'city' by 'town'. In one place, the *Cambridge* text reads 'Oh Cambr.', presumably because the whole word would not fit into the space left by 'Oxford'. This is the feature that leads me to believe that the *Oxford* text was printed first.

35. For the complete passage in Mather's sermon, see Phyllis Mack, 'Women as Prophets During the English Civil War', *Feminist Studies*, 8, 1982, p. 24.

36. Casey Miller and Kate Smith, *Words and Women: New Language in New Times*, 1979.

37. David Latt, (ed.), *Women's Speaking Justified (Margaret Fell) (1667)*, California, 1979, p. v.

38. This same logic is adopted in several later women's prophecies, including Sarah Blackborow, *The Just and Equal Balance*, and Katherine Evans, *A Brief Discovery*.

39. Claire Cross, 'The Church in England 1646–1660', in G.E. Aylmer, (ed.), *The Interregnum*, 1972, shows that such disputes were not unusual, although she does not cite Parr's case.

40. George Keith, *The Woman Preacher of Samaria*, p. 11.

41. Vann, op. cit., p. 100.

42. Page 5 refers to a 'printed paper' by Aldridge, which appears not to have survived. For another attack on a travelling woman, see John Furly, *The Substance of a Letter*, which reproves Sarah Hayward as a false prophet and a thief.

43. Elizabeth Bathurst, *Truth's Vindication*; Isabel Yeamans, *An Invitation*.

44. Wright, op. cit., p. 80. Wright also describes (pp. 104–5) Judith Boulbie's brushes with Quaker censors after 1686.

45. *A Brief Relation of the Persecutions and Sufferings*, 1662, pp. 35–6.

46. These biographical details comes from the remarkable *Dictionary of Quaker Biography*, a typescript at Friends' Library, London. Mary Howgill is identified there as 'an unsuitable minister', and Ann Gargill as 'an example of the Ranter type which associated itself with Friends and was not immediately disowned by them'.

47. Writing in 1680, Mary Elson refers to the origin of the London Women's Meeting as being 'betwixt three or four and twenty years ago': 'A True Information' in Anne Whitehead, *An Epistle*.

48. Whitehead, op. cit., p. 6.

49. Brailsford, op. cit., p. 15.

50. See especially Dorcas Dole and Margaret Fell.
51. Anne Whitehead, et al, *Piety Promoted*; Ann Gardner, et al, *A Brief Relation*; John Furly, *A Testimony*.
52. Joan Vokins, et al, *God's Mighty Power*, p. 29. I have found no official Quaker record on the attempt to abandon women's meetings that this passage refers to.
53. Elizabeth Bathurst, *Truth's Vindication*, 'The Contents'.
54. Alice Curwen, *A Relation*.
55. For another late-seventeenth-century visionary, see articles on Jane Lead by Catherine Smith: 'Jane Lead: The Feminist Mind and Art of a Seventeenth-Century Protestant Mystic', in Rosemary Ruether and Eleanor McLaughlin, op. cit.; 'Jane Lead: Mysticism and the Woman Cloathed with the Sun', in Sandra Gilbert and Susan Gubar, (eds.), *Shakespeare's Sisters*, Bloomington, Indiana, 1979; 'Women, Property, and Prophecy in Seventeenth Century England', unpublished conference paper, 1981.
56. Revelation, p. 10. Knowles is probably Hanserd Knollys, whose *The Life and Death*, p. 15, also claims direct inspiration from God in dreams.

Two: Religious Poetry, Meditations and Conversion Narratives

1. *Divine Songs and Meditacions* is unpaginated, and many of the poems are entitled simply 'Another Song'. I have therefore referred to such verses by quoting the first line as well as the title. A modern facsimile of part of Collins's book has been printed by the Augustan Reprint Society.
2. Mary Simpson's account is published with the sermon preached at her funeral by John Collings, in *Faith and Experience*. Sermons preached at women's funerals might prove a rich source of forgotten women's writings.
3. Edmund Calamy, *The Godly Man's Ark*, p. 203.
4. 'Dedicatory Epistle' by Thomas Weld. In this same year, Weld published a defence of his doctrines, after his refusal to baptise children had led him into trouble with other church officers. The Council of State removed his opponents. For details, see Michael Watts, *The Dissenters*, Oxford, 1978. Perhaps this incident encouraged Weld to publish Venn's writings and use them to promote his own theological position. She had died four years previously.
5. See Dorothy Ludlow, ' "Arise and Be Doing": English "Preaching" Women, 1640–1660', unpublished PhD thesis, Indiana University, 1978; Murray Tolmie, *The Triumph of the Saints*, 1977; Watts, op. cit.
6. Ludlow, op. cit., p. 159.
7. Tolmie, op. cit.; H.N. Brailsford, *The Levellers and the English Revolution*, ed. Christopher Hill, 1961.
8. According to Owen Watkins, *The Puritan Experience: Studies in Spiritual Autobiography*, 1972, after 1670 almost all the printed conversion experiences written by men were also posthumous publications.
9. The prefatory remarks to Davy's text are signed 'A.P.'. A likely identity for this anonymous Baptist minister is Anthony Palmer of Pinners' Hall, London.
10. Brooks, along with Jessey, was one of the supporters of the 1647 *Declaration by Congregational Societies in and about London*, which 'solemnly repudiated polygamy, and community of property, and ... defined liberty exclusively in terms of religious liberty' (Tolmie, op. cit., pp. 170–1).
11. Many diary manuscripts were discovered and printed in private editions in the nineteenth century. See, for instance, *The Priuate Diarie of Elizabeth, Vicountess Mordaunt*.
12. See also chapter 3 for a related discussion of Mary Rich.

Three: Autobiographies and Biographies of Husbands

1. Quoted in George Williamson, (ed.), *Lady Anne Clifford Countess of Dorset, Pembroke and Montgomery 1590–1676: Her Life, Letters and Work*, 1967, pp. 173–4. The original work for this chapter was shared with Dr Sandra Findley, published as Sandra Findley and Elaine Hobby, 'Seventeenth-Century Women's Autobiography', in Francis Barker, (ed.), *1642: Literature and Power in the Seventeenth Century*, Essex, 1981. See also Elaine Hobby, 'English Women's Writing 1649–1688', unpublished PhD thesis, Birmingham University, 1984.

2. Rich's autobiography was published 1848, extracts from her diary in 1847. I have also consulted the diary manuscripts in the British Library (Add. MSS 27, 351–27, 355). Other manuscript autobiographies not discussed at all here include those by Anne Clifford and Anne Halkett. See Hobby, op. cit.

3. Thornton, *The Autobiography*, pp. 131–2.

4. Margaret Bottrall, *Every Man a Phoenix*, 1958; Anna Burr, *The Autobiography: A Critical and Comparative Study*, Boston, 1909; Richard Butler, *The Difficult Art of Autobiography*, Oxford, 1968; Paul Delany, *British Autobiography in the Seventeenth Century*, 1969; Dean Ebner, *Autobiography in Seventeenth-Century England: Theology and the Self*, The Hague, 1971; William Matthews, *British Autobiographies: An Annotated Bibliography of British Autobiographies Published or Written before 1951*, 1968; Harold Nicolson, *The Development of English Biography*, 1947; Wayne Shumaker, *English Autobiography: Its Emergence, Materials, and Form*, California, 1954; Donald Stauffer, *English Biography Before 1700*, Cambridge, Mass., 1930; Joan Webber, *The Eloquent 'I': Style and Self in Seventeenth-Century Prose*, Wisconsin, 1968. For contrast, see Mary Mason, 'The Other Voice: Autobiographies of Women Writers', in James Olney, (ed.), *Autobiography*, 1980; Cynthia Pomerleau, ' "Resigning the Needle for the Pen": A Study of Autobiographical Writings of British Women Before 1800', unpublished PhD thesis, Penn. State University, 1974; and the forthcoming collection of seventeenth-century women's autobiographies edited by Elspeth Graham, Hilary Hinds, Elaine Hobby and Helen Wilcox (Routledge, Winter 1988/9).

5. John Loftis, (ed.), *The Memoirs of Anne, Lady Halkett and Ann, Lady Fanshawe*, 1979, p. 102.

6. Lucy Hutchinson, *Memoirs of the Life of Colonel Hutchinson*, ed. by Harold Child, 1904, p. 46.

7. Theodosia Alleine, *The Life and Death of . . . Joseph Alleine*, 1672, p. 78. There were several 1672 editions of the *Life*. All quotations are taken from Wing A1012.

8. In his edition of the autobiography, Mason points out that Cavendish shifts the question from 'why this *Lady*?' to 'why *this* Lady?'

Four: Romantic Love – Prose Fiction

1. See also, for instance, *The Women's Petition against Coffee* and *The Womens Complaint Against Their Bad Husbands*.

2. Margaret Cavendish, *Natures Picture*, 1671, pp. 663–4.

3. Lawrence Stone, *The Family, Sex and Marriage in England 1500–1800*, 1977; Roger Thompson, *Unfit for Modest Ears: A Study of Pornographic, Obscene and Bawdy Works Written or Published in England in the Second Half of the Seventeenth Century*, 1979. See also Edmund Shorter, 'Capitalism, Culture and Sexuality: Some Competing Models', *Social Science Quarterly*, 53, 1972.

4. For example *The Dutchess of Monmouth's Lamentation*; *The Dutchess of*

Portsmouths and Count Coningmarks Farvvel; *A Letter from the Dutchess of Ports-mouth*; *A Pleasant dialogue*; *Portsmouths Lamentation*; *The Poor Whores Petition*; *The Whores Petition*. Mabel Brailsford, *Quaker Women 1650–1690*, 1915, comments on the case of Lucy Walter's children. Her son, the Duke of Monmouth, actually made a bid for the throne. Her daughter Mary received no title, and married in succession two commoners.

5. Quoted in Angeline Goreau, *Reconstructing Aphra: A Social Biography of Aphra Behn*, New York, 1980, p. 166.

6. David Foxon, *Libertine Literature in England 1660–1745*, 1964, p. ix, first suggested that 'pornography seems to have been born and grown to maturity in a brief period in the middle of the seventeenth century'. His evidence actually indicates, as I argue here, that this growth took place after the Restoration.

7. See also *The Women's Fegaries*. See also Birmingham Rape Crisis and Research Centre, *First Annual Report*, Birmingham, 1980; Donna-Lee Weber, 'Fair Game: Rape and Sexual Aggression on Women in some early Eighteenth-Century Prose Fiction', unpublished PhD thesis, University of Toronto, 1980.

8. Mead's work on the Arapesh is quoted in Susan Brownmiller, *Against Our Will: Men, Women and Rape*, 1976, p. 284: 'Nor do the Arapesh have any conception of male nature that might make rape understandable to them'. The propensity to rape is socially created, not the result of an irresistible 'natural' urge.

9. Gary Kelly, ' "Intrigue" and "Gallantry": The Seventeenth-Century French *Nouvelle* and the "Novels" of Aphra Behn', *Revue de Littérature Comparée*, 55, 1981; Bruce Morrissette, *The Life and Works of Madame Desjardins*, 1947; Mary Palgrave, *Mary Rich, Countess of Warwick 1625–1678*, 1901; Ioan Williams, *The Idea of the Novel in Europe, 1600–1800*, 1979.

10. George Hickes's translation and adaptation of Fénelon's *Traité de l'éducation des filles, Instructions for the Education of a Daughter*, p. 8.

11. Suzanne Hull, *Chaste, Silent and Obedient*, Los Angeles, 1982, pp. 80, 232; Bridget MacCarthy, *The Female Pen*, Cork, 1948, pp. 53–64.

12. The introductory preamble to *Arcadia* indicates that Mary Sidney undertook editing and some revisions of the text; also, that Sidney wrote much of it in her presence, reading it out to her. We can only speculate how much of the final product was composed by her.

13. Maurice Evans, (ed.), *Sir Philip Sidney 'The Countess of Pembroke's Arcadia'*, 1977, pp. 14–19.

14. This discussion omits Cavendish's *Sociable Letters*, a semifictional work that could be read as an early epistolary novel.

15. Dolores Paloma, 'Margaret Cavendish: Defining the Female Self', *Women's Studies*, 7, 1980.

16. Marie-Catherine Desjardins' *The Memoires* pp. 45–6 also shows the heroine shooting the man (her adopted father) who tries to assault her.

17. Diary entries for 29 May and 7 June 1663.

18. Gillian Beer, *The Romance*, 1970, p. 50. See also Ernest Bernbaum, *The Mary Carleton Narratives*, 1914; Maximillian Novak, ' "Appearances of Truth": The Literature of Crime as a Narrative System 1660–1841', *Yearbook of English Studies*, 11, 1981; Robert Singleton, 'English Criminal Biography, 1651–1722', *Harvard Library Bulletin*, 18, 1979; Theodore Spencer, 'The History of an Unfortunate Lady', *Harvard Studies and Notes in Philology and Literature*, 20, 1938. All these male accounts side with John Carleton.

19. Accounts of the first trial include *The Arraignment, Tryal and Examination of Mary Moders*; *The Articles and Charge of Impeachment*; F.B., *Vercingetorixa*; John Carleton, *The Replication* and *The Ultimum Vale*; *The Great Tryall and Arraignment*; *The Lawyer's Clarke trappan'd*; *A Vindication of a Distressed Lady*; *The Westminster Wedding*; and Mary Carleton's *A True Account*.
20. *The Deportment and Carriage*; *An Elegie on the Famous and Renowned Lady*; *An Exact and True Relation*; Francis Kirkman, *The Counterfeit Lady*; *The Life and Character*; *The Memoires of Mary Carleton*; *News from Jamaica*; *Some Luck Some Wit*.
21. The summary that follows is my reconstruction based on texts by both Carletons.
22. The pagination of *The Case* is erratic in this gathering, running [37] 46 47 40 41 43 42 45 38 [48]. The pages appear in the correct order, however. The passage quoted appears on pages numbered 45–38.
23. Perhaps she had help in the preambles to her books, which, unlike the main body of them, are rather laboured and include classical references.
24. This idea is proposed by Goreau, op. cit., although developed by her along rather different lines. My discussion of Behn's prose fiction might properly be extended to include the semifictional *Loveletters from a Nobleman to his Sister*.
25. Studies of the story include Charles Batten, 'The Source of Aphra Behn's *The Widow Ranter*', *Restoration and Eighteenth-Century Theatre Research*, 13, 1974; Martine Brownley, 'The Narrator in *Oroonoko*', *Essays in Literature*, 4, 1977; B. Dhuicq, 'Further Evidence on Aphra Behn's Stay in Surinam', *Notes and Queries*, 26, 1979; Edwin Johnson, 'Aphra Behn's *Oroonoko*', *Journal of Negro History*, 10, 1975; J. Ramsaran, '*Oroonoko*: A Study of the Factual Elements', *PMLA*, 205, 1960; Edward Seeber, '*Oroonoko* in France in the XVIII Century', *PMLA*, 51, 1936.
26. In general, page references to Behn's works are to the first edition as a separate. References to *The Fair Jilt* (not issued separately) are to *Histories and Novels*, 1696. Quotations from *The Adventure of the Black Lady* are from Montague Summers's edition of her *Works*, 1915, volume 5.
27. Ian Watt, *The Rise of the Novel*, 1957; Maureen Duffy, *The Passionate Shepherdess: Aphra Behn 1640–1689*, 1977.
28. See also, for instance, *The Court of the King of Bantam*.

Five: Romantic Love – Plays

1. Nancy Cotton, *Women Playwrights in England ca. 1363–1750*, Pennsylvania, 1980, p. 39. See also Lucyle Hook, *Mrs Elizabeth Barry and Mrs Anne Bracegirdle Actresses: Their Careers from 1672 to 1695*, New York, 1949; John Hotson, *The Commonwealth and Restoration Stage*, Cambridge, Mass., 1928; G. Sensabaugh, 'Platonic Love and the Puritan Rebellion', *Studies in Philology*, 37, 1940.
2. Nathan Starr, (ed.), '*The Concealed Fansyes*: a Play by Lady Jane Cavendish and Lady Elizabeth Brackley', *PMLA*, 46, 1931, suggests instead that the man addressed is Elizabeth Brackley's husband.
3. Emmett Avery, 'The Restoration Audience', *Philological Quarterly*, 65, 1966.
4. This is a hotly debated issue. See Avery, op. cit.; Andrew Bear, 'Criticism and Social Change: The Case of Restoration Drama', *KOMOS*, 2, 1969; Robert Hume, *The Development of English Drama in the Late Seventeenth Century*, 1976; Harold Love, 'The Myth of the Restoration Audience', *KOMOS*, 1, 1967; Arthur Scouten, ed., *Restoration and Eighteenth-Century Drama*, 1980; William Van Lennep, (ed.), *The London Stage 1660–1800*, Illinois, 1965.
5. Van Lennep, op. cit., p. liii.

6. Katherine Philips, *Letters from Orinda to Polarchus*, 1705, especially pp. 78–80, 83, 90, 104, 110, 115, 119, 122, 127, 194.
7. Scouten, op. cit,. p. 2.
8. William Clark, *The Early Irish Stage: the Beginnings to 1720*, Oxford, 1955, p. 62.
9. Philips Souers, *The Matchless Orinda*, Cambridge, Mass., 1931, misidentifies Lady Mary Cavendish, confusing her with Margaret Cavendish who would have been known not as 'Lady M. Cavendish' but as 'Lady Newcastle'.
10. Judith Milhous and Robert Hume, (eds.), *'The Frolicks or The Lawyer Cheated' (1671) by Elizabeth Polwhele*, New York, 1977, introduction. See also Hume, op. cit.; Van Lennep, op. cit.
11. Virginia Birdsall, *Wild Civility: The English Comic Spirit on the Restoration Stage*, Indiana, 1970; see also F.W. Bateson, 'L.C. Knights and Restoration Comedy', *Essays in Criticism*, 8, 1957; Jean Gagen, *The New Woman: Her Emergence in English Drama, 1600–1730*, New York, 1953; Norman Holland, *The First English Comedies: The Significance of Etherege, Wycherley and Congreve*, 1959; Robert Jordan, 'The Extravagant Rake in Restoration Comedy', in Harold Love, (ed.), *Restoration Literature*, 1972; Donald Wall, 'The Restoration Rake in Life and Comedy', unpublished PhD thesis, Florida State University, 1963.
12. Charles Barber, *The Idea of Honor in the English Drama*, Gothenburg, 1957, shows that (in works by men) the dichotomy between women's reputation for chastity and their actual profligacy grows steadily 1661–1700.
13. Scouten, op. cit., p. 3.
14. Donald Bruce, *Topics of Restoration Comedy*, 1974, p. 135. See also Guy Montgomery, 'The Challenge of Restoration Comedy', *University of California Publications in English*, 1, 1929; John Smith, *The Gay Couple in Restoration Comedy*, Cambridge, Mass., 1948; P. Vernon, 'Marriage of Convenience and the Moral of Restoration Comedy', *Essays in Criticism*, 12, 1962.
15. See afterword in Margaret Cavendish, *Playes* 'To the Readers'. The three copies of *Playes* in the British Library are gathered differently. An examination of the catchwords indicates that copy G19153 is closest to the ideal copy, and so page references are made to this copy. The initial sheets are gathered in twos, the signed leaves bearing sigs. [A2] A3–A7. The intermediate halfsheets gathered with them are therefore described here as A3/2–A7/2.
16. Richard Goulding, *Margaret (Lucas) Duchess of Newcastle*, Lincoln, 1925, p. 33; Virginia Woolf, *The Common Reader*, 1925, p. 106; A. Turberville, *A History of Welbeck Abbey and Its Owners*, 1938, pp. 191–2.
17. *Playes*, sig. A4. See also her *The Female Academy* in the same collection.
18. During this period the dominant meaning of 'original' shifted from implying something that had existed 'from the beginning' to referring to something newly invented (OED).
19. *Playes*, p. 2. A similar discussion of women writers occurs in Cavendish's *Wits Cabal*, *Playes*, p. 270, where Satyrical condemns women's writing to the fire while the matron defends women's mental fire. Satyrical insists that women's only 'heat' is lasciviousness, and that it leads to madness.
20. Plays of the first type are *Love's Adventures, Youths Glory and Deaths Banquet, The Lady Contemplation, The Unnatural Tragedie, The Matrimoniall Trouble, The Religious, Natures Three Daughters*. Plays of the second type include *The Several Wits, Wits Cabal, The Publique Wooing, The Comical Hash*. An exception to these groupings is *Bell in Campo*, where all parts of the play are integrated.
21. cf. Aphra Behn, *The Forc'd Marriage*; also much Jacobean tragedy, especially John Ford *'Tis Pity She's a Whore*.

22. The 'honesty' that is challenged is not in fact Lady Innocence's chastity. She is charged with theft in a trick devised by Lady Incontinent.

23. *Playes*, p. 47. See also Lady Happy in *The Convent of Pleasure*, who agrees to marry a man who has lived disguised as a woman, and so experienced all the limitations and joys of femininity.

24. For plays and male education, see Hotson, *The Commonwealth and Restoration Stage*, Cambridge, Mass., 1928, p. 134.

25. From the *Tixall Letters*, volume 2, p. 60, quoted by Van Lennep, op. cit., who believes it refers to Behn. Boothby seems a more likely candidate since Behn's first play was not performed until autumn 1670. See also Cotton, op. cit., for women playwrights not discussed here.

26. Van Lennep, op. cit., p. 163. The play was entered in the *Term Catalogues* in November 1669.

27. Milhous and Hume, op. cit., pp. 8, 13, 29.

28. Milhous and Hume, op. cit., explain that Prince Rupert was a good choice of patron as he was friendly with the owner of the King's Company, Thomas Killigrew, and was lover with one of the company's actresses (Margaret Hughes) from 1668 to 1670, when he removed her from the stage.

29. Milhous and Hume, op. cit., p. 44. They suggest she could have been the daughter of Theophilus Polwhele, vicar of Tiverton, a prominent nonconformist minister. He had a daughter named Elizabeth, born *ca.* 1651, by his first wife. She married the Reverend Stephen Lobb before 1678 when she bore him a son, one of five known children. She died in 1691.

30. Hotson, op. cit., p. 227.

31. Commented on in John Cunninghame, *Restoration Drama*, 1966, pp. 153–6; Henry Hargreaves, 'The Life and Plays of Mrs Behn', unpublished PhD thesis, Duke University, 1961, pp. 96–112; Hume, op. cit., p. 375; Frederick Link, *Aphra Behn*, New York, 1968, pp. 22, 101; Richard Southern, *Changeable Scenery: Its Origin and Development in the British Theatre*, 1952, pp. 146–9; Montague Summers, (ed.), *The Works of Aphra Behn*, 1915, pp. 2, 304, 388.

32. Van Lennep, op. cit., p. 175; Hume, op. cit., p. 23.

33. Goreau, op. cit., records that Behn did continue to make enough to live, and to help out more desperate fellow-writers, although the 1680s found her ill and in desperate straits.

34. Elisabeth Mignon, *Crabbed Age and Youth: The Old Men and Women in the Restoration Comedy of Manners*, Washington, 1947, suggests that Behn's 'elderly' characters fuse the scorned characteristics of old age and the 'constricting morality' of commonwealth Puritanism.

35. Goreau, op. cit., pp. 88–113.

36. George Whiting, 'The Condition of the London Theatres 1679–1683: A Reflection on the Political Situation', *Modern Philology*, 25, 1927; Hume, op. cit., pp. 318–19, 357.

37. The reference in the epilogue to Shaftesbury's acquittal gives the likely date of the first performance as autumn 1679. The play's dedication asserts that it was 'The first essay of my infant-poetry', and that it was written in America. The dedication appears on a sheet signed a, which has been tipped in. It is reasonable to speculate that this late dedication to 'Philaster' was made to earn money.

38. Alfred Leja, 'Aphra Behn – Tory', unpublished PhD thesis, University of Texas, 1962, p. 110; Mignon, op. cit., p. 93; Link, op. cit., pp. 68–9; Scouten, op. cit., p. 4. On one occasion at least Behn went too far in the eyes of the authorities. Her prologue to Dryden's (?) *Romulus and Hersilia* led to her arrest. She seems to have been very badly frightened as she fell silent for three years.

39. The others are *The Feign'd Curtizans*, 1679, a comedy of intrigue; *The Luckey*

Chance, 1686; and *The Younger Brother* (published posthumously 1696 with a preface explaining that references to Whig/Tory clashes have been removed. It is therefore impossible to know how close the text is to the one written by Behn). Summers, op. cit., and Link, op. cit., give sources for the rest of the plays. See also Marston Balch, (ed.), *Thomas Middleton's 'A Trick to Catch the Old One' and Aphra Behn's 'City Heiress'*, Salzburg, 1981; Charles Batten, 'The Source of Aphra Behn's *The Widow Ranter*', *Restoration and Eighteenth-Century Theatre Research*, 13, 1974; Anne Witmer and John Freehafer, 'Aphra Behn's Strange News from Virginia', *Library Chronicle*, 38, 1968.

40. See texts cited in note 31, and Susan Zuther, 'The World of Love and Ethic in Aphra Behn's Comedies', unpublished PhD thesis, University of Kansas, 1980.
41. *The Rover*, p. 85. See also introduction to Frederick Link, (ed.), *Aphra Behn: The Rover*, 1967.
42. See Link, op. cit.; Kenneth Muir, *The Comedy of Manners*, 1970; Summers, op. cit.
43. Judith Ludwig, 'A Critical Edition of Aphra Behn's Comedy *The Feigned Courtesans* (1679) with Introduction and Notes', unpublished PhD thesis, Yale University, 1977, p. 18.
44. Hargreaves, op. cit.
45. From 'The First Epistle of the Second Book of Horace', lines 209–19.
46. Hume, op. cit., p. 290. For Behn's principles of adaptation see Hargreaves, op. cit.; Link, op. cit.; see also Bear, op. cit.
47. Cotton, op. cit.; Bear, op. cit.; Van Lennep, op. cit.
48. For the popularity of 'female' prologues, see Autrey Wiley, 'Female Prologues and Epilogues in English Plays', *PMLA*, 48, 1933.
49. The heroine of Behn's novel *The Nun; or the Perjur'd Beauty* also finds that falling in love makes her vulnerable to exploitation.
50. Hume, op. cit., p. 305; Link, op. cit., p. xv.
51. The August 1984 production of *The Luckey Chance* at The Royal Court Theatre, London, could not cope with Julia Fulbank at all. She was played as a lecherous, flighty figure who is quite insincere in her final rejection of her husband and her beloved.

Six: Romantic Love – Poetry

1. I am now (April 1988) working on a study of seventeenth-century women's sexuality. My use of the term 'lesbian' when discussing this period is contentious.
2. *Letters from Orinda to Poliarchus* was published in 1705, 1714, 1729. An anonymous poem of Philips's appeared in Tottel's *Miscellany* in 1716 and 1727. She is praised in Dryden's poem to Anne Killigrew, which was published in 1693, 1701, 1716, 1727, and reference was made to her in 1743 by the anonymous satirist who wrote *The Crooked Sixpence*. Her poems appear in *Poems by Eminent Ladies*, 1757. In 1764 her achievements were noted by David Erskine in *Biographia Dramatica*. In 1776 William King praised her in *The Art of Love*, and in 1780 John Nicolls reprinted William Temple's *Elegy* on her, appending a biographical note. Articles also appeared in *Theatrum Poetarum* 1800 and 1812, and *Biographia Dramatica* 1782, 1812. In 1861 she was mentioned in Jane Williams's *The Literary Women of England*. Edmund Gosse's *Seventeenth-Century Studies* mentioned her in 1883, and John Aubrey's *Brief Lives* in 1898. 1904 saw the beginning of the 'Orinda Booklets', a series which opened with L.I. Guiney's edition of a selection of Philips's poems. Thorn-Drury's *A Little Ark*, 1921, included J.C.'s *Elegy* on her. In many of these instances, some familiarity with her work is assumed , so reference to her was clearly much wider than this.
3. Marjorie Plant, *The English Book Trade: An Economic History of the Making and*

Sale of Books, 1965; David Vieth, *Attribution in Restoration Poetry: A Study of Rochester's 'Poems' of 1680*, New Haven, Connecticut, 1963.

4. Jeremy Taylor, *A Discourse of the Nature, Offices, and Measures of Friendship*, 1657, p. 9.

5. William Roberts, 'The Dating of Orinda's French Translations', *Philological Quarterly*, 49, 1970.

6. Philips chose this prologue and epilogue from many others offered to her, *Letters from Orinda to Poliarchus*, pp. 119–20.

7. See, for example, Philip Souers, *The Matchless Orinda*, Cambridge, Mass., 1931.

8. Another cool critic of Margaret Cavendish was Dorothy Osborne, who, having asked her fiancé William Temple to obtain a copy of *Poems and Fancies* for her, the following month wrote: 'You need not send me my Lady Newcastle's book at all for I have seen it, and am satisfied there are many soberer people in Bedlam. I'll swear her friends are much to blame to let her go abroad' (*Letters of Dorothy Osborne*, ed. E.A. Parry, 1903, p. 113). Perhaps this judgement was well-known, since Philips wrote to Dorothy Osborne Temple after the appearance of the 1664 *Poems*, asserting that she had not been so immodest and unfeminine as to seek publication (quoted in Julia Longe, *Martha, Lady Giffard: Her Life and Correspondence (1664–1722). A Sequel to the Letters of Dorothy Osborne*, 1911, pp. 38–43).

9. The editor was probably Charles Cotterell. The edition was entered in the *Stationers' Register* on the same day as Cotterell's *Relation of the Defeating of Cardinal Mazarin* (21 January 1667).

10. She also refers to an earlier surreptitious edition of some of her poetry in *Letters to Poliarchus*, p. 127: 'I am sure it [*Pompey*] will be as false printed as was my copy of verses to the queen'. I have been unable to identify this text, and believe it might have been a Dublin imprint.

11. Lines were omitted in 1664 from 'On the Fair Weather just at the Coronation'; 'To the Noble Palaemon on his Incomparable Discourse of Friendship'; 'To My Dear Sister Mrs C.P. on her Marriage'. Significant variations between editions affect, for instance, 'Friendship'; 'To the Queen's Majesty'; 'In Memory of F.P.'; 'In Memory of that Excellent Person, Mrs Mary Lloyd'. See also Paul Elmen, 'Some Manuscript Poems by the Matchless Orinda', *Philological Quarterly*, 30, 1951; Catherine Mambretti, ' "Fugitive Papers": A New Orinda Poem', *Papers of the Bibliographical Society of America*, 71, 1977.

12. I suspect she was brought in as a stepmother for James's nine-month-old daughter, Frances.

13. Richard Greaves and Robert Zaller, *Biographical Dictionary of English Radicals*, 1982.

14. Souers, op. cit., argues that the Society of Friendship was limited to women, but a letter to Lucasia from Dering quoted in William Clark, *The Early Irish Stage: the Beginnings to 1720*, Oxford, 1955, p. 51, shows that men were included. I agree with Souers, though, that relationships with women are celebrated with more intensity than those with men.

15. Maren-Sofie Røstvig, *The Happy Man: Studies in the Metamorphoses of a Classical Ideal*, Oslo, 1962.

16. Jeremy Taylor, op. cit., pp. 88–9 and Martin Kornbluth, 'Friendship and Fashion: The Dramatic Treatment of Friendship in the Restoration and Eighteenth Century', unpublished PhD thesis, Pennsylvania State University, 1956.

17. In *Letters to Poliarchus*, p. 124, Philips reports receiving an adulatory poem by an unknown woman; this is probably that one.

18. In 1655 the singer Mary Knight had contributed a poem to Lawes's *Second Book of Ayres*.

19. Vieth, op. cit., also refers to some manuscript poems by women at the Bodleian Library. Since Behn herself was dead by 1692, perhaps this second collection was assembled by someone else.

20. Gould's poem is one in a series of anonymously printed attacks on women and defences of them which have been omitted from this discussion. The first of this series is a collection of four poetic attacks on women, collectively entitled *Female Excellence*, 1679; the first poem in the book, which might well have appeared either then or subsequently as a separate, is 'A General Satyr on Women'. This book, and in particular the first poem, was replied to in 1688 by *Sylvia's Revenge*, which has wrongly been attributed to Richard Ames. The style of this forthright riposte makes me believe it is the work of Aphra Behn. In 1692 the debate was continued by a poem which, though anonymous, is commonly believed to be the work of Richard Ames: *Sylvia's Complaint*. This poem is closely based on the earlier *Sylvia's Revenge*, and I believe that a misreading of an ambiguous reference to *Sylvia's Revenge* in the preface to *Sylvia's Complaint* is the source of the mistaken attribution of the earlier text to Ames. *Sylvia's Complaint* also draws heavily on another early defence of women, *Triumphs of Female Wit*, 1683. *Triumphs* is a collection of several poems, some of them ostensibly by women. The main thrust of the pamphlet, however, is an attack on the uselessness of some aspects of male university education, and I think it likely that the book is entirely the product of male endeavour. Regardless of whether the authors of *Triumphs* are male or female, however, it is clearly a source of Ames's *Sylvia's Complaint*. Between them, these poems provide rich material for comparing male and female strategies in defending women.

21. From Hilda Smith, *Reason's Disciples: Seventeenth-Century English Feminists*, 1982, p. 22.

22. Perhaps this is a reference to Rochester's famous deathbed repentance. See Vieth, op. cit.; Graham Greene, *Lord Rochester's Monkey, being the Life of John Wilmot, Second Earl of Rochester*, New York, 1974.

23. I have been unable to find any such suggestion in Wheatley's published works. Dr P. Lyons of Glasgow University has suggested to me that Ephelia might not have existed at all; that the *Female Poems* were written by a group of male rakes. The idea is challenging, but I am not convinced: to me, Ephelia's voice is unmistakeably female.

24. A copy of the broadside is in the British Library, although the catalogue does not identify *A Poem To His Sacred Majesty, On the Plot. Written by a Gentlewoman* as Ephelia's work.

25. It seems reasonable to assume that the poet is the same, as *Advice to his Grace* is signed 'Ephelia'.

26. The copy of the '1682 edition' in the Huntington Library also has the title page changed again, this time by a manuscript addition, so that the date reads '1684'.

27. The sources for the additional songs appear to be the Rochester 1680 *Poems*; *Choice Ayres and Songs*, 1681; Katherine Philips, *Pompey*, 1663 (reprinted in *Choice Songs and Ayres*, 1673, 1675, 1676): John Crowne, *The Destruction of Jerusalem*, 1677 (reprinted in *New Ayres and Dialogues*, 1678). Cyrus Day and Eleanore Murrie, *English Song Books 1651–1702: A Bibliography*, 1940, identifies some of the songs in the '1682' *Female Poems* as first appearing there, but it is possible that they were printed on earlier broadsides that have not survived.

28. For example, *Female Poems* omits the last verse of the poem known as 'The Maim'd Debauchee'. The publisher also changed the opening line of Aphra Behn's 'The Counsel' to read 'Oh fie upon this needless scorn', rather than Behn's more strident 'A pox upon . . .'. The last four poems in the 1679 edition are also probably not the work of Ephelia (the first of these, 'Ephelia to Bajazet', is probably by Etherege: Vieth, op.

cit.). They fill what would otherwise be blank pages in the final gathering.

29. Acrostics are written around the names of Venetia Powney, Rachell Powney and Anne Bury.

30. Gosse, op. cit.; Vieth, op. cit. Moira Ferguson is pursuing Lucyle Hook's unpublished suggestion that J.G. was a slave trader.

31. 'My Fate' pp. 95–7 also records her early loss of her parents, and the history of J.G.'s marriage to another woman.

32. For an interesting discussion of another woman using conventional imagery to discuss the economic relations of marriage, see Catherine Smith, 'Jane Lead: The Feminist Mind and Art of a Seventeenth-Century Protestant Mystic', in Rosemary Ruether and Eleanor McLaughlin, (eds.), *Women of Spirit: Female Leadership in the Jewish and Christian Traditions*, New York, 1979, and 'Jane Lead: Mysticism and the Woman Cloathed with the Sun', in Sandra Gilbert and Susan Gubar, (eds.), *Shakespeare's Sisters*, 1979.

33. See the letter by Robert Wolseley written in 1685 quoted in John Wilson, (ed.), *Court Satires of the Restoration*, Columbus, 1966, p. xvii.

34. 'Last Farewell to J.G.', *Female Poems*, p. 66. Ephelia includes several farewells to her lover, each written in a different voice. Between them, these poems sketch out the available stances for a woman rejecting or being rejected by a man.

35. Behn's version of this poem is based on a prose translation by another writer. The precise sentiments are therefore hers.

36. Richard Morton, (ed.), *Poems (1686) by Mrs Anne Killigrew: A Facsimile Reproduction with an Introduction*, Gainesville, Florida, 1967.

37. Michael Heyd, 'The Reaction to Enthusiasm in the Seventeenth Century: Towards an Integrative Approach', *Journal of Modern History*, 53, 1981.

38. G. Gibbons, 'Mrs Jane Barker', *Notes and Queries*, 11, 1922; William McBurney, 'Edmund Curll, Mrs Jane Barker, and the English Novel', *Philological Quarterly*, 37, 1958.

39. This leads Joan Kinnaird to argue, wrongly, that there was a causal connection between royalism and 'feminism' ('Mary Astell and the Conservative Contribution to English Feminism', *Journal of British Studies*, 19, 1979).

40. Aphra Behn, 'The Golden Age', *Poems*, 1684, pp. 7–12.

Seven: Skills Books – Housewifery, Medicine, Midwifery

1. Alice Clark, *Working Life of Women in the Seventeenth Century*, 1919; Christina Hole, *The English Housewife in the Seventeenth Century*, 1953; Doris Stenton, *The English Woman in History*, 1957. See also Introduction.

2. Suzanne Hull, *Chaste, Silent and Obedient*, Los Angeles, 1982.

3. Hull, op. cit.; Marjorie Plant, *The English Book Trade: An Economic History of the Making and Sale of Books*, 1965; William London, *A Catalogue of the Most Vendible Books*, 1657.

4. Leonard Beck, 'Two Loaf-Givers, or a Tour through the Gastronomic Libraries of Katherine Golden Bitting and Elizabeth Robins Pennell', *Quarterly Journal of the Library of Congress*, 38, 1981.

5. The false biography appears in *DNB* and in *Notes and Queries*, July 1852.

6. *The Gentlewomans Companion* went through three editions. Only the first, entered in the *Term Catalogues* 21 November 1672, was sold by Dorman Newman. The next two were sold by Edward Thomas and do not differ substantially from the first. I have found no record of the transfer of copyright. Neither this book nor *A Supplement* was entered in the *Stationers' Register*.

7. Hannah Wolley, *A Supplement*, p. 10, says she married at twenty-four. Her husbands' names are given in the *Victoria County History of England (Essex)*, volume 2, p. 542 (*VCH*). There is a discrepancy of three years between Wolley's account of Benjamin's headmastership of Newport School and that given in the *VCH*.

8. The date of this second marriage is given in *VCH*. The description of her will is in British Record Society, *Wills at Chelmsford*, volume 2, p. 399.

9. *A Supplement*, p. 140, says she has four sons and two grandchildren living. Her son's address is given at the beginning of *A Supplement*.

10. The quotation is taken from the 1662 edition of *The Ladies Directory*. The only known copy of the first edition, 1661, was destroyed in bombing. A. Oxford, *Notes from a Collector's Catalogue: With a Bibliography of English Cookery Books*, 1909, p. 76, has a transcription of its title page and a detailed comparison with the second edition.

11. Perhaps the family of Sir Peter Wroth, to whom she dedicates *The Cook's Guide*.

12. *The Ladies Directory* pp. 30–1. This is reprinted, verbatim, as many of her recipes are, in her later books: see *The Ladies Delight*, p. 50, and *The Queen-like Closet*. Not all recipes with similar titles in her various books are identical, however. The recipe for 'Rare Cakes without Sugar' in *The Ladies Directory*, p. 100, for instance, is completely different from that of 'To make sweet Cakes without Sugar' in *The Queen-like Closet*, p. 140.

13. Wolley dedicated *The Queen-like Closet* to another baronet's daughter, Grace Buzby.

14. Robert May *The Accomplisht Cook*, fourth edition for O. Blagrave, 1678; sig. A4^v–A6^v. All page references are to this edition. The book first appeared in 1660.

15. Her directions to servants are also explicitly ungendered (p. 375), and her remedies in *A Supplement* also employ this kind of linguistic device to keep indefinite the gender of the patient.

16. See May's life described by W.W. in May's *The Accomplisht Cook*, sig. A6$^{r–v}$. The quotation is from Wolley, *A Supplement*, pp. 82–3. For women and apprenticeship, see Dorothy Gardiner, *English Girlhood at School: A Study of Women's Education Through Twelve Centuries*, 1929; Leonore Glanz, 'The Legal Position of English Women under Early Stuart Kings and the Interregnum, 1603–1660', unpublished PhD thesis, Loyola University, 1973.

17. Oxford, op. cit., p. 82.

18. Those quoting this passage include Alice Clark, op. cit.; Kate Hurd-Mead, *A History of Women in Medicine from the Earliest Times to the Beginning of the Nineteenth Century*, New York, 1938; Myra Reynolds, *The Learned Lady in England 1650–1760*, Gloucester, Mass., 1964, first published 1920; Stenton, op. cit.; Lawrence Stone, *The Family, Sex and Marriage in England, 1500–1800*, 1977; Roger Thompson, *Women in Stuart England and America. A Comparative Study*, 1976.

19. Contrast Mary Carleton's use of romance convention, discussed in chapter four.

20. The earliest attribution of *The Accomplish'd Lady's Delight* to Wolley that I have found appears in the Index to Edward Arber's transcription of the *Term Catalogues*. The attribution may actually be a clerical error: Arber lists the book twice, once with 'T.P.' as author, then immediately below this attributing it to Wolley. The Index, according to Arber, simply provides information that he has compiled by consulting the texts themselves. Since no copy of *The Accomplish'd Lady's Delight* I have seen gives Wolley as its author, it seems possible that Arber simply confused the two similar titles when making his Index.

21. 1690 edition. I have not found a copy of the first edition, 1678.

22. See also John Webb, 'Some passages in the Life and Character of a Lady resident in

Herefordshire and Worcestershire during the Civil War [Mrs Joyce Jeffries]', *Archaeologia*, 37, 1857.

23. *The Tryall and Examination of Mrs Joan Peterson*, p. 8. See also Christina Larner, *Enemies of God: the Witch-hunt in Scotland*, New York, 1981; Keith Thomas, *Religion and the Decline of Magic. Studies in Popular Beliefs in Sixteenth- and Seventeenth-Century England*, 1978. For Lady Powel, see p. 5.

24. *The Witch of Wapping* p. 3. Page 8 of this pamphlet describes the execution of Prudence Lee for the 'abominable murther' of her adulterous husband. Finding him in a tavern with another woman, she drew a knife and stabbed him.

25. W. Copeman, *Doctors and Disease in Tudor Times*, 1960, p. 26; Muriel Hughes, *Women Healers in Medieval Life and Literature*, 1943, p. 85; Charles Webster, *The Great Instauration: Science, Medicine and Reform 1626–1660*, New York, 1976, p. 251.

26. Charles Goodall, *An Historicall Account of the College's Proceedings*, 1684, pp. 316–19. See also Hurd-Mead, op. cit.

27. Jane Donegan, *Women and Men Midwives*, Westport, Conn., 1978, p. 14. See also Michael MacDonald, *Mystical Bedlam: Madness, Anxiety, and Healing in Seventeenth-Century England*, 1981; Webster, op. cit., pp. 250–1.

28. Margaret Searl's advertisement appears in a British Library broadside collection, shelfmark 551 a 32 (number 59). Mary Clark's in volume shelfmark c112 f 9 (number 18).

29. 551 a 32 (13).

30. 551 a 32 (86).

31. 551 a 32 (31), (71); c112 f 9 (26).

32. Henry Thomas, 'The Society of Chymical Physitians: An Echo of the Great Plague of London, 1665', in E. Underwood (ed.), *Science, Medicine and History*, volume 2, 1953; Charles Webster, 'English Medical Reformers of the Puritan Revolution: A Background to the "Society of Chymical Physitians" ', *Ambix*, 14, 1967. Webster wrongly describes the Society as the first organised attempt to challenge the Physicians. They were in fact predated by the midwives.

33. *Shinkin-ap-Shone Her Prognostication* appears from its title to be by a woman, but the 'her' is simply an index of the 'humour' of the pamphlet, which is an anti-Welsh parody.

34. Copeman, op. cit.; Webster, *Great Instauration*. See also many entries in *Notes and Queries*, 1900. Of limited use, because he believes midwives to have been evil witches are several works by Thomas Forbes: *The Midwife and the Witch*, New Haven, Conn, 1966; 'Midwifery and Witchcraft', *Journal of the History of Medicine*, 17, 1962; 'The regulation of English midwives in the sixteenth and seventeenth centuries', *Medical History*, 8, 1964.

35. Jean Donnison, *Midwives and Medical Men: A History of Inter-Professional Rivalries and Women's Rights*, 1977, p. 10. See also Donegan, op. cit., p. 13; Forbes, 'The regulation', p. 238; Ann Oakley, 'Wisewoman and Medicine Man', in Juliet Mitchell and Ann Oakley, (eds.), *The Rights and Wrongs of Women*, 1976.

36. *The Book of Oaths*, 1649 and 1689. See also Donegan, op. cit., pp. 11–12; and *The Midwives Ghost*, 1680.

37. James Aveling, *English Midwives: Their History and Prospects*, 1967, first published 1872; Stone, op. cit.

38. Charles Goodall, *An Historicall Account*, 1684, pp. 463–5; Forbes, 'The regulation', p. 240. Hurd-Mead, op. cit., also deals with the petitions, but her interpretation is suspect: she sees the result of Peter Chamberlen's 1634 petition, for instance, as him gaining a licence and so achieving the recognition he sought. Since her verifiable remarks are untrustworthy, it is unwise to accept her unreferenced assertion,

p. 395, (repeated by Donnison, op. cit.) that Hester Shaw was involved in the 1634 petition.

39. Hugh Chamberlen, *The Diseases of Women with Child*, 1672, sig. a2ᵛ. See also Donegan, op. cit., pp. 49–50.

40. Nicholas Culpeper, *A Directory for Midwives*, 1651, 1675. Quotations from 1675 edition. After his death in 1655 his wife Alice appears to have seen to the publication of his works.

41. Mary Rich, *Autobiography*, ed. by T.C. Croker, 1848; Alice Thornton, *The Autobiography of Mrs Alice Thornton*, Surtees Society, 1875; John Evelyn, *The Life of Mrs Godolpin*, ed. Harriet Sampson, 1939; *Eliza's Babes*, 1652; Sarah Goodhue, *The Copy of A Valedictory and Monitory Writing, Left by Sarah Goodhue*, 1681, reprinted Boston, 1850. See also Anne Bradstreet and Ann Fanshawe.

42. These include *The English Midwife Enlarged*; Thomas Chamberlayne, et al, *The Compleat Midwifes Practice*; Richard Bunworth, *The Doctresse*. See also Patricia Crawford, 'Attitudes to Menstruation in Seventeenth-Century England', *Past and Present*, 91, 1981; Barbara Ehrenreich and Deidre English, *Witches, Midwives and Nurses: A History of Women Healers*, 1973; Samuel Radbill, 'Pediatrics', in Allen Debus, (ed.), *Medicine in Seventeenth-Century England*, California, 1974; Hilda Smith, 'Gynaecology and Ideology in Seventeenth-Century England', in Berenice Carroll, (ed.), *Liberating Women's History*, Illinois, 1976.

43. Cellier's *Scheme* was published in 1745 (*Harleian Miscellany*, volume 4). References are to this edition.

44. Elizabeth Cellier, *To Dr ——*, p. 7.

45. Aveling, op. cit., p. 84, who has nothing but praise for the Chamberlens, slights Cellier's scheme as one intended primarily to line her own pockets.

46. *To Dr ——*, p. 7, says that the king promised the previous September to establish a College of Midwives.

47. Oakley, op. cit.

Eight: Education

1. Christopher Hill, *The World Turned Upside Down*, 1975.

2. Margaret Spufford, 'Schooling 1575–1700', *Agricultural History Review*, 18, 1970; David Cressy, *Literacy and the Social Order*, 1980. For Theodosia Alleine, see chapter three; for all others, see chapter one.

3. For Dury, see George Turnbull, *Hartlib, Dury and Comenius: Gleanings from Hartlib's Papers*, Liverpool, 1947, pp. 120–1. For Carleton, see chapter four. See also Josephine Kamm, *Hope Deferred: Girls' Education in English History*, 1965; Dorothy Gardiner, *English Girlhood at School: A Study of Women's Education Through Twelve Centuries*, 1929.

4. Foster Watson, *The English Grammar Schools to 1660, Their Curriculum and Practice*, 1968, first published 1908, p. 531; William Vincent, *The State and School Education 1640–1660 in England and Wales*, 1950.

5. Lawrence Stone, 'The Educational Revolution in England, 1560–1640', *Past and Present*, 28, 1965.

6. Marjorie Nicholson, (ed.), *Conway Letters*, 1930, pp. 107, 145, 234. Huntington Library MS HA14332 is a letter from Conway dated 1674, in which she reports that, after ten years of enforced withdrawal from the world, her migraines had not abated. For feminist discussion of migraine, see *Spare Rib*, August and September 1979.

7. I give an oversimplified picture of the universities' role. In *Behemoth*, 1680, Thomas Hobbes argues the need to abolish them because they were hotbeds of sedition.

8. See also Margret Braidley, et al, *Certain Papers*; Mary Cary, *New and Exact Mappe*; Elizabeth Hooton, et al, *False Prophets*; Rebeckah Travers, A Testimony. For royalist alarm at such proposals, see Vincent, op. cit., pp. 87–8.

9. Turnbull, op. cit.; Vincent, op. cit.; Charles Webster, *The Great Instauration, Science, Medicine and Reform 1626–1660*, New York, 1976. For the link to empiricism, see Watson, op. cit., p. 90 and Webster, op. cit.

10. Margaret Cavendish, *The New Blazing World*, in *Observations*, 1666, pp. 57–8.

11. Cavendish's visit was made on 30 May 1667, and according to Pepys, in his diary entry for that date, the question of whether she should be invited to attend had been hotly debated. The record of the decision in Thomas Birch *The History of the Royal Society*, volume 2, 1756, pp. 175–6, is carefully explicit that the Duchess attended at her own desire and not as a result of the free invitation of the Society.

12. Rufus Jones, *Ancients and Moderns. A Study of the Rise of the Scientific Movement in Seventeenth-Century England*, Washington, 1936, and *The Seventeenth Century. Studies in the History of English Thought and Literature from Bacon to Pope*, California, 1951.

13. More also received a copy of her books, and wrote mockingly about this to Anne Conway. In her *Philosophical Letters* Cavendish mentions that a woman has refuted her ideas in print. I have not found this text.

14. A more extensive analysis of the continuities and differences between these texts needs to be made. Those informing the present discussion include William Austin, *Haec Homo*, 1637; Charles Gerbier, *Elogium Heroinum*, 1651; Thomas Heywood, *Generall History of Women*, 1657; William Hill, *New-years-gift for Women*, 1670; J. Golborne, *A Friendly Apology*, 1674; Poulain de la Barre, *The Woman as Good as the Man*, 1677; John Shirley, *The Illustrious History of Women*, 1686.

15. For van Schurman's international reputation, see J.R. Brink, (ed.), *Female Scholars. A Tradition of Learned Women Before 1800*, Montreal, 1980. The translator of the 1659 edition of *The Learned Maid* refers to an earlier English edition which does not appear to have survived.

16. Wilbur Howell, *Logic and Rhetoric in England, 1500–1700*, Princeton, 1956.

17. *The Learned Maid*, p. 48, Van Schurman mentions 'the most learned matron, Madam Bathsua Metkins' who 'so highly commended my industry in sublimer studies'.

18. For further biographical information, see Vivian Salmon, 'Bathsua Makin; a pioneer linguist and feminist in seventeenth-century England', in Brigitte Asbach-Schnitker and Johannes Roggenhofer (eds.), *Neuere Forschungen zur Wörtbildung und Historiographie der Linguistik: Festgabe für Herbert E. Brekle*, Tubingen, 1987. See also Paula Barbour, (ed.), *Bathsua Makin, An Essay to Revive the Antient Education of Gentlewomen (1673)*, California, 1980; Veena Kasbekar, 'Power Over Themselves: The Controversy About Female Education in England, 1660–1820', unpublished PhD thesis, University of Cincinatti, 1981.

19. Bathsua Makin, *An Essay*, p. 17. Unlike male authors who merely state that the muses are female, Makin uses this idea to suggest that 'women were the inventors of many of these arts' (p. 21).

20. Makin, p. 4. She also says that 'persons of higher quality, for want of this education, have nothing to employ themselves in, but are forced to cards, dice, plays, and frothy romances, merely to drive away the time' (p. 26).

Postscript: Beginning Again

1. For information on William Strong, see Ira Boseley, *The Ministers of the Abbey Independent Church*, 1911.

BIBLIOGRAPHY

PRIMARY SOURCES

This listing is in four major sections rather different from one another.

1. Works by English women published 1649–88. Some *but not all* earlier and later works by women publishing in this time-frame are included, if consulted by me. A few texts by foreign women are also included.
2. Works by sixteenth- and seventeenth-century men consulted for this study. (Many of these are commonly falsely attributed to women. The others are about or for women.)
3. Modern editions of works by English women written 1649–88 (many not published then). This list is designed as a guide only, and does not pretend to be complete.
4. Manuscripts consulted.

1. Works by English women published 1649–88

Explanatory Note. This listing is in two parts:

a) works by named women
b) works by anonymous or pseudonymous women.

This list is designed to aid others interested in researching English women's writing of the period, and therefore includes some works that I have not consulted, marked +. It was originally compiled by reading Donald Wing, *Short-Title Catalogue 1641–1700*, but has been altered on the basis of textual evidence. Original spelling and punctuation are maintained. Reference numbers from the *Second Edition* of Wing are given (except volume 3: no second edition yet available). Locations are given for texts omitted from Wing. Works are given both Wing numbers in cases of erroneous double-listings. Where I dispute Wing's datings, my amended date appears in **bold print**. Since my aim is to identify as many women writers as possible, texts with multiple authorship have subsidiary entries under the names of joint or minor authors. (Titles to part-texts appear in inverted commas, not italics.)

Key   + work not seen by me but believed to have been published by an English woman writing 1649–88
        * work by foreign woman consulted for this study

a. works by named women

Abbott, Margaret, *A Testimony Against the False Teachers*, [1659?], A70B
Adams, Mary, *A Warning To The Inhabitants of England*, 1676, A489
+   – *A warning to the inhabitants of England*, 1678, not in Wing, see *NUC*
     – *The Ranters Monster*, [male work, see under title]
Alexander, Mary, *The State of the Case*, *see* Levingston, Anne, L1824 & S5685
     – *To the Right Honourable, the Parliament*, [1654], T1705A
     – *To the Supream Authority Of the Nation*, [1654], T1730A
+ Alleine, Theodosia, *The life and death of Mr Joseph Alleine*, 1671, A1011
     – *The Life and Death Of . . . Joseph Alleine*, 1672, A1012
     – *The Life and Death Of . . . Joseph Alleine*, 1672, A1013
     – *The Life & Death Of . . . Joseph Alleine*, 1672, A1013A
     – *The Life & Death Of . . . Joseph Alleine*, 1673, A1014
     – *The Life & Death Of . . . Joseph Allein*, 1677, A1015
+   – *The life and death of . . . Joseph Alleine*, 1693, A1016
Allen, Hannah, *Satan his Methods and Malice Baffled*, 1683, A1025
Anderdon, Mary, *A Word to the World*, [1662], A3084A
Anne, Queen of England, *The Princess Anne of Denmark's Letter*, [1688], [actually several editions in Huntington Library] A3224
Atkinson, Elizabeth, *A Breif and plain discovery*, 1669, A4129A
     – *The Weapons Of the People*, 1669, A4129B
Audland, Anne, et al, *The Saints Testimony*, 1655, S365
     – and Jane Waugh, *A True Declaration*, 1655, A4195
     – 'Letter' and 'Testimony' part of Camm, John, *The Memory*, 1689, C390
Aulnoy, Marie Catherine, *see* La Mothe, Marie Catherine, A4221, A4222
Austill, Bridget, 'Her testimony', part of Whitehead, Anne, *Piety Promoted*, 1686, W1885
Barker, Jane, *Poetical Recreations*, 1688, B770
Barwick, Grace, *To all present Rulers*, 1659, B1007A
Bastwick, Susannah, *To the High Court of Parliament*, [1654], B1073
Bateman, Susanna, *I matter not how I appear to man*, [1657], B1097
Bathurst, Anne, *An Expostulatory Appeal*, *see* Bathurst, Elizabeth, B1135A
Bathurst, Elizabeth and Anne Bathurst, *An Expostulatory Appeal*, [**1679?**], B1135A
Bathurst, Elizabeth, *The Sayings of Women*, 1683, B1135B
     – et al, *Truth Vindicated*, 1691, B1135C
     – et al, *Truth Vindicated*, 1695, B1136
     – *Truth's Vindication*, 1679, B1137
     – *Truth's Vindication*, 1683, B1138
     – *Truth's Vindication*, 1683, B1139
Bathurst, Grace, 'Her testimony', part of Bathurst, Elizabeth, *Truth Vindicated*, 1691, 1695, B1135C, B1136
     – 'Her testimony', part of Whitehead, Anne, *Piety Promoted*, 1686, W1885
Baxter, Margaret, 'Diary', part of Baxter, Richard, *Breviate*, 1681, B1194
Beck, Margaret, *The Reward of Oppression*, 1655, B1648

+   – *The reward of oppression*, 1656, B1649
      Beck, Sarah, *A certain and true*, [male work, *see* under title] C1686A
      Behn, Aphra, *The Histories and Novels*, 1696, B1711
        – *Histories, Novels, And Translations*, 1700, B1711A
        – *All the Histories And Novels*, 1698, B1712
+   – *All the histories and novels*, 1699, B1713
+   – *The histories and novels*, 1700, B1714
        – *Abdelazer*, 1677, B1715
        – *Abdelazer*, 1693, B1716
        – *et al*, *Aesop's Fables With His Life*, 1687, A703
+   – *Agnes de Castro*, 1688, B4693A
        – *The Amorous Prince*, 1671, B1717
+   – *The amours of Philander and Silvia*, 1687, [part of *Love Letters*, 1685?],
          B1718
        – *The City-Heiress*, 1682, B1719
        – *The City-Heiress*, 1698, B1719A
        – *The City-Heiress*, 1698, B1720
      Behn, Aphra, ed., *A Collection Of Poems*, 1672, C5177
        – ed., *A Collection Of Poems*, **1693**, C5178
+ Behn, Aphra, *A congratulatory poem to her most sacred*, 1688, B1721
        – *A Congratulatory Poem To Her Most Sacred*, 1688, B1722
        – *A Congratulatory Poem to . . . Queen Mary*, 1689, B1723
+   – *A congratulatory poem to the king's*, 1688, B1724
        – (?), *The Counterfeit Bridegroom*, 1677, M1983
        – (?), *The Debauchee*, 1677, B4869
      Behn, Aphra, tr., *A Discovery Of New Worlds*, 1688, F1412
+   – tr., *A discovery of new worlds*, 1688, F1412A
      Behn, Aphra, *The Dutch Lover*, 1673, B1726
        – *Emperor of the Moon*, 1687, B1727
        – *The Emperor of the Moon*, 1688, B1728
        – *The Fair Jilt*, 1688, B1729
        – *The False Count*, 1682, B1730
        – *The False Count*, 1687, B1731
+   – *A farce call'd The false Count*, 1682, B1732
        – *The Feign'd Curtizans*, 1679, B1733
        – (?), *Floriana*, 1681, D2505
        – *The Forc'd Marriage*, 1671, B1734
        – *The Forc'd Marriage*, 1688, B1735
        – *The Forc'd Marriage*, 1690, B1736
      Behn, Aphra, tr., *The History Of Oracles*, 1688, F1413
+   – tr., *The history of oracles*, 1699, F1413A
      Behn, Aphra, *The History Of The Nun*, 1689, B1737
+   – *The lady's looking-glass*, 1697, B1738
+   – *The lives of sundry notorious villains*, 1678, B1739
+   – *Love letters between a noble-man and his sister*, 1684, B1740
+   – *Love letters between a noble-man and his sister*, 1694, B1742
+   – *Love letters between Polydorus*, 1689, B1743

    – *Love Letters From A Noble Man ... Second Part*, 1685, not in Wing [British Library, part of B1740?]

+   – *Love letters from a nobleman ... second part*, 1693, [part of an edition of *Love letters between a noble-man?*] B1743A

    – *The Luckey Chance*, 1687, B1744

    – *The Lucky Mistake*, 1689, B1745

Behn, Aphra, tr., *Lycidus*, 1688, T129

    – 'Memoirs on the court', 1697, B1746, part of her *All the Histories and Novels*, 1698, B1712

Behn, Aphra, ed., *Miscellany, Being A Collection of Poems*, 1685, M2230

Behn, Aphra, tr., *La Montre*, 1686, B3596

+ Behn, Aphra, *A new song sung in Abdelazar*, 1695, B1747

    – *Oroonoko*, 1688, B1749

    – *A Pindarick On The Death Of Our Late Sovereign*, 1685, B1750

+   – *A pindarick on the death of our late sovereign*, 1685, B1751

+   – *A pindarick on the death of our late sovereign*, [1685?], B1752

    – *A Pindarick Poem on the Happy Coronation*, 1685, B1753

    – *A Pindaric Poem To The Reverend Doctor*, 1689, B1754

    – *A Poem Humbly Dedicated*, 1685, B1755

    – *A Poem to Sir Roger L'Estrange*, 1688, B1756

    – *Poems Upon Several Occasions*, 1684, B1757

    – *Poems Upon Several Occasions*, 1697, B1758

    – *A Prologue By ... to her New Play*, 1682, B1759

+   – *Prologue spoken by Mrs Cook*, 1685, B1759A

    – *Prologue to Romulus*, 1682, B1760

    – (?), *The Revenge*, 1680, B2084

    – *The Roundheads*, 1682, B1761

    – *The Roundheads*, 1698, B1762

    – *The Rover*, 1677, B1763

    – *The Rover*, 1697, B1764

    – *The Second Part Of The Rover*, 1681, B1765

    – *Sir Patient Fancy*, 1678, B1766

    – *Three Histories*, 1688, B1766A

    – *To Poet Bavius*, 1688, B1767

    – *To the Most Illustrious Prince Christopher*, 1687, B1768

    – *The Town-Fopp*, 1677, B1769

    – *The Town-Fopp*, 1699, B1770

+   – *The town raves*, [1696], B1770A

    – *Two Congratulatory Poems*, 1688, B1771

    – *The Unfortunate Bride*, 1698, B1772

    – *The Unfortunate Bride*, 1700, B1773

    – *The Wandering Beauty*, 1698, B1773A

+   – *The wandering beauty*, 1700, B1773B

    – *The Widdow Ranter*, 1690, B1774

    – *Young Jemmy*, [ca. 1681], B1775

    – *The Young King*, 1683, B1776

    – *The Young King*, 1698, B1777

    – *The Younger Brother*, 1696, B1778

    – 'Poems', part of Gildon, Charles, ed., *Miscellany Poems*, 1692, G733A

Bell, Susanna, *The Legacy Of A Dying Mother*, 1673, B1802

Bennet, Dorcas, *Good and seasonable counsel*, [male work, *see* under Bennet, Dorcas, pseud.] B1883A

Benson, Mabel, 'Testimony', part of Camm, John, *The Memory*, 1689, C390

Bettris, Jeane, *A Lamentation*, 1657, B2085

+   – *Spiritual discoveries*, 1657, [no copy found] B2086

Biddle, Hester, *Oh! wo, wo, from the Lord*, 1659, B2864C

    – *To the inhabitants*, 1659, B2864D, [same as her *Oh! wo, wo, from the Lord*, 1659] B2864C

+   – *The trumpet of the Lord God*, 1662, [no copy found] B2864E

    – *The Trumpet Of the Lord Sounded forth*, 1662, B2865

    – *A Warning From The Lord God*, 1660, B2866

    – *Wo to thee town of Cambridge*, [**1655**], B2866A

    – *Wo to thee City of Oxford*, [**1655**], B2867

    – 'Something in short', part of Woodrow, Thomas, *A brief*, 1659, W3474

* Birgitta, Saint, *The Most Devout Prayers*, 1659, B2958

*   – *The Most Devout Prayers*, 1686, B2959

Blackborow, Sarah, *Herein is held forth the Gift*, 1659, B3063

    – *The Just and Equal Balance discovered*, 1660, B3064

    – *The Oppressed Prisoners Complaint*, [1662], B3064A

    – *A Visit to the Spirit in Prison*, 1658, B3065

    – 'Dear Friends', part of Hubberthorne, Richard, *A Collection*, 1663, H3216

Blaithwaite, Mary, *The Complaint of*, [1654], B3129

Blaugdone, Barbara, *An Account Of The Travels*, 1691, A410

Booth, Mary, 'Preface', part of Nayler, James, *Milk for Babes*, 1661, 1665, 1668, N299, N300, N301

Boothby, Frances, *Marcelia*, 1670, B3742

Boulbie, Judith, *A Few Words To the Rulers of this Nation*, [1673], B3827A

    – *A Testimony for Truth*, [1665], B3828

    – *To all Justices of Peace*, [**1688**], B3828A

+   – *A warning and lamentation*, 1679, [no copy found] B3828B

* Bourgeois, Louise, 'Instructions', part of Chamberlayne, Thomas, *The Compleat*, 1656, C1817C

*   – 'Serious ... secrets', part of Chamberlayne, Thomas, *The Compleat*, 1659, 1663, and *The Complete*, 1680, C1817D, C1817E, C1817F

+ Bradmor, Sarah, *Prophecy of the wonders*, 1686, B4139

* Bradstreet, Anne, *The Tenth Muse*, 1650, B4167

Braidley, Margret, et al, *Certain Papers which is the Word*, [1655], T260

Braytwhaite, Elizabeth, [passage], part of C., T., *A brief relation*, [1684], C128

Brégy, Charlotte, *see* Flecelles, Charlotte de, B4342

Brooksop, Joan, *An Invitation of Love*, [1662], B4983

Camfield, Elizabeth, 'Many are the testimonies', part of Whitehead, Anne, *Piety Promoted*, 1686, W1885

Carleton, Mary, *The Case of*, 1663, C586A

    – *An Historicall Narrative*, 1663, H2106

    – *The memoires of*, 1673, [male work, *see* under title], C587 & G35B

    – *A True Account Of The Tryal*, 1663, not in Wing

Cartwright, Joanna, *The Petition of the Jewes*, 1649, C695

Cartwright, Ursula, *The Case Of*, [1680?], C1191

Cary, Mary, *The Little Horns Doom and Downfall*, 1651, C736

    – *The Resurrection of the Witnesses*, 1648, C737

    – *The Resurrection of the Witnesses*, 1653, C738

    – *Twelve Humble Proposals*, 1653, R51

    – *A Word in Season*, 1647, C739

Castlemayne, Barbara, *see* Patison, Barbara, C4653

Cavendish, Margaret, *De Vita et Rebus Gestis*, 1668, N848

    – *The Description of a New World*, 1666, N849

    – *The Description of a New World*, 1668, N850

    – *Grounds of Natural Philosophy*, 1668, N851

    – *Letters*, 1676, [male text, *see* under title] L1774

    – *The Life of the thrice Noble ... Duke*, 1667, N853

    – *The Life Of The Thrice Noble ... Duke*, 1675, N854

    – *Natures Pictures*, 1656, N855

    – *Natures Picture*, 1671, N856

    – *Observations*, 1666, N857

    – *Observations*, 1668, N858

    – *Orations*, 1662, N859

    – *Orations*, 1662, N860

+   – *Orations*, 1663, N861

    – *Orations*, 1668, N862

·   – *The Philosophical and Physical Opinions*, 1655, N863

    – *The Philosophical and Physical Opinions*, 1663, N864

    – *Philosophicall Fancies*, 1653, N865

    – *Philosophical Letters*, 1664, N866

    – *Plays, Never before Printed*, 1668, N867

    – *Playes*, 1662, N868

    – *Poems, and Fancies*, 1653, N869

    – *Poems, and Phancies*, 1664, N870

    – *Poems, or, Several Fancies in Verse*, 1668, N871

    – *CCXI Sociable Letters*, 1664, N872

    – *The Worlds Olio*, 1655, N873

    – *The Worlds Olio*, 1671, N874

+ Cellier, Elizabeth, *Answers to queries*, 1687/8, [Wing 1st ed. only] C1660

    – *Madam Celliers answer*, 1680, [male work, *see* under title] C1659

    – *Malice Defeated*, 1680, C1661

    – *The Matchless Rogue*, 1680, C1662

    – *To Dr. —— An Answer*, [1688], C1663

+   – (?), *The ladies answer*, 1670, C1660

    – *Mistris Celliers lamentation*, 1681, [male work, *see* under title] C1660A

    – *A true copy*, 1681, [male work, *see* under title] C1663A

Channel, Elinor, and Arise Evans, *A Message From God*, 1654, C1936

Chevers, Sarah, 'To All People', part of Evans, Katherine, and Sarah Chevers, *A*

True Account, 1663, [listed in Wing as separate, C3776A]
+ Cholmley, Elisabeth, and Sarah Cholmley, *The case of*, [1673], C911
* Christina, Queen of Sweden, *A Declaration*, 1652, C3964
*   – *A Letter*, 1652, C3965
    – *A declaration*, 1649, [male work, *see* under title] C3963
    Clarke, Frances, *A Briefe Reply To The Narration*, [1653], C4439
    Clark, Margaret, *The true confession*, 1680, [male work, *see* under title] C4482
    – *Warning*, 1680, [male work, *see* under title] C4483
    Clark, Mary, *The Great and Wonderful Success*, [1685], C4483A
    Clayton, Anne, *A Letter to the King*, [1660], C4609
    Cleveland, Barbara, *see* Palmer, Barbara, C4653
    Clipsham, Margery, *see* Ellwood, Mary and Margery Clipsham, C4716A, C4716B & S4994
    Cobb, Alice, 'Testimony', part of Curwen, Alice, et al, *A Relation*, 1680, M857
    Cole, Mary, *see* Cotton, Priscilla and Mary Cole, C6474
    Coleman, Elizabeth, *see* Travers, Ann, and Elizabeth Coleman, C6925
    Collins, An, *Divine Songs and Meditacions*, 1653, C5355
    Conway, Anne, *see* Finch, Anne, Lady Conway
    Cook, Lucretia, 'A short testimony', part of Whitehead, Anne, *Piety Promoted*, 1686, W1885
+ Cottington, Angela, *The case of*, [1680], C882
+ Cotton, Priscilla, *A briefe description*, [1659], C6473B
    – *As I was in the Prison-house*, 1656, not in Wing [Friends' Library, London]
    – and Mary Cole, *To the Priests*, 1655, C6474
    – *A Visitation of Love*, 1661, C6475
    Cromwell, Elizabeth, *The court*, 1664, [male text, *see* under title] C7036
    Crouch, Ruth, 'Her tsetimony' [sic], part of Whitehead, Anne, *Piety Promoted*, 1686, W1885
    Culpeper, Alice, 'Preface', part of Culpeper, Nicholas, *Last Legacy*, 1657, C7519
    – 'Preface', part of Culpeper, Nicholas, *Treatise*, 1656, C7549
    Curwen, Alice, et al, *A Relation Of The Labour*, 1680, M857
    Davies, Eleanor, *see* Douglas, Eleanor
    Davy, Sarah, *Heaven Realiz'd*, 1670, D444
* Desjardins, Marie Catherine de, *The Memoires*, 1672, D1191
*   – *The Unfotunate [sic] Heroes*, 1679, D1193
    Dew, Susanna, 'A testimony', part of Whitehead, Anne, *Piety Promoted*, 1686, W1885
* Dirrecks, Gertruyde, *An Epistle*, [1677], D1558
+ Docwra, Anne, *An apostate conscience exposed*, 1699, D1777
    – *A brief Discovery*, 1683, B1777A
    – *An Epistle of Love*, [1683], D1778
    – *A Looking-Glass For The Recorder*, [1682], D1779
+   – *The second part*, 1700, D1780
    – *Spiritual Community, vindicated*, [1687], D1781
    – *True Intelligence to be Read*, 1683, not in Wing [Friends' Library, London]
    Dole, Dorcas, *Once more A Warning*, 1683, D1834
    – *Once more A Warning*, 1684, D1834A

– *A Salutation and Seasonable Exhortation*, 1683, D1835
– *A Salutation and Seasonable Exhortation*, 1700, D1835A
– *A Salutation Of My Endeared Love*, 1685, D1836
– *A Salutation Of My Endeared Love*, **1687**, D1836A
– 'To you', part of Stirredge, Elizabeth, *A Salutation*, [1683], S5685A
Douglas, Anne, *The Countess of Morton's*, 1666, [male text, *see* G., M., *The Countess of Morton's*] M2817
Douglas, Eleanor, *Amend, Amend*, [1643], D1967
  – *And without proving what we say*, [1648?], D1968
  – *Apocalyps*, Chap. 11., [164-?], D1969
  – *Apocalypsis Jesu Christi*, 1644, D1970
  – *The Appearance*, 1650, D1972A
  – *The Arraignment*, 1650, D1972B
  – *As not unknowne, This Petition*, [1645], D1973
  – *Before the Lords second coming*, 1650, D1974
  – *The Benediction . . . I have an Errand*, 1651, D1975
  – *The Benidiction [sic] . . . I have an Errand*, 1651, D1976
+ – *The Benediction . . . I have an errand*, 1651, D1977
+ – *Bethlehem signifying the house of bread*, 1652, D1978
  – *The Bill of Excommunication*, 1649, D1979
  – *The Blasphemous Charge Against Her*, 1649, D1980
+ – *The blasphemous charge against her*, 1649, D1981
  – *The Brides Preparation*, 1644/5, D1982
  – *The Crying Charge*, 1649, D1982A
  – *The Day Of Iudgements Modell*, 1646, D1983
  – 'The dragons', 1651, D1984, part of her *Given to* [1651], D1993
  – *Elijah the Tishbite's Supplication*, 1650, D1985
+ – *The everlasting gospel*, 1649, D1986
  – *The Excommunication Out Of Paradice*, 1647, D1987
  – *Ezekiel, Cap. 2.*, [164-?], D1988
  – *Ezekiel The Prophet Explained*, 1649, D1988A
  – *For the blessed Feast Of Easter*, 1646, D1989
  – *For the most Honorable States*, 1649, D1989A
  – *For the Right Noble, Sir Balthazar Gerbier*, 1649, D1989B
  – *For Whitsontyds Last Feast*, 1645, D1990
  – *From the Lady Eleanor, Her Blessing*, 1644, D1991
  – *The Gatehouse Salutation From*, 1646 [=**1647**], D1991A
  – *Given to the Elector Prince Charles*, [1648], D1992
  – *Given to the Elector Prince Charls* [sic], [1651], D1993
  – *Great Brittains Visitation*, 1645, D1994
+ – *Hells destruction*, 1651, D1995
  – *I am the first, and the last*, [1644/5], D1996 [fragment, seized in press, part of her *A Prophesie*, 1645, D2004?]
  – *Je Le Tien*, 1646, D1996A
  – *The Lady Eleanor Douglas, Dowager*, 1650, D1996B
  – *The Lady Eleanor, Her Appeale*, 1641, D1971
+ – *The Lady Eleanor her appeal*, 1646, D1972

     – *The Lady Eleanor Her Remonstrance*, 1648, D2006
     – *The Mystery Of General Redemption*, 1647, D1996C
     – *The New Jerusalem At Hand*, 1649, D1997
     – *The New Proclamation*, 1649, see Hastings, Lucy, D1998
     – *Of Errors Ioyned With Gods Word*, 1645, D1999
     – *Of the general Great Days Approach*, 1648, D1999A
     – *Of Times and Seasons Their Mystery*, 1651, D2000
     – *A Prayer or Petition For Peace*, 1644, [**1649?**], D2001
+   – *A prayer or petition for peace*, 1645, D2002
+   – *A prayer or petition for peace*, [1647], D2003
     – *A Prophesie Of The Last Day*, 1645, D2004
+   – *Prophetia de die*, 1644, D2005
     – *Reader, The heavy hour*, 1648, D2005A
+   – *The restitution of prophecy*, 1651, D2007
     – *The Restitution of Reprobates*, 1644, D2008
     – *The Revelation Interpreted*, 1646, D2009
     – *Samsons Fall*, 1649, D2010
+   – *Samsons legacie*, [1642], D2011
     – *The [second] Co[mming]*, 1645, D2012
     – *The Serpents Excommunication*, 1651, D2012A
     – *A Sign Given them*, 1649, D2012AA
     – *Sions Lamentation*, 1649, D2012B
     – *The Star to the Wise*, 1643, D2013
     – *Strange and Wonderfull Prophesies*, 1649, D2014
     – *To The Most Honourable*, [1643], D2015
     – *Tobits Book*, 1652, D2016
     – *Wherefore to prove the thing*, [1648], D2017
     – *The Word Of God*, 1644, D2018
     – *The Writ of Restitution*, 1648, D2019
     – *Zach. 12. And they shall look*, [1649], D2020
Dyer, Mary, [brief passage], part of Stephenson, Marmaduke, *A Call*, 1660, S5466
+ Ebbs, Joyce, *The last speech, confession & prayer*, 1662, E126A
Eeds, Judith, *A Warning to all the Inhabitants*, 1659, E241A
Egerton, Sarah, see Fige, Sarah
+ Elestone, Sarah, *The last speech and confession*, 1678, L504F
Elizabeth, Queen, *The Golden Speech of*, [1659], E528
+   – *The last speech and thanks of*, 1679, E530
     – *Queen Elizabeth's Opinion*, 1688, E532
+   – *A speech made by*, 1688, E533
Elizabeth, Queen of Bohemia, *The Declaration*, 1652, D532
Ellis, Sarah, 'Testimony', part of Whitrow, Joan, *The Work*, 1677, W2039
+ Ellwood, Mary and Margery Clipsham, *The Spirit that works*, [1685], C4716A
     – *The Spirit that works*, 1685, C4716B & S4994
Elson, Mary, et al, *A Tender and Christian Testimony*, [1685], E642
     – 'A testimony', part of Whitehead, Anne, *Piety Promoted*, 1686, W1885

   – 'A true Information', part of Whitehead, Anne, *An Epistle*, 1680, W1882

Evans, Katherine, *A Brief Discovery*, 1663, E3453

   – and Sarah Chevers, *This is a short Relation*, 1662, B487

   – *A True Account*, 1663, not in Wing [Friends' Library, London]

+ Evelyn, Mary, *The picture of the Princesse*, 1660, [lost] E3523A

Fairman, Lydia, *A few Lines given forth*, 1659, F257

Fell, Lydia, *A Testimony and Warning*, [1676], F625

Fell, Margaret, *A Call to the Universall Seed of God*, 1665, F625A

   – *A Call Unto The Seed of Israel*, [1668], F626

+   – *The citie of London reprov'd*, [1660] F626A

   – 'Concerning ministers', 1659, F626B, part of her *A Paper*, 1659, F634A

   – *The Daughter of Sion Awakened*, 1677, F627

   – *A Declaration And An Information*, 1660, F628

   – *An evident Demonstration to Gods Elect*, 1660, F629

   – *An Evident Demonstration to Gods Elect*, 1660, F630

   – *The Examination and Tryall*, 1664, E3710

   – et al, *False Prophets, Anticrists*, [sic], 1655, F631

   – *For Manasseth Ben Israel*, 1656, F632

   – *A Letter Sent to the King*, [1666], F633

   – *A Loving Salutation, to the seed*, 1656, F634

+   – *A loving salutation to the seed*, 1660, F634aA

   – *A Paper concerning such as are made ministers*, 1659, F634A

   – *The Standard of the Lord Revealed*, 1667, F635

   – *A Testimonie Of The Touch-Stone*, 1656, F636

   – *This is to the Clergy*, 1660, F637

   – *This Was Given to Major Generall Harrison*, 1660, F638

   – *To the Generall Councill of Officers*, [1659], F638A

   – *To the General Council of Officers*, 1659 [male work, *see* under title] F638B

   – *To The General Councel*, 1659, F638C

+   – *To the magistrates and people of England*, 1664, F638D

   – *A Touch-Stone, Or, A Perfect Tryal*, 1667, F639

   – *A True Testimony*, 1660, F640

   – *Two General Epistles To the Flock of God*, 1664, F641

   – *Womens Speaking Justified*, 1666, F642

   – *Womens Speaking Justified*, 1667, F643

   – 'John Wigan', part of Curwen, Thomas, *This is An Answer*, 1665, C7703

   – 'Testimony', part of Carter, William, *The Memory*, 1690, M1701A

   – 'A few lines', part of Coale, Josiah, *The Books*, C4751

Fige, Sarah, *Female Advocate*, 1686, E251A

   – *The Female Advocate*, 1687, E251B

Finch, Anne, *The Principles Of . . . Philosophy*, 1692, C5989

Fisher, Abigail, 'Testimony', part of Whitehead, Anne, *Piety Promoted*, 1686, W1885

* Flecelles, Charlotte de, *The Royal Standard*, 1660, B4342

Fletcher, Elizabeth, *A few Words in Season To all*, 1660, F1328

Ford, Bridget, 'Testimony', part of Whitehead, Anne, *Piety Promoted*, 1686,

W1885
Forster, Mary, *A Declaration of the Bountifull*, 1669, F1603
  – *A Declaration of the Bountiful*, 1693, F1603A
  – *Some Seasonable Considerations*, 1684, F1604
  – et al, *These Several Papers*, 1659, F1605
  – et al, *A Living Testimony*, 1685, L2598A
  – 'Testimony', part of Whitehead, Anne, *Piety Promoted*, 1686, W1885
Freeman, Ann-Mary, 'Testimony', part of Whitehead, Anne, *Piety Promoted*, 1686, W1885
Furly, Anna, et al, *A Testimony To The True Light*, 1670, F2541A
  – et al, *A Testimony To The True Light*, 1670, F2542
Gardner, Anne, 'The Testimony', part of C., T., *A Brief Relation*, 1684, C128
Gargill, Ann, *A Brief Discovery*, 1656, G258
  – *A Warning To all the World*, 1656, G259
Gaunt, Elizabeth, *Mrs Elizabeth Gaunt's Last Speech*, [1685], G381A
Gilman, Anne, *An Epistle to Friends*, 1662, G768
  – *To the Inhabitants of the Earth*, **1663**, G768A
Gotherson, Dorothea, *To all that are Unregenerated*, 1661, G1352
Gould, Ann, et al, *An Epistle To all Christian Magistrates*, 1659, G1414
Greenway, Margret, *A Lamentation against the Professing*, [1657], G1861
Grey, Elizabeth, *A Choice Manuall*, [male work, *see* Jarvis, William], K310
  – *A True Gentlewomans*, [male work, *see* Jarvis, William], K317A
Hall, Anne, *A brief representation*, [male work, *see* under title] H324
+ Hamilton, Elizabeth, *To the Parliament*, [1651], H477A
Hastings, Lucy, *The New Proclamation*, 1649, D1998
+ Hatt, Martha, *To the right honourable, the Commons*, 1660, H1141A
+   – *To the right honourable, the Lords*, [1660], H1141B
Haynes, Elizabeth, 'Testimony', part of Whitehead, Anne, *Piety Promoted*, 1686, W1885
* Hendericks, Elizabeth, *An Epistle to Friends*, 1672, H1447
+ Henrietta Maria, Queen, *The Queens majesties letter*, [1649], H1461
+   – *The Queens majesties message*, [1649], H1462
Henshaw, Anne, *To the Parliament of . . . England*, 1654, H1477
+ Herring, Anne, *The case of*, [1678], H1600A
+ Heusde, Sarah Cornelius de, *Loving reader . . . secret arts*, [1670?], G1672A
Hewitt, Mary, *To the . . . Parliament. The humble petition*, [1660], H1640
Hincks, Elizabeth, *The Poor Widows Mite*, 1671, H2050
Holden, Mary, *The Womans Almanack . . . 1688*, 1688, A1827
  – *The Womans Almanack . . . 1689*, 1689, A1827A
Hooton, Elizabeth, et al, *False Prophets and false Teachers*, 1652, A894B
  – 'Testimony', part of Simpson, William, *The life*, 1671, L2042
  – 'To the King', part of Taylor, Thomas, *To the King*, 1670, H2710A
Hopton, Susannah, *Daily Devotions*, 1673, H2761
+ Howard, Arabella, *The case of Mrs Arabella Thompson*, 1680, C960
Howgill, Mary, *A Remarkable Letter*, 1657, H3191
  – *The Vision Of The Lord of Hosts*, 1662, H3192
Huntingdon, Lucy, *see* Hastings, Lucy, Countess of Huntingdon

Hyde, Anne, *A Copy Of A Paper*, 1682, Y46

+   – *Reasons of her leaving the communion*, [1670], Y47
+ James, Elinor, *Mrs James's advice*, [1688], J415
+   – *Mrs James's apology*, [1694], J415A
+   – *Mrs James's application*, [1695], J415B
+   – *The case between a father and his children*, 1682, J416
+   – *Dear soveraign*, [1687], J416A
+   – *Mrs James's defence*, 1687, J417
+   – *Mrs James's humble letter*, [1699], J417aA
+   – *I can assure your honours*, [1699?], J417bA
+   – *An injur'd prince vindicated*, [1688], J417A
+   – *May it please your honours*, [1699?], J417AB
+   – *May it please your Majesty*, [1689], J417AC
+   – *May it please your most sacred Majesty*, [1685], J417B
+   – *Most dear Soveraign*, [1689], J417C
+   – *My Lord*, [1687], J418
+   – *My Lords, I can assure*, [1688], J419
+   – *My Lords, I did not think*, [1690], J419A
+   – *My Lords, you can't but be sensible*, [1688], J419B
+   – *Mrs. James her new answer*, [1681], J420
+   – *Sir, my Lord Mayor*, [1690?], J421
+   – *This being your Majesty's birth-day*, [1690], J421aA
+   – *To the honourable convention*, [1688], J421A
+   – *To the honourable House of Commons*, [1685], J421B
+   – *To the honourable House of Commons*, [1699], J421C
+   – *To the Honourable the House of Commons*, [1696], J422
+   – *To the Kings most excellent majesty*, [1685], J422aA
+   – *To the right honourable Convention*, [1688], J422bA
+   – *To the right honourable the House of Lords*, [1688], J422A
+   – *To the right honourable, the Lord Mayor*, [1683], J422B
+   – *Mrs James's vindication*, 1687, J423
+ Jermyn, Rebecca, *A true state of the right and claime of*, [1655], J681bA
   Jesserson, Susanna, *A Bargain for Bachelors*, 1675, J686
   Jevon, Rachel, *Carmen*, 1660, J729
     – *Exultationis Carmen*, 1660, J730
   Jinner, Sarah, *An Almanack Or Prognostication . . . 1658*, 1658, A1844
     – *An Almanack Or Prognostication . . . 1659*, 1659, A1845
     – *An Almanack Or Prognostication . . . 1660*, 1660, A1846
     – *An Almanack For . . . 1664*, 1664, A1847
     – *The Womans Almanack*, [male work, *see* Ginnor, Sarah, pseud.]
+ Joceline, Elizabeth, *The mother's legacy*, 1684, J756
   Jones, Sarah, *This is Lights appearance in the Truth*, 1650, J989
+ Juliana of Norwich, *XVI revelations*, 1670, C6903
   Kemp, Anne, *A contemplation*, [male work, *see* under title], K257
   Kent, Elizabeth, *see* Grey, Elizabeth, Countess of Kent
   Killigrew, Anne, *Poems*, 1686, K442
   Killin, Margaret and Barbara Patison, *A Warning*, 1655, K473

Knight, Mary, 'To the most honoured', part of Lawes, Henry, *Second Book*,
    1655, L641
+ Lamb, Catherine, *A full discovery*, 1688, L205C
  Lambert, Lady, *To his Excellency*, [male work, *see* Lambert, Lady, pseud.]
* La Mothe, Marie Catherine, *The Novels Of Elizabeth*, 1680, A4221
* La Porte, Ortensia, *The Memoires*, 1676, S355
+ Lead, Jane, *The heavenly cloud*, 1681, L785
+   – *The revelation of revelations*, 1683, L789
  Leigh, Dorothy, *The Mothers Blessing*, 1656, L980
+   – *The mother's blessing*, 1663, L981
+   – *The mother's blessing*, 1667, L981A
+   – *The mother's blessing*, 1674, L982
  Levingston, Anne, *Some Considerations*, 1654, L1825A
    – *The State of the Case*, 1654, L1824 & S5685
    – *A true Narrative of the Case*, 1655, L1825
  Love, Mary, et al, *Loves Name Lives*, 1651, L3141
    – et al, *Loves Name Lives*, 1660, not in Wing [Bodleian Library]
    – et al, *Loves Name Lives*, 1663, L3142
  Lynam, Margaret, *The Controversie of the Lord*, 1676, L3564
    – *For the Parliament*, 1659, L3564aA
    – *A Warning from the Lord*, [1680?], not in Wing [Friends' Library, London]
  Mackett, Ann, 'Testimony', part of Whitehead, Anne, *Piety Promoted*, 1686,
    W1885
  Major, Elizabeth, *Honey on the Rod*, 1656, M305
  Makin, Bathsua, *An Essay To Revive the Antient Education*, 1673, M309
  Martin, Ann, 'Concerning that False Report', part of Whitrow, Joan, *The Work*,
    1677, W2039
  Martindall, Anne, 'A Relation', part of Curwen, Alice, *A Relation*, 1680, M857
  Mazarin, Ortensia, *see* La Porte, Ortensia, Duchess de Mazarin
  Meekings, Margaret, 'Testimony', part of Whitehead, Anne, *Piety Promoted*,
    1686, W1885
+ Melvill, Elizabeth, *A godly dream*, [1686], M1649A
  Moore, Elizabeth, 'Evidences for Heaven', part of Calamy, Edmund, *Godly*
    Man's Ark, 1669, C247
  Moore, Mary, *Wonderful news*, [male work, *see* under title]
* More, Gertrude, *The Holy Practices*, 1657, M2631A
*   – *The Spiritual Exercises*, 1658, M2632
  Morey, Dewans, *A true and faithful Warning*, [1665], M2726A
  Morton, Anne, Countess of, *see* Douglas, Anne, Countess of Morton
  Mudd, Ann, *A Cry, a Cry: a sensible Cry*, 1678, M3037
  Newcastle, Margaret, Duchess of, *see* Cavendish, Margaret
+ Northumberland, Elizabeth, *Meditations*, 1682, M1308
+   – *Meditations*, 1687, M1308A
+   – *Meditations*, 1693, M1309
+   – *Meditations*, 1700, M1309A
  Oliver, Elizabeth, *A catalogue*, [male work, *see* under title]
  Osborne, Alice, *The case of the Lady Wandesford*, 1660, C1102A

Bibliography

Oxford, Wendy, [male name]
Oxlie, Mary, [poem], part of Drummond, William, *Poems*, 1656, D2201
Palmer, Barbara, *The gracious answer*, [male work, *see* under title] C4653
Parr, Susanna, *Susanna's Apologie against the Elders*, 1659, P551
Patison, Barbara, *see* Killin, Margaret and Barbara Patison, K473
Pendarves, Theodosia, 'A Letter', part of Poole, Elizabeth, *An Alarum*, 1649,
    P2809
Pennyman, Mary, *Something formerly writ*, 1676, P1429
Perrot, Luce, *An Account Of Several Observable Speeches*, 1679, P1643
Pettus, Katherine, *Katherine Pettus, Plaintiffe*, [1654], P1913
Philips, Joan, *see* Ephelia, pseud.
Philips, Katherine, *Letters from Orinda to Poliarchus*, 1705
    – *Letters from Orinda to Poliarchus*, 1729
    – *Poems*, 1664, P2032
    – *Poems*, 1667, P2033
    – *Poems*, 1669, P2034
    – *Poems*, 1678, P2035
    – *Pompey*, 1663, C6317
    – *Pompey*, 1663, C6318
    – [poem], part of Cartwright, William, *Comedies*, 1651, C709
    – [poem], part of Lawes, Henry, *Second Book*, 1655, L641
    – 'Letters to Berenice' part of Wilmot, John, *Familiar Letters*, 1697, R1743
Plumley, S., 'Testimony', part of Whitehead, Anne, *Piety Promoted*, 1686, W1885
Plumsted, Mary, 'Testimony', part of Whitehead, Anne, *Piety Promoted*, 1686,
    W1885
Poole, Elizabeth, *An Alarum of War*, 1648/9, P2808
    – *An Alarum of War*, 1649, P2909
    – *A Prophecie Touching the Death of King*, 1649, P2809A
    – *A Vision*, 1648/9, P2810
+ Pope, Mary, *Behold, here is a word*, 1649, P2903
+   – *A treatise of magistracy*, 1647, P2904
Powys, Elizabeth, *A ballad*, [male work, *see* Gadbury, John]
+ Rone, Elizabeth, *A reproof to those church-men*, 1688, R1914A
Scaife, Barbara, et al, *A short Relation*, 1686, S806
Scarborow, Ann, *A looking-glass*, [male work, *see* under title]
* Schurman, Anna Maria van, *The Learned Maid*, 1659, S902
Sharp, Jane, *The Midwives Book*, 1671, not in Wing [British Library]
Shaw, Hester, *Mrs Shaw's Innocency restored*, 1653, S3018
    – *A Plaine Relation of my Sufferings*, 1653, S3019
Shinkin ap Shone, *Shinkin ap Shone her prognostication*, [male work, *see* under
    title]
Shipton, Ursula, *Mother Shipton's Christmas carols*, [male work, *see* under title]
Simmonds, Martha, *A Lamentation For The Lost Sheep*, 1655, S3791
    – *A Lamentation For the Lost Sheep*, 1656, S3792
    – et al, *O England; thy time is come*, [1656–65], S3793
    – *When the Lord Jesus came*, [1655], S3794
Simpson, Mary, et al, *Faith and Experience*, 1649, S3818

Smith, Mary, *These few lines are to all*, 1667, S4130

Smith, Rebecca, *The foundation* [male work, *see* under Smith, R.] S4150

Smyth, Anne, *The Case of*, 1650, S4358

Somerset, Margaret, *To the Parliament of the Commonwealth*, [1654], W3537

Sowle, Jane, 'Testimony', part of Whitehead, Anne, *Piety Promoted*, 1686, W1885

Stiff, Mary, *The good womens*, 1650, [male work, *see* Stiff, Mary, pseud.]

Stirling, Mary, Countess of, *see* Alexander, Mary

Stirredge, Elizabeth, et al, *A Salutation*, [1683], S5685A

Stone, Katherine, *To the High Court of Parliament*, [1654], S5731

Stout, Mary, 'Ah William Haworth', part of Crook, John, *Rebellion*, 1673, C7212

    – 'Testimony', part of Whitehead, Anne, *Piety Promoted*, 1686, W1885

Stranger, Hannah, 'Consider I beseech you', part of Simmonds, Martha, *O England*, [1656–65], S3793

Strong, Damaris, *Having seen a paper printed*, [1655], S5988

Sutton, Katherine, *A Christian Woman's Experience*, 1668, S6212

Taylor, Mrs., [three songs], part of Behn, Aphra, *Miscellany*, 1685, M2230

+ Tillinghast, Mary, *Rare and excellent receipts*, 1678 [destroyed] T1182

    – *Rare and Excellent Receipts*, 1690, T1183

Townsend, Theophila, et al, *An Epistle of Love*, [1686?] T1987A

+   – et al, *An epistle of tender love*, 1690, T1988

    – et al, *A Testimony*, 1676, T1989

    – *A Word of Counsel*, [1687], T1990

Trapnel, Anna, *The Cry of a Stone*, 1654, T2031

    – *A Legacy for Saints*, 1654, T2032

    – *Anna Trapnel's Report and Plea*, 1654, T2033

    – *Strange and Wonderful Newes*, 1654, T2034

    – *A Voice for the King Of Saints*, 1658, T2035

+   – [untitled volume of verse in Bodleian Library], 1658, not in Wing

Travers, Ann, 'Testimony', part of Whitehead, Anne, *Piety Promoted*, 1686, W1885

    – and Elizabeth Coleman, 'Unto which', part of Crisp, Stephen, *A Backslider*, 1669, C6925

Travers, Rebeckah, *For Those that meet to worship*, 1659, T2059

    – *Of that Eternal Breath*, [1659], T2060

    – *A Testimony Concerning the Light*, 1663, T2061

    – *A Testimony for God's Everlasting Truth*, 1669, T2062

    – *This Is For all or any*, 1664, T2063

    – *This is for any of that generation*, **1659/60**, T2064

    – 'Testimony', part of Whitehead, Anne, *Piety Promoted*, 1686, W1885

Trye, Mary, *Medicatrix, Or The Woman-Physician*, 1675, T3174

Turner, Jane, *Choice Experiences*, 1653, T3294

Venn, Anne, *A Wise Virgins Lamp Burning*, 1658, V190

Vokins, Joan, et al, *God's Mighty Power Magnified*, 1691, V685

Vokins, Joan, *A Loving Advertisement*, [**1670/1**], V686

+   – *A tender invitation*, 1687, V687

Wails, Isabel, *A Warning To the Inhabitants of Leeds*, 1685, W221

Waite, Mary, *A Warning To All Friends Who Professeth*, 1679, W224

Walker, Mary, *The Case of*, [1650], W395

Wandesford, Lady Alice, *see* Osborne, Alice

+ Warren, Elizabeth, *A warning-peece from heaven*, 1649, W961

Waters, Margaret, *A Warning from the Lord*, [1670], W1058

Waugh, Jane, *see* Audland, Anne and Jane Waugh

Waugh, Dorothy, 'A Relation', part of *The Lambs Defence*, 1656, L249

Weamys, Anna, *A Continuation of . . . Arcadia*, 1651, W1189

Webb, Mary, *I being moved of the Lord*, 1659, W1205

Wells, Mary, *A Divine Poem*, 1684, W1296

  – *A Divine Poem*, 1690, not in Wing [British Library]

+ Wentworth, Anne, *A true account of*, 1676, not in Wing [Folger Library]

  – *The Revelation Of Jesus Christ*, 1679, W1355

  – *A Vindication of*, 1677, W1356

Wentworth, Henrietta Maria, *The Case of*, 1677, C1102

Weyer, Florence, [male name]

Wharton, Anne, 'Copies of Verses', part of Young, Edward, *The Idea of Christian Love*, 1688, Y61

White, Dorothy, *An Alarum Sounded forth*, 1662, W1744

  – *An Alarm Sounded To Englands Inhabitants*, 1661, W1745

  – *A Call from God*, 1662, W1746

  – *The Day Dawned*, 1684, W1747

  – *A Diligent Search*, 1659, W1747A

  – *An Epistle of Love*, 1661, W1748

  – *Friends*, [**1660?**], W1749

  – *Greetings of pure Peace*, 1662, W1750

  – *A Lamentation*, [**1661**], W1751

  – *A Salutation*, [1684], W1752

  – *This to be delivered*, 1659, W1753

  – *To all those that Worship*, **1664**, W1754

  – *A Trumpet*, 1662, W1755

  – *Universal Love*, [1684], W1756

  – *Unto All Gods Host*, [1660], W1757

  – *Upon the 22nd day*, 1659, W1758

  – *A Visitation Of Heavenly Love*, 1660, W1759

  – *A Visitation Of Love*, 1684, W1760

  – *The Voice of the Lord*, 1662, W1761

White, Elizabeth, *The Experiences*, 1696, W1762

+ – *The experiences*, 1698, W1763

Whitehead, Anne, *An Epistle for True Love*, 1680, W1882

+ – *An epistle for true love*, [1680?], W1883

  – et al, *For the King and both Houses*, [1670], W1884

  – et al, *Piety Promoted*, 1686, W1885

Whitrow, Joan, et al, *The Work of God In A Dying Maid*, 1677, W2039

Whitton, Katherine, *An Epistle To Friends*, 1681, W2050

  – et al, *A Testimony For The Lord*, [1688], W2051

Wight, Sarah, *A Wonderful Pleasant . . . Letter*, 1656, W2106

+ Wigington, Leticia, *The confession*, [1681], W2110

Wilmot, Elizabeth, [poem], part of Wilmot, John, *Poems*, 1680, R1753

With, Elizabeth, *Elizabeth fool's*, [male work, *see* With, Elizabeth, pseud.]

Wolley, Hannah, *The Accomplish'd Lady's Delight*, [male work, *see* P., T.]

    – *The Compleat Servant-Maid*, [male work, *see* under title]

    – *The Cooks Guide*, 1664, W3276

    – *The Gentlewomans Companion*, [male work, *see* under title]

    – *The Ladies Delight*, 1672, W3279

+   – *The ladies directory*, 1661 [destroyed], W3280

    – *The Ladies Directory*, 1662, W3281

    – *The Queen-Like Closet*, 1670, W3282

+   – *The queen-like closet*, 1672, W3283

    – *The Queen-like closet*, 1675, W3284

    – *The Queen-like Closet*, 1681, W3285

    – *The Queen-like Closet*, 1684, W3286

    – *A Supplement To The Queen-Like Closet*, 1674, W3287

    – *A Supplement To The Queen-Like Closet*, 1680, not in Wing [Huntington Library]

    – *A Supplement To The Queen-Like Closet*, 1684, W3288

Woolley, Mary, 'Testimony', part of Whitehead, Anne, *Piety Promoted*, 1686, W1885

Worcester, Margaret, Countess of, *see* Somerset, Margaret

Wyndham, Anne, *Claustrum Regale Reseratum*, 1667, [male work?] W3772

Yeamans, Isabel, *An Invitation Of Love*, 1679, Y20

    – et al, *A Lively Testimony*, 1676, J514

York, Anne, Duchess of, *see* Hyde, Anne

* Zins-penninck, Judith, *Some Worthy Proverbs*, 1663, Z13

b. works by anonymous or pseudonymous women

Advice To the Women and Maidens of London, 1678, A644

An Answer to Pereat Papa, 1681, A3373

+ *The case betwixt Thornton Cage, Esq., and his wife*, 1684, C860

+ *The case of the poor widow*, 1685, C1143

+ *The confession . . . of . . . young gentlewoman*, 1684, C5802

Eliza's Babes: or the Virgins-Offering, 1652, E526

Ephelia, pseud., *Advice to his Grace*, [1681–2], P2029

    – *Female Poems*, 1679, P2030

    – *Female Poems*, 1682, [reissue of 1679 edition] P2031

    – *A Poem To His Sacred Majesty, On The Plot*, [1678], P2707

H., M., *The Young Cooks Monitor*, 1683, H95

    – *The Young Cooks Monitor*, 1690, H96

Lady of Quality, 'The female wits', part of Behn, Aphra, *Miscellany*, 1685, M2230

Philophilippa, pseud., 'To the excellent Orinda', part of Philips, Katherine, *Poems*, 1667, 1669, 1678, P2033, P2034, P2035

* S., D. *Good Thoughts For Every Day of the Month*, 1656, G1082

Sylvia's Complaint, 1692, [male text, *see* Ames, Richard, (?)]

Sylvia's Revenge, Or; A Satyr Against Man, 1688, [Behn, Aphra, (?)] A2992D

A Tender and Christian Testimony, 1685, *see* Elson, Mary, et al, E642

To the Supreme Authority of England, 1649, T1724

To the Parliament . . . humble Petition of . . . Women, 1653, T1585

To the Supreme Authority . . . severall Wives and Children, [1650], T1734

Triumphs of Female Wit, 1683, [male work?, *see* under title]

Unto every individual Member . . . Women-Petitioners, 1653, U99

The Womens Petition, 1651, W3332

2. Works by Sixteenth- and Seventeenth-Century Men

Explanatory Note. Editions listed are those consulted for this study. Although due care has been taken, no claims of bibliographical accuracy are made, and works are only included if directly relevant.

A., I., *The good womans champion*, 1650, A9A

The academy of pleasure, 1665, A159

An advertisement from the Society of Chymical Physitians, 1665, A615B

Agrippa von Nettesheim, Heinrich, *Female pre-eminence*, 1670, A784

The ale-wives complaint, 1675, A905

All is ours and our husbands, [1675–80], A936

Ames, Richard, *The folly of love*, 1691, A2980

 – (?), *Sylvia's complaint*, 1692, A2992A

Animadversions on the Lady Marquess, 1680, A3196

The arraignment, tryal and examination of Mary Moders, 1663, A3764

The articles and charge of impeachment against the German lady, 1663, A3805

Austin, William, *Haec homo*, 1637

B., F., *Vercingetorixa: or, the German princess*, 1663, B65

The bashful virgin, 1670, B1014

Batchiler, John, *The virgin's pattern*, 1661, B1077

Baxter, Richard, *Breviate of the life of Margaret Baxter*, 1681, B1194

Bedell, M., *The ladies cabinet enlarged and opened*, 1654, B135

Bennet, Dorcas, pseud., *Good and seasonable counsel*, 1670, B1883A

Blake, William, *The ladies charity school-house*, 1670, B3152

 – *A new trial of the ladies*, 1658, B3153

 – *A serious letter sent by a private Christian*, 1655, B3153A

 – *The trial of the ladies*, 1656, B3153B

 – *The yellow book*, 1656, B3153D

Bolton, John, *A justification . . . Elizabeth Atkinson*, 1669, B3508

The book of oaths, 1649, G264

Brathwait, Richard, *The English gentleman*, 1630

 – *The English gentlewoman*, 1631

A brief relation of the persecutions . . . Quakers, 1662, B4629

A brief representation and discovery of . . . Anne Hall, 1649, H324

Brinsley, John, *A looking-glasse for good women*, 1645, B4717
Brown, David, *The naked woman*, 1652, B5014
Bunworth, Richard, *The doctresse*, 1656, B5474
Burrough, Edward, *Something in answer to . . . Jane Turner*, 1654, B6025
C., J., *An elegy upon the death of . . . Katherine Philips*, 1664, C53
C., T., *A brief relation of . . . Elizabeth Braytwhaite*, 1684, C128
Calamy, Edmund, *The godly man's ark*, 1669, C247
Camm, John, *The memory of the righteous revived*, 1689, C390
Care, Henry, *The glory of women*, 1652, A787
Carleton, John, *The replication*, 1663, C585A
  – *The ultimum vale of*, 1663, C586
Carter, William, *The memory of William Carter*, 1690, M1701A
Cartwright, William, *Comedies, tragi-comedies*, 1651, C709
A catalogue of valuable books . . . sold . . . Elizabeth Oliver's, 1689, C1416 &
    O274
A certain and true relation of . . . Sarah Beck, 1680, C1686A
Chamberlayne, Edward, *An academy or colledge*, 1671, C1818
Chamberlayne, R., *The English midwife enlarged*, 1682, E3104
Chamberlayne, Thomas, *The compleat midwifes practice*, 1656, C1817A
  – *The compleat midwife's . . . enlarged*, 1659, C1817D
  – *The complete midwife's . . . enlarged*, 1680, C1817F
Chamberlen, Hugh, *The diseases of women with child*, 1672, M1371B
Chidley, Samuel, *Cloathing for the naked woman*, 1652, C4736
The city-dames petition, 1647, C4350
The citie matrons, 1654, C4356
The citizens reply to the whores petition, 1668, C4344
Coale, Josiah, *The books and divers epistles of*, 1671, C4751
A collection of letters and poems . . . Duchess of Newcastle, 1678, C5146
The complaint of Mis. Page, 1680, C5613A
The complaint of Mrs Celiers, 1680, C5613
The compleat servant-maid, or the young maidens, 1677 [British Library]
The compleat servant-maid . . . a supplement, 1682, [British Library]
The compleat servant-maid . . . a supplement, 1685, W3274
A contemplation of Bassets down-hill, [1658?], K257
Cook, John, *A true relation*, 1650, C6022
The court and kitchen of Elizabeth . . . Cromwel, 1664, C7036
Crisp, Stephen, *A backslider*, 1669, C6925
Crook, John, et al, *Rebellion rebuked*, 1673, C7212
Culpeper, Nicholas, *Culpeper's last legacy*, 1657, C7519
  – *A directory for midwives*, 1651, C7488
  – *A directory for midwives*, 1675, C7493
  – *Mr. Culpeper's treatise*, 1656, C7549
Curwen, Thomas, et al, *This is an answer to John Wiggans*, 1665, C7703
Dalton, James, *A strange . . . young woman possest*, 1647, D142
Dangerfield, Thomas, *The case of . . . with . . . Cellier*, 1680, C1181
  – *Mr Tho. Dangerfeilds [sic] narrative*, 1679, D192
  – *Mr Tho. Dangerfeild's [sic] second*, 1680, D193

Davies, John, *Hymen's praeludia*, 1659, L119

Death's master-peece . . . sudden fire in Towerstreet, 1650, D503

A declaration from . . . Adolphina, queen of Sweden, 1649, C3963

A declaration from Oxford of Anne Greene, 1651, C586

A declaration of the maids of the city of London, 1659, D710

The deportment and carriage of the German princess, 1672, D1077A

The devil pursued . . . a satyr upon Madam Celliers, 1680, D1220

A dialogue between Mistris Macquerella, 1650, D1318

A dialogue between the Duchess of Cleveland, 1682, D1328

A dialogue between the Dutchess of Portsmouth and Madam Gwin, 1682, D1329

A discourse of auxiliary beauty, 1656, G355

Donne, John, *Poems with elegies*, 1654, D1870

Drummond, William, *Poems*, 1656, D2201

The dumb lady; or, no, no, not I, 1680, D2523

The dutchess of Mazarines farewel, 1680, D2424

The dutchess of Monmouth's lamentation, 1683, D2425

The Dutchess of Portsmouths and Count Coningsmarks farvvel, 1682, D2426

E., T., *The lawes resolution of women's rights*, 1632

An elegie on . . . Madam Mary Carlton, 1673, E417

An exact and true relation of . . . the German princesse, 1672, E3619

The examination, confession and execution of Ursula Corbet, 1660/1, E3711

An exhortation and admonition . . . to all maid-servants, 1672, E3865A

F., E., *The emblem of a virtuous woman*, [1650], F12

Farnworth, Richard, *A woman forbidden to speak in the church*, 1654, F514

Female excellence: or, woman display'd . . . satyrick poems, 1679, F1749

Female liberty regained, [Houghton Library]

Filmer, Robert, *Patriarcha: or the natural power of kings*, 1680, F922

Finch, Francis, *Friendship*, 1654, F930A

Fontanus, Nicholas, *The womans doctour*, 1652, F1418A

Fox, George, *The woman learning in silence*, 1656, F1991

Furly, John, et al, *The substance of a letter . . . Sarah Hayward*, 1666, S8108

G., M., *The Countess of Morton's daily exercise*, 1666, M2817

Gadbury, John, *A ballad . . . written by a lady of quality*, 1679, G75 & P1118

   – *A new narrative of the Popish plot*, [1680?] G93A

   – *A true narrative*, [1682], G99

The gallant she souldier, 1655, G174B

The gentlewomans companion, 1673, [British Library]

The gentlewomans companion, 1675, W3277

The gentlewomans companion, 1682, W3278

Gerbier, Charles, *Elogium heroinum*, 1651, G583

Gildon, Charles, *Miscellany poems*, 1692, G733A

Ginnor, Sarah, pseud., *The womans almanack*, 1659, A1848

Golborne, J., *A friendly apology . . . womens excellency*, 1674, G1009

Goodall, Charles, *An historical account of the College's*, 1684, G1091

Gouge, William, *Of domesticall duties*, 1622

Gould, Robert, *Love given o're . . . satyr against . . . woman*, 1682, G1422

The gracious answer of . . . Countess of Castlem——, 1668, C4653

The great tryall and arraignment of . . . *German Princess*, 1663, G1758

H., I., *A strange wonder or a wonder in a woman*, 1642, H50

Heale, William, *An apologie for women*, 1609

Heydon, John, *Advice to a daughter*, 1658, H1664

Heywood, Thomas, *Generall history of women*, 1657, H1784

Hill, William, *A new-years-gift for women*, 1660, H2035

Hubberthorne, Richard, *A collection*, 1663, G3216

Jarvis, William, *A choice manuall* . . . *the Countesse of Kent*, 1653, K310
   – *A true gentlewomans delight*, 1653, K317A

Jessey, Henry, *The exceeding riches of grace* . . . *Sarah Wight*, 1652, J691

Keith, George, *The woman preacher of Samaria*, 1674, K236

Kirkman, Francis, *The counterfeit lady unveiled*, 1673, K7

Knollys, Hanserd, *The life and death of*, 1692, K715

The lady besieged. A new song, 1670, L163A

The ladyes champion, 1660, L151

The ladies answer to that busiebody, 1670, C1660

The ladies companion, or, a table furnished, 1654, L152

The ladies lamentation for the loss of the land-lord, 1651, L155

The ladies remonstrance, 1659, L160

The ladyes vindication, 1662, L162

The lambs defence, 1656, L249

Lambert, Lady, pseud., *To his Excellency General Monck*, 1660, T1344

The lamentation of Mr. Pages wife, 1680, D965

The lamenting ladies last farewel to the world, 1650, L294

Lawes, Henry, *The second book of ayres, and dialogues*, 1655, L641

The lawyer's clarke trappan'd . . . *Mary Mauders*, 1663, L739F

Lemoyne, Peter, *The gallery of heroick women*, 1652, L1045

A letter from the Dutchess of Portsmouth to Madam Gwyn, 1682, L1518

A letter from the Lady Creswell to Madam C. the midwife, 1680, L1529

Letters and poems . . . *Margaret, Dutchess of Newcastle*, 1676, L1774

The life and character of Mrs Mary Moders, 1679, [British Library]

A list of some of the grand blasphemers and blasphemies, 1654, L2406

Livingston, Patrick, *Truth owned and deceit denyed* . . . *womens*, 1667, L2607

London, William, *A catalogue of the most vendible books*, 1657, L2849

A looking-glass for maids . . . *Ann Scarborow*, 1655, S821

M., W., *The compleat cook*, 1662, M92
   – *The queens closet opened*, 1655, M96
   – *The queens closet opened*, 1662, M100A

Madam Celliers answer to the Popes letter, 1680, C1659

The maids complaint against the batchelors, 1675, M276

The maids complaint for the want of a dil-doul, 1690, M277

The maids lamentation, 1680, M279

Markham, Gervase, *The English huswife*, 1664, M633

May, Robert, *The accomplisht cook*, 1678, M1393B

The memoires of Mary Carleton, 1673, G35B

Memoires of the life of the famous Madam Charlton, 1673, M1700

The midwife unmask'd . . . *Mrs Cellier's meal-tub*, 1680, M2002

The midwives ghost, 1680, M2003

The mid-wives just petition, 1643, M2005

The mid-wives just complaint, 1646, M2006

Mistris Cellier's lamentation for the loss of the liberty, 1681, C1660A

Modesty triumphing over impudence . . . Elizabeth Cellier, 1680, M2379

Mother Shiptons Christmas carols, 1668, S3442

Narrative of the process against Madam Brinvilliers, 1676, N220

Nayler, James, *Milk for babes*, 1661, N299

   – *Milk for babes*, 1665, N300

   – *Milk for babes*, 1668, N301

Newgate salutation: or, a dialogue . . . Mrs Cellier, 1680, N918A

The new way of marriage, [1672–95], N793

News from Jamaica . . . the Germane princess, 1671, N976B

Osborne, Thomas, *The new popish sham-plot . . . Mrs Celier*, 1681, [British
   Library]

P., T., *The accomplish'd lady's delight*, 1675, W3268

   – *The accomplish'd lady's delight*, 1677, W3269

   – *The accomplish'd lady's delight*, 1677, [British Library]

   – *The accomplish'd ladies delight*, 1683, W3270

   – *The accomplish'd ladies delight*, 1684, W3271

   – *The accomplish'd ladies delight*, 1685, W3272

   – *The accomplish'd ladies delight*, [1696?] W3273

   – *The English and French cook*, 1674, E3079

Parkhurst, Nathaniel, *The faithful and diligent . . . Lady E. Brooke*, 1684, P489

The Parliament of women, 1646, P505

A pleasant dialogue . . . Portsmouth, 1685, [British Library]

The poor-whores lamentation, [1685–92], P2896

The poor-whores petition, 1668, P2897

The Popes letter to Maddam Cellier, 1680, P2935

Porter, Thomas, *A witty combat: or, the female victor*, 1663, P2998

Portsmouth's lamentation, 1685, P3008

Poulain de la Barre, Francis, *The woman as good as the man*, 1677, P3038

The prentices answer to the whores petition, 1668, A3584

The ranters monster . . . Mary Adams, 1652, A488

Ray, John, *A collection of English proverbs*, 1670, R386

Reflections upon the murder . . . Mrs. Cellier, 1682, R731

A remonstrance of the shee-citizens of London, 1647, R1014

Rich, Barnaby, *The excellency of good women*, 1613

Rochester, John Wilmot, Earl of, *see* Wilmot, John

Rogers, John, *Ohel or beth-shemesh*, 1653, R1813

Savile, George, *The lady's new year's gift*, 1688, H304

Sermon, William, *The ladies companion, or the English midwife*, 1671, S2628

Shaw, John, *Mistris Shawe's tomb-stone*, 1658, S3029

Shinkin ap Shone, Her Prognostication for . . . 1654, 1654, A2385

Shirley, John, *The illustrious history of women*, 1686, S3508

Simpson, William, *The life of William Simpson*, 1671, L2042

Smith, R., *The foundation of true preaching*, 1687, S4150

Some luck some wit . . . Mary Carlton, 1673, S4516
Sowerby, Leonard, *The ladies dispensatory*, 1651, S4781
Stephenson, Marmaduke, et al, *A call from death to life*, 1660, S5466
Stiff, Mary, pseud., *The good womens cryes*, 1650, S5551
Strong, William, *The saints communion with God*, 1656, S6006
Swetnam, Joseph, *The arraignment of . . . women*, 1615
The swimming lady; or, a wanton discovery, [1680?] S6259
Taylor, Jeremy, *A discourse of . . . friendship*, 1657, T317
Taylor, Thomas, et al, *To the King*, 1670, H2710A
To the general council of officers, 1659, F638B
To the praise of Mrs Cellier the popish midwife, 1680, T1596
The triall of Elizabeth Cellier . . . June the 11th, 1680, T2187
Triumphs of female wit, 1683, T2295
The true confession of Margaret Clark, 1680, C4482
A true copy of a letter of consolation . . . meal-tub midwife, 1681, T2618
The tryal and sentence of Elizabeth Cellier, 1680, T2171
The tryal of Elizabeth Cellier, the popish midwife, 1680, T2187A
The tryall and examination of Mrs Joan Peterson, 1652, T2167
Tuke, Thomas, *A treatise against painting and tincturing*, 1616
Vaughan, Henry, *Olor Iscanus*, 1651, V123
Verses . . . an aspersion upon the Lady G[rey], 1681, S4696
A vindication of a distressed lady, 1663, V463B
Vives, Luis, *A very fruteful . . . boke . . . the instruction of a christen woman*, 1558
W., L., *The new made gentlewoman*, 1680, W80
Walker, Anthony, *The virtuous woman found . . . Mary . . . of Warwick*, 1687, W314
Walker, Clement, *The case between . . . and Humphrey Edwards*, 1650, W323
Walker, Henry, *Spirituall experiences of sundry believers*, 1653, W387
Walsh, William, *A dialogue concerning women*, 1691, W645
Warning for servants . . . Margaret Clark, 1680, C4483
The Westminster wedding; or Carlton's epithalamium, [1663], W1472
The whores petition, 1668, W2069
Wilmot, John, *Familiar letters*, 1697, R1743
 – *Poems on several occasions*, 1680, R1753
The witch of Wapping . . . Joan Peterson, 1652, W3137
With, Elizabeth, pseud., *Elizabeth fools warning*, 1659, W3139
The woman outwitted: or, the weaver's wife cunningly catch'd, 1685, W3320
The woman to the plow and the man to the hen-roost, 1683, W3321
The womens complaint against their bad husbands, 1676, W3328
The women's complaint against tobacco, 1675, W3328A
The women's fegaries, 1675, W3329
The women's just complaint: or, a mans deceitfulness, [1672–95], W3330
The women's petition against coffee, 1674, W3331
Wonderful news, 1650, M2581
Wood, Hugh, *A brief treatise of religious women's meetings*, 1684, W3393
Woodrow, Thomas, *A brief relation*, 1659, W3474
Young, Edward, *The Idea of Christian Love*, 1688, Y61
The young-womans complaint, 1680, Y134

Bibliography

3. Modern Editions of Works by English Women Written 1649–88

Explanatory Note. More editions are now being published, and this list does not pretend to be complete. Place of publication is London unless otherwise stated.

Andrews, 'An Account of the Birth, Education and Sufferings for the Truth's Sake', *Journal of the Friends Historical Society*, 26, 1929

Beaumont, Agnes, *The Life of Mrs Agnes Beaumont*, 1978

Behn, Aphra, *The Works of*, edited by Montague Summers, 1915
— *Selected Writings*, New York, 1950

Brooke, Elizabeth, selections from her writings in *The Lady's Monitor*, 1828

Cavendish, Jane and Elizabeth Brackley, 'The Concealed Fansyes', edited by Nathan Starr, *PMLA*, 46, 1931

Cavendish, Margaret, *The Cavalier in Exile: being the lives of the first Duke and Dutchess of Newcastle*, 1903
— *The Life of William Cavendish, Duke of Newcastle*, edited by C.H. Firth, 1886
— *The Life of William Cavendish Duke of Newcastle to which is added The True Relation of my Birth and Breeding*, edited by C.H. Firth, [1906]
— *The Lives of William Cavendish, Duke of Newcastle, and of his Wife*, 1872
— *The Life of the First Duke of Newcastle and Other Writings by Margaret, Duchess of Newcastle*, [1915]
— *The Phanseys of William Cavendish, Marquis of Newcastle addressed to Margaret Lucas and her Letters in Reply*, edited by Douglas Grant, 1956
— *Poems and Fancies*, [facsimile reproduction], 1972
— *Sociable Letters*, [facsimile reproduction], 1969

Cellier, Elizabeth, 'A Scheme for the Foundation of a Royal Hospital', *Harleian Miscellany*, volume 4, 1745

Clifford, Anne, *The Diary*, introduction by Vita Sackville-West, 1923
— *Lives of Lady Anne Clifford and of her Parents Summarized by Herself*, edited by J.P. Gibson, The Roxburghe Club, 1916

Collins, An, *Divine Songs and Meditacions*, [facsimile reproduction], edited by Stanley Stewart, Los Angeles, 1961

Conway, Anne, *Conway Letters*, edited by M.H. Nicholson, 1930

Fanshawe, Ann, *The Memoirs of Anne, Lady Halkett and Ann, Lady Fanshawe*, edited by John Loftis, Oxford, 1979

Fell, Margaret, *Women's Speaking Justified, 1667*, [facsimile reproduction], edited by David Latt, Los Angeles, 1979

Halkett, Anne, *see* Fanshawe, Ann

Hutchinson, Lucy, *Memoirs of the Life of Colonel Hutchinson*, edited by Harold Child, 1904

Jefferies, Joyce, 'Account-book', edited by John Webb, *Archaeologia*, 37, 1857

Killigrew, Anne, *Poems*, [facsimile reproduction], edited by Richard Morton, Gainsville, Florida, 1967

Lynam, Margaret, *Extracts from Letters, written about the year 1660*, edited by John Bellows, Gloucester, n.d.

Makin, Bathsua, *An Essay To Revive the Antient Education of Gentlewomen*, [facsimile reproduction], edited by Paula Barbour, Los Angeles, 1980

Osborne, Dorothy, *Letters from Dorothy Osborne to Sir William Temple*, edited by E.A. Parry, 1903

Penington, Mary, *Some Account of the Circumstances of the Life of Mary Penington from her Manuscripts*, 1821

Polwhele, Elizabeth, *The Frolicks, or, The Lawyer Cheated*, edited by Judith Milhous and Robert Hume, New York, 1977

Rich, Mary, *Autobiography*, edited by T.C. Croker, 1848
    – *Diary*, 1847

Thornton, Alice, *The Autobiography of Mrs Alice Thornton*, Surtees Society, 1875

Wriothesley, Rachel, Lady Russell, *Letters*, 2 volumes, 1819

4. Manuscripts Consulted

Beale, Mary, 'Discourse on friendship', British Library, Harleian MSS

Cavendish, Margaret, 'Letter to Constantin Huygens', British Library, Add. MSS

Anne Finch, Lady Conway, Letters dated 1662, 1663, Huntington Library

Doggett, Mary, 'Her book of receipts', British Library, Sloane MSS

Evelyn, Mary, Letter, July 16, 1686, Library of Congress, Rosenwald MSS

Rich, Mary, 'Diary', British Library Add. MSS

SELECTED BACKGROUND AND FURTHER READING

Place of publication is London unless otherwise specified.

Arber, Edward, (ed.), *Term Catalogues*, 1903–05

Aveling, James, *English Midwives: Their History and Prospects*, 1967, first published 1872

Avery, Emmett, 'The Restoration Audience', *Philological Quarterly*, 65, 1966

Balch, Marston, (ed.), *Thomas Middleton's 'A Trick to Catch the Old One' and Aphra Behn's 'City Heiress'*, Salzburg, 1981

Barber, Charles, *The Idea of Honor in the English Drama*, Gothenburg, 1957

Barbour, Paula, (ed.), *Bathsua Makin 'An Essay to Revive the Antient Education of Gentlewomen' (1673)*, Los Angeles, 1980

Bateson, F.W., 'L.C. Knights and Restoration Comedy', *Essays in Criticism*, 8, 1957

Batten, Charles, 'The Source of Aphra Behn's *The Widow Ranter*', *Restoration and Eighteenth-Century Theatre Research*, 13, 1974

Bear, Andrew, 'Criticism and Social Change: The Case of Restoration Drama', *KOMOS*, 2, 1969

Beck, Leonard, 'Two Loaf-Givers, or a Tour through the Gastronomic Libraries of Katherine Golden Bitting and Elizabeth Robins Pennell', *Quarterly Journal of the Library of Congress*, 38, 1981

Beer, Gillian, *The Romance*, 1970

Bibliography

Berg, Christine and Philippa Berry, 'Spiritual Whoredom: An Essay on Female Prophets in the Seventeenth Century', in Frances Barker, (ed.), *1642: Literature and Power in the Seventeenth Century*, Essex, 1981

Bernbaum, Ernest, *The Mary Carleton Narratives*, 1914

Bernikow, Louise, (ed.), *The World Split Open: Women Poets 1552–1950*, 1979

Besse, Joseph, *A Collection of the Sufferings of the People called Quakers*, 1753

Birch, Thomas, *The History of the Royal Society*, 1756

Birdsall, Virginia, *Wild Civility: The English Comic Spirit on the Restoration Stage*, Indiana, 1970

Birmingham Rape Crisis and Research Centre, *First Annual Report*, Birmingham, 1980

Boseley, Ira, *The Ministers of the Abbey Independent Church*, 1911

Bottral, Margaret, *Every Man a Phoenix*, 1958

Brailsford, H.N., *The Levellers and the English Revolution*, ed., Christopher Hill, 1961

Brailsford, Mabel, *Quaker Women 1650–1690*, 1915

Braithwaite, William, *The Beginnings of Quakerism*, 1912

Brink, Jeanie, (ed.), *Female Scholars: A Tradition of Learned Women Before 1800*, Montreal, 1980

British Record Society, *Wills at Chelmsford*

Brown, Louise, *The Political Activities of the Baptists and Fifth Monarchy Men*, Oxford, 1912

Brownley, Martine, 'The Narrator in *Oroonoko*', *Essays in Literature*, 4, 1977

Brownmiller, Susan, *Against Our Will: Men, Women and Rape*, 1976

Bruce, Donald, *Topics of Restoration Comedy*, 1974

Burr, Anna, *The Autobiography: A Critical and Comparative Study*, Boston, 1909

Burrage, Champlin, 'Anna Trapnel's Prophecies', *English Historical Review*, 26, 1911

Butler, Richard, *The Difficult Art of Autobiography*, Oxford, 1968

Capp, Bernard, *English Almanacs 1500–1800: Astrology and the Popular Press*, New York, 1979

Capp, Bernard, *The Fifth Monarchy Men: A Study in Seventeenth-Century Millenarianism*, New York, 1972

Carroll, Kenneth, 'Early Quakers and "Going Naked as a Sign" ', *Quaker History*, 67, 1978

Carroll, Kenneth, 'Martha Simmonds, a Quaker Enigma', *Journal of the Friends' Historical Society*, 53, 1972

Chaytor, Miranda, 'Household and Kinship: Ryton in the late sixteenth and early seventeenth centuries', *History Workshop Journal*, 10, 1980

Clark, Alice, *Working Life of Women in the Seventeenth Century*, 1968, first published 1919

Clark, William, *The Early Irish Stage: the beginnings to 1720*, Oxford, 1955

Cohen, Alfred, 'The Fifth Monarchy Mind: Mary Cary and the origins of Totalitarianism', *Social Research*, 31, 1964

Cole, W. Alan, 'The Quakers and the English Revolution', in T. Aston, (ed.), *Crisis in Europe 1560–1660*, 1970

Copeman, W., *Doctors and Disease in Tudor Times*, 1960

Cotton, Nancy, *Women Playwrights in England ca. 1363–1750*, Lewisburg, Pennsylvania, 1980

Coward, Barry, *The Stuart Age*, 1980

Cragg, Gerald, *Puritanism in the Period of the Great Persecution*, 1957

Crawford, Patricia, 'Attitudes to Menstruation in Seventeenth-Century England', *Past and Present*, 91, 1981

Cressy, David, *Literacy and the Social Order*, 1980

Cross, Claire, 'The Church in England 1646–1660', in G.E. Aylmer, (ed.), *The Interregnum*, 1972

Cunninghame, John, *Restoration Drama*, 1966

Day, Cyrus, and Eleanore Murrie, *English Song Books 1651–1702: A Bibliography*, 1940

Delany, Paul, *British Autobiography in the Seventeenth Century*, 1969

Dhuicq, B., 'Further Evidence on Aphra Behn's Stay in Surinam', *Notes and Queries*, 26, 1979

Donegan, Jane B., *Women and Men Midwives*, Westport, Connecticut, 1978

Donnison, Jean, *Midwives and Medical Men: A History of Inter-Professional Rivalries and Women's Rights*, 1977

Douglas, Mary, (ed.), *Witchcraft, Confessions and Accusations*, 1970

Duffy, Maureen, *The Passionate Shepherdess: Aphra Behn 1640–1689*, 1977

Dworkin, Andrea, 'Pornography and Grief', in Laura Lederer, (ed.), *Take Back the Night*, New York, 1980

Easlea, Brian, *Witch-Hunting, Magic and the New Philosophies*, 1980

Ebner, Dean, *Autobiography in Seventeenth-Century England: Theology and the Self*, The Hague, 1971

Ehrenreich, Barbara and Deidre English, *Witches, Midwives and Nurses: A History of Women Healers*, 1973

Elmen, Paul, 'Some Manuscript Poems by the Matchless Orinda', *Philological Quarterly*, 30, 1951

Evans, Maurice, (ed.), *Sir Philip Sidney 'The Countess of Pembroke's Arcadia'*, 1977

Fea, Allan, *The Flight of the King*, 1897

Findley, Sandra and Elaine Hobby, 'Seventeenth-Century Women's Autobiography', in Francis Barker, (ed.), *1642: Literature and Power in the Seventeenth Century*, Essex, 1981

Forbes, Thomas, *The Midwife and the Witch*, New Haven, Connecticut, 1966
 – 'Midwifery and Witchcraft', *Journal of the History of Medicine*, 17, 1962
 – 'The regulation of English midwives in the sixteenth and seventeenth centuries', *Medical History*, 8, 1964

Foxon, David, *Libertine Literature in England 1660–1745*, 1964

Gagen, Jean, 'Honor and Fame in the Works of the Duchess of Newcastle', *Studies in Philology*, 56, 1959

Gardiner, Dorothy, *English Girlhood at School: A Study of Women's Education Through Twelve Centuries*, 1929

George, Margaret, 'From "Goodwife" to "Mistress": the Transformation of the Female in Bourgeois Culture', *Science and Society*, 1973

Bibliography

Gibbons, G., 'Mrs Jane Barker', *Notes and Queries*, 11, 1922

Glanz, Leonore, 'The Legal Position of English Women under Early Stuart Kings and the Interregnum, 1603–1660', unpub. PhD thesis, Loyola University, 1973

Goreau, Angeline, *Reconstructing Aphra: a social biography of Aphra Behn*, New York, 1980

Gosse, Edmund, *Seventeenth-Century Studies*, 1883

Goulding, Richard, *Margaret (Lucas) Duchess of Newcastle*, Lincoln, 1925

Goulianos, Joan, (ed.), *By a Woman Writt*, 1976

Greaves, Richard, and Robert Zaller, *Biographical Dictionary of English Radicals*, 1982

Grant, Douglas, *Margaret the First: A Biography of Margaret Cavendish Duchess of Newcastle 1623–1673*, 1957

Greene, Graham, *Lord Rochester's Monkey, being the Life of John Wilmot, Second Earl of Rochester*, New York, 1974

Hamilton, Roberta, *The Liberation of Women: A Study of Patriarchy and Capitalism*, 1975

Hargreaves, Henry, 'The Life and Plays of Mrs Behn', unpublished PhD thesis, Duke University, 1961

Heyd, Michael, 'The Reaction to Enthusiasm in the Seventeenth Century: Towards an Integrative Approach', *Journal of Modern History*, 53, 1981

Higgins, Patricia, 'The reactions of women', in Brian Manning, (ed.), *Politics, Religion and the English Civil War*, 1973

Hill, Christopher, *The World Turned Upside Down*, 1975

Hindle, Christopher, *A Bibliography of the Printed Pamphlets and Broadsides of Lady Eleanor Douglas*, second edition, 1936

Hobby, Elaine, 'The Fame of the Honest Margaret Cavendish', unpublished M.A. dissertation, Essex University, 1979
  - 'English Women's Writing 1649–1688', unpublished PhD thesis, Birmingham University, 1984

Hole, Christina, *The English Housewife in the Seventeenth Century*, 1953

Holland, Norman, *The First Modern Comedies: The Significance of Etherege, Wycherley and Congreve*, 1959

Hook, Lucyle, *Mrs Elizabeth Barry and Mrs Anne Bracegirdle Actresses: Their Careers from 1672 to 1695*, New York, 1949

Hotson, John, *The Commonwealth and Restoration Stage*, Cambridge, Mass., 1928

Howell, Wilbur, *Logic and Rhetoric in England, 1500–1700*, Princeton, 1956

Huber, Elaine, 'A Woman Must Not Speak', in Rosemary Ruether and Eleanor McLaughlin, (eds), *Women of Spirit: Female Leadership in the Jewish and Christian Traditions*, New York, 1979

Hughes, Muriel, *Women Healers in Medieval Life and Literature*, 1943

Hull, Suzanne, *Chaste, Silent and Obedient*, Los Angeles, 1982

Hume, Robert, *The Development of English Drama in the Late Seventeenth Century*, 1976

Hurd-Mead, Kate, *A History of Women in Medicine from the Earliest Times to the Beginning of the Nineteenth Century*, New York, 1938

Johnson, Edwin, 'Aphra Behn's *Oroonoko*', *Journal of Negro History*, 10, 1975

Jones, Richard, *Ancients and Moderns: A Study of the Rise of the Scientific Movement in Seventeenth-Century England*, Washington, 1963

Jones, Richard, 'Science and English Prose Style in the third quarter of the Seventeenth Century' in his *The Seventeenth Century*, Stanford, 1951

Jordan, Robert, 'The Extravagant Rake in Restoration Comedy', in Harold Love, (ed.), *Restoration Literature*, 1972

Kamm, Josephine, *Hope Deferred: Girls' Education in English History*, 1965

Kaplan, Cora, (ed.), *Salt and Bitter and Good: Three Centuries of English and American Poets*, New York, 1975

Kasbekar, Veena, 'Power Over Themselves: The Controversy About Female Education in England, 1660–1820', unpublished PhD thesis, University of Cincinatti, 1981

Kelly, Gary, ' "Intrigue" and "Gallantry": The Seventeenth-Century French *Nouvelle* and the "Novels" of Aphra Behn', *Revue de Littérature Comparée*, 55, 1981

Kenyon, John, *The Popish Plot*, 1974

Kett, Joseph, 'Review of *The Family, Sex and Marriage*', *Chronicle of Higher Education*, 1978

Kinnaird, Joan, 'Mary Astell and the Conservative Contribution to English Feminism', *Journal of British Studies*, 19, 1979

Kornbluth, Martin, 'Friendship and Fashion: The Dramatic Treatment of Friendship in the Restoration and Eighteenth Century', unpublished PhD thesis, Pennsylvania State University, 1956

Larner, Christina, *Enemies of God: The Witch-hunt in Scotland*, New York, 1981

Latt, David, (ed.), *'Women's Speaking Justified' (Margaret Fell) (1667), Epistle from the Womens Yearly Meeting at York (1688), A Warning to all Friends (Mary Waite) (1688)*, Los Angeles, 1979

Leja, Alfred, 'Aphra Behn – Tory', unpublished PhD thesis, University of Texas, 1962

Levack, Brian, 'The Great Scottish Witch Hunt of 1661–62', *Journal of British Studies*, 3, 1975

Link, Frederick, *Aphra Behn*, New York, 1968
– *Aphra Behn: The Rover*, 1967

Loftis, John, (ed.), *The Memoirs of Anne, Lady Halkett and Ann, Lady Fanshawe*, 1979

Longe, Julia, (ed.), *Martha, Lady Giffard: Her Life and Correspondence (1664–1722). A Sequel to the Letters of Dorothy Osborne*, 1911

Love, Harold, 'The Myth of the Restoration Audience', *KOMOS*, 1, 1967

Ludlow, Dorothy, ' "Arise and Be Doing": English "Preaching" Women, 1640–1660', unpublished PhD thesis, Indiana University, 1978

Ludwig, Judith, 'A Critical Edition of Aphra Behn's Comedy *The Feigned Courtesans* (1679) with Introduction and Notes', unpublished PhD thesis, Yale University, 1977

MacArthur, Ellen, 'Women Petitioners and the Long Parliament', *English Historical Review*, 24, 1909

McBurney, William, 'Edmund Curll, Mrs Jane Barker, and the English Novel', *Philological Quarterly*, 37, 1958

MacCarthy, Bridget, *The Female Pen*, Cork, 1948

MacCormack, John, *Revolutionary Politics in the Long Parliament*, 1973

MacDonald, Michael, *Mystical Bedlam: Madness, Anxiety, and Healing in Seventeenth-Century England*, 1981

MacFarlane, Alan, 'Lawrence Stone, *The Family Sex and Marriage in England*: Review Essay', *History and Theory*, 18, 1979

Mack, Phyllis, 'Women as Prophets During the English Civil War', *Feminist Studies*, 8, 1982

MacLean, Ian, *The Renaissance Conception of Woman*, 1980

Main, C., 'The German Princess: or, Mary Carleton in Fact and Fiction', *Harvard Library Bulletin*, 10, 1956

Mambretti, Catherine, ' "Fugitive Papers": A New Orinda Poem', *Papers of the Bibliographical Society of America*, 71, 1977

Manners, Emily, *Elizabeth Hooton, First Quaker Woman Preacher (1600–1672)*, 1914

Mason, Mary, 'The Other Voice: Autobiographies of Women Writers', in James Olney, (ed.), *Autobiography*, 1980

Mason, Wilmer, 'The Annual Output of Wing-Listed Titles 1649–1684', *Library*, 29, 1974

Matthews, William, *British Autobiographies: An Annotated Bibliography of British Autobiographies Published or Written before 1951*, 1968

Mignon, Elisabeth, *Crabbed Age and Youth: The Old Men and Women in the Restoration Comedy of Manners*, Washington, 1947

Milhous, Judith and Robert Hume, (eds), *'The Frolicks or The Lawyer Cheated' (1671) by Elizabeth Polwhele*, New York, 1977

Miller, Casey and Kate Swift, *Words and Women: New Language in New Times*, 1979

Monter, Edward, 'Pedestal and Stake: Courtly Love and Witchcraft', in Rosa Bridenthal, (ed.), *Becoming Visible: Women in European History*, 1977

Montgomery, Guy, 'The Challenge of Restoration Comedy', *University of California Publications in English*, 1, 1929

Morrissette, Bruce, *The Life and Works of Madame Desjardins*, 1947

Morton, Arthur, (ed.), *Freedom in Arms: A Selection of Leveller Writings*, 1975
 – *The World of the Ranters*, 1970

Morton, Richard, (ed.), *Poems (1686) by Mrs Anne Killigrew: A Facsimile Reproduction with an Introduction*, Gainesville, Florida, 1967

Muir, Kenneth, *The Comedy of Manners*, 1970

Nicholson, Harold, *The Development of English Biography*, 1947

Notestein, Wallace, *A History of Witchcraft in England from 1558 to 1718*, Washington, 1911

Novak, Maximillian, ' "Appearances of Truth": The Literature of Crime as a Narrative System 1660–1841', *Yearbook of English Studies*, 11, 1981

Oakley, Ann, 'Wisewoman and Medicine Man' in Juliet Mitchell and Ann Oakley (eds), *The Rights and Wrongs of Women*, 1976

O'Malley, Thomas, ' "Defying the Powers and Tempering the Spirit": A Review of Quaker Control over their Publications 1672–1689', *The Journal of Ecclesiastical History*, 33, 1982

Oxford, A., *Notes from a Collector's Catalogue: With a Bibliography of English Cookery Books*, 1909

Palmer, Mary, *Mary Rich, Countess of Warwick 1625–1678*, 1901

Paloma, Dolores, 'Margaret Cavendish: Defining the Female Self', *Women's Studies*, 7, 1980

Plant, Marjorie, *The English Book Trade: An Economic History of the Making and Sale of Books*, 1965

Plumb, J., 'Review of *The Family, Sex and Marriage*', *New York Review*, November 24, 1977

Pomerleau, Cynthia, ' "Resigning the Needle for the Pen": A Study of Auto-biographical Writings of British Women Before 1800', unpublished PhD thesis, University of Pennsylvania, 1974

Radbill, Samuel, 'Pediatrics', in Allen Debus, (ed.), *Medicine in Seventeenth-Century England*, California, 1974

Ramsaran, J., '*Oroonoko*: A Study of the Factual Elements', *PMLA*, 205, 1960

Reay, Barry, 'The Quakers, 1659, and the Restoration of the Monarchy', *History*, 63, 1978

Reynolds, Myra, *The Learned Lady in England 1650–1760*, Gloucester, Mass., 1964, first published 1920

Roberts, William, 'The Dating of Orinda's French Translations', *Philological Quarterly*, 49, 1970

Røstvig, Maren-Sofie, *The Happy Man: Studies in the Metamorphoses of a Classical Ideal*, Oslo, 1962

Scouten, Arthur, (ed.), *Restoration and Eighteenth-Century Drama*, 1980

Seeber, Edward, '*Oroonoko* in France in the XVIII Century', *PMLA*, 51, 1936

Sensabaugh, G., 'Platonic Love and the Puritan Rebellion', *Studies in Philology*, 37, 1940

Shammas, Carole, 'The Domestic Environment in Early Modern England and America', *Journal of Social History*, 14, 1980

Shorter, Edward, 'Capitalism, Culture and Sexuality: Some Competing Models', *Social Science Quarterly*, 53, 1972

Shumaker, Wayne, *English Autobiography: Its Emergence, Materials, and Form*, California, 1954

Singleton, Robert, 'English Criminal Biography, 1651–1722', *Harvard Library Bulletin*, 18, 1979

Smith, Catherine, 'Jane Lead: The Feminist Mind and Art of a Seventeenth-Century Protestant Mystic', in Rosemary Ruether and Eleanor McLaughlin, (eds), *Women of Spirit: Female Leadership in the Jewish and Christian Traditions*, New York, 1979

– 'Jane Lead; Mysticism and the Woman Cloathed with the Sun', in Sandra Gilbert and Susan Gubar, (eds), *Shakespeare's Sisters*, 1979

Smith, Hilda, 'Gynaecology and Ideology in Seventeenth-Century England', in Berenice Carroll, (ed.), *Liberating Women's History*, Illinois, 1976

– *Reason's Disciples: Seventeenth-Century English Feminists*, 1982

Smith, John, *The Gay Couple in Restoration Comedy*, Cambridge, Mass., 1948

Bibliography

Souers, Philip, *The Matchless Orinda*, Cambridge, Mass., 1931

Southern, Richard, *Changeable Scenery: Its Origin and Development in the British Theatre*, 1952

Spencer, Theodore, 'The History of an Unfortunate Lady', *Harvard Studies and Notes in Philology and Literature*, 20, 1938

Spufford, Margaret, *Contrasting Communities: English Villagers in the Sixteenth and Seventeenth Centuries*, 1974

– *Small Books and Pleasant Histories*, 1981

Starr, Nathan Comfort, (ed.), 'The Concealed Fansyes: A Play by Lady Jane Cavendish and Lady Elizabeth Brackley', *PMLA*, 46, 1931

Stauffer, Donald, *English Biography Before 1700*, Cambridge, Mass., 1930

Staves, Susan, *Players' Scepters: Fictions of Authority in the Restoration* Nebraska, 1978

Stenton, Doris, *The English Woman in History*, 1957

Stone, Lawrence, 'The Educational Revolution in England, 1560 –1640', *Past and Present*, 28, 1965

– *The Family, Sex and Marriage in England 1500–1800*, 1977

Summers, Montague, (ed.), *The Works of Aphra Behn*, 1915

Thirsk, Joan, '*The Family, Sex and Marriage in England*: Review', *Past and Present*, 27, 1978

Thomas, Henry, 'The Society of Chymical Physitians: An Echo of the Great Plague of London, 1665', in E. Underwood, (ed.), *Science, Medicine and History*, volume 2, 1953

Thomas, Keith, *Religion and the Decline of Magic. Studies in Popular Beliefs in Sixteenth- and Seventeenth-Century England*, 1978

– 'Review of L. Stone *The Family, Sex and Marriage*', *Times Literary Supplement*, 21 October 1977

– 'Women and the Civil War Sects', *Past and Present*, 13, 1955

Thompson, Edward, 'Happy Families', *New Society*, 8 September 1977

Thompson, Roger, *Unfit for Modest Ears: A Study of Pornographic, Obscene and Bawdy Works Written or Published in England in the Second Half of the Seventeenth Century*, 1979

Tolmie, Murray, *The Triumph of the Saints*, 1977

Turberville, A., *A History of Welbeck Abbey and Its Owners*, 1938

Turnbull, George, *Hartlib, Dury and Comenius: Gleanings from Hartlib's Papers*, Liverpool, 1947

Van Lennep, William, (ed.), *The London Stage 1660–1800*, Illinois, 1965

Vann, Richard, *The Social Development of English Quakerism*, Cambridge, Mass., 1969

Vernon, P., 'Marriage of Convenience and the Moral of Restoration Comedy', *Essays in Criticism*, 12, 1962

Vieth, David, *Attribution in Restoration Poetry: A Study of Rochester's 'Poems' of 1680*, New Haven, Connecticut, 1963

Vincent, William, *The State and School Education 1640–1660 in England and Wales*, 1950

Wall, Donald, 'The Restoration Rake in Life and Comedy', unpublished PhD thesis, Florida State University, 1963

Walzer, Michael, *Revolution of the Saints: a Study in the Origins of Radical Politics*, Cambridge, Mass., 1965

Watkins, Owen, *The Puritan Experience: Studies in Spiritual Autobiography*, 1972

Watson, Foster, *The English Grammar Schools to 1660, Their Curriculum and Practice*, 1968, first published 1908

Watt, Ian, *The Rise of the Novel*, 1972; first published 1957

Watts, Michael, *The Dissenters*, Oxford, 1978

Webber, Joan, *The Eloquent 'I': Style and Self in Seventeenth-Century Prose*, Wisconsin, 1968

Weber, Donna-Lee, 'Fair Game: Rape and Sexual Aggression on Women in some early eighteenth-century prose fiction', unpublished PhD thesis, University of Toronto, 1980

Webster, Charles, 'English Medical Reformers of the Puritan Revolution: A Background to the "Society of Chymical Physitians" ', *Ambix*, 14, 1967
 – (ed.), *Samuel Hartlib and the Advancement of Learning*, 1970
 – *The Great Instauration: Science, Medicine and Reform 1626–1660*, New York, 1976

Whiting, Charles, *Studies in English Puritanism from the Restoration to the Revolution, 1660–1688*, 1931

Whiting, George, 'The Condition of the London Theatres 1679–1683: A Reflection on the Political Situation', *Modern Philology*, 25, 1927

Wiley, Autrey, 'Female Prologues and Epilogues in English Plays', *PMLA*, 48, 1933

Williams, Ethyn, 'Women Preachers of the Civil War', *Journal of Modern History*, 1, 1929

Williams, Ioan, *The Idea of the Novel in Europe, 1600–1800*, 1979

Williamson, George, (ed.), *Lady Anne Clifford Countess of Dorset, Pembroke and Montgomery 1590–1676: Her Life, Letters and Work*, 1967

Wilson, John, (ed.), *Court Satires of the Restoration*, Columbus, 1966

Witmer, Anne and John Freehafer, 'Aphra Behn's Strange News from Virginia', *Library Chronicle*, 38, 1968

Wing, Donald, *Short-Title Catalogue 1641–1700*, New York, 1945–51

Woodhouse, A., *Puritanism and Liberty*, 1950

Woolf, Virginia, 'The Duchess of Newcastle' in her *The Common Reader*, 1925

Wright, Luella, *The Literary Life of the Early Friends 1650–1725*, New York, 1966

Zaretsky, Eli, *Capitalism, the Family and Personal Life*, 1976

Zuther, Susan, 'The World of Love and Ethic in Aphra Behn's Comedies', unpublished PhD thesis, University of Kansas, 1980

INDEX

Abbott, Margaret, 41
adultery, in ballads, 85; legal position, 12; predicted by Jinner, 181; theme in women's plays, 103, 108, 125; woman executed for murdering adulterous husband, 225
affairs of state, women's exclusion from, 3; women's involvement in, 15–18, 26–45, 55, 60–1, 107–8, 115–16, 134–5, 152; *see also* petitioners; sectaries; tithes
Aldridge, Elizabeth, 46, 213
Alexander, Mary, Countess of Stirling, 5, 209
Alleine, Theodosia, 79, 80–1, 191, 206, 215
Allen, Hannah, 69, 72–4
almanacs, almanac-makers, 180–2; popularity of 5, 73; *see also* astrology; Holden, Mary; Jinner, Sarah; witchcraft
amazons, characters in Margaret Cavendish, 91–2, 109, 111; characters in Anne Killigrew, 157; discussion of women's autonomy, 197; metaphor, 52
Ames, Richard, 222
Anderson, Mary, 213
androgyny, 91; *see also* cross-dressing
apprenticeship, metaphor for suffering, 64; midwives', 183, 185; offered to cooks, 171; part of family, 208; women Quakers responsible for, 47
army, parliamentary, 12, 35, 39; royalist, 81; women's, 91–2, 109
astrology, studied by Mary Carleton, 96; and almanac-making, 180; *see also* almanacs
Atkinson, Elizabeth, 37
audience, Behn's need to please, 117–18; composition of, 102, 115–16
Audland, Anne, 212, 213
aunts, 5, 73

authorship, women's, challenged or doubted, 37, 95–6, 155
autobiography, 76–84, 191–2; Quaker, 37, 49; and romance, 88, 90, 92–6; spiritual, 66–75; in verse, 59; *see also* autonomy, women's
autonomy, women's, asserted, 133; and autobiography, 79–84; threatened by love, 99, 125; ways of achieving, 8, 27, 68, 109–10, 135

babies, death of, 9, 70; imprisoned with mother, 38; metaphor, 42, 57, 63; murdered by mothers, 188; will not die following millennium, 31
ballads, woman-hating, 22, 85–7, 142
Bancroft, Margaret, 4, 208
baptists, Anabaptists, 36; expel Elizabeth Poole, 30; ideas of, 13; and women's writing, 40, 41, 49–53; *see also* sectaries
Barker, Jane, 142, 143, 148, 159–63
Barwick, Grace, 39, 53, 213
Bastwick, Susannah, 14, 209
Bateman, Susanna, 212
Bathurst, Elizabeth, 43, 46, 49, 213
bawds, 22–3; *see also* prostitutes
Beck, Margaret, 15
Behn, Aphra, 6, 25, 88, 96–100, 103, 104, 114–27, 142, 143, 148, 151, 152–5, 164, 182, 189, 196, 208, 217, 219, 222; *The Adventure of the Black Lady*, 97–8; *Agnes de Castro*, 98; *The Amorous Prince*, 116, 121, 122; *The City Heiress*, 115–16, 124; *The Dumb Virgin*, 98; *The Dutch Lover*, 115, 119, 124, 125, 127, 196; *The Emperor of the Moon*, 115, 117; *The Fair Jilt*, 97, 98–9; *The False Count*, 117, 121; *The Feign'd Curtizans*, 115, 116, 127; *The Fair Vow-Breaker*, 99–100; *The Forc'd*

Behn, Aphra — cont.
Marriage, 115, 116, 120, 218;
Loveletters from a Nobleman, 217; *The
Luckey Chance*, 116, 118–19, 121,
124, 125, 220; *The Nun*, 98, 220;
Oroonoko, 96; *The Rover*, 116–17,
121, 122–4, 125, 126; *The
Roundheads*, 115, 116; *The Second
Part of the Rover*, 116; *Sir Patient
Fancy*, 117, 120; *The Town-Fopp*, 122;
The Unfortunate Bride, 98; *The
Younger Brother*, 121
Bell, Susannah, 69, 71
Bettris, Jeane, 212
Bible, Book of Daniel, 13, 27, 32; Book of
Proverbs, 201; Book of Revelation, 13,
28; comfort from, 73–4; examples used
from, 43, 146, 186, 188; language in
prophecies, 27–8, 41, 51; popularity
of, 5; replaced by Inner Light, 194; and
women's passivity, 47; and women's
preaching, 44–5
Biddle, Hester, 41, 43, 45, 46, 157, 212,
213
bigamy, 93–5
Beck, Margaret, 15
biography, of Mary Carleton (spurious),
92, 95; of husbands, related to
autobiography, 76–84; of Hannah
Wolley (spurious), 166, 172, 173; *see
also* deathbed testimonials
Blackborow, Sarah, 36, 37, 42, 212, 213
Blaithwait, Mary, 14, 15
booksellers, 89, 103, 161, 165, 167, 172,
174
Booth, Mary, 206
Boothby, Frances, 103, 104, 111, 114, 219
Boulbie, Judith, 213
Brackley, Elizabeth, 102, 185
Bradstreet, Anne, 202, 226
Brathwait, Richard, *The English
Gentlewoman*, 3, 191
Braidley, Margret, 37, 212, 213
Braytwhaite, Elizabeth, 48
breastfeeding, metaphor of, 42
Brégy, Charlotte, 210
brothers, death of, 70; greater
opportunities of, 193; matchmaking
for, 94; threatening rape, 122;
tyrannical, 114
Brooksop, Joan, 37, 213

Calamy, Edmund, 66, 73
Care, Henry, translator of *Female
Pre-eminence*, 197, 199, 200, 202
Carleton, John, 93–6

Carleton, Mary, 88, 92–6, 97, 101, 192,
224
Cartwright, Joanna, 16
Cary, Mary, 30–1, 34, 41, 53, 163, 210,
227
Catherine of Braganza, and Catholicism,
20; Ephelia's connections with court of,
146; illness subject of poem by
Katherine Philips, 131; Rachel Jevon
petitioning to be servant of, 19;
Catholics, called Whore of Babylon, 43;
and Charles II's court, 20; and Popish
Plot, 20–3, 115, 188; seen as virtuous
in women's poetry, 158, 159; thought
tyrannical, 12, 43
Cavendish, Jane, 102
Cavendish, Margaret, 5, 9, 79, 81–4, 85,
90, 102, 104, 105–11, 119, 131, 163,
168, 192, 193, 195–7, 202, 208, 215,
218, 221; *Grounds of Natural
Philosophy*, 196; *Natures Pictures*,
81–4, 88, 90–2; *Observations*, 196;
Philosophical Fancies, 81; *Philosophical
Letters*, 227; *Philosophical and Physical
Opinions*, 190; *Playes*, 105–11, 218;
Plays, Never before Printed, 106–11;
Poems and Fancies, 81, 209; *Sociable
Letters*, 216; *The Worlds Olio*, 190,
191
Cellier, Elizabeth, 21–3, 78, 187–9, 210
Chamberlen, Hugh and Peter, 9, 183–4
Channel, Elinor, 29, 192
Charles I, and civil war, 12, 13, 18; cooked
for, by Hannah Wolley, 167; death
predicted by Lady Eleanor, 27;
execution of, 11, 25; execution of
opposed by Elizabeth Poole, 29–31; his
daughter tutored by Bathsua Makin,
199; poem about execution by
Katherine Philips, 134; poem to, in
Eliza's Babes, 55
Charles II, letter to, by Anne Clayton, 41;
poem to, by Ephelia, 146–7; and
religious toleration, 20, 40; Restoration
of, celebrated by Rachel Jevon, 18–9;
sent poems by Katherine Philips, 129,
131; and Society of Chemical
Physicians, 178; and the theatre, 102;
see also court (royal); Succession Crisis
chastity (honesty, honour, reputation),
women's, asserted by authors, 65–6,
79, 81–4, 156; becoming central for
Quaker women, 47–8; Margaret
Cavendish's, 81–4, 91–2, 108–11,
131, 219; Elizabeth Cellier's
questioned, 21–3; jeopardised by
learning, 199–200; jeopardised by

chastity—cont.
  writing, 10, 57, 83; lost by falling in
  love, 123–5; protected by anonymity,
  207; punishment for breaking vow of,
  99–100; required, 2–3, 9; seen as
  empty obsession, 104, 118, 154–5; *see
  also* modesty; virtue; virgins
Chevers, Sarah, 38, 48, 212, 213
Chidley, Katherine, 69
childbirth, causing madness, 46; in
  conversion narratives, 69–72; fatal,
  184, 185; illegitimate, 97; Mary Love's
  delaying husband's execution, 15;
  painful, 57, 183; women gathering at,
  91, 165; *see also* midwives
children, education of, 193; fatherless
  objects of pity, 15; left by mother
  committed to prophecy, 29, 37, 38; as
  metaphor for writing, 57–61, 63, 120;
  as petitioners (with mothers), 14; as
  symbol of male debauchery, 113; *see
  also* young people
Christ, body of, image of interdependency,
  40–1; as bridegroom or husband,
  35–6, 46, 56–9, 61–2; resurrection of,
  witnessed by women, 34; Second
  Coming of, expected, 12, 20, 32, 35;
  women claiming to be pregnant with,
  28; women and men equal in, 44
civil war, commented on by women writers,
  55, 59–62, 91, 158, 182; and sectaries,
  26, 35; source of women's petitioning,
  6, 13–14
Clarendon Code, 20, 26, 40
Clark, Mary, 178
Clayton, Anne, 41, 210
Clifford, Anne, 215
Clipsham, Margery, 46
Cole, Mary, 43, 44, 45, 212, 213
Coleman, Elizabeth, 37
Collins, An, 59–62, 214
Commonwealth, state of, lamented by
  Anna Trapnel, 32
conduct books, 8, 88
conversion narratives, 66–75
Conway, Anne, *see* Finch, Anne
cookery, male incursions into, 169–70;
  women's control of, 6, 168–9
cookery books, 5, 165–75
Cotton, Priscilla, 43, 44, 45, 212, 213
court (royal), and Margaret Cavendish, 81,
  83; as centre of licentiousness, 85–6,
  127, 145, 150–1, 156, 202;
  relationship with theatre, 102, 115
courtly love conventions, in *Eliza's Babes*,
  56–8; in Anne Killigrew's poems,
  158–9; and misogyny, 85, 142–3;

parodied by Aphra Behn, 117, 120–1,
  126, 152–4; in Katherine Philips's
  poems, 128, 134–40; *see also* mistress
courtship, advice on, by Sarah Jinner, 181;
  parodied, by Aphra Behn, 117–27, by
  Frances Boothby, 112–13, by Anne
  Killigrew, 159, and by Elizabeth
  Polwhele, 113–14; Alice Thornton
  threatened with rape or purchase in,
  77–8
critics, scorned by Aphra Behn, 117–20;
  scorned by Margaret Cavendish, 106–
  7; threatening to Boothby, 111; Waller
  critical of Margaret Cavendish, 131
Cromwell, Oliver, addressed by *The
  Women's Petition*, 16; petitioned by
  Mary Blaithwait, 15; told by Anna
  Trapnel to abandon title of Lord
  Protector, 35
cross-dressing, women as men, 91, 124,
  188; men as women, 91, 219
Culpeper, Alice, 206
Culpeper, Nicholas, 184–5, 186, 206
Curwen, Alice, 37, 49, 213
daughters, Charles II's left unsupported,
  86; Lady Eleanor's pamphlet addressed
  to her, 27; parody of letter from, 171–2

Davies, Lady Eleanor, *see* Douglas, Lady
  Eleanor
Davy, Sarah, 66, 67, 69, 70–1, 72, 192,
  214
death, accepted as God's will, 49; in
  childbed, 72, 188; description of
  violent, 90; of family members, 70, 179;
  of husband, 73–4, 80, 99–100;
  imminence of, causing women to write,
  66, 82, 166–7; reuniting with woman
  friend after, 137
deathbed testimonies, 40, 71, 78, 206; *see
  also* autobiographies
debtors, women's petitions concerning, 4,
  16, 29; Aphra Behn's imprisonment for
  debt, 114
Declaration of Breda, 19, 40
dedicatory epistles, *see* prefaces
delinquents, petitions by wives of, 14; *see
  also* sequestered property
Desjardins, Marie-Catherine, 88, 216
dialogues, 63, 107, 137, 159
diary, Samuel Pepys's, 82; reading own for
  comfort, 73; survival of, 76–9, 185,
  214
Dirrecks, Geertruyde, 48
Dole, Dorcas, 214
Douglas (or Davies), Lady Eleanor, 27–9,
  34, 49, 163, 211

dower rights, 8, 15, 183
dreams, 73, 161, 214
Dryden, John, 155, 160
Dumb Lady, The, 87
Dury, Dorothy, 192
Dyer, Mary, 212

E., T., *The Lawes Resolution of Women's Rights*, 4, 17, 76
editing, by men of women's work, 66, 156; by women of men's work, 19, 207; *see also* prefaces
education, men's, classical, 119, 174, 179; from plays, 219; universities, 161–2, 185, 189, 192–9, 222, 226; university towns threatened by Hester Biddle, 41; *see also* Latin
education, women's, Mary Carleton's unusual, 96; differs from men's, 89, 105–6, 119; need to improve, 110–11, 176, 181, 190–203; a source of women's subordination, 109, 171, 173; *see also* Latin; schools
Elizabeth of Bohemia, praised in *Eliza's Babes*, 55
Eliza's Babes, 55–9, 75, 159, 185
Elson, Mary, 38, 213
enthusiasm, abandonment of, 26, 39, 46–9, 157, 164; criticism of women for, 52; *see also* sectaries
Ephelia, 142, 146–52, 164, 222
Etherege, George, 104
Evans, Katherine, 38, 48, 212, 213
Eve, denial of guilt of, 144; proof of women's evil, 143, 145, 197, 201; model for women's autonomy, 133, 162
Exhortation and Admonition, An, 47

Fairman, Susanna, 213
family, appeal for unity in, 60–1; control over marriage, 99, 120; importance of, 80, 91, 102; as metaphor for state, 29; rejected by women, 55–7, 62, 76, 78; woman's place, 31, 48, 71; women's position in, 2–5, 208; *see also* marriage
Fanshawe, Lady Ann, 78, 192, 226
fathers, defence of, 178–80; power of, 120–1, 151; rage at daughter's publishing, 143, 146; source of woman's identity, 82; *see also* parents
Fell, Margaret, 43, 45, 212, 213, 214
Female Excellence, 222
femininity, defined, 7–8; *see also* chastity, modesty, obedience, virtue
Fifth Monarchists, 13, 20, 40; and Anna Trapnel, 32–5
Fige, Sarah, 143–6

Finch, Anne, Viscountess Conway, 134, 193, 226, 227
Forster, Mary, 47–8, 213; *These Several Papers*, 194, 212
Fox, George, 36, 43
freedom, through acceptance of constraints, 62, 135–7; in celibacy, 145, 159–61; fought for by women warriors, 109; lost by falling in love, 150–3; in relationship with God, 52, 54–8, 63–6; in relationship with woman, 138–40; in state, argued for, 16, 39, 40; woman's dependent on men, 121
friends, female, enduring value of, 98, 112–13; gathering at childbirth, 10; poems written to, 134–41, 147, 161; sectaries, 32, 37–8, 50, 52, 70–1, 72; Society of Friendship, 134, 147, 221; suggesting lesbianism, 70–1, 128, 134–41; threatening to men, 160
friendship, between men, 112, 117, 136; as source of support, 74; between wife and husband, 4, 139
Friends, Society of, and autobiography, 46–8, 78, 206–7; and education, 194; rejected, 69; women's role in, 36–40, 43–4, 46–9, 163; *see also* sectaries
Furly, Elizabeth, 48

Gargill, Anne, 46, 212, 213
Gentlewomans Companion, The, 166, 172–4, 223
Gerbier, Charles, 197, 201, 202
Gilman, Anne, 213
God, appealed to as ally, 16, 34; claimed as origin of message, 26, 29, 30–1, 39, 41, 45, 48, 50–2, 55, 60, 63, 67, 72, 170; denied as origin of message, 46, 49–52; female deity or qualities, 28, 42; as father and teacher, 63–6; justification of male authority, 203; source of experience, 66–7; source of knowledge, 194; his will leading to equality of all people, 41; his will leading to equality of women and men, 33, 36–7, 58–9, 68; his will a motive for action, 6, 9, 12–13, 34, 37, 48–9, 55, 57–8, 70–1; working through weak women, 17, 26, 30, 38
Godolphin, Margaret, 185
Goodhue, Sarah, 185
gossip, better to write than to, 9; creating female solidarity, 107–8; at childbed, 10, 91
Gould, Ann, 213
Gould, Robert, 143, 144, 145, 222; not author of *Sylvia's Revenge*, 222

H., M., *The Young Cooks Monitor*, 175
Halkett, Anne, 215
Hampshire, 19, 97
Hastings, Lucy, Countess of Huntingdon, 202
Hayward, Sarah, 213
Hendericks, Elizabeth, 213
Henrietta Maria, acting at court of, 102; Margaret Cavendish at court of, 81–3; purported source of *The Queen's Closet Opened*, 165
Henshaw, Anne, 14
Hewitt, Mary, 19
Hincks, Elizabeth, 40–1, 42
Holden, Mary, 181, 182
home, becoming private place, 3, 53; books sold from, 21; Margaret Cavendish's plays to be read at 105–11; place of limited freedom, 59–62, 135; as prison, 64, 190; woman's place, 9, 11, 46–7, 100
honesty, *see* chastity; modesty
honour, *see* chastity; modesty
Hooton, Elizabeth, 36, 37, 210, 212, 213, 227
housewifery, making a living from, 175, 189; must take priority over education, 198, 203; prison enforced by men, 91; women's books about, 165–75; women's proper concern, 88
Howgill, Mary, 46, 212, 213
Huntingdon, Lucy, *see* Hastings, Lucy
husbands, autonomy from, 68, 76, 98, 133–4; biographies of, 76–84; Christ a better alternative, 46, 56–9, 61–2, 63; deaths of, 73–4, 166; forcing wife to change will, 5; made to pay for sex, 181; murder of, 99–100; petitioned for by wives, 14–15, 19; power over wives, 2–4, 6, 28, 29, 43–5, 47, 69, 71, 107–8, 120–2, 135, 138–40, 151, 203; preventing wives writing, 27, 49–53, 91, 110; published argument with, 92–6; violence to wives, 85, 87, 121, 125, 171; women leaving to prophesy, 29, 36–8; *see also* marriage; wives
Hutchinson, Lucy, 79

illness, women's, resulting in writing, 59–62; *see also* medicine; nursing
immodesty or immorality, women charged with, 22, 30, 86, 117, 181
imprisonment, for bigamy, 92–3; for debt, 4; of husband, 15, 80; of John Lilburne, 16–17; for malicious slander, 21–2; metaphor for suffering, 64; in Newgate

prison, 21–2, 40, 46, 92–3; for prophecy, 27, 32–4, 36, 38, 39, 40, 46, 47; writing from, 32, 38, 40, 45, 172
Inner Light, rejection of, 69; source of women's independence, 13, 36, 44, 194; *see also* Friends, Society of
Inquisition (Spanish), 38, 48
Ireland, women visiting, 38, 130–3

James II, appealed to by Cellier, 187–9; dedicatee of Aphra Behn's *Second Part Of The Rover*, 116
Jarvis, William, *The Countess of Kent's Choice Manuall*, 165
Jessey, Jenry, 67, 69
Jevon, Rachel, 18–19
Jews, and circumcision, 186–7; petition of, 16
Jinner, Sarah, 114, 181–2, 189
justification for writing/publishing, 9–11, 46, 55, 65, 119, 168–70 *see also* prefaces

Killigrew, Anne, 142, 143, 148, 155–9, 164, 220
Killin, Margaret, 41, 46, 212, 213
Knight, Mary, 206, 221

Ladies Remonstrance, The, 18
La Mothe, Marie Catherine, 88
Latin, men's promotion of, 173–4, 186; women's grasp of 19, 27, 192, 198, 203; women's rejection of, 105–6, 194, 195–6
Laverent, Anne, 178
law, imagined changes in, 109; impotence over, 100; petitioning over, 14–17; rejection of, 39; woman studying, 96
Lawes Resolution of Women's Rights, The, see E., T.
lawyers, drafting women's petitions, 13–14, 19; tricked, 92–6, 113
Lead, Jane, 214, 223
lesbians, 24, 128, 187, 220
letters, 4, 38, 41, 67, 88, 128, 130–2, 193–4, 196; instructions on writing, 171–2
Levingston, Anne, 4, 209
liberty, *see* freedom
Lilburne, John, 16–17
love, women falling in, with a man, 3, 99, 123–4, 150, 153; with a woman, 69–70; *see also* marriage; sexuality (women's)
Love, Mary, 15, 19
Lynam, Margret, 213

Index

madness, Margaret Cavendish seen as mad, 82; and circumcision, 186–7; jealousy is, 121; love or marriage would be, 109, 114; from oppression, 15; prophets accused of, 27–8, 34, 46, 52; *see also* melancholy

Major, Elizabeth, 63–6

Makin, Bathsua, 199–203

male backlash, pamphlets parodying petitioning, 17–18; pornography, 85–8

manuscripts, circulation of, 103, 129, 132, 155; presented to Charles II, 19; survival of, 76–7, 102, 222

marriage, and crisis of faith, 72; divorce, 50; effacing woman's identity, 82–4; with God or Christ, 56–8; leading to silence, 70, 110; for love, 77, 80, 84; love irrelevant to, 69, 113; relieving melancholy, 74; resisted, 33, 57–9, 77–8, 91, 96–100, 114, 160; woman's control over, 77–8, 91–2, 109, 124, 126–7; *see also* family; husbands; wives

Mary II, Bathsua Makin's *Essay* dedicated to, 199

Mary of Modena, Elizabeth Cellier midwife to, 188; Anne Killigrew at court of, 156–7

May, Robert, 169–70, 171, 174

Meal-Tub Plot, *see* Cellier, Elizabeth

medicine, cost of, 184–5; and witchcraft, 177, 180; women prescribing or making, 162–3, 165, 166–7, 177, 178–80, 181–2; *see also* illness; physicians

meditations, 54–75, 77

melancholy, causing suicide attempts, 71–4; husband's, 77; *see also* madness

midwifery, Elizabeth Cellier, 21–3, 187–9; Mary Holden, 182; male incursions into, 9, 182–5, 186, 188–9; midwives' oath, 9, 183; Jane Sharp, 185–7; Hester Shaw, 9–11

millinarianism, *see* enthusiasm

ministers, making sexual advances, 93; marriage to, 80–1; publishing women's work, 66–72, 80, 206; women's disputes with, 9–11, 39, 43–5, 194

misogyny, of court, 85–6; and courtly love, 142–3, 147, 159–60; *see also* pornography

mistress, ill-treatment of, 113–14; lack of real power, 4, 150–2; lesbian, 136–40; marriage of, 112–13; murder of, 108, 120–1; *see also* courtly love conventions; pornography

modesty, women's, asserted by authors, 23, 57, 65–6, 68–9, 80, 89–90, 130–2, 142, 168; barrier to health, 181; seen by men as empty obsession, 104, 144–5; *see also* chastity, virtue; weakness

money, and female independence, 30, 109, 160–1; and marriage, 77–8, 94–5, 121–4; petitioned for, 4–5, 191; stolen by minister, 10–11; women's income, 30, 35, 177–8, 183; from writing, 103, 114–16, 155, 167–72, 175, 176, 180–2; *see also* poverty

Monmouth, Duke of, *see* Scott, James

Moore, Elizabeth, 66

Mordaunt, Elizabeth, 214

mother, death of, 70, 71, 179; educating daughters, 192; God a nursing mother, 42; mock-letter to, 171–2; to one's poems, 57–9, 61–2, 63; support from, 76–8; *see also* parents

Mudd, Ann, 37

Newcastle, Margaret, *see* Cavendish, Margaret

Nayler, James, 20

New England, women visiting, 37–8, 48–9, 71

news-sheets, reports of women in, 10, 97, 211

novels, of Aphra Behn, 96–100, 122; of Margaret Cavendish, 90–2; and crime narrative, 92–6; and romance, 88–90

nunneries, place of courtship, 98–100; tedious place, 94–5; *see also* single women

nursing, of husband, 80–1

obedience, women's, asserted, 83–4; excuse for writing or action, 9, 37–9, 64–5, 160–1; rebelled against, 108; required, 6, 43, 122; *see also* chastity; modesty

Osborne, Alice, 19

Osborne, Dorothy, 4, 88, 196, 221

P., T., *The Accomplish'd Ladies Delight*, 166, 167, 175, 224

parents, religious, 73; tyrannical, 96, 113, 122; *see also* fathers; mothers

parliament, 11, 12, 13, 20, 86, 102, 195; prophecy addressed to, 30–2, 39; women petitioning, 4–5, 13–19, 208–9

Parr, Susannah, 44–5

Patison, Barbara, 212, 213

Pembroke, Mary, *see* Sidney, Mary

Pendarves, Theodosia, 30

Pennyman, Mary, 37
Pepys, Samuel, 82, 92, 227
Perrot, Luce, 66
petitions, mock, 22, 85, 210; personal,
    4–5, 13–15, 19, 21; social issues, 14,
    16–17, 39, 184
Pettus, Katherine, 4, 208
Philips, Katherine, 128–42, 147, 151, 161,
    173, 192, 202, 205, 222; *Letters from
    Orinda to Poliarchus*, 88, 130–2;
    Poems, 132–41; *Pompey*, 103, 129,
    130, 132, 140, 222
Philophilippa, 140–1
philosophy, Margaret Cavendish's, 81, 85,
    106–8, 110–11, 195–7; desire for,
    162–3, 201; dismissal of men's, 179,
    195–7, 200; Anne Finch's, 193–4
physicians, College of, 9, 177–80, 183–4,
    189; women, 162–3, 171, 174,
    177–80
plague, 71, 179
plays, 102–27, 128, 129, 147, 185, 219;
    Aphra Behn's themes, 114–27;
    Margaret Cavendish's themes, 107–11;
    Mary Carleton acting in, 93; male
    conventions of, 103–5; male
    conventions of, rejected by Aphra Behn,
    119–20, Margaret Cavendish, 105–6;
    as metaphor, 145; royalist
    preoccupation with, 102–3; suitable
    for woman to write, 196
poets, 128–64, 212, 222; Jane Barker,
    159–64; Aphra Behn, 152–5; seeking
    identity as poet 118–19; Margaret
    Cavendish, 90–1, 106; An Collins,
    59–62; *Eliza's Babes*, 54–9; Ephelia,
    146–52; Sarah Fige, 143–6; Anne
    Killigrew, 155–9; Elizabeth Major,
    63–6; Katherine Philips, 128–41;
    Philophilippa, 140–1; Hannah Wolley,
    168, 170, 172; *see also* ballads
politics, *see* affairs of state
Polwhele, Elizabeth, 103, 104, 111, 113,
    114
Poole, Elizabeth, 29–30, 211
Popish Plot, *see* Catholics
pornography, Aphra Behn's rejection of,
    118; Restoration growth of, 18, 85–8
posthumous publication, 66–74, 88, 132,
    142, 155, 214
poverty, 178, 192; duty to relieve, 47, 169,
    180, 183, 188; end promised to, 31, 41;
    rich reproached for, 41, 43, 184–5;
    wealthy's ignorance about, 164; *see also*
    money
Powell, Lady Mary, 5, 177
prefaces, by men to women's work, 54, 63,

66–74, 80, 89, 198; by women,
    discussing their writing, 82, 84, 105–6,
    111, 117–21, 132, 143–4, 168, 172;
    see also editing; readers
pregnancy, medical help with, 181, 184–9;
    preventing travel, 71; unmarried, 97
prophecies, 26–53
prose fiction, *see* novels; romance
prostitutes, actresses seen as, 106;
    mistresses seen as, 86; in plays, 113,
    117, 122–7; prostitution of muses,
    156, 160; prostitution related to
    marriage, 122–6; *see also* bawds

Quakers, *see* Friends, Society of
Queen's Closet Opened, The, 165, 174
rape, 24, 216; in Aphra Behn's work,
    96–9, 122–6, 152–3; in Margaret
    Cavendish's work, 91–2, 108; in Sarah
    Fige's work, 145–6; for forced
    marriage, 77, 87, 125; metaphor, 140;
    and murder, 108; prevented by woman,
    91–2; for male vengeance, 122

Ray, John, 1–2
readers, appealed to, 10–11, 15, 30–1, 59,
    68, 82, 94, 105–6, 118–19, 143–4,
    161–2, 167–8, 176, 200; *see also*
    prefaces, by women
reading, women's ability to, 5; importance
    to writers, 68, 72, 73; of romances,
    88–9
reason, a guard against love, 150; and
    rejection of enthusiasm, 157–9, 163–4
Remonstrance of the Shee-Citizens, A, 18
reputation, *see* chastity; modesty
Restoration of the Monarchy, celebrated,
    18–19; effects on women's writing, 6,
    26, 45–9, 52, 85–8, 102–5, 129,
    157–9, 199–203, 204–5
Rich, Mary, 76, 79, 84, 134, 185, 214
Rochester, John, Earl of, *see* Wilmot, John
romance, Mary Carleton using conventions
    of, 92–6; Margaret Cavendish's, 90–2;
    parodied, 22; ridiculed, 116–17;
    Hannah Wolley, described as romance
    heroine, 174, transforming conventions
    of, 170; women reading, 72, 88–90
royalists, 90, 100, 157, 163, 223; attacking
    women, 17–18; celebrating
    Restoration, 19; during Commonwealth
    period, 55, 129, 133–5, 190–1;
    petitioning, 14–15, 19; petitioning
    against, 15, 31
Russell, Rachel, Lady, *see* Wriothesley,
    Rachel

Saints Testimony, The, 40, 43
Schurman, Anna Maria van, 173, 197, 198–9, 200, 202, 227
schools, women working at, 80–1, 166–7, 191; *see also* education
scold's bridle, 39
Scott, James, Duke of Monmouth, 21, 147; addressed by Ephelia, 146–7; and the Meal-Tub Plot, 21–3
sectaries, 17, 26–53, 54, 55, 60, 66–75, 134, 145–6, 163–4, 182, 191, 194, 202; *see also* Baptists, Friends, Society of
de Scudéry, Madeleine, 88
Searl, Margaret, 178
sequestered property, 77, 84; James Philips Commissioner for Sequestration, 133; should not be resold, 31; *see also* delinquents
servants, 31, 208, 224; training of, 166–75, 224; work for, 47
sewing, used in murder plot, 99–100; women's work, 9, 171, 176
sexuality (men's), debauchery, 112–13, 121–7, 143–4; *see also* court; rape; sexuality (women's)
sexuality (women's), believed lustful, 2–3, 18, 85–8, 98, 182; lesbian, 205; in male writings, 22, 103–5; women advocating celibacy, 52–66, 155–64; women analysing sexual 'freedom', 96–100, 107–8, 111–14, 122–7, 152–5; women giving advice on, 181–2, 186–7; *see also* adultery; chastity; courtly love conventions; lesbians; mistresses; prostitutes; widows
Shaw, Hester, 9–11, 21, 226
Sharp, Jane, 185–7, 193
Sidney, Mary, Countess of Pembroke, 89, 216
silence, women's, broken by writers, 10, 50–3, 55, 80–1; challenged, 44–5; characteristic of witches, 34–5; described, 31; required, 3, 6, 43, 45; self-silencing, 29, 65–6, 80–1, 83–4
Simmonds, Martha, 46, 210, 212
Simpson, Mary, 66, 214
single women, admonitions to, 47–8; economic inviability, 3; spinsterhood preferable to marriage, 61, 91, 109, 145, 159–61; *see also* marriage
sisters, dominated by brother, 144, 122; poem to, 135; sisterhood in radical sects, 33, 37–8, 43–4, 48–9; *see also* Friends, Society of
Smyth, Anne, 4, 208

Somerset, Margaret, Countess of Worcester, 14
sons, autobiography written for, 78; mother living with, 166–7; petition on behalf of, 15; writing for mother, 71
songs, 129, 142–3, 207; from divine inspiration, 34, 49–53; in plays, 106–7, 117, 147–8; singing a female accomplishment, 174, 192
spelling, women's, 5, 171–2, 196
spinsters, *see* single women
Stirling, Mary, *see* Alexander, Mary
Stone, Katherine, 14
Strong, Demaris, 205
Succession Crisis, 115–16
Swimming Lady, The, 87

Taylor, Mrs, 142, 148
Temple, William, 4, 221
Tender and Christian Testimony, A, 47
Thornton, Alice, 77–8, 79, 84, 185
Tillinghast, Mary, 175
tithes, 13, 28; women attacking, 26, 35, 39, 194
Tories, 20; Aphra Behn working for, 100, 115
Townsend, Theophila, 37, 212, 213
trances, 29, 31–2, 67
translations, by Aphra Behn, 154–5; by Katherine Philips, 103, 128–32, 134–5, 140–1; paid for by Jane Sharp, 185; of Anna Maria van Schurman, 198–9, 227
Trapnel, Anna, 29, 31–6, 51, 53, 67, 157, 191–2, 194, 210, 211
travel, husband's, 73; women's, 29, 32, 37–8, 46, 48–9, 71, 84
Travers, Anne, 37
Travers, Rebeckah, 37, 49, 211, 213, 227
trials, Hester Biddle, 46; Mary Carleton, 93–6, 217; Elizabeth Cellier, 21, 22; proceedings in Latin, 12; Hester Shaw, 11; Anna Trapnel, 33–5; women storming court, 188
Tryal of Elizabeth Cellier, The, 22
Trye, Mary, 178–80, 193
Turner, Jane, 67, 68–9

utopia, 31

Venn, Anne, 67, 72, 214
violence, male, 50–2, 85, 98, 100, 121; *see also* rape
virginity, asserted by writers, 57–9, 198; requirement of, 2–3, 77, 123, 187; virgins as philosophers, 91, 108; wise

virginity—cont.
virgins, 35–6, 67; *see also* chastity; modesty; virtue
virtue, 62; of necessity, 11–23, 100; superior to warfare, 157–8; undermined by men, 159–60; woman's asserted, 71, 79, 143–6; *see also* chastity, modesty
Vives, Luis, 3
Vokins, Joan, 38, 48–9

Waite, Mary, 213
Wales, 128, 133
Walker, Mary, 15
Wandesford, Mary, *see* Osborne, Alice
Warwick, Mary, Countess of, *see* Rich, Mary
Waters, Margaret, 213
Waugh, Dorothy, 39
Waugh, Jane, 212, 213
weakness, women's, caused by love, 123–4; concept subverted, 15, 17, 30, 44, 55, 63; disproved, 109–10; reasserted, 203; *see also* modesty
Weamys, Anne, 88, 89–90
Webb, Mary, 213
Wentworth, Anne, 49–53, 212
Wentworth, Henrietta Maria, 210
West Indies, women visiting, 38, 49; deportation to, 93
Whigs, 20, 115
whipping, of women, 39, 87
White, Dorothy, 212, 213
White, Elizabeth, 69, 71–2
Whitehead, Anne, 47, 48, 206, 213
Whitehead, Jane, 37
Whitrow, Joan, 213
whores, *see* prostitutes
Whore of Babylon, *see* Catholics
widows, madness of, 72–4; petitioning, 4, 14–15; sexuality of, 2, 124–5; travelling, 37; working, 176, 178

Wight, Sarah, 67, 69
Wilmot, John, Earl of Rochester, 116, 147, 148, 222
witchcraft, metaphor, 72, 114, 152; and midwifery, 183; women charged with, 5, 34–5, 38, 177
withdrawal from public world, advocated by writers, 55–66, 134–5; lamented, 161–3
wives, duties of a model for state, 29–30; financial rights of asserted, 31; loneliness of, 80–1; maintaining autonomy, 133–4; obedience of, 71, 79; oppressed, 49–53, 85, 91; petitioning, 14–15; position of, 2–4, 100, 108–10, 121, 138–40, 172, 200; scold's bridle, 39; working with husband, 177–8; *see also* marriage
Wolley, Hannah, 78, 114, 166–75, 176, 189; *The Queen-like Closet*, 166, 168–70, 175, 224; *A Supplement*, 166, 170–3, 223, 224
woman-hating, *see* misogyny
women's meetings, *see* Friends, Society of
Women's Petition, The, 16
women's preaching, *see* Friends, Society of
Worcester, Margaret, Countess of, *see* Somerset, Margaret
Wriothesley, Rachel, Lady Russell, 192
Wroth, Mary, 89
Wycherley, William, 104
Wyndham, Anne, 19, 210
writing, process of, 27–8, 30, 32, 38, 59–60, 80; women's inability to, 5, 29

Yeamans, Isabel, 46, 49, 213
Young-womans Complaint, The, 85
young women, books addressed to, 70, 174; education of, 195, 198–203; reprimanded, 47–8; sexual desire of, 182; philosophers, 108, 158; writing, 143–6, 147